MEET THE LOVE OF YOUR LIFE

DR JAN YAGER

HINKLER BOOKS

Copyright © 2005, 2004 by Jan Yager, Ph.D.

This is a new edition with additional anecdotes and a completely revised Appendix of Resources based on original research by the author related to Australia, New Zealand, England, Ireland and South Africa. It is based on the US edition, published under the title *125 Ways to Meet the Love of Your Life*, first published in the United States by Hannacroix Creek Books, Inc. www.hannacroixcreekbooks.com

'My story' by Jan Yager in Chapter 1 is an edited and updated version of an article that originally appeared in *Cleo* under the title, 'What Type of Woman Advertises for Love? Here's One Who Did', April 1989.

Suggestions for getting over rejection in Chapter 16 are based on 'The Power of "No!"' by Jan Yager, published in *National Business Employment Weekly*, Managing Your Career, Fall, 1988.

'Maintain Speed: Love Zone Ahead' by Jan Yager originally appeared in *Newsday* newspaper, 20 September, 1984.

HINKLER BOOKS

First published in 2005 by Hinkler Books Pty Ltd
17-23 Redwood Drive
Dingley Victoria 3172 Australia
www.hinklerbooks.com

All rights reserved. No part of this publication may be reproduced, stored in a retrieval system, or transmitted in any way or by any means, electronic, mechanical, photocopying, recording or otherwise, without the prior written permission of the copyright holders.

ISBN 1 7415 7003 4

Cover design: Sam Grimmer

Printed and bound in Australia

Contents

Part 1   Gearing Up   1

1 Why You Need This Book   3
2 A Love Story   8
3 How to Have a More Productive Search and Increase the Odds   15
4 Staying Safe During Your Search   23
5 Getting Ready for Your Search   27
6 Getting to Know You   41

Part 2   The Search Begins: 125 Ways to Meet the Love of Your Life   49

7   Making Introductions (1–18)   51
8   School, Work or Business (19–34)   72
9   Personal Ads (Print or Online) (35–40)   82
10 Trips, Travel and Vacations (41–49)   94
11 Cultural, Educational or Volunteer Activities and Singles Associations (50–78)   101
12 Commercial Social Settings (Bars, Clubs and Restaurants) (79–88)   111
13 Sports Activities (89–99)   117
14 Seasonal Opportunities: Holidays and Summer (100–109)   121
15 Miscellaneous 'How to Meet' Ideas (109–25)   125

Part 3   The Next Steps   131

16 Continuing the Search   133
17 When You Find 'The One'   139
Bibliography   148
Appendix: Resources   155
Index   170
About the Author   179

Other books by Jan Yager, Ph.D.
(a/k/a J.L. Barkas/Janet Lee Barkas)

Nonfiction
Single in America
Friendshifts:® The Power of Friendship and How It Shapes Our Lives
When Friendship Hurts
Who's That Sitting at My Desk?
Creative Time Management for the New Millennium
Creative Time Management
Making Your Office Work For You
Business Protocol: How to Survive & Succeed in Business
Effective Business and Nonfiction Writing
Victims
The Help Book
Road Signs on Life's Journey
Career Opportunities in the Film Industry (with Fred Yager)
The Vegetable Passion: A History of the Vegetarian State of Mind
365 Daily Affirmations for Creative Weight Management
Sleeping Well (with Michael J. Thorpy, M.D.)
The Encyclopedia of Sleep and Sleep Disorders
  (with Michael J. Thorpy, M.D.)

Fiction
Untimely Death (with Fred Yager)
Just Your Everyday People (with Fred Yager)
The Cantaloupe Cat (illustrated by Mitzi Lyman)

*This book is dedicated with love and friendship
to the love of my life, my husband Fred Yager,
and to our sons, Scott and Jeffrey*

Disclaimer

This publication contains the opinions of its author and is designed to provide useful information in regard to the subject matter covered. It is sold with the understanding that the author and publisher are not engaged in rendering legal, psychological, matchmaking or other professional services. If the reader requires expert assistance or legal advice, a competent professional should be consulted.

Inclusion in this book does not imply a recommendation of any service or product, nor does omission imply criticism. Readers should consider any listings in this book with the caution and 'buyer beware' attitude that applies when considering any service or product. Nor can the accuracy of any listings be guaranteed since companies may change names and contact information, or even disband overnight. Furthermore, website addresses may be replaced, acquired by others or removed.

Although in this book there may be references to websites and companies that rely predominantly on the Internet, it is not necessary to have a computer or to have access to the Internet to benefit from this book. Every effort has been made to leave out any questionable sites with adult content. However, there are instances where domain names or ownership change and questionable content suddenly appears. This is an extenuating circumstance that is beyond the control of the author or the publisher.

Exercise extreme caution and protect your identity when communicating with anyone you do not know, whether by e-mail, mail or phone and certainly in person.

Most online dating sites require participants to be at least 18 years of age; some brick-and-mortar dating services do not accept clients younger than 21. In the United States, entertainment establishments where drinking is permitted require customers to be at least 21 years of age. Readers must know what laws apply in their particular state, region, or country.

You may put a great deal of time and effort into reading this book and it still may not give you the results you wish. Neither this book nor its author or publisher in any way promise love, finding a date or a mate, happiness or any other results.

The author and publisher specifically disclaim any responsibility for any liability, loss or risk, personal or otherwise, which is incurred as a consequence, directly or indirectly, of the use and application of any of the contents of this book.

Acknowledgements

For this edition, the author wishes to express her gratitude to the men and women, whether named or anonymous, from Australia, New Zealand, England, Ireland, South Africa and Canada, who were gracious enough to complete and return her survey or were interviewed. Thanks especially to Rex Finch, Lorna Patten of Open Up Communication, Colin Chapman, Charlotte Funck-Brentano, and to those individuals, lists and associations who posted the author's request for information including the PUBLISH-L list, Fran Silverman's Book Promotion e-zine, the International Association for Relationships Research (IARR), the forum at www.homesick.com.au and AED. Thanks also to the dedicated staff at Hinkler Books for helping to make this edition a reality: Tracey Ahern, Ruth Coleman, Louise Coulthard, Stephen Ungar, Nadika Garber, Gretta Blackwood, Wendy Ungar, Leanne O'Sullivan and Gary Coppen.

part 1

GEARING UP

chapter 1

WHY YOU NEED THIS BOOK

The goal of this book is to help you find someone to share your life with whether you decide to date or mate. Although the core of this book is the annotated *Meet the Love of Your Life*, it is more than just a how-to manual for finding a date or a mate. This book explores some of the obstacles to finding a romantic partner, and how to overcome them, as well as how to have a more productive search, how to motivate yourself to continue your search, plus advice on becoming and remaining a happy couple.

Since I wrote *Single in America* two decades ago, the number of singles in the United States and internationally has skyrocketed. According to an article in *Family Matters*, written by David De Vaus, Lixia Qu and Ruth Weston, the number of married people in Australia declined from 65 per cent, or two-thirds, of the population in 1971 to just 52 per cent, or a little over half, in 2001. Here are some of the reasons for this global increase in singleness.

1 The need for more education and the increased social acceptance of spending one's twenties or thirties as a single has led to the delaying of entering a first marriage.

2 The widespread quest for a fulfilling, romantic marriage and the acceptance of divorce rather than remaining in an unhappy union means there are more divorced singles. Some may prefer to remain single and unattached but most want to find a new romantic partner or mate.

3 There are more single widows and widowers due to increased life expectancy, as well as spousal deaths from accidents, disease or war.

4 Couples who live together, since unmarried households have become more acceptable, may be considered as singles even though they are in a committed monogamous relationship.

5 The stigma that used to be associated with the never-married woman (spinster) or the single male (bachelor), as well as those who divorce, has been minimized or removed, paving the way for more singles.

6 In those countries where single parenting is acceptable, starting a family is no longer enough of a reason to get married, or to stay married.

7 As sexual intimacy has continued to be available without marriage, postponing marriage until it is for the 'right' reasons means it is easier to remain single longer.

8 As more women have become economically self-sufficient and able to enjoy the freedom to travel and commit to a career, the motivation for marriage has changed, as has the timing of it.

There is still, of course, some fortune and coincidence at work in this whole process and, once you find Mr or Ms Right, a commitment to working hard on your relationship so it flourishes and lasts. That's what makes it such an exciting and challenging experience. Love and romance can happen in the most commonplace situations or the most unexpected ways, as you'll note throughout *Meet the Love of Your Life*. For example, Joanne McCall met her future husband by chance at her job: she was working as a disk jockey at a radio station in Minnesota when she started getting threats from a caller. Her future husband, Gary, was then a policeman and he responded to Joanne's call. They married eight years later. (Joanne shares about their meeting and courtship at the beginning of Chapter 8, 'School, Work or Business').

Five years ago, Wayne, who grew up in Australia and now lives in Canada, went on an African safari. On the safari, he met the woman he would marry two years later. When Penny was 28 and in Beijing, China, where she lives and works, she met her husband, who was then 33 and visiting Beijing on business, because he asked her for directions. A long-distance relationship ensued and they married two years later. Pamela, who is 47 years old, met Karl, her partner of 22 years, through work. These residents of Perth in Western Australia, who both work in the healthcare field, started dating seven months after they met and became an exclusive couple three months later.

But for so many others, finding a date or a mate takes a determined and concerted effort, whether it's because you have been so busy that you stopped putting the time and energy into your social life that it deserves, or you are working in a career or business that offers few of the spontaneous opportunities to meet that often characterized your school, college or graduate school years or your first job experiences. Or perhaps you suddenly want to find a mate before the childbearing years are over, or you just broke up with someone, or you are divorced or widowed and need some help getting back into the dating game.

Not only have the number of singles multiplied, but also the singles industry has expanded into the billion-dollar range. There are an expanding number of websites on the Internet for finding a mate as well as everything from posting a personal ad (profile) to electronic matchmaking, to providing information on clubs and activities for singles that are not Internet-related. There are also non-Internet-based companies and services to sort through, from dating services or clubs for singles to travel opportunities for singles, books on finding a mate, to quick dating single events as a way to meet eligible singles.

With all these companies, associations, services and books for singles, I realized it was time to write a sequel to *Single in America*. In this second book I would focus on how to meet someone as well as exploring blocks to a successful search and how to improve the possibility of becoming, and remaining, a happy couple. I wanted to write a book to answer the question that so many singles had asked me over the years: 'Where do I find "the one"?'

I was also concerned that those with a financially vested interest in one type of meeting option over another were putting down the competition to make their own method seem like 'the' best or only way for singles to spend their time or money in their quest for a romantic partner. Instead, each way of meeting someone has its benefits and drawbacks; what works for one may not work for another for a variety of personality, economic, geographic or even cultural reasons.

As a happily married relationships expert and sociologist without any vested interests in one approach to meeting versus another, I knew that I could describe a wide range of how-to-meet options and let you – the reader – decide what you want to try. I also share in this book what I have learned over the years from researching singleness, as well as romance, marriage, divorce, friendship and even time management.

Success stories throughout the book, including my own, are not recommendations that you go out and try that method. Although placing a personal ad worked for me, it may not be the method that is comfortable for you or most likely to provide you with the outcome you want. Dating services certainly have countless success stories and there are others who find the love of their life through online matching programs, cyberspace dating, at a party, through a blind date, at school, work or by going on a singles cruise.

Ultimately you have to decide what options for meeting you want to try. Financial cost is just one factor; even if a service or program is free, there is the time and effort involved to consider. A key question is: What ways are more likely to help you to achieve your relationship goals?

I interviewed an accomplished professional woman in her mid-40s who lives in Melbourne, Australia. She confided, 'I don't date at all. I haven't had a relationship for a long time'. For her, the new trend toward fast dating, whereby you have numerous dates in a short period of time, would probably *not* be the singles activity to try when she does decide to start dating again. Perhaps being introduced by a mutual friend at a party where she and one or more potential dates were in attendance and then letting 'nature take its course' might be a more low-key way for her to re-enter the dating world. (See Chapter 7, 'Making Introductions', for more on parties and related meetings.)

In the next chapter, I tell the story about how, when I was 35 years old, I met my husband Fred. Since I also wanted you to share our 'how we met' story from my husband's perspective, Fred next provides his account of our meeting and courtship.

Chapter 3 applies time management principles to your romantic search. Everyone should read Chapter 4, 'Staying Safe During Your

Search', since it is essential that singles be especially careful about protecting themselves.

Chapter 5 offers suggestions for 'Getting Ready for Your Search' including overcoming possible obstacles. 'Getting to Know You', Chapter 6, helps you to zone in on what you are looking for in a date or a mate as well as 110 questions that will help you to learn more about someone.

Part 2, 'The Search Begins: 125 Ways to Meet the Love of Your Life', Chapters 7 through 15, contains the 125 annotated ways to find the love of your life, organized into nine separate categories to help you more easily find ways that are suited to your preferences and interests. Examples of successful matches are intertwined throughout those chapters.

'The Next Steps', Part 3, in Chapter 16 offers help in continuing the search till you reach your goal. Chapter 17, 'When You Find "The One"', covers 'How Do You Know?' and 'Tips for Becoming and Remaining a Happy Couple'.

There is a bibliography of works cited in the book and additional references plus an Appendix with the contact information for companies, organizations or associations mentioned in the book plus additional resources.

As noted in the Disclaimer, there are no promises made to you because you read this book. However, I welcome feedback from you about your search and about this book. Thanks for sharing about your search including a successful match, engagement or marriage.

Send your feedback to: Dr Jan Yager, P.O. Box 8038, Stamford, CT 06905-8038, USA, jyager@aol.com.

Good luck on your search! Most of all, be safe and careful, and have fun!

chapter 2

A LOVE STORY

When I was 35, I reached a point in my life where I wanted more than being a writer, sociologist and college professor; I also wanted to find a mate and start a family. Of course I could have continued to leave my love life just to chance or fate. I had been married briefly between the ages of 20 and 23, and had just gotten over the end of a four-year relationship, including two years as an engaged couple. But as my biological clock ticked loud and strong, I wanted to see if there was a way I could help luck along with actions that might increase the likelihood of success.

Yes, I am the author of *Single in America* and I've been researching relationships for two decades. But in this chapter, I want to share the story of how my husband Fred and I met each other, so you know that I've been where you are now. Hopefully you may find our story encouraging as you begin your own search for the love of your life.

My Story
I was Determined to Find the Man of My Dreams

'Your mother and I have resigned ourselves to the fact that you may never marry or have children,' my father said.

'But it's not all right with *me*,' I shouted back.

Even my own parents failed to understand the isolation I felt as a single. I had tried to be a joyful single, filling my life with friends, work and relationships. But it was no longer enough. As I wrote in my diary just before I placed the personal ad that led to meeting the man I would marry, 'Oh, how lonely I am at night when I'm alone'.

I had just broken up with someone whom I had met through conventional means – a friend introduced us. We had been together from the first week I started my doctorate till a few weeks before graduation, four years later.

This break-up was different, however. It left me feeling more determined than ever that I wanted to get married. I was clearer in my vision. Determined, not desperate. I no longer apologized for what I wanted.

After a few months of getting over my four-year relationship, I started dating again. A relationship of six months ensued, but it also led to a break-up.

I decided I needed to become more efficient in my search, increasing the number of potential suitors from which to choose. Placing an ad in the personals seemed like a way to accomplish that.

I had placed ads a couple of times before and although I had not met 'Mr Right' from those previous ads, I had dated a lot. The best of those responses had led to one or two dates with interesting and pleasant men. I rarely met the worst, since I pre-screened them on the basis of their letters. Results from these previous ads were satisfactory enough that I was willing to try the method again. Besides, one of my close friends reminded me that her friend had met his wife through *The Village Voice* newspaper.

I put an ad in *New York* magazine, a publication that was one of the 'in' places for personal ads at that time, especially since I was then living in an apartment in Manhattan. That first ad led to several dates, but I had not yet met the man of my dreams.

Based on an evaluation of the men who were responding to my first ad, I decided to re-write my ad and try again. This time I decided to specify the age and height range that I was looking for. I also changed the emphasis in my occupation from a college professor to a writer. I also decided to state very bluntly my wish to get married and have a family; being subtle about that in the first ad led to too many respondents who were only looking to date or for a fling.

This is the second ad that ran in *New York* magazine:

---

*Cicero wrote – 'Love is the attempt to form a friendship inspired by beauty.'
I'm a successful nonfiction writer looking for an equally exciting successful
man, 5'9 plus, 33–45, who wants a wife and children. I'm pretty, 35, fun.
I like movies, theatre, travel, and sports.*

Some 70 responses soon arrived. (I received a total of 120 letters from the first and second ads.) Overall, the men tended to be creative and successful – artists, writers, editors, financial advisers and lawyers – if not in their jobs, certainly in their spirits.

At that time, because of my fulltime college teaching job, I restricted my dating during the week to just one or two nights. Over the weekends, I tried to schedule dates for breakfast, lunch, drinks and dinner. If it sounds like I was interviewing for a job, you're right: I was interviewing for the job of 'spouse'.

There was a timetable to this hunt as I sensed my biological clock ticking. But, ironically, as I got involved in the process of meeting new people, I began to actually enjoy my singleness more than ever. I could not remember having so much fun just dating since my high school years. I was being wined and dined by numerous eligible men, and it felt good to be fussed over. Lunch or dinner at an 'in' restaurant. Movies. Theatre. Dancing.

By the second week of responses to the ad, I was also meeting more men than usual in other ways such as at parties or through blind dates. I had become much more open to meeting people, comforted that there were many eligible men eager to meet me.

I was not being coy when someone asked me out and I said I was booked for two weeks. While some singles were moaning, 'Where can I find someone?' as they stayed home alone and watched TV, or ran to singles bars where they got discouraged when they met mostly younger men or married men, I was actively dating.

I had developed guidelines about how to deal with meeting men through the personals to better assure my safety. The first rule was never to give out my home address. (I had been provided with a mailing address by the magazine; periodically an envelope with the responses was forwarded to me by the magazine, keeping my identity and address concealed.)

The second rule was that the first meeting was always in a public place. The third rule was to keep the initial meeting to a cup of coffee or a drink, instead of an open-ended dinner, in case I wanted to make a quick getaway. The fourth rule was to leave a record with someone as to my whereabouts, in case of any kind of emergency.

Out of the letters that I received in response to my second ad, I phoned about 25 men. Enough was said during those conversations that I wanted to actually meet 12. I went to lunch with an erudite yet agreeable entertainment lawyer, but he was not my type physically. I went out for coffee with a tall, handsome and kind former high-level city administrator. But there was not enough chemistry to go out on a second date. I dated an intriguing researcher but decided to limit it to two dates when I realized he was definitely not ready to give up being a bachelor any time soon.

One respondent turned out to be someone I had spoken to in a business capacity a few years before. We finally met, but that mysterious spark of connection and attraction was missing. After six phone calls, I never did get to meet an out-of-town stockbroker. He wanted me to meet his train at Penn Station and somehow that just struck me as odd; I thought meeting at a restaurant would have been a more appropriate first encounter.

The best date through the personals, of course, followed my reading of the letter from Fred, the man I would marry. Fred's letter broke one of my other rules since he typed it, and I preferred handwritten, but at least it was original and not a photocopy! It was strong, clear, open and honest and on a piece of beige note paper that had 'Great Ideas' printed in bold letters at the top. Rather than trying to sell himself to me, Fred's letter began, quite simply:

Dear Writer,
Well now you've done it. You've gotten me to answer one of these ads. Now what do I do?

I suppose one way to answer an ad IS with an ad. Is that proper? Here's what I'd say:

Successful screenwriter, looking for collaborator in love and work. I'm 38, 6'4, handsome, with a background in film and a BA in psychology.

Like you, I'm looking for someone who's exciting and wants a family. 'A life unshared isn't worth . . . etc.' I don't know who said it.

I'm compelled to tell you more about myself but I'd rather do that in person or at least over the phone.

You can reach me at --- ---- I look forward to hearing from you.
Sincerely,
(Signed) Fred Yager

I called Fred as soon as I finished his letter. I expected to talk to a phone machine since it was during the day but he answered the phone. (He was a freelance writer working from home at the time.)

I immediately liked his soothing voice and his comfortable conversational style. Usually I ended a conversation by being vague about a get-together, preferring a cooling-off period between phone calls so I could reassess what had transpired. But there was something magical about Fred from the very beginning that caused me to ignore all such rules and at his insistence agree to meet him later that night.

We met at a restaurant after I attended a business networking party – I was instantly attracted to him – but ended up talking till two in the morning. I accepted a date for the next day that I planned to sandwich in between a lunch date and a party, and Fred put me in a cab.

The next day, Fred and I went to an afternoon movie. Fred had just come from visiting a female friend in hospital who had had surgery. That's the kind of caring man Fred is, and my awe for his selflessness continues and deepens with each wonderful day of our relationship.

There are many things Fred said and did that caused me to fall in love with him. I read and admired his writing. He could also verbally express his feelings and needs. (Some writers are only comfortable with their emotions on paper.) I could be my true self with him. He could be outgoing and somewhat shy at the same time. He knew how to say, 'I'm sorry'.

Within two weeks, I knew I was deeply in love with Fred and that I wanted to spend the rest of my life with him. I asked him if he wanted to get married and he said he needed more time to decide. I told him that was fine but he couldn't expect me to wait around for him to decide and that I would keep on dating till he made up his mind.

I didn't know if he needed weeks, months, years or if it was just a stall tactic. Much to my delight and surprise, a few days later, Fred proposed. (I had to cancel my registration with a dating service because we became engaged the day before my scheduled interview.)

We married five days later at a wonderful afternoon wedding that we put together quickly, attended by amazed friends and family. It was just three weeks after we had met.

I'm not saying the personal ads are for everyone. I remember that a 39-year-old woman sought me out because she had heard of my success with the personals. She had placed an ad, and was not pleased with the results. She wanted to know if I had a formula I could pass on, or if I had just been lucky.

I showed her what I wrote in my ad. 'Your ad wasn't very specific,' she said. 'I'm surprised you got any good responses.'

I quickly re-read my ad, silently counting no less than nine specific traits about myself!

Of course there's some luck and chance involved in all of this. I also believe I would have fallen in love with Fred if I had met him at the corner bus stop. But there's a positive mental attitude and that's not luck. I learned to view everyone I met through the personals as valuable special adventures, looking for the good in everyone I met.

The personal ads taught me that if the ways you are using to meet people are not working, try new ways, however unconventional, as long as they're legitimate and safe. The very same people who gasp at your methods will applaud your success. Looking for a mate, or even just for a new date, is like looking for a new job, of most concern to you. You can ask your friends or family for help, but after all their leads, it just might be time to venture out into wider circles.

The One for Me
by Fred Yager

Falling in love was never easy for me. Each time it seemed to take a larger amount of raw courage to re-open my heart to potentially harmful forces. While many of the women I loved caused me excruciating pain when that love was no longer returned, I recall each with a special fondness because they prepared me for the ultimate search that led to the one true love of my life.

To me, love, true love, is one of life's miracles. True love, like true north, is love with direction, with purpose. True love doesn't fear rejection, or abandonment. True love is active, not passive. It is a giver, not a taker; it fills from within, not from without. It makes you strong and daunting, not weak and wanting. People who find true love are envied by anyone who hasn't and are therefore vulnerable to attack by the majority of those who are still searching or have given up all together.

For finding true love is a search, a quest. It takes time when you find it and courage to say 'no' when you don't. I had just ended a four-year relationship with a woman I thought was my true love. But the relationship never grew to that pivotal level where we both shared the same dream for the future. When I realized there was no way I was going to change her mind about wanting a family, I began the process of dissolving an otherwise wonderful relationship.

When it was over, it took me nearly a year before I was even ready to meet someone new. But when I was ready, it didn't take long to find her.

It was the autumn of 1984. After a year of putting all my time and energy into a freelance screenwriting career, I emerged from my cavernous apartment and headed out into the world in search of a partner. Someone to share my life and my dreams.

I went to all the regular places, singles bars and networking salons. I read the personals in *New York* magazine and *The Village Voice*. I even circled a few possibilities. I met women in bars and discos, on blind dates, at the gym, in the supermarket, at the museum, on the subway and through work. No one seemed to click.

Still, I knew what I wanted, to meet someone I could fall in love with, who also wanted a family. I met a few women who were definitely attractive enough, or nice enough personality-wise, but they still lacked the other main ingredient of wanting children.

So I kept searching, refusing to settle. I knew she was out there. I just had to be ready to move when I found her. Now, I've never been a very aggressive person. I tend to be a little shy. And when it came to love, having been burned so often, I was also a bit gun-shy. But I knew I didn't want to spend the rest of my life living alone with my two cats.

I was reading the personals in *New York* magazine when an ad leaped out at me. There was something special about it. I could tell a creative force was behind the writing, a force that I connected with. So I dashed off a quick note in response.

A few days later, I got a call from Jan. She was answering my letter to her ad. I knew immediately I wanted to meet her. But she said she was booked for several weeks. So I said either meet me tonight or forget about it. So we met. Three weeks later we got married. And all it took to meet her was raw courage and knowing what I wanted.

Now we've been married 19 years. We have two great sons and a beautiful marriage. Jan is truly the love of my life.

When people ask how we did it, we say we followed our hearts. All it takes is guts, a belief in love, and a commitment to togetherness. Most of all, it takes being ready, but sometimes you don't know if you are ready until you do it. That's how we found out.

chapter 3

How to Have a More Productive Search and Increase the Odds

After a time of mourning, a widow in her fifties decided she wanted to find a new mate. Every night after work for the next year, she went out, dedicated to her goal of finding a second husband, and she did.

When I first heard that anecdote in my early thirties, I didn't appreciate the message to that story. Like so many of my baby boom peers, I was putting work before all else and I also didn't yet understand time management and how those concepts could be applied to love as well as work. Furthermore, I was content to let love 'happen', getting asked out, and falling in love, as chance permitted. After a four-year relationship ended, I initially went about social life in the same 'purely by chance' fashion as before.

Then I got the phone call from my older sister that changed my life by providing the motivation and clarity about what I wanted that had been eluding me. My sister Eileen is 17 months older than I am and I figured as long as my older sister was not worried about starting a family, I had plenty of time as well. My sister had married at the age of 20 but she and her husband had not rushed into parenthood since both their careers involved a lot of travel. But when I got that phone call announcing that my 36-year-old sister was three months pregnant, I of course congratulated my sister but when I got off the phone I wondered, 'What about me?' I did not have a boyfriend – let alone a mate – so what were my prospects of getting married and starting a family any time soon? Maybe it was time to go about searching for a mate in a more concerted way since I suddenly became conscious of my ticking biological clock.

I had learned a great deal about the power of taking control of your time with proven techniques, such as goal setting and prioritizing, during the previous two years as I conducted original research for my first business book, *Creative Time Management*. Why not apply those methods to my love life and see what I could accomplish? I decided to apply time management techniques to my search for a mate.

As a single self-supporting woman, I had to find time to search for love without jeopardizing my job. Old-fashioned dating, although an investment of time is, in the long run, the typical way most find what we wanted all along, someone with whom we truly can be ourselves and with whom love can grow and deepen. Most of us have to go through the numbers because dating helps you to find out who you are as well as what turns you on, or off, so that you have a wider basis of comparison, and more confidence, in your decision when chemistry and everything else seems to be there.

An effective love search campaign may benefit by turning it into a time management issue. In contrast to a haphazard or disorganized approach, if you apply the basics of time management – goal setting, planning, getting organized, prioritizing, 'to do' lists, improving communication skills – your love search may be more productive.

Creative Time Management Basics

In my second book on time management, *Creative Time Management for the New Millennium*, I identify seven principles of creative time management.

1. Be active, not just reactive.
2. Set goals.
3. Prioritize actions.
4. Keep your focus.
5. Create realistic deadlines.

6. D-O I-T N-O-W.
7. Balance your life.

Here are those principles applied to searching for a date or a mate:

1. Be Active, Not Just Reactive

There are two approaches to the way someone manages his or her time – reactive, whereby you respond to the demands of others, and active, whereby you generate your own options.

How you manage your time during your love search will be affected by whether this is a reactive search, whereby you just go about your business and hope that he or she will notice you across a crowded room, or waiting for the bus; or an active search, whereby you deliberately go about creating social opportunities for yourself.

For some, the reactive approach does work. As initially noted in Chapter 1, Penny, a consultant in China, was stopped on the street by a visitor from Australia who asked her for directions. A long-distance relationship ensued and finally her future husband relocated to Beijing, where they were married two years after that initial meeting and where they live today.

For others, especially those who are older and for whom it is harder to find an available mate because the majority are married or going with someone rather than single and available as they were during the school years, taking a more active role in the search, rather than leaving it to chance, may be what is called for.

An active approach means you decide what is important to you and you say 'no' to anything or anyone that interferes. For example, you want to get married and after three dates you learn your date is committed to remaining single. Or you meet someone who is pleasant to be around but there are just too many incompatibility issues so you do not want a long-term relationship. What will you do in either situation so you have an active control of your search?

Being active, however, also means being open to those reactive opportunities that occur. For example, someone calls you and asks you if you would like to go out on a blind date, or you meet someone at a party and you feel chemistry toward each other and you are both eligible and looking.

Job-search campaigns employ a variety of tactics, such as reading alumni newsletter job listings or 'help wanted' newspaper

17

advertisements. They also employ word of mouth networking. Similarly, don't be shy about telling everyone you know, or meet, that you're looking for a date or a mate. Get invited to parties, or give them. If you give a party, ask your guests to use it as an opportunity to bring along any single people they know that you might be interested in.

Whether you are trying to find new friends, or new dates, visibility is usually the key. That usually means getting out and being active and involved in community, educational, sports, or volunteer activities.

One of the most effective time management tools when it comes to any kind of search is a written 'to do' list. Since finding the love of your life, or someone to date, is a key concern, have activities related to achieving that goal on your 'to do' list.

It will be easier to be active in your search for the love of your life if you also follow creative time management principle number two, namely, set goals.

2. SET GOALS

If you don't know where you're going, how will you know how to get there, or what you're striving for? It's tempting to be concerned only with 'the next relationship', but a one-, five- or ten-year romantic plan will aid this and every love search. A broad goal, such as 'I'd like to be married' or 'I'd like to have two children', differs from a well-conceived plan. A plan includes figuring out what kind of person you would be most comfortable with, how you're going to find that person, and what you will do once you find him or her. You need to specify the steps you will take to achieve your goal or you'll be back to the reactive approach, leaving one of the two most important aspects of your life – one is love, two is work – to pure chance.

Take a few minutes to ponder the following questions, writing down your considered answers.

Three weeks from now, I plan to accomplish:

_____

Six months from now, I plan to accomplish:

_____

One year from today, I plan to accomplish:
_____

In five years, I plan to accomplish:
_____

To achieve these goals, my dating activity plan is:
_____

Now that you have a long-term romantic plan, and a 'next step' short-term plan, you can zero in on your current date search, more confident that there is a focus and an active component to your explorations. In this way, you will be less likely to just react to each and every date offer, no matter how at odds it is with your romantic plan.

Paul Falzone, CEO of Together Dating® and The Right One® dating services, a brick-and-mortar franchise throughout the United States of in-person matchmakers, emphasizes that the most successful clients of his dating services are the ones with clear goals. Says Falzone:

Some [clients] come for companionship, some to get married, or maybe someone just moved into the area and wants to network to meet more people. If you come to us with a positive attitude, a realistic set of expectations, and a willingness to work with us – we're going to need honest feedback once a match is made if it was a good match – your chances of success are very good.

---

3. PRIORITIZE ACTIONS

Remember that this romantic search may just have to be your number one priority. Yes, of course there are those who can just take this search in stride, and that might have worked for you at other times in your life. But this time, for a variety of reasons, you are trying this new, more focused, approach to finding the love of your life.

Until you achieve your goal of a new love, learn to say 'no' to optional requests on your time that interfere. Furthermore, each romantic search will have priorities unique to that search so clarify what is most important to you, whether that includes rewriting your personal ad, getting some new clothes, or going on a two-week vacation where you might meet hundreds of eligible singles.

Until you find a loved one, your priority task is your romantic search. Since dating takes time you may have to be even more efficient at work by applying the same time management techniques to your job. In that way, you will get more accomplished in less time so you'll be out of the office before eight and you won't have to do work on the weekends as often if at all.

I knew a woman when she was single and in her late forties who admitted to me that she purposely worked till nine each night so by the time she came home, had dinner and watched a little TV, it was time to go to bed (alone) to prepare for work again the next day. She somehow managed to get through the weekends and the cycle kept going on. And it would probably go on unless she decided to take a more active stand and prioritize dating and finding a mate. (When I ran into her after 15 years, she was still single, unattached, working long hours, and still longing for a romantic relationship.)

Short-term planning will revolve around all the background research, phone calls and interviews you will have to carry on in order to achieve your short-term goal, namely finding the love of your life. Once again, long-term plans aid short-term planning since you will be doing things, if you haven't been doing them all along, that will make each search easier. You may decide, for example, that staying in touch with recommended matchmaking services is a time-saver, as well as going to parties or sharing with others who are searching about online or print personals that are working well for them.

You may also decide to update or revise your personal ad, or get a new photograph, if you decided to post one, if you aren't getting the results that you want.

4. Keep Your Focus

To achieve your goal of finding the love of your life, you may need to keep that as your focus even if others tell you to just 'let nature take its course'. Although some may find that love just 'happens', for others, it helps to make it the focus in your life. Of course you want to get ahead at work, but you also need to keep your focus so you accept a date rather than using work or other activities as an excuse for being too busy.

Since you may be dating more frequently than you have in a long time, you definitely want to keep the names and details clear about the various people you are meeting. You certainly do not want to call someone by the wrong name, or forget a detail you have been told between the first and second date. If necessary, after a date, if you do plan to see someone again, write down as many of the key details you can remember that were shared, such as favorite color, birthday, occupation and so forth.

5. Create Realistic Deadlines

Women who are of childbearing age who want to find a mate before their biological clock stops ticking may have more of a reason to set a deadline for their romantic search than most others. However, there can be an emotional need to find someone regardless of someone's age or wish for a family that also makes a deadline a useful technique for the romantic search.

Deadlines help someone to focus. 'I want to be married in a year' or 'I'd like to find someone to settle down with by the time I'm 40' could be helpful in motivating you to have a plan to your search.

6. D-O I-T N-O-W

Once you create a plan, and you are focused, just do it *now*. Here is a convenient way to help you recall this sixth principle of creative time management.

D = Divide and conquer what you have to do.

Break up an overwhelming task into smaller, more manageable ones, and give each part of that task a realistic deadline.

O = Organize your materials, how you will do it.

Take notes as you read this book. When you find a way out of the 125 ways that you want to explore, do your homework. Do research, online or by making phone inquiries.

I = Ignore interruptions that are annoying distractions.

You are the one who will most benefit from finding the love of your life. Keep yourself on task.

T = Take the time to learn how to do things yourself.

What ways are working for you? What new, effective ways can you come up with?

N = Now, not tomorrow. Don't procrastinate.

Unless there's a good reason to delay, get going on your search now.

O = Opportunity is knocking. Take advantage of excellent opportunities.

Timing can be crucial when dating and mating.

W = Watch out for time gobblers.

The Internet can help your search, or keep you away from connecting. TV can be a source of relaxation, entertainment and information, or it can be a 24-hour companion that keeps you from reaching out to real people.

How do you deal with time gobblers? Keep track of, and in control of, how much time you spend on the Internet, reading and sending e-mails, watching TV or talking on the phone. Watching some TV, of course, is educational as well as a way to relax, reduce stress and for entertainment. The Internet may of course be helpful in your search but it could also be a time gobbler and a way of avoiding interactions.

7. Balance Your Life

You don't want to lose your job while you're dating, nor do you want to misuse your work as an excuse to avoid dating. A balanced life includes time for work, intimate relationships, friends, family, community activities and relaxation.

chapter 4

STAYING SAFE DURING YOUR SEARCH

I have researched crime, crime victimization, and crime prevention for my book *Victims* (Scribner's, 1978), for my masters in criminal justice, and, more recently, for a study of adult survivors of childhood and teenage sexual abuse. Although it is important not to blame the victim for what happens to him or her, it is also known that taking certain precautions to decrease the likelihood that someone might become a victim is useful in helping to prevent victimization in the first place.

Singles need to walk the line between taking as many precautions as possible so they are not extremely vulnerable but not being so overly paranoid that they use a fear of becoming a victim as a justification to avoid meeting new people or going out on a date.

There are cases, however, of first meetings that end tragically that emphasize the potential dangers. Just one recent example is the murder of a 14-year-old girl by a 17-year-old boy whom she had met on the Internet and with whom she had been talking on the phone for nine months before their one meeting. According to Andrew Jacobs' article in *The New York Times*, the victim, who was living with her grandfather, waited until he went away overnight to invite her suitor to her isolated home. The teen allegedly confessed to stabbing the girl to death and then setting her and her home on fire, telling the arresting officers, 'I just snapped'.

Dr Signe Dayhoff, who is now in her fifties, shared with me what happened to her when she was 28. A healthcare professional she met through a computer dating service 'tried to press his advantage' when she made the mistake of going 'out in the boonies to see his newly refurbished office and the exotic Hollywood-style pad above it'. After 20 minutes, she talked him out of his plan. It could have had a tragic ending but it did not although what occurred was still traumatic and frightening.

Don't become a crime statistic; take precautions to stay safe during your search. Homicide is of course the worst possible outcome but there's also date rape, assault, kidnapping, robbery and even burglary to be concerned about.

Here are tips for increasing your personal safety during your search for the love of your life.

Personal Safety Tips

- The number one rule: never meet alone in an isolated situation or at someone's apartment or home. Stay in public places surrounded by others until you are absolutely secure about someone.

- Don't reveal your complete name, phone number or home address to a stranger whether you meet over the Internet, through a dating service or at a bar. For safety reasons, use a post office box or only e-mail.

- Be very careful about any personal information that you reveal and certainly do not brag about any financial assets or personal wealth.

- Once you meet or connect with someone, keep your emotions in check while you weigh carefully what someone says in terms of how reliable or believable it sounds.

- If you have an instinctive feeling of fear about someone, trust your gut and keep yourself safe.

- If you need a second opinion, consider bringing a friend along.

- If necessary, check out the implausible parts of someone's autobiography so you feel more comfortable that what you're hearing is true.

- Take the relationship at whatever pace is comfortable for you. Don't let anyone pressure you into an intimate relationship before you want to engage in one.

- You have a right to ask someone to take a blood test and to show you the results if you have any suspicions that someone might be HIV+ or have any kind of sexually transmitted diseases.

- You have a right to ask someone to use protection if you wish your relationship to become sexual.

- If sexual intimacy is mutually desired, take the necessary steps to protect yourself from any unwanted pregnancies or sexually transmitted diseases.

- Be on the lookout for any signs that someone is hiding that he or she is married, engaged, living with someone or otherwise romantically unavailable, such as a reluctance to ever ask you out on a Saturday night or weekend, unwillingness to let you call him or her at home, too many missing personal details, or a tan line where a wedding band is usually worn.

- Create business card-size cards with just your phone number, or get an outside phone service that requires you to call in for messages, and use that number instead. Do not include your address or any other personal information on the card.

- Make sure at least one person knows your whereabouts at all times. If you are meeting someone for a date even if it is in a public place, give his or her phone number and contact information to someone you trust so there is documentation about your whereabouts.

- Carry a fully charged cell phone with you at all times so you are able to call for help or a taxi or car service if you have car trouble, if necessary.

- Men have to be careful that they are not being solicited by prostitutes misusing the Internet or any other type of entrée to dating by posing as an eligible single looking for a legitimate relationship.

- Everyone has to be on guard against websites that are not legitimate dating sites but are really porn sites. Check out a website's legitimacy before you visit it or share any information including your e-mail address.

- College or graduate school students should follow the crime prevention guidelines issued by your school to reduce placing yourself in vulnerable dating situations.

- If traveling, check if there is a government travel warning advisory. (See Appendix for listing.)

- Whether you're 60 or 30, the advice your parents told you when you were a child or teen still holds: Never ever get into a car with a stranger.

- Be careful about attending any private or commercial establishments where there is drinking; you must be of legal drinking age and there has to be a designated driver who does not drink.

- Keeping in mind the tragedy in Rhode Island in 2003 where 100 people died because of a fire that broke out at a club, be careful that you choose to attend concerts, clubs or restaurants where the building is safe, and that there are ample available exit signs in case of an emergency.

- Remember that even if you are careful, other drivers may not be as diligent. If possible, stay off the roads on holidays including New Year's Eve. Attend nearby parties or arrange for overnight accommodations.

chapter 5

GETTING READY FOR YOUR SEARCH

Be Open to All Kinds of New Relationships

Getting ready means keeping an open mind about love and being open to meeting new potential dates. It also means meeting people and being open to new relationships, such as friendships. As a 32-year-old single musician wrote to a 30-year-old divorced woman who was using her work to avoid people: 'Personal growth comes from interaction with people'.

Sometimes you meet someone and even though it does not lead to a romance, it could lead to a friendship and that friend might introduce you to her or his friends who might turn out to be the one. But even if that does not happen, 18-year-old Angel Rivera, a freshman at the University of Connecticut at Storrs and a cheerleader for football and men's basketball, is glad that the girl he met at a party has become his friend. Angel shares what transpired:

'Aren't you a UConn cheerleader?' a tall brunette asked me.

I was wearing a UConn cheerleading sweatshirt that said 'UConn Cheerleader'.

'Yeah, do you go to my games?' I replied.

From there, the conversation got more intense and initially I was interested in her because physically she was my type. Finally it got to the point where we exchanged numbers.

We did call each other a couple of times and we did hang out, but it didn't work out. She's a friend now. Not only do I get a friend but also I have someone who could introduce me to other possible candidates for the love of my life.

Meeting People is an Art and a Skill

Have you noticed that some people always seem to be meeting new and interesting people, while others continue within the same circle of acquaintances and friends? Meeting people is an art and skill that can be learned and developed just like cooking or bicycle riding.

The primary asset of persons who are able to meet people easily is that they make the most of each situation, no matter how fleeting or inconsequential. For example, you are having dinner alone in a neighborhood restaurant. The person at another table is also alone. How do you begin a conversation? Should you both pass the meal in silence? If you have cultivated the friendship of the waiter or waitress, he or she may be able to act as an intermediary and introduce you to the other patron, especially if you are both regular customers and he knows that the patron is single and looking to meet someone.

I remember a time I was having dinner in a Japanese restaurant with my sister and brother-in-law on a Friday night. Behind us there was a woman who told the waiter she was waiting for a party of six to arrive. To her right, there was a single man eating dinner alone. Within a few minutes, I observed that she had moved and was now sitting next to the man, talking to him as he sipped his soup. About ten minutes later, five other men and women arrived – the friends she had been waiting for. The single woman invited the single man to join her friends. They all introduced themselves and shared the rest of their meal.

One of the most helpful insights that I gained from *A New Look at Love* by Elaine and G. William Walster is that the ability to be relaxed is rated the highest factor in attraction to the opposite sex. It's a useful concept to keep in mind when psyching oneself up to go to a party or on a blind date or into any new situation, for that matter.

Another useful classic book, illustrated with line drawings, is *How*

To Read a Person Like a Book by Gerald I. Nierenberg and Henry H. Calero. The authors point out that it is not just what you say that indicates whether you are relaxed or not, or projects a certain image; it is also how you sit or stand. If you are continually attracting men or women who completely contradict the type of person you would like to meet and get to know, perhaps you are sending off impressions and images that are diametrically opposed to what you think you are transmitting. Are your gestures indicating openness or, as Nierenberg and Calero point out in their book, are you instead indicating defensiveness, evaluation or suspicion?

What about phoning? This is often a challenge for many who are trying to meet, and follow up with, new people. A successful arbitrator who has been trained in group dynamics advises: unless it's an emergency, late-hour calls indicate panic and desperation. Why is this important to someone who is trying to improve, or re-establish a social life? Because what you perceive as being spontaneous and natural in calling whenever you want may be misinterpreted as despondency or hysteria, or an inability to 'get through the night'. Try to call no earlier than ten am (at home) or after 10 pm (in the evening). You may also want to consider whether it is a weekday night or a date night (Friday or Saturday) and modify your calling behavior accordingly. Especially in the beginning of a relationship, you may want to be cautious about how early you call on a Sunday morning, if you are unsure of what transpired Saturday night.

Be Friendly

Most people will agree that when you are down and out, it is hard to be a people magnet. Ironically, those who 'need' someone the most have to work hardest not to communicate that need too soon. If you evince an ability to make it alone – even though you still want to be with others – there is a lot more room for peer or romantic relationships.

Of course you have to use your judgment about whom you want to meet or get to know, but friendliness is a quality that propels you forward in both your personal and professional life. Good conversationalists know what to reveal and what to disclose; how to titillate without overwhelming; how to be remembered favorably; and how not to be ignored; how to show interest nonverbally by flirting and body language.

Becoming a Better Friend May Help

How good a friend are you? Working on your friendship skills and friendship relationships so you feel loved and special could help you to have more confidence, a definite plus in finding a romantic partner.

You may also find that committing to a friendship, if you have intimacy issues, may help you to develop the resiliency to deal with the ups and downs of a romantic relationship. For example, if you and your friend are supposed to get together but something comes up, learning to cut your friend some slack and not over-react to a change in plans may be helpful when someone you just met or are dating has to adjust your plans.

Although romantic relationships of course have even more levels and expectations than a friendship, some of the same skills, such as having fun together and feeling you trust each other and are compatible, will be similar in both intimate relationships.

Build Your Self-Confidence

Do whatever it takes to build your self-esteem from within, feeling good about your personality and the kind of person you are. The better you feel about yourself, the more attractive you become to other people.

Work on building up your self-confidence from within. Tell yourself, 'I'm wonderful and I deserve to share myself with someone who finds me wonderful and whom I like and love'. Believe it. Believe in yourself. Believe in the possibilities and love.

Dress the Part

Yes, those who are dating and trying to find a mate put a great deal of effort into how they look and they should. You want to show that you are ready, available and desirable, not only on the inside but on the outside as well.

Put your best foot forward by taking an interest in every aspect of your appearance, including:

- your attitude

- your clothes

- your figure

- your hair

- your skin.

You will enhance your self-confidence by improving your appearance. If necessary, buy new clothes, work out, eat a better diet, and lose or gain weight, as needed. Michelle, a conference manager living in Melbourne, Australia shared with me how being poorly dressed was one of the reasons that she had just one date with a man she met through Internet dating. Michelle explains: 'He arrived very badly dressed like what my father would wear around the house to go gardening'.

Keep Believing in Love and being a Romantic

Here's an article I wrote that was published in *Newsday* newspaper just four months before I received the letter from my future husband, Fred.

I'm reprinting it because it pinpoints the commitment to dating and the strength to face the outcome of a romantic relationship, even if it does not lead to finding 'the one', as a positive pro-dating philosophy that, in my case certainly, kept my heart open to the possibility of love. Perhaps the point of view expressed in this article will inspire you or someone you know to keep looking, and dating, without bitterness or hostility (but of course always with safety and common sense to help keep you safe during the search).

Maintain Speed: Love Zone Ahead

Sometimes I wonder if one's friends truly know what's best. In their well-meaning desire to protect you from possible disappointment, they admonish you to 'take it slow', 'don't plunge', 'see what happens', especially in regard to love. I understand their caution. Yet how are you to get to the middle of a relationship, if your fear of its ending arrests its beginning?

Eight months ago, after meeting my most recent ex-boyfriend, I was so euphoric that I sent a contribution to charity to celebrate our first 18 days together. We both tried our best in that relationship; it ended because we were not meant to share the rest of our lives together. Is that a failure, or a triumph of giving love a best effort in the hope that someday, with someone, it will be forever?

I swore that next time I would be more cautious, using divine wisdom to foretell the future of any romantic exhilaration. I didn't know exactly how I'd accomplish that, since love depends on interaction, not fantasies. In theory, being cautious makes sense, especially if you're 35 and no longer a kid. Yet how can one truly know someone else without peeling pretense? Do you ask for references, as for a job? Do you look over a 'love resumé?' What could those other experiences really mean anyway, when it comes to the sublime combination of the you at this moment and the him of now, not yesterday. How you get along together can only be understood by being together.

To my great surprise, 'the next time' evolved out of a business lunch the day after I broke up with my boyfriend. I tried playing hard to get with this new man, continuing to meet, and date, others, even shouting to him, and to a few choice friends, that I was going to fight these feelings because I didn't want to get hurt again. But the magic happened for both of us, and we've decided to see if it grows.

I look around at so many frightened and jaded single people. They want guarantees; they have laundry lists for ideal spouses, and never date, or date 25 people that they never see a second time. I once was that scared, throwing my love into work, a surer road to fulfillment, or friends, a safer way to gain nurturance. But I've gotten stronger in the last few years, and I will only know him, and the me he brings out, by knowing him.

I'm not making contributions to charity this time, but I am having fun and letting him know I care. Despite the 'here she goes again' censures of some friends, I am optimistic about these loving feelings. I used to hold back, but I can't anymore; this time it just might be 'right'. Refusing to love is the tragedy, not that love may end.

I'm telling my cynical friends that I'm a big girl, and I'll be fine even if it doesn't last, if that's what has to be. I will not be apologetic for the fact that I did not have to wait very long for another chance at love. There is too much cynicism and too little joy in this world to risk happiness passing by. I'm all for reflecting on past experiences as a learning process, but that can be done privately and in the midst of newfound joy. My willingness to love again so soon shows that my last boyfriend, even if not 'Mr. Right', reaffirmed my commitment to romantic partnership.

I actually bought a book about making a man fall in love with you, hoping I might learn new scripts for success. It said that almost everything I was doing was wrong, and I should not 'send him every adorable card' that I find, nor 'bake his favorite oatmeal raisin cookies for him on every visit'. But I sent him a musical card, and he liked it, and I baked his favorite brownies, and he was grateful for that too. I can't follow that book's advice, because it's my nature to give, and maybe this time he'll be the one I can always give to.

Consider Cultural Differences in Meeting, Dating and Mating

It is also crucial to keep dating customs in mind by region as well as by religion, country or culture. What is acceptable and typical in contemporary India, for example, may vary compared to what is typical for those who live in Australia, New Zealand, the United States, England, Canada, France, Spain, Italy, Korea, Ireland, Taiwan, South Africa, or first-generation Indians from India who are now United States citizens.

If you are using an online dating service and you indicate that you are open to considering possible dates or matches from around the world, being aware of the customs and attitudes in those cultures may help you to avoid heartbreak or heartache down the road.

Dating customs are subject to change; sometimes it is an overnight change that only time will tell if it is a fad, such as the quick dating singles events as noted in Chapter 7, 'Making Introductions'. Sometimes the changes take decades or even centuries and are more profound and fundamental. Or sometimes the differences are cultural as well as semantics. For example, as a 47-year-old business coach who lives in Sussex, England, pointed out to me: 'For a start, in the UK we don't call it "dating". We call it "going out". These days it usually involves sex, but not always.' (He met his wife 21 years ago on a sailing holiday in Greece.)

Even within a country, there may be regional differences in dating. As a psychologist in Perth, Western Australia, who counsels couples points out: 'I would think that the social scene in Sydney and Melbourne would be much more active than in Perth. Perth is quite a distance from every other major city in Australia and I think it suffers somewhat from a "small town" attitude'.

You also have to be careful not to assume that cultures are exactly the same because the same language is spoken. As the Perth psychologist points out about England, Australia, the United States, New Zealand and Canada: 'People from each culture see themselves as totally separate and different... I think Australians have more similarities to Canadians than Americans and New Zealanders, well, that's a whole other story!'

In some countries, the changes and contrasts are more dramatic. For instance, in South Korea arranged marriages are a thing of the past as paid dating services or asking parents and colleagues for introductions are more common, according to an article in the *Seattle Post-Intelligencer*. One dating agency, with more than 4000 members, charges 200,000 won (approximately $230) to members. An investigator does a background check and, in contrast to typical dating services in the United States which require the complete fee up front, only if a couple gets married through the agency there is an additional 'thank-you fee' of $1100 paid by both the groom and the bride.

Marriage is still a goal in most cultures even as the stigma of remaining single, even for women, has subsided a little; and even where the divorce rate has escalated, so too has the remarriage rate.

But the fear of making the wrong choice, and possibly feeling the necessity of remaining in an unhappy marriage since, even today, in some cultures or religions, divorce may still bring shame to the family, may cause women, and men, to avoid dating or marriage altogether rather than make a 'mistake'. As a 23-year-old single woman living in Seoul shared with me: 'I feel bored at being single and trying to fall in love as well. I am poor at how to find a date or a mate.'

Finding the right person to share your life with is one of the life's greatest challenges. Twenty-six-year-old Catherine, who lives in Melbourne, Australia, is content to be single but she would like to 'eventually get married if I meet the right person'. Catherine discloses: 'It is extremely hard to meet people of the opposite sex'. Fifty-five-year-old Gavan, a single writer living in Melbourne, would also like to 'find a life partner'; he finds that by being single he is 'missing the "wow" factor'. Hopefully the pages that follow will offer hope, insights, inspiration and suggestions for you as you search for the love of your life.

Overcoming Potential Blocks to Your Search

I've observed several consistent themes in why men or women give up on 'the search', as well as key factors that doom some relationships from the start.

Sometimes it may be a question of changing one's attitude about the search that helps someone to meet new potential dates or mates in a variety of happenstance or planned situations; *Meet the Love of Your Life* includes advice about finding a way to enjoy the search and how to make it more productive so you are more likely to be optimistic and upbeat.

It is of course hard to take the search in stride when there is a time element or someone feels pressured – emotionally, by his or her family, or by a multiplicity of other factors – to find someone *now*. Yet pressure is a very complex and insidious thing. As I've learned in researching time management, a little bit of pressure is a motivator; too much usually shuts someone down and pushes others away. So it's a question of walking the fine line between being motivated so you are actually searching and not ignoring your emotional or physical needs for love and finding a mate, but not so determined and goal-oriented that you are not fun to be with or able to let romance unfold in the pace and manner that it is meant to between you and a particular person. (In my friendship research, I also similarly observed that too much pressure on a new friend, or even on an existing friendship, could lead to a failed friendship or a friendship that eventually fades away.)

What have I noticed are the biggest blocks to even starting a search?

Seven Blocks to Beginning Your Search

1. Fear of rejection.

We've all been at that point where we just ended a relationship and the recovery time from that failed relationship is taking just as long as it's going to take. Once you are ready to deal with dating again it will be possible to get out there and search until you find 'the one' whether it takes five more relationships, five months or five years.

2. Too much loss.

Whether a relationship ends because one or both of you decide you're not right for each other and you break up or divorce, or a partner dies, grieving for a failed or ended relationship takes time. Until that grief work is done, it may be hard to even have the motivation to find someone new. Grief work, like overcoming a fear of rejection, is highly individual. For some, it takes weeks or months, for others it takes years, or it seems to be dealt with almost instantaneously.

3. School, work or family pressures.

Some are able to 'do it all', school, work, taking care of a family or even a pet, community or volunteer activities and so forth. Others need to be at a point in their lives where they are able to add to the mix the time and energy that it takes to date and explore a new relationship.

Dating does take time. It's time well spent but you need to be ready, willing and able to devote that time to dating. Sometimes that means over the weekend, semester or summer breaks from college or graduate school, at work when you no longer have to work overtime for weeks at a time or even the graveyard shift at some jobs, or, if you are a single parent, when you have the childcare help that allows you the time and peace of mind to date.

4. You like dating but you don't want to commit to 'the one' right now.

Knowing that you're at a point in your life that you just want 'a date' but not the emotional commitment to 'the one', whether a boyfriend or girlfriend, exclusive romantic partner or even a spouse, can be useful information so you can give out the right signals to others. As an 80-year-old widow recently told me, 'I don't want a love affair, I want companionship. Someone to go with, someone to dance with.'

5. 'I'll start looking when I lose weight.'

If you feel you need to lose weight, do it, although there will be someone who cares for you, whether you have to lose a couple of pounds or 50.

But whatever it is about yourself that you feel you need to change before you begin your search, deal with it, and get on with the search. Or accept yourself as you are and look anyway. The key is not to use a quest for perfectionism to keep you from finding true love. But if you think you will be more confident and attractive by making some external changes in your appearance, then that is fine, too.

6. Misconceptions about Romance or Marriage.

Are there attitudes about romance or marriage, holdovers from your formative years, your first dating experiences or even a failed marriage, that you need to re-evaluate and change? Perhaps your parents had an unhappy marriage and you question if marital bliss is possible? Maybe you were in an abusive relationship and question if all partners will mistreat you like that? On your own, or with counseling, if necessary, re-examine your attitudes toward romance and marriage so that antiquated or inaccurate notions do not hold you back from finding the love of your life.

7. Unresolved intimacy issues.

If you have unresolved intimacy concerns, there is help for you to overcome those fears that may be stopping you from starting your search. (For referrals, see the 'Getting Help' listings in the Appendix.)

For some, you may also have to deal with obstacles to finding the love of your life. Here are some of those possible obstacles.

Eight Obstacles to Finding 'The One'

1. Perfectionism.

No one should settle. But if you're unwilling to accept even the tiniest insecure flaw in a suitor, you may find yourself forever single. Look long and hard at the pattern to your dating to see if your perfectionism got in the way of taking a relationship to the next level.

Are you a perfectionist? If you learn to be kinder to yourself about your own faults, you might be more accepting of the imperfection of others.

2. Not knowing yourself and what you need in a mate for it to work.

You might find it helpful to read through and give yourself, or even someone you are dating or considering as a date, the self-evaluation questionnaire in Chapter 6, 'Getting to Know You'. When I met my future husband, Fred, we talked on that first date for around six hours, sharing with each other in an informal way information that this self-evaluation formally asks.

3. Failing to get to know the other person on a deep level.

Whether you do it formally through a questionnaire or informally through conversation, listening intently to someone's answers to key questions as well as sharing about your goals and dreams will help you have a better chance to know each other on a deeper level. Hopefully you are physically attracted to each other but for the long haul, compatibility and sharing basic values may be a better predictor of marital bliss.

4. Being in sync about timing.

Each person, each couple, will have its own timetable for how long it will take to figure out if there's a likelihood that you will make it as a couple.

If your timetables are dramatically different, one or both may back off because it's not 'the right time'. You may decide to patiently wait till you are both on the same romantic schedule, or you may prefer to look for someone else.

5. You just might need a catalyst to begin your search, and that's okay.

For whatever reason someone is not ready for the search, or to make a commitment, a catalyst may be needed. For example, your best friend announces his engagement, a raise enables you to give up a second job so you have more time to date, or you celebrate your birthday and feel it is time to find 'the one'.

Or you might be the kind of person who just dates and explores a new relationship until a particular person unleashes the romantic muse – a muse that inspire love like the muse some believe is necessary for creativity – in all its passion and intensity.

6. Ignoring the rules of dating and courtship.

Fussing over a date, going out and having fun, are all parts of dating as much as keeping your eye on the bigger goal of finding the love of your life. Although it is far more common today for a woman to call a man and not to have to wait for the man to call her, there is still the expectation that a man will take the lead in the courtship rituals. There's an old cliché that a woman chases the man until he catches her. From what I've observed, it's still true today.

7. Giving up too soon.

Whether it takes one, 20 or 200 dates, if your goal is to find the love of your life, you have to keep going till you find him or her. The philosophy behind this book is that if you somehow find a way to enjoy the search, relishing in the process, not just the ultimate outcome, it will be easier to keep going till you achieve your goal.

8. Being afraid of change.

Becoming a couple will cause changes in your life. If either of you have children from a previous marriage, those changes will impact on even more individuals. Change, even if all the changes are going to be positive ones, can be scary. There is a temptation to cling to the old and familiar, and that pull toward the status quo has to be overcome.

chapter 6

GETTING TO KNOW YOU

What Are You Looking For?

There are no right or wrong criteria for dating or mating. But you can increase the likelihood of finding what you want in a date or a mate if you know what you need to have in a partner. What is important to you in a date or a mate as a reflection of the culture or society in which you were raised or as a departure from that if you wish to follow your own standards?

There may, of course, be cultural considerations. Although since 1999 it is no longer illegal to marry someone with the same last name in Korea, it is still frowned upon. Therefore, if you are Korean, finding out someone's last name may be high on your list of concerns for a date (or being introduced to someone) who might become a mate.

It might be helpful to ask yourself what you care most about in a future spouse, ranking the criteria below in order of importance for you:

Criteria	Ranking (with 1 the highest)		
Appearance	_____	Place of origin	_____
Education	_____	Race	_____
Income	_____	Religion	_____
Intelligence	_____	Status	_____
Last name	_____	Marital status	_____
Occupation	_____	Nationality	_____
Personality	_____	Hobbies/Interests	_____
Parents' choice	_____	Political views	_____
Romantic love	_____	Other	_____

There are also lifestyle issues to consider. For example, for those who live in cultures where there are still arranged marriages, especially in the rural areas, such as in India, it might also be important to find out the answers to the following lifestyle questions before you commit to a relationship: Will we live with your parents or on our own? Will you allow me to work after we are married? In what country (community) will we live?

In Australia, New Zealand, the United Kingdom, the United States and other countries with the romantic love approach to dating and marriage, there are still other lifestyle issues that couples need to explore, such as: Will you live in a city, the suburbs, or a rural community? What are your religious orientations? What are your attitudes toward money, including spending and saving, and are you from the same socio-economic or social class? Do you expect one or both spouses to work after you have children? What about how household chores will be divided?

Practice Describing Yourself in a Succinct Way

Whether or not you plan to place a personal ad, you might find it useful to write one below to help you pinpoint what is most important to you in a date or mate as well as how you would describe yourself:

Compose your ad here:

_____
_____
_____
_____

_____
_____
_____
_____

If you want to find a quote to use in your ad, seek out a book of famous quotations such as *Bartlett's Familiar Quotations* or *The Oxford Dictionary of Quotations*. *Microsoft Bookshelf* is a CD-ROM with thousands of quotations from *The Columbia Book of Quotations*, searchable by topic or by author.

Put your ad aside for at least a few hours; preferably at least a day or two. You might also consider showing your ad to family and friends and get their opinions and ask for feedback. Then re-read your ad with a fresh eye. What's your instant, knee-jerk response to your ad? Does it make you want to send a response and get to know the writer better? Does it convey who you are and what you most want known about you?

Check your ad for typos, misspellings, and grammatical errors. If you are not a professional writer and you think your ad does a disservice to you, consider asking a friend or family member who has excellent writing skills to proofread or edit your personal ad (often referred to as a 'profile' when placed on an online site). The online dating site, Match.com, now offers reasonable ghostwriting services to its customers for editing a current profile or developing a new one. (For prices, visit their website.)

Use the space below to compose your edited or revised personal ad or profile:

_____
_____
_____
_____
_____
_____
_____
_____

Getting To Know Yourself and Your Date
Compatibility

That's the word you hear most of all when experts talk about the best predictor of whether or not a couple is more likely to get along, and last. No one of course has a crystal ball that can predict the future but there may be clues or very strong hints that, for the long haul, one person might be more suitable over another.

There are well-regarded personality tests you can take to find out more about your own personality, such as the Myer-Briggs Psychological Type Indicator, based on the work of Carl Jung, which puts test takers into 16 personality types, with these four general types: Extroversion versus Introversion; Sensation versus Intuition; Thinking versus Feeling; and Judging versus Perceiving.

Professor David H. Olson, Ph.D. of the University of Minnesota and President of Life Innovations has developed a couples quiz known as the PREPARE/ENRICH Inventories. The complete inventory has 195 questions in 20 relationship areas. Test results are used during premarital counseling sessions. Being able to work on areas of potential conflict has been tied to decreasing the likelihood of a couple getting a divorce.

The suggested questions that I developed that follow are not part of a scientific study. The goal is to get you thinking, and your date talking, about what you value as well as childhood, teen and adult experiences that might help you to see what you have in common, where you have key differences, and if those disparities are manageable or cautionary warning signs.

The 110 questions below suggest topics that you might want to talk about, or find out about, on the phone or during that important first date. Answering these questions will also help you find out more about yourself.

Pick out the questions that are most meaningful to you. Add to the list any considerations that you need to find out about that are unique to your situation.

1. Have you ever taken a trip with less than a week's planning?
2. What do you usually do to celebrate your birthday?
3. Do you like to spend time alone?
4. What man or woman from history would you like to be able to meet and talk to? Why?
5. What's your favorite holiday? Why?

6. How many friends do you have? How many are best friends? Close? Casual?
7. What's the most generous thing you've ever done?
8. What's your earliest childhood memory?
9. When did you start dating?
10. What's your favorite vacation? Why?
11. Where would you like to go on your next vacation?
12. What's your ideal for a wonderful evening?
13. What is your ideal age group for a mate?
14. What is the height range you're looking for?
15. Is there an occupation that you would like your ideal partner to have? If yes, what is it?
16. What do you do for a living?
17. Give a numerical ranking from 1 to 5 to your key considerations about someone with 1 as the highest ranking:
    _____ participates in sports
    _____ likes to read
    _____ enjoys going to the movies
    _____ likes to go to the theatre
    _____ enjoys the outdoors
    _____ likes to talk on the phone
    _____ likes to travel
    _____ prefers going out every night
    _____ likes to stay home and watch TV or cable
    _____ enjoys regularly getting together with friends
    _____ likes to work a lot
    _____ has a sense of humor
    _____ is demonstrative about feelings
    _____ is physically attractive
    _____ is a certain weight
    _____ earns a certain salary or income
    _____ is creative
    _____ is intelligent
18. What is your favorite movie? Why?
19. What's your best-liked novel? Why?
20. Do you believe in marriage? Why?
21. Do you want to have children? Why?
22. When you have children, where do you want to raise them?
23. Whose decision would it be if one of you discontinued work after you had children?
24. What's the highest educational degree you obtained?

25. Do you want to live in a rural town, a suburb or a city for the next five years? Why?
26. What's the most money you've ever spent on a present for a romantic partner?
27. Do you go to a religious house of worship regularly?
28. What religion are you?
29. How important is it for the love of your life to be the same religion as you?
30. Are you active in your block or neighborhood association?
31. What is your favorite athletic activity?
32. Do you have any siblings? If yes, what are their ages and gender?
33. What was your relationship like with your siblings growing up?
34. What is your relationship like now with your siblings?
35. What was your relationship like with your father growing up?
36. What was your relationship like with your mother growing up?
37. What is your relationship like now with your father?
38. What is your relationship like now with your mother?
39. What's the nicest thing you ever did for a friend?
40. What's the nastiest thing you ever did to a friend?
41. Do you believe in a monogamous romantic relationship?
42. Do you take the vacation time that you are allowed to take from your job every year?
43. How important is family to you?
44. Have you ever told a lie?
45. What did you do during the summers when you were growing up?
46. Do you consider yourself a neat or messy person?
47. Do you like to cook?
48. Do you like to go out to restaurants?
49. Do you like to go to parties?
50. Do you like to give parties?
51. Have you ever seen a therapist?
52. What do you think of psychotherapy?
53. What do you want to be doing in five years?
54. What do you want to be doing in ten years?
55. Do you like to write letters?
56. Do you own or use a computer?
57. How long do you spend on the Internet each day?
58. If your best friend got sick, what would you do?
59. If we had a date and your best friend asked you to help out with a move at the very same time, what would you do?
60. What do you like most about me?

61. What would you do if your best friend told you that I'm not the right 'one' for you?
62. What's your favorite magazine? Why?
63. If you read a daily newspaper, what is it? Why?
64. Who do you most admire from history? Why?
65. Do you like pets? If yes, what kind?
66. What do you like most about yourself?
67. What's your favorite current TV show?
68. What's your favorite TV show from the last decade? Why?
69. What's are the key values you have about life?
70. Who's your favored movie star?
71. Who did you vote for in the last presidential election? Why?
72. What political party do you belong to? Why?
73. Do you pay off your credit card expenses every month when you receive the bill or do you let a balance accumulate?
74. How often do you go shopping at the mall 'just to look'?
75. What do you like to do on New Year's Eve?
76. Will you tolerate my interests even if they don't interest you?*
77. Where would you go on your ideal date?
78. How often do you see your parents?
79. How often do you get together with your extended family, your cousins, aunts or uncles?
80. Do you smoke?
81. Do you drink?
82. Can you dance?
83. Do you like to go dancing?
85. Do you belong to any professional or community associations?
85. If you needed an escort for a business function or an important social event, and you weren't dating anyone seriously, what would you do?
86. Did you go to your last high school reunion?
87. Do you contribute to any humanitarian causes?
88. Have you ever done volunteer work?
89. What business leader do you most admire?
90. Have you ever had any conflicts with the law?
91. What would you do if your beloved gained a lot of weight?
92. Are there any cultural considerations because of your heritage that I should know about that would help me to understand you better?
93. What else would you like to know about me that might help you get to understand me better?

* My son Jeffrey Yager suggested this question.

94. How do you feel about someone rearranging your stuff?
95. What should I ask you that I haven't asked yet that would help me understand you better?
96. If you had to write a personal ad about yourself, what would you write?
97. If you had to pick one word to describe your best attribute, what would that word be?
98. If your parents objected to our relationship, what would you do?
99. What would you do if the person you deeply loved were required to move far away for the sake of the job?
100. What does your father do? What does your mother do?
101. How would you describe your current emotional state: happy, sad, eager, depressed, joyful, intense, optimistic, calm? Why?
102. What college did you attend?
103. (If you believe in astrology) What sign are you?
104. When do you relax? What relaxes you?
105. What room in your house or apartment do you spend most of your free time in?
106. If you could trade places with one person, who would that person be? Why?
107. Do you ever get angry? If yes, when? How do you usually deal with it?
108. What's the wildest thing you've ever done?
109. Where do you see yourself in 20 years?
110. What's the longest romantic relationship you've had till now?

part 2

THE SEARCH BEGINS: 125 WAYS TO MEET THE LOVE OF YOUR LIFE

Instead of just listing the 125 ways to meet the love of your life, I divided those options into nine categories giving each one its own chapter. For example, the category I call 'Making Introductions' covers meetings that are set up by friends, family members, matchmakers, dating services or at parties.

Please also note: contact information for the selected examples that appear throughout the 125 ways is included in the Appendix along with additional listings.

chapter 7

MAKING INTRODUCTIONS

Widening one's circle is really what meeting through introductions from friends or family members (as well as blind dates, whether from Aunt Sally or a co-worker) is all about. They are acting as informal matchmakers, but there are professional ones as well, including dating services (introduction agencies) and online sites, that match up clients who visit their offices or subscribers to their Internet sites.

Blind Date Protocol

Who hasn't been set up on a blind date, or hasn't set someone up, only to have the experience turn out to be disastrous and, even worse, a low point, or the catalyst to the end of your friendship? I remember when I was single and dating and my sister introduced me to a very nice, successful and interesting man with whom I spent a pleasant enough two hours over dinner. But there was no chemistry between us. I then set him up with a friend of mine at the time.

Afterwards, she called me up and became bombastic about the date.

Not only did she find him unattractive, but she also questioned what I thought of her because I thought she would want to date him.

I've heard similar blind date or fix-up stories from others who have set up friends as well as the laments and regrets of those who have been set up: instead of saying 'thanks for thinking of me' the typical response to a blind date that backfires is, 'How could you?'

But there are also enough blind date 'how we met' success stories that it is a way of meeting a date or mate that is definitely worth considering. For example, Jody Jaffe, 50, who has two teenage sons, met her future husband six years ago when she was 'going through a difficult divorce'. Jody asked her friend Laura Lippman, a mystery writer who was working at *The Baltimore Sun,* if she knew any eligible men at the newspaper. Her friend described two possibilities. As Jody recalls:

'I know two', Laura said. 'One's brash, the kind of guy who stands up in the middle of the newsroom and shouts, "Hey Lippman, are we going to edit this %$#%^ story or what?" He'd be good for dating practice. The other's heartfelt and kind. He'd be good for later on.'

Having been out of the dating scene for more than 20 years, I said, 'Let's go for dating practice'.

Laura gave Jody's name and e-mail address to John Muncie, who was then the arts and entertainment editor of the *Baltimore Sun*. Jody continues:

John e-mailed me the most clever of notes. We went on a blind lunch date and haven't been apart since.

They co-wrote a novel about their blind date and courtship called *Thief of Words*; they married six months after the book was published.

Hearing an uplifting blind date success story like that one, juxtaposed with quite the opposite – those blind date from you-know-where stories – led me to evaluate, long and hard, the blind date as a potential for meeting someone, from both the perspective of the person setting up the blind date and that of the person who is fixed up.

There are, fortunately, ways to help minimize the negative consequences of blind dates that fail to work out (as well as increase the possibility that it will be a positive experience even if it does not lead to true love). Here are some suggestions:

If You Are Fixing Up Someone

- **Make sure your friend (acquaintance or family member) and the other person are ready.**
  First of all, make sure your friend is at a point in his or her life when he or she really wants to meet someone new. If your friend is getting over a marriage or long-term relationship that just ended, or is in the midst of a major work-related project taking total concentration and 18-hour workdays and nights, this might not be the time to play Cupid.

- **Describe each person realistically, not embellishing, although the less said, the better.**
  If your friend is open to meeting someone new, provide a thumbnail sketch with some of the key attributes of the person you are matching him or her up with, such as age, career, how you know the person, personality and so forth. If there's a particular reason you think they would hit it off, say so. For example, 'I've known Bob through work for the last few years and he's hard-working, and diligent, but he's got a great sense of humor and he's kind and thoughtful.'

- **Lower expectations.**
  The key, however, is to take the pressure off. You're not setting up your friend because you think he could be the love of her life. You just think they should meet and see what happens.

- **Instead of also setting up the 'when' and 'where' of the first meeting, with permission, just provide your friend's phone number and/or e-mail address.**
  By just providing the contact information, it is more likely there will be a dialogue in advance of the meeting. That way, after their initial communication by phone, or exchange e-mails, if either one feels it's just not going to work out, trust your friend's judgment and don't push for taking the blind date to the next level. Say you tried

and better luck next time. No hard feelings, hopefully, and on to the next.

- **If they still want to meet, suggest double dating if that will reduce the pressure.**
  Having a drink, lunch, or dinner with someone where it's just not working or there's nothing in common or compatible can be the longest period of time anyone can remember. To avoid that happening, suggest double dating and, if possible, combining the get-together with an activity, such as playing tennis, bowling or going to the movies as well as having a cup of coffee and dessert afterwards. Avoid setting up a friend with a blind date for an extended event, such as a three-hour concert that requires a four-hour round trip drive or a weekend getaway.

- **Lessen the pressure inviting the pair you're fixing up to a dinner party of eight or more.**
  If you invite the couple you are trying to fix up to a dinner party of eight or more, especially if at least two or more are single and unattached as well, it might minimize the stress and risk of a blind date. If you invite the couple to a large party, you could still introduce them at the party but then it will be a question of nature taking its course rather than you sticking your neck out by more directly suggesting that your friend should have a blind date with someone else.

- **If you get together for a double date and your friend needs to leave early because she feels the event is going badly, don't take it personally.**
  She's rejecting the person you've introduced her to, not you. And she's not even rejecting the blind date, just the combination of her and the blind date. On his own, he could be a perfectly fine person, just not her type or for her.

- **After the blind date, be open to hearing your friend's thoughts about it.**
  This will help you decide if you ever want to do this again. You might also learn about what your friend is looking for in a date from the feedback your matchmaking efforts get. Keeping that feedback in mind might help you to be more successful in your next blind date efforts.

- **If your friend is totally unraveled by the blind date, try not to regret having put yourself out in this way.**
  It takes courage to recommend someone to another but remember that you are likely to hear about whether your judgment call was right or wrong with as much, or even more, fervor as when you recommend a movie, play or restaurant, only to find out that the one to whom you made the referral is far less enchanted with your taste or choice than you are.

If Someone Fixes You Up on a Blind Date

- **Be grateful but only say 'yes' if you really want to do it, not just to please your friend (family member or acquaintance).**
  Remember that your friend is doing this because she wants you to meet someone with whom you will be happy. She is not a professional matchmaker who is getting any kind of economic reward from setting you up on this blind date. If the blind date is someone she knows through work or through her own friendship or family network, she is taking professional and emotional risks on your behalf. It is far easier to do nothing than to set someone up since it could be a positive experience or completely backfire.

- **Whether or not it leads to a second date or something more, try to have a good time.**
  Why two people click or not is so complicated and so individual that no one can predict the short- or long-term outcome of a blind date. Rather than dwelling on what the blind date leads to, try to enjoy the experience.

- **If you think having a blind date is too much pressure, offer other suggestions.**
  You could thank her for wanting to introduce you to this blind date, but you could also offer alternative situations where you will be more comfortable. For example, you could suggest to your friend that you'd rather you and this potential blind date be included in a dinner party situation or that she has, or you have, a party and that he is invited so it is less of a two-some situation.

- **You might meet someone who becomes an acquaintance or even a new friend.**
  You might find this blind date is positive enough, although you do not have a romantic interest, or perhaps you do but your date does not, that you still want to get to know each other better and eventually become friends. But be careful to suggest this if your blind date is romantically interested in you and the feelings are not returned. That old line, 'Can't we be friends?' has to be uttered at the right moment, and in the right way, in a new relationship or it could be seen as a put-down of your date's feelings.

- **If you do not want a second outing with your blind date, be careful about offering an alternative to you.**
  Although some might welcome your suggestions and see it as a gesture of concern and kindness, others might see it as trivializing the situation as if you're offering an alternative as a runner-up prize when he wants the first prize. Timing is important, however. It's possible a week, or a month, down the road, a suggestion to your blind date, or to the friend that you have in common, about alternative dates for him might be welcomed and favorably acted upon.

- **Whatever the outcome, remember to thank your friend for her efforts on your behalf.**
  It's important to be grateful initially for the blind date, but it's far harder to say 'thank you' if your dream date is less than ideal. But it could be the difference to whether or not your friend ever facilitates another blind date for you or, even more important, how this experience impacts on your friendship. Send your friend a thank-you card or even a little gift reinforcing her efforts on your behalf.

- **Be careful about getting a reputation for kissing and telling.**
  Remember that people usually suggest someone as a blind date because they have some sort of a connection to that other person, whether through friendship, a family tie, school or work. Whatever you learn about the person on the date, or even how you feel about the person's appearance, demeanor or personality, should be shared in a way that maintains the blind date's privacy and integrity. Also, if you are not smitten after the first date, but you do give the blind date another chance and romance does blossom, you do not want to regret any badmouthing or any conclusions you jumped to that

you have to take back if your initial opinion changes down the road. Bottom line: be honest and open, but discreet as well.

- **If the friend who set you up is also single, find out if she wants you to fix her up on blind dates before you assume she wants that.**
  Just because your friend fixed you up on a blind date, do not automatically assume that this is something she wants you to do for her. Just as it was polite for your friend to ask, rather than insist, that you might want to pursue a particular blind date, you owe her the same courtesy. Suggesting someone as a date is a lot different than being the one who will actually go out on the date.

Parties

Parties may provide the opportunity to meet new people with less pressure than a blind date. Psychologist and mystery writer Dr Sandra Levy Ceren shares how she met her second husband through an introduction and a party:

I was a divorced mom, raising two children on my own, and a part-time faculty member at a local college. It was a tough time in my life. A colleague, familiar with my doctoral dissertation, which included a test for extra sensory perception, recommended that I have an adventure. She urged me to make an appointment with Leonora, an incredible psychic. She told me that for $25, Leonora would predict my future.

Curious, I phoned for the appointment.

I spent over an hour with Leonora. Several things she told me about myself and my life, she could have figured out without ESP, but one specific item caught my attention: 'Someone will ask you to meet a certain man. At first you won't be interested because he is much older than you, but meet him, because he will be very important to you. He is famous in the field of optics. I see two sons in the picture, but can't tell whether they are his, but they're connected with this image.'

Several years later, a woman I knew called me. 'I'd like you to meet a friend of mine.' She told me that he was the inventor of the zoom lens . . . I felt a strange chill. A tingle throughout my body. Shades of Leonora!

I agreed to attend his luncheon. The food wasn't memorable, and his collection of fine art was incredible, but I felt no budding connection in terms of a friendship, and a little disappointed.

But he invited me to a party at his house on July 4th.

It was there, at his party, that I met Ely, who was divorced and who had two sons.

After a long courtship, when my children went off to university, Ely and I were married. I would have loved to invite Leonora [the psychic] to the wedding, but could not locate her.

For additional comments about parties, see the entries for #3 and #4 that follow.

Dating Services (Introduction Agencies)

Although one of the more costly ways to meet, there are certainly countless satisfied customers who have met and dated or mated through dating service introductions. Paul Falzone, CEO of Together Dating® and The Right One® dating services, told me about one employee at a franchise in Massachusetts who is responsible for 650 successful marriages over the last 20 years.

The average cost for clients of those dating services ranges from $1000 to $3000 depending upon the region as well as the range of services that are selected and the time frame that is covered.

I spoke with Amy Distefano, who has worked at a dating service based in Lawrenceville, New Jersey, that is part of the Together® franchise of dating services throughout the United States. Amy, who has been happily married for 12 years and is the mother of identical twin toddlers, has worked at Together Dating® for nine years.

Explaining that she personally meets with every single client, interviewing him or her for an hour, on average, but up to two or three hours, if necessary, Amy shares how her company's approach works:

We weed them out for you and you don't spend a lot of time schlepping into bars. When someone comes in, they tell me exactly what they're looking for. They tell me the age range, the [geographic] area, religion, the best qualities of that person [that they're looking for].

I want to know everything they've ever dreamed about and also the qualities they don't like. I also want to know how many brothers and sisters they have, and the very best qualities of the people who raised them – mother, father, or caretaker – since I think we search for the very best qualities of those whom we most admired and respected in our life as well as people who make us feel absolutely fabulous about ourselves when we're with them.

We absolutely do a criminal background check. They cannot just give a cell phone number. We have to know everything about them. We need to know where they live, who they work for, when they were divorced. We need to know about their children. We really ask a lot of questions.

I interviewed Signe Dayhoff, Ph.D., a social effectiveness coach, who met her husband through a computer dating service in Boston in 1972 when computer use in the matchmaking process was in its infancy. Here is her story:

My husband and I were signed up with a computer dating firm but I nearly didn't meet him because just before he called me, I had had a very unpleasant and frightening experience with another client [as noted in Chapter 4, 'Staying Safe During Your Search']. But Bob, my husband-to-be, called and while I was in the process of turning him down, he mentioned that he worked with someone with whom I had gone to school. This high school chum had seen my name on Bob's list from the dating service and had urged him to call me. With this reassurance, I made a date to meet him at a restaurant.

Someone wearing his described dress arrived and I nearly ran from the restaurant. I hunkered down at the counter where I was drinking a cup of tea. This was not someone I wanted to date.

Five minutes later, as I was getting ready to leave, Bob arrived . . . He was a big improvement. A year-and-a-half later, we were married.

Online Dating Services

As discussed below (see #18, 'Cybermatching,' in this chapter and #37, 'Cyberspace personal ads,' in Chapter 9, 'Personal Ads (Print or Online),' online dating services are quite different from the in-person brick-and-mortar services. Online dating, such as singleSearch.com, MatchNet.com, eHarmony.com, Match.com, and PerfectMatch.com, is done electronically and online. Online dating or matchmaking services are distinctive from the online sites that instead have personal ads posted (called 'profiles' on the Internet) and those who post or answer ads are using the Internet in the same way they might use a newspaper or magazine.

Ways to Meet Through Introductions

1. INTRODUCTIONS BY FRIENDS OR FAMILY MEMBERS.

The benefit of being introduced by a family member or the friends of friends is that there is a POR – point of reference. You are not total strangers. You know the family background. This, of course, can backfire if too much pressure is put on you and your date because the family member knows about the glimmer of interest in each other. But ask your parents, aunts or uncles or cousins to ask all of their friends if they have any relatives who are single or recently single and looking again.

A 2003 poll of men and women by Jill Bourque, director of the San Francisco-based improvisation romantic comedy troupe, 'How We First Met,' found that 30 per cent of the respondents met their partner through a friend, followed by 29 per cent who introduced themselves at a shared activity. (The next most popular ways to meet were online, 8 per cent, followed by a family member introduction, 3.5 per cent.)

Friends and relatives are such popular ways to meet other singles because you have someone in common: you both know the same person. That helps to legitimize who you both are. No need for criminal background checks. You can ask your friend for details or Uncle Harry for 'the scoop'.

Meeting through friends or family could involve an informal introduction, because you happen to be at the same party together, or a more formal type of introduction where the introducer may or may not be present when the date takes place, known as the 'blind date' and discussed above, in the section on 'Blind Date Protocol'.

You should always try to be friendly, because that woman at work or who knows your second cousin just might ask if you'd like to be introduced to an eligible person she knows. But be careful about putting someone on the spot. There's a more subtle but distinctive way to say, 'Keep me in mind if you know anyone you think I should meet who's also single and looking', so you announce your availability, but you don't sound too desperate or needy, which usually pushes potential matchmakers (and suitors) away.

An electronic version of being introduced through friends is friendster.com. The difference between friendster.com and other on-line services is that it is necessary to have a mutual friend (or a friend of a friend) who is also registered at the site for a new connection to occur.

2. Introduce yourself. Take the initiative.

If you meet someone new, just introduce yourself and let the conversation flow from there. No one wants a line. Be yourself and show an interest in finding out about the other person.

You might consider sending a seasonal, birthday or no-occasion greeting card to someone eligible that you've met and see what kind of response you get.

And ladies, you don't have to wait to ask a man out till Sadie Hawkins Day, celebrated every 15 November since 1938, or Leap Year Day, celebrated on 29 February whenever there is a leap year. Those two days have become associated with a woman asking out (or even proposing to) a man without those actions getting her labeled as aggressive. But if you have tickets for a concert or a benefit, or a special event that requires an escort, and you ask in a matter-of-fact way, without any pressure, taking the initiative might work out well.

3. Going to private parties.

A party provides an informal atmosphere with lots of distractions – food, music, dancing, and other guests – so there may be less pressure on an initial meeting than if your first meeting is a blind or first date. Attending a party is usually less expensive and time-consuming than hosting one.

Since you usually get invited to a party because you know the host or hostess, that person can vouch for you if you meet someone as well as tell you about the person you meet.

At a party, unlike the typical blind date over lunch or dinner, you can find an excuse, such as needing to 'circulate', or wanting to refill your beverage or drink, as a way to cut a conversation short if your first impression of someone is less than favorable.

If a friend asks you to join him or her at a party, even if the host didn't invite you, take advantage of the opportunity and go! That's what Tom Jaffee, 41, and Cathy, 31, did three years ago; two years later they were married. Says Tom, founder of minuteDating.com: 'We met at a party at the Head of the Charles Regatta. It's the largest crew race in the world. There was a party and neither of us was invited by the host.' But Tom went with his friend, and Cathy went with her roommate.

If you do go to a party with a friend, once you get there, mix and mingle. If no one new approaches, you could ask the host or hostess to introduce you to other guests. But if the host or hostess is unavailable, you could also approach someone yourself and break the ice by simply saying, 'Hello, my name is – . It's nice to meet you.'

According to the college students I interviewed, parties are the number one way that they socialize, especially at a rural campus. As Angel Rivera, an 18-year-old freshman at the University of Connecticut in Storrs, told me:

At Storrs, the parties work well because it's a rural campus situation in the middle of a very rural area. It's a big farm. Plain and simple, there's nothing else to do. But at a school like NYU [in Manhattan], you could go to a museum or to a club [to meet someone].

---

4. HOST YOUR OWN PARTY.

Years ago I gave a birthday party for a friend and I invited her entire network as well as a few of my friends. The birthday girl ended up falling in love with and marrying one of my platonic friends who was a guest at her party.

Other reasons for throwing a party for a friend? Celebrating your friend's accomplishments, such as a job promotion or an award, a significant anniversary, such as a decade on the job.

Or you could invite the men and women you know to a party; include those in your apartment house or on your block. Ask your guests to bring along at least one single friend, and request an introduction. Even if those guests are not right for you, you might develop a new friendship or someone might think of someone else that you should meet.

5. Bring a movie home and invite people over to watch it on videocassette or DVD.

Invite friends over to watch a movie with you. Ask them to bring acquaintances or friends whom you might enjoy meeting. Having the film to talk about will help break the ice and also reduce the pressure 'to meet' that is typical in purely social situations, such as a party.

Sharing video footage taken during an exotic trip is another event that could bring family and friends – including singles – together.

6. Attend family functions.

Family gatherings where you might meet someone because a family member brings along a friend or they facilitate an introduction to others at the event include: weddings, christenings, funerals, engagement parties, holiday celebrations, reunions, birthday parties, anniversary parties and bridal or baby showers.

Joy Kuby, who is a college instructor teaching computer software as well as the author of *The Fortunate Four: Other Journeys of the Heart,* has celebrated 27 years of marriage to her husband Keith. She shares her story of how they met as teenagers:

I was a country girl from Stanchfield, Minnesota, and he was a city boy from St Paul, Minnesota. Keith and I were just teenagers one warm summer day back in August 1969 when we met tubing on the Apple River in Somerset, Wisconsin. My family and his family were both mutual friends of the Swenson family. The trip would take three to four hours and would end after maneuvering through some exciting rapids.

Naturally, the adults floated down together, and we teenagers formed our own linked group – talking, laughing, and teasing each other as we bobbed along. The rapids were exhilarating and scary.

Keith and I had our next encounter a year later at the little county fair in my hometown . . . [But] we didn't actually begin dating until later that fall when I began college in the big city and he called to ask for our initial date.

For three years we attended colleges located about 200 miles apart, so

*our relationship was on and off again as we explored other relationships . . .
Six years after that day on the river, we were married.*

7. Use a matchmaker, professional or amateur.

Did you ever know someone at high school, college or work who also seemed to have a knack for introducing a couple to each other and before you know it, there's a wedding being planned? *The Washington Post* columnist Bob Levey interviewed Tommy 'The Matchmaker' Curtis, the owner and operator of the Yacht Club of Bethesda, Maryland. Levey cites Curtis' matchmaking success rate: 138 engagements and marriages. *The Washingtonian* magazine gave Tommy the title of 'Maestro of dating'.

Curtis explained that the first step is, of course, the all-important introduction that breaks the ice: Levey points out that each person who goes to the Yacht Club will be introduced that night by owner Tommy Curtis to at least one other person. He quotes Curtis as explaining: 'Some people can hit a ball or throw a pass – I just know who should be with whom. It's a sixth sense . . .'

Having a second career, like Curtis, is not uncommon for matchmakers. In 2003, this even became the theme to an American TV show, *Miss Match*, whereby a divorce lawyer also becomes a professional matchmaker. Esther Jungreis is a 68-year-old Talmudic scholar as well as a matchmaker. Jungreis brings her philosophical teachings and insights to her role as a matchmaker. In the article about Jungreis, 'Scholar, Matchmaker and Convention Presence', Marek Fuchs writes in *The New York Times*:

. . . The central problem with matchmaking, she [Jungreis] said, is that people too often look for the wrong attributes in a potential mate. She recalls one woman who wanted a man who was five things: bright, accomplished, a great personality, cute and athletic.

'I said to her, "Good luck, but your big five amount to a bunch of zeroes. After all, looks will turn, brightness can mock you, monetary success can be used to control you, and you want someone to be athletic?" The rebbetzin waved a hand. 'Go get a trainer. That's good enough.'

You can find matchmakers everywhere, in your own family or in the phonebook. Professional matchmakers may charge thousands of dollars. They tend to specialize so do your research before you sign a check or a contract. Referrals from satisfied customers are often the best sources. If you cold call a matchmaker, ask for the names and phone numbers of successful matches who are willing to talk to you about their experience.

A 33-year-old single woman who works in Seoul, Korea, in the media shared with me about her experiences with a matchmaker. She notes: 'One day my mother had been watching TV. In the TV program, a woman was introduced. She was a hair designer and matchmaker. She succeeded in making approximately 100 couples [to] marry. So my mother put me on her list. Therefore I met lots of men.' None of those introductions have yet led to a successful match, but she's still optimistic about this as a possibility in the future.

8. The musical chair dating game.

Quick date options are a growing trend. It's a fast, easy and relatively inexpensive way to meet several singles in person. One example is 8minutedating.com. This is a phenomenon that has taken off quickly since it was started by Tom Jaffee in Boston in 2001. It has expanded to more than 60 cities throughout the United States and Canada with plans to expand to Australia and other countries as well. (The company's website updates the availability of the events nationally and internationally.)

There is a moderate fee for each event, which consists of eight one-to-one dates, each date lasting eight minutes, with a 20-minute intermission. After the event, participants log in to the company's website and enter the names of people they'd like to meet again, either for a second date, for friendship or for business. Whenever the interest is mutual, contact information is provided to both parties.

8minuteDating enables singles to converse with numerous people throughout the evening. Participants can determine if there's any initial physical attraction and if whatever information shared about each other is enough to spark curiosity and a wish to see each other again.

Original Dating is a company in the United Kingdom that organizes fast dating events in London.

In Australia and New Zealand, there are several fast dating options including Fast Impressions (in Sydney, Melbourne, Brisbane and

Auckland), and Fast Date Australia. In Perth, Western Australia, it is called Hot Seat Speed Date. (For contact information, see the Appendix.)

Another example is SpeedDating™, started by Aish HaTorah, a global Jewish educational network. This is a dating event for only Jewish singles whereby a man and a woman are paired together for seven minutes and then they switch. After an hour and a half, each participant has met seven persons of the opposite sex. At the website, there is a section that lists upcoming SpeedDating™ events.

9. Widen your net.

Let everyone you meet know that you are single and looking. Ask them to keep you in mind for any single colleagues, friends or relatives.

10. Attend reunions.

There may be friends from elementary, junior or middle school, high school, college, graduate school or camp who might introduce you to other former classmates or campmates, as well as friends or relatives in their current networks.

Becoming involved in the planning of the reunion will enable you to get more involved with the attendees; you might rekindle an old friendship, or begin a new one through the months that most reunions take to organize and carry out.

11. Go to a wine tasting.

There are wine-tasting events sponsored by wine companies that are either free or for a fee bring people together who belong to an association or for whom the only connection is a wish to learn more about wine, and meet people. Check your local paper, as well as the newsletter for any associations you belong to and their websites, for wine-tasting events.

12. Attend a charity function.

Fundraisers, or charity balls, can be a wonderful way to expand your network, leading to possible friendships or even business relationships, as well as a romantic relationship. If you pick charities to attend that truly reflect your interests and concerns, such as a fundraiser for the renovation of a theatre, or a non-profit association dedicated to disadvantaged children, you will be more likely to meet others who share your same concerns.

The Wall Street Journal columnist Jeffrey Zaslow, in his 'Moving On' column entitled, 'Have I Got a Girl for You: Helping Your Friends Dump the Dating Service', shared about the matches that resulted from a charity event that he hosted each September during the 14 years that he was a columnist at the *Chicago Sun-Times*. Zaslow writes that 'at least 78 marriages' resulted from those events attended by 7000 single readers.

13. Help organize a fundraising event.

By getting involved and helping to actually organize a charity function, you increase the likelihood that you will meet new people who may become friends since you are spending a lot of time together. Not only may these new acquaintances or friends have suggestions about how to meet people, but also they may have eligible friends, family or co-workers to introduce you to. They may also be more likely to make such introductions since they are getting to know you over the weeks or months that you are working together on a praiseworthy cause.

Even if you do not have time to organize the event, you could volunteer to help out in some way. Perhaps you could help put together the 'goodie bags' for any giveaways, or you could offer to help set up or decorate.

14. Attend a party or discussion group for singles.

Whether a religious institution or community center sponsors the group or party, if it is for singles you will at least know that everyone you meet is supposed to be available. Whether you go to a party on one particular night, or you participate in a weekly discussion group, you will start off knowing that those you meet are probably the same religion, if that is important to you in dating or mating, and, if they attend the discussion group, that they find the same topic of interest. If you want to increase the likelihood that you meet a loved one of the same religion, going to a party organized by a local organized religious institution that you believe in will increase that probability.

15. Have a dinner party and ask each guest to bring one single acquaintance or friend whom you don't know.

A smaller and more intimate dinner party might provide a better opportunity to get to know six or eight people. Even if you do not hit it off with the one person who you invited as a date or who was invited with you in mind, that person as well as the other guests may get to know you well enough to recommend other eligible singles with whom you might click.

16. Reconsider someone you've known previously who may now be available.

Times change, circumstances change, but if there were strong positive feelings, it might be possible that those feelings will be rekindled given another chance. Previous unavailable friends or former romantic partners who are now single again because of a breakup, divorce or widowhood might be worth a second look.

Is there someone from your past who you always wanted to look up to see if the timing would now be right to try to reconnect? Through various search engines, such as classmates.com, you might be able to find out enough information about your former crush or paramour, if they are a registered user, to know if they are married or available.

You might also want to contact old acquaintances that you had in common and ask, 'Whatever happened to so-and-so?'

17. Professional dating services.

Dating services will pre-screen candidates and provide introductions for a fee. What each service offers, how much they charge, what geographic area, economic level or professional group they draw from, may differ widely. Word-of-mouth referrals by satisfied customers are one way to explore dating service options. Searching online or through the telephone directory, and following up with a phone call or a free consultation, is another way to learn about reputable dating services that you might hire.

Sydney and Melbourne-based Yvonne Allen & Associates is an introduction agency founded and run by Allen, who is a psychologist. She founded her company in 1976 to provide consulting services for singles as well as introductions. Allen is the author of *Successfully Single, Successfully Yourself*.

Together® and The Right One® is a brick-and-mortar franchise of dating services discussed at the beginning of this chapter. Another long-standing dating service with more than 50 local offices throughout the United States, in business since 1976, is Great Expectations®. Clients are interviewed; they also have the option of creating a videotape that is available for viewing by other clients.

To find out about local franchises of these dating services in your community, check the telephone directory or the corporate sites on the Internet.

For any dating service that you're considering, ask the same questions you would ask of any business that you are considering, such as cost, any contractual agreements, what period of time and costs are covered and any penalties if you wish to cancel, what you can get for your money, how your privacy will be protected, if you can talk with any previous clients to ask them their opinion of the company and so forth.

There are also dating services that have a very different model from the franchised brick-and-mortar matchmaking franchises with in-person pre-screening. For instance, artist and editor Rodelinde Albrecht founded Concerned Singles in 1984. Its more than 1000 paid members follow up on their own by e-mail or regular mail. Ads for the service reflect the singles to whom it appeals, including *Mother Jones*, *Vegetarian Times*, and *The Environmental Magazine*.

Single Booklovers describes itself as a 'national dating service for people who enjoy reading'. It's been around since 1970 and has members throughout the United States, Canada, and globally.

18. Cybermatching.

Each online matching site has a slightly different approach to the way matches are conducted or the policies regarding pricing so contact each one for details. Here is a sample of some of the popular sites for Internet matching.

SingleSearch.com, co-founded by a counselor, Lisa Bentsen, and her husband Robert, who is a computer programmer, started in 1989 as an offline service but became an online service in 1994.

It now has more than 400 affiliate sites throughout the United States and several other countries including England, France, Germany, Malaysia and the Philippines. It is based on a matchmaking principle: those who register for the service have to have a match of 60 per cent on more than 350 questions that they are asked to complete. Fees are based on the number of purchased matches.

A therapist and mate selection expert, Neil Clark Warren, Ph.D. founded eharmony.com, another singles matchmaking online service. Dr Warren, married for 40 years, has authored several bestsellers on mate selection. His membership Internet dating site is based on his 29 dimensions of compatibility.

Perfectmatch.com has teamed up with relationships expert Dr Pepper Schwartz for its matchmaking site. To increase the potential of finding Mr or Ms Right, this membership site offers Dr Pepper's Personality Test, to increase the likelihood of finding a compatible partner.

Find My Australian Soul Mate is a local version of the Findmymate.com site, which asks participants to answer questions based on the works of Nathaniel Branden.

Greatboyfriends.com has the unique principle that everyone who is registered with the website has to be recommended by someone: an ex-girlfriend or spouse, a sister, a friend or a co-worker.

Match.com allows you to post or search for free for either dating or friends. In order to contact other members by anonymous e-mail or instant messaging, you have to become a paid subscriber. There is a list of the international sites of Match.com, which rely on the local language and currency, including sites for Australia and New Zealand.

Millionairematch.com is another matchmaking site. It has a free trial and then you may elect to subscribe. Profiles are divided into two categories when you create your profile: annual income below or above $100,000.

Oneandonly.com is a subscriber site that allows creating and posting an ad for free. Subscribers can search for a match on criteria such as zip code, physical traits and lifestyle habits.

Matchnet.com consists of several sites including its AmericanSingles.com (United States); CollegeLuv.com (for college students ages 18 to 24), and JDate.com and jdate.co.il for Jewish singles in the United States and in Israel. Profiles are searched for on specific criteria. Instant messaging and chats are available to members.

Matchmaker.com is another subscription site with an estimated 8 million users internationally. At their site you will find a very upbeat slide show of dozens of testimonials of satisfied couples who met through this site.

Friendfinder.com, started in 1996, has grown to a global network with an estimated 18 million+ registered members.

chapter 8

SCHOOL, WORK OR BUSINESS

School, especially college, along with work, and business are typical ways for singles to meet, after introductions. For example, Lisa, a 46-year-old retail manager who grew up in Melbourne, Australia, met her husband at a technical college there. Twenty-nine-year-old Suzanne, who lives in Brisbane, Australia, met her husband at work seven years ago. They married a year later. Suzanne's advice: 'Look for someone who makes you laugh'.

Freshman year at Fairfield University in Connecticut was the setting where 29-year-old Kristen Finello met her husband, Matt Wilson. Here is Kristen's account:

We had the same group of friends but Matt and I weren't really any more than acquaintances. We sat next to each other in Microeconomics class and every Monday Matt would come in and say, 'Hi, Kristen. How was your weekend?' And I would always answer, 'Fine. How was yours?'

I was polite, but shy. Finally, after a few weeks of this he got kind of frustrated and said, 'How come you always give me the same answer?' And I said seriously, 'Because you always ask me the same question!' and that kind of broke the ice between us. But still we only saw each other in class and sometimes out on the weekend.

Eventually, Matt would stop by my room after class to hang out with me and my roommate, Dawn, and Matt and I became better friends. Then at the end of freshman year, we went to the annual Dogwoods Dance, just as friends, and had a great time. Then right before we left Fairfield for summer break, Matt invited me to go down to his parents' house in Baltimore and go to a concert with him over the summer. We ended up seeing each other a few times over the summer.

By the time we got back to school in September, we were a couple.

We broke up for a year right after graduation. During that year we had broken up, we dated other people but we would talk every month or so.

After we talked for a while, then we made plans to get together. We started seeing each other more frequently. At that point, we knew after we started dating again that down the line we would get married.

Kristen and Matt married eight years after they met.

Forty-five-year-old Joanne McCall, who runs McCall Public Relations in Aloha, Oregon, a public relations company specializing in book promotions, met her future husband, Gary, through work back in 1988 when she was a 30-year-old disk jockey at a radio station in Minneapolis and he was 41. Says Joanne:

I worked seven till midnight. I had phone calls after every record, five hours of crazy wildness. I started getting this creepy guy who was making death threat phone calls to me, which is not that uncommon in the radio business.

So I immediately called the cops. I had an officer come to see me the next day shortly before I went on the air and it was Gary.

He asked me all kinds of questions – what did the guy sound like, what specifically did I say? While I was giving him that report, I had to go on the air. He came in the studio with me and as he was leaving, he asked me to play one of the oldie songs that he liked.

The next day, he just started showing up at the station a lot. He told me that they were working on finding that guy. I'd say hello.

I guess after about three days of this, I said to myself, 'I bet he doesn't do this with everybody'.

We had a huge blizzard. Gary showed up at my apartment and asked if I wanted to go out for a cup of hot chocolate.

I wouldn't buzz him up but I came downstairs and we went to a nearby restaurant. We had a cup of hot chocolate and that started the more personal thing.

He picked me up in a snowplow later that night and brought me to work. He was turning into a knight in shining armor.

After a year and a half, Joanne accepted a job offer from a station in Oregon because she couldn't handle the harsh winters. Five years later, Gary telephoned her.

He said, 'I don't want to live without you anymore and I'm coming out there'.

Of course I didn't really believe him so I said, 'When?'

He answered, 'Memorial Day weekend'.

So he came out for three days and we just decided that that was it, and he moved out here.

They married the next year, eight years after they met.

Office Romance Protocol

Fortunately Joanne and Gary's story had a happy ending but there are unhappy endings that begin at work that may have drastic work consequences, for one or both, not to mention possible accusations of sexual harassment. So, be careful, if you initially meet in a work or business-related capacity. Here are guidelines from office romance, excerpted and updated from my book *Friendshifts*®.

- Especially if you are at different levels within the company, avoid drawing attention to your romantic relationship to reduce the likelihood of any bad feelings developing because of perceived favoritism.

- Avoid acting passionate around each other at work including such obvious romantic gestures as staring into each other's eyes, hand-holding or kissing.

- Try not to call each other by such demonstrative terms as 'honey', 'deary', 'sweetie', 'sweetheart' or a special, intimate nickname you may have for each other.

- Do not let your romance affect your productivity. The managers I interviewed seemed concerned if a developing romance competed for a worker's attention.

- Work friendship that turns to romance implies a risk; if the relationship ends, and being around each other is too stressful for the ex-couple or those around them, someone may have to consider leaving.

But the issues are certainly not insurmountable; we have all heard of lots of happily married couples who first met in a work or business situation.

Ways to Meet through School, Work or Business

19. IN THE CLASSROOM.

Whether you're an undergraduate, graduate or just taking courses because you like a subject, the classroom is a great place to meet people. It's a shared experience. If you see someone you might want to introduce yourself to, you can partner up for a project, do a scene together for acting class, or sit next to each other in lab.

Continuing education courses in subjects that you are interested in will put you close to others who share these same interests so you have something in common.

20. STUDY DATES.

A popular way to meet someone of the opposite sex at college or graduate school is by going to the study lounge or asking someone before or after class to study with you. The college library is another opportunity where studying might lead to meeting someone.

21. Extracurricular activities.

Extracurricular activities, whether sports or working on a project in the art studio, offer an opportunity to meet others who share your interests. The atmosphere is usually more relaxed and conducive to mixing and mingling than it is before or after class. You might also check out if there is a TV or game room in the student activity center or dorm where students congregate to meet others.

22. Co-ed dorms.

'I know two couples that met this year because they were on the same floor', says 18-year-old Stan Bashmashnikov, a freshman at Ithaca College majoring in business administration. Angel Rivera, also a freshman, concurs: 'In that kind of community, you leave the doors open so it makes it easier to interact with the opposite sex'.

Here's an example of how living in a co-ed dorm indirectly led to a marriage, 11 years after the couple first met as freshmen at Fairfield University. Michelle Grady, a 29-year-old human resource manager, shares how a co-ed dorm association (it was a townhouse in this case) led to reconnecting with Sean Grady, who is also 29 and an employee benefits consultant specializing in IT projects:

Three years ago, in August, my townhouse roommate married Sean's townhouse roommate. Sean and I both attended the wedding without dates. We began to dance in the same circles towards the end of the wedding and Sean asked me to dance the final dance of the evening, 'Wonderful Tonight'.

At the conclusion of the wedding, he mentioned he was going to the hotel bar. I met him there and we continued dancing the night away. I later found out that our friends had a hand in pushing us together. Our first kiss was that night and our first date was the following weekend.

---

23. Go back to school.

Whether you go back to get an advanced degree or to take non-credit courses, school opens up opportunities to meet new people while you learn. If you do not find the love of your life in one of your classes, you may become friends with other students who might know eligible singles to introduce you to.

24. WORKPLACE ROMANCE.

After school, work is the most common place for people to meet and date because that's where most of us spend the bulk of our time.

When he was 58, Tom Blake, who had been divorced three times, 'finally got it right' when he met Greta, then 57, through his job. Blake, a former public relations executive who is the author of *Finding Love After 50* and the owner of a delicatessen on the Pacific Coast Highway in Dana Point in California, explains about their meeting.

She came in and ordered a fresh carrot juice. I looked at her and I said, 'This woman has a radiance about her face. I can tell she's kind'. I went over to her and I asked her if she would like to have dinner.

'That would be nice,' she said.

We were both out somewhere and we took the opportunity as it presented itself and we seized the moment.

They've been together more than five years now.

Of course at each job there are considerations if you meet someone you want to date. At some companies, dating between co-workers or supervisors and subordinates is strictly forbidden. Other companies permit it; others ask that one party request a transfer to another department especially if it is a supervisor/subordinate situation.

Cupid can strike at any time, however, and sometimes it is so powerful that you have to go with it yet do the ethical thing when it comes to your job. For example, a psychologist shared that he was smitten with a social worker who reported to him. He told his boss that he wanted to date the social worker, his boss said fine, and assigned her to another supervisor. (The psychologist married his former social worker a year later.)

25. Attend activities sponsored by companies dedicated to building relationships.

Check out local activities sponsored by national, regional or local companies. For example, magazine editor and writer Laurel Touby founded mediabistro.com, a site with job postings for those in the media which also organizes parties in New York City, Denver, Chicago and other cities. Basic membership is free; you can sign up to be notified about parties in your geographic area.

Another grassroots relationship-building network with local activities is Company of Friends (CoF), an outgrowth of the magazine *Fast Company*. These events attract working young professionals, who tend to be single, throughout the United States and internationally; business relationships or romance could bloom through these events. Membership is free; some of the events that CoF organizes locally may have modest participation fees to cover food and drink. There is a calendar at the website that lists upcoming events.

26. Go out after work with co-workers and suggest they invite others along.

At the end of the workday, or after work on Friday, unwinding from work is a common way to connect with others outside of a strictly work context. You could also ask co-workers to invite others, from your company or from other companies or businesses, to join in as a way of expanding your network of potential dates.

27. Reconnect with alumni from school or previous jobs.

You can reconnect by networking among your former co-workers, those who are still at the old company or at other companies, or through an online service, such as classmates.com, which has a worker reunion section in addition to old classmates, or School Friends, which helps to reconnect former school friends throughout Australia and New Zealand. (See the Appendix for additional sites or search engines for finding old classmates, previous co-workers or military buddies.)

There are of course former classmates or employees who stay connected through their own efforts, through e-mail and annual or less frequent get-togethers depending upon the distance that alumni or former co-workers have to go to reconnect.

Even if former classmates or co-workers are not the love of your life, you can always ask them if they know someone who is currently single. A recommendation or referral by old classmates or former co-workers may be advantageous since they have known you through school or work, and so they may have a better idea about the type of person to whom you'd want to be introduced.

28. Get a part-time job.

If you can make the time, getting an additional part-time or freelance job will open up opportunities to meet people. For example, you could become an event organizer for 8minutedating.com, which has events in 55 cities. In addition to earning money, you will have a chance to socialize with everyone you meet through the events.

Consider a part-time job where there will be a lot of customer or client contact, such as working in a bookstore, department store, electronics store, computer store, record or video store.

29. Switch jobs to improve your odds.

If you think being in a new work setting would open up new social (as well as career) opportunities for you, and you want to make a change anyway, this might be a strategy that helps you. It might be the type of work you do, or if you like the work but the particular location has few opportunities for meeting someone, you might change the environment without changing your career. For example, if you are a nurse and you have been working as a private nurse with home duty, you might instead switch to working in a hospital where there are nurses, doctors and administrative staff who might be single and eligible.

30. Create networking breakfasts, lunches and dinners.

Stop eating alone. Eat out. Gather together other singles for regular meals. Let your 'meal-mates' know they can bring along other singles as well.

31. Go to trade shows.

Trade shows, such as the Book Expo for the publishing industry, the American Library Association annual meeting for librarians and publishers, or the annual technology show in Las Vegas, or meetings of professional associations or organizations, such as the National Speakers Association of Australia or the Professional Speakers Association of Europe, are opportunities for meeting since there is a heightened friendliness at these shows only rivaled by the geniality you often find from those sitting next to you on airplane trips.

In addition to possibly taking you out-of-town, removed at least temporarily from the pressures of day-to-day work, phone calls and e-mails, trade shows usually offer multiple social opportunities, such as lunches and dinners, and educational programs as well as open-ended hours walking the exhibit hall.

32. Attend association meetings.

If you belong to an association, try to get to the meetings that are offered. You will have a common bond with those you meet; in addition to advancing your career and learning about your profession or industry, you will become better known to other members who might have a family member, co-worker or acquaintance to introduce you to.

33. Participate in your alumni associations.

Volunteer to be a mentor to current students. Attend reunions for your year as well as the annual homecoming. Let former classmates know that you are single and open to an introduction to eligible singles.

34. Take a job in another city, state or country.

You might just need a dramatic change to jump-start your social life such as relocating to one of the top cities for singles. (See #122 in the last chapter for a list of the top United States and the top international cities for singles, according to Forbes.com.)

In addition to moving to a city with the nightlife and housing situations that singles will find especially convenient, if you are moving because you have been offered a wonderful job that is a great opportunity, you will be in a very upbeat mood and possibly even have more disposable income than if you remain in a dead-end job.

Of course you can find the love of your life anywhere, including where you currently live and work, but moving to further your career just might also further your social life.

chapter 9

Personal Ads (Print or Online)

Florida-based Lisa Bentsen met her husband Robert through a personal ad in a local newspaper. Together they now run Singlesearch.com. Lisa shares their 'how we met' story:

I had been divorced and I had been looking around for a permanent partner. My kids were at the age that I could consider getting married again. I had dated a lot in my particular region. I was living in Boca Raton, Florida, at the time but I wasn't finding the kind of person I wanted. So I thought, 'Why don't I make this a science project and let me sit down and write down all the things when you reach a certain age that I knew about me that were flexible and the things about me that were inflexible'.

My game plan was to write all this down on paper, to compose an ad. I found a paper in South Florida, a single's publication that drew from Palm Beach and Broward Counties, and I wrote an ad. It was a pretty good size ad and it would have been rather expensive [to run] so I made a deal with the publisher: I would write articles for singles in exchange for the newspaper running the ad for free.

Four hundred people wrote to me over about a year and a half. I weeded it down to around forty with potential. [Then] I got it down to around two when I got Robert's letter. It was remarkably different. It had a spiritual overtone to it. It was honest and it had integrity. Here was a person interested not just in the mundane functions in life but in the why we are here and what is our job on earth.

I responded to it and we talked for hours but our schedules were such that we couldn't get together for a week and a half. But we spent hours on the phone.

I think I knew the moment I saw him. He was a very good-looking man but it didn't matter. He had this personality and was unlike anyone I had dated before. He said the same thing to me.

We were married four months later and that was 15 years ago.

There are countless success stories about couples who met through a personal ad. However, there are also occasional horror stories, as well as instances of lies and deception. I do not have a scientific reference for this, but in doing research for this book I heard the statistic bandied about that as many as 30 per cent of those who post ads online are actually married and unavailable.

If you decide to place an ad in a publication, or post one online, there are safety and privacy considerations. Be careful to guard your identity until you feel confident about whom you are dealing with. (See additional suggestions in Chapter 4, 'Staying Safe During Your Search'.)

Tips for Writing an Ad

The pluses for writing and placing the ad, rather than answering someone else's, is that you get to pick and choose exactly where you want it to appear, such as online (and if online, at what site?) or in print (and if in print, in what magazine or newspaper, local or national, or even international)?

You can place the ad when you've got the time and motivation to look, and wade through the responses, and you can also decide if you want to include your photo, or if you want to request a photo or video.

Some personals are free but most do have a cost per word. That usually forces you to write as little as possible but telling as much about yourself as you can. You also want to try to get positive attention through either a quote or a unique expression that sets you apart from everyone else.

A personal ad is, first and foremost, an ad. You are trying to attract the ideal date or mate. You are selecting from all your traits and attributes the ones that you think will be valued by others but also that you want to be distinguished by. (You may wish to refer back to Chapter 5, 'Getting Ready for the Search'. Review the sample ad or revised ad that you wrote or, if you did not write an ad before, try writing one now.)

Here are key suggestions for writing a personal ad.

- Choose where you place your ad as carefully as you choose the words in your ad. Spend the necessary time to research each website or publication offering ads. Read through typical ads. Do those placing the ads seem to reflect men or women similar to you in terms of socioeconomic status, level of ambition, accomplishments, goals, or interests? If not, keep searching for the ideal publication or website.

- Write and rewrite your ad until you are satisfied. Share it with trusted friends or family members. See what they think of the ad.

- Be as clear and specific as possible about who you are as well as what you want. If you want to get married, say it. If you want to have children, make that known. If you are just looking for a date but without a long-term commitment, state that, too.

- To set your ad apart, use a catchy phrase or a famous quote.

- When you place the ad, study the responses you initially receive. Are you attracting the kind of person you had hoped to attract? Do you see any traits those respondents have in common? How might it tie to what you wrote or failed to write in your ad? Keeping those issues in mind, try rewriting your ad, placing it again, and seeing if this time the respondents are closer to what you had hoped to find.

- Think through what you will say and do when your ad starts to generate responses. Have a clear plan about how you will make sure you keep yourself safe through the search.

- If the cost of the ad seems prohibitive but your instinct is that this would be the right forum for it, see if you can work out a barter arrangement with the publication or the website like Lisa Bentsen did (as described at the beginning of this chapter).

Tips for Answering an Ad

You can avoid the cost and effort of composing and placing your own print ad by instead answering someone else's. (Check with each website, however, to determine whether it is free to respond to someone else's ad even if you do not place your own.)

When you answer someone else's ad, you are now the one who is contacted, or passed over, rather than the one making those decisions and taking charge of the search, but this approach might suit you better. A counselor I know called to say that her own ad failed to get the results she wanted, but she answered someone else's and they're marrying in May. Her fiancé went on dates with ten out of the 90 women who responded to his ad; she was the tenth date.

Here are some guidelines if you do answer an ad.

- Avoid general statements about you; key in on specifics about the interests, dreams and goals of the person to whom you're responding.

- Let your answers reflect who you are, without giving away so much to a total stranger that it's inappropriate.

- If responding to printed ads, select the paper, pen and even the way of responding – handwritten, typewriter or computer – as carefully as you do your words.

- Enjoy the self-discovery that answering an ad provides so the experience is useful and pleasant, whether or not you receive an answer.

- If you are responding to an online ad (profile), be aware that your response, like any e-mail on the Internet, may not be a secure communication. You may wish to write as little as possible and instead request a regular mailing address, fax or phone number so you could communicate in a more secure way.

Should You Include a Photo or Video?

This is of course a matter of personal taste but consider some of the reasons asking for a photograph or a video could be a disservice to your search. A picture sets up expectations so instead of reacting to someone's personality, or how someone actually looks, the response is, 'You don't look like your picture', or 'You're much prettier than your picture'.

Some, however, need a picture to make the decision that you are enough of their 'type' that they want to go further. But pictures may be outdated, let alone unflattering.

Others will disagree; for them, asking for a picture or video is as vital as asking whether someone is allergic to animals, or wants to marry and have children.

Considerations When Using an Online Dating Site

When using an online dating site, keep in mind all the concerns in Chapter 4, 'Staying Safe During Your Search', as well as the guidelines for sending, or answering, an ad or profile as noted previously in this chapter. There are, however, additional considerations when you are dealing with online dating sites. Remember that every site is different in some small or major ways and sites may change ownership at any time as well as what types of singles they are appealing to in their databases. So check back regularly to make sure a site is still appealing to you as well as the kind of potential dates you want to meet.

Here are some general guidelines when evaluating if a site will work best for you.

- **Cost**
  Although some sites profess to be completely free, if you read further you discover that you can post your profile for free but you cannot respond to, or receive, e-mails about your post without paying a fee. Make sure you are clear about what the fee for getting responses is as well as whether or not that fee covers accessing a certain number of profiles, such as one or five or more, or an unlimited number of profiles for a specific period of time, such as one month, three or even for a year.

- **Customer service**
  Some sites will tell you bluntly that they offer absolutely no customer service and that is why their site is so much less expensive than other sites. Other sites offer customer service or help to site users only through e-mail. Some also offer a telephone number you can call to talk to a real person. Figure out what your comfort level is in terms of having the ability to get your questions answered about the site or a profile and, before you sign up and post your profile or pay your money, if a particular online dating site will meet your needs.

- **What's the refund policy?**
  Most online dating sites do not offer a refund. That's not as big a problem if you pay for just a few profiles at a time, or just one month, but what if you sign up for the year and you are lucky enough to meet Mr or Ms Right the very first day. Will you be able to get your annual fee back or not?

- **How good is the screening to make sure married or unavailable men or women are not signing up as single?**
  Some online dating sites provide or offer background checks. Others rely on the honor system.

- **Testimonials and referrals from other satisfied customers**
  Are there testimonials at the site and do those testimonials seem authentic? Are the photos or details about those success stories matching your own needs so you feel confident this site is attracting what you're looking for in a partner? Does the site have any current or previous members who have agreed to answer questions from prospective members?

- **What is the purpose of the site participants?**
  Some sites offer a chance to find someone who is looking for friendship, romance, marriage or just fun. Other sites are more focused on the pursuit of a serious relationship leading to marriage. See if the goals of those participating at the site seem to closely match your own.

- **How easy is it to get your profile removed?**
  If you meet someone and no longer want to be listed at the site, or if there is any other reason you prefer to take down your profile,

how easy or hard is it to have that done? How long will it take? A few hours? A week? A month? You can't get anyone to even answer your question about that?

- **How easy is it to report any potential abuses?**
What system does the dating service have in place for reporting of any abuses, such as a married person misrepresenting him or herself as single?

- **Will your anonymity be maintained?**
If you wish to keep all your postings anonymous, especially initially, will this online dating site enable you to do so or do you have to include your real name, real e-mail address and any other personal contact information?

- **Is there a free trial?**
Does the site allow you to have a free trial and what do you get for that free trial, e.g. actual site members who can be contacted or just general information?

- **Is there a FAQ or 'About Us' part of the site that describes its history?**
Usually it is better to know as much about the site and its founders as possible, such as when was it established, who started it, and whether someone has taken the time and shown the effort to put together frequently asked questions (FAQ) so you can get answers to typical concerns without having to contact customer service.

- **Are there any press clippings you can read?**
Does the site have any press materials posted about it? If you do a search on the Internet, do you find articles or references to the site and what it offers that are favorable?

Ways to Meet Using Personal Ads

35. PLACE A PERSONAL AD (OR ANSWER ONE) IN A NEWSPAPER.

When Bill Allin, who lives in Ontario, Canada, was 42, he decided to try another way to meet someone besides the dating services. So he placed an ad twice in the *Toronto Star.* Here's his ad:

I believe in honesty, integrity, and much caring and affection. I am a professional, 42, interested in music, theatre, film, outdoors, good conversation and a good sense of humor. You are a woman 35 to 45, single, emotionally secure and would like to see if we could make a pair for life. Write and tell me about yourself.

Bill received 130 letters from the two ads. He says:

Needless to say I did not meet 130 women but I went through a screening system. I probably met as many as 20 and my wife was the twentieth.

She really took care in the way she worded her letter. It gave me the impression that this was someone who had a somewhat similar view of life to mine and that is to say more rural than big city urban. Our childhoods were spent in rural areas so we had similar kinds of values.

Ten months after following up on the letter that his future wife sent, they were married. That was 17 years ago.

36. PLACE OR ANSWER A PERSONAL AD IN A GENERAL OR SPECIAL INTEREST MAGAZINE (IN PRINT OR AT THE ONLINE VERSION).

Subscribe to magazines or newsletters that have personals for those with a shared interest. For example, animal lovers could find 'the one' through a magazine such as *Cats*, which has personal ads. See if the city magazine where you live runs personal ads like *New York* magazine.

37. CYBERSPACE PERSONAL ADS.

There are lots of sites that have personal ads; each site has a slightly different population that it attracts as well as a theme or unifying shared interest to its members or subscribers. For example, the website for media professionals, mediabistro.com, has nationwide media personals at its site for finding friendship or love.

You can find countless testimonials from clients who met through an online personal ad site at the sites of the various dating sites. It may, however, be harder to find couples who are boasting that this is the way that they met since in some circles it is still seen as a controversial way to find romance. A single business coach in Melbourne, Australia, whom I interviewed told me that her closest friend, who just got married, met her husband through online dating 'but she doesn't like to talk about that. It's very hush hush.'

A 27-year-old single woman, who has lived in Seoul, Korea all her life, shared with me that she used an online dating site but, she explains, 'It wasn't exactly for dating.' She was more concerned with finding someone with whom she could just converse about topics of interest. This attitude may help those who are embarrassed about using an online dating site for finding romance to get to the site and try it out; if romance occurs, that would be fine, but they feel less self-conscious about using this method because they are not 'looking' for love.

For those who use online dating for finding someone new to just have discussions, sometimes it does advance from just conversation to romance. (See #67, 'Post a message or chat online on a subject of interest to you', for an example of this approach that worked.) Of course both parties have to agree that the relationship should become closer and develop into something more than just friends or correspondents.

Five years ago, Florida-based Karen Bryson, who is now 37, a counselor and coordinator of a program for disadvantaged university students at the University of South Florida, put an ad in the personals @ yahoo.com!® Why use the personals at yahoo.com? Karen explains:

I have a Yahoo!® e-mail address and one day I was just looking around on Yahoo!® I noticed the personals and I wondered what that was all about. I thought it looked interesting. I had no idea really what would happen. I was very surprised at the enormous response that I got from my ad. I had no idea there were that many single people out there looking for somebody.

What did Karen's ad say?

It was very brief and it just basically said I was interested in meeting people that I could talk with about some of my interests in theatre, writing and art.

I had two dogs at the time and so I needed someone who liked dogs. I also said that I was a vegetarian.

Close to 100 persons answered including her future husband, Tony Bryson, who wrote to her and said, 'I'm not a vegetarian [but] I hope this won't deter you from wanting to meet me'. It didn't. Karen only met two out of the 100: 'One other guy and my husband'. Exactly one year from when they met, they married.

There are numerous online personal ad possibilities today, in addition to the personals at Yahoo.com. Each site or online service may have a slightly different system or niche population that tends to use its site but the basic principle is the same: you post an ad about who you are and what you're looking for in a date or a mate. You may or may not want to include, or request, a photograph; today some even provide, or request, a video in addition to or in place of a still photograph. Sites range from free to a membership fee, by the month; one site described below, The Singles Resource Network, charges a one-time lifetime membership fee.

The person who places the ad, whether male or female, will follow-up in some way, through an e-mail or a phone call if a phone number is shared. It is up to the person who gets all the responses to decide who, if any, he or she will respond to.

Some ads may generate literally hundreds of responses. As with responses to ads in newspapers or magazines, a screening system is necessary for figuring out what ads you want to pursue as well as staying organized about follow-up in terms of what information you learn about someone, general and specific impressions, and any other details that will help you to decide if you want to consider further communication with someone.

Here is a sampling of websites for personal ads; sites are also listed in the Appendix.

Uk.match.com is an affiliate of Match.com that has grown to become one of the most popular online dating sites in the United Kingdom. There are also sites in Australia and New Zealand that are part of Match.com: au.match.com and nz.match.com

Personals@yahoo.com enables you to post an ad for free; subscribers pay a monthly fee to get as many responses as favored. They sponsored a competition in summer 2003 and 38,000 responded to become one of the 50 Real People of Yahoo!®Personals to show who was using the site. There are numerous local Yahoo!®Personals throughout the world including Australia and Ireland.

Friends Reunited Dating is a UK-based site that is also available in Australia, South Africa, New Zealand and Italy that allows you to search for old friends by place or by name.

Udate.co.uk is the UK site of the online dating site known as udate.com. One, three and six-month registration packages are available for purchase. It is free to register but you need to pay to communicate with other site members.

UBlove.com is an international site with participants from Australia and New Zealand that has posting profiles at its main site, searchable by country and other factors.

Date.com was launched on Valentine's Day in 1997. In 2003, it added non-Internet events including a New Year's Eve party and a Caribbean cruise. A couple who met in a date.com chat room married in Las Vegas in 2003 with approximately 70 date.com chat room members as guests. Articles posted at the website include flirting tips, love quizzes and dating advice.

Friendfinder.com is a membership site for posting or answering an online personal ad. It also maintains several sites for singles wanting to post or respond to specific ads, including asiafriendfinder.com (for Asians), amigos.com (Spanish version of the main site), indianfriendfinder.com (for Indians), and seniorfriendfinder.com (for those over 50).

Jdate.com is a global site for Jewish singles to post their profile (for free); there is a monthly fee to communicate with members.

In 2003, AOL launched love.com, another site for singles looking for love and marriage to post profiles and pictures and use instant messaging to communicate.

Lavalife.com is a membership site with an estimated one million active members during any one-month period throughout the United States, Canada or Australia. Posting a profile is free; if you see a profile that you like, it is also free to send a 'smile' (to show interest) to that profile.

The Singles Resource Network is a members-only site with a one-time life membership charge of $99. Fifty dollars is for the background check that their private investigators do on each member.

DatingDirect.com is a membership site based in England. In addition to the online ads, the company sponsors singles events in various cities.

Personal ads are also listed by city, state, and internationally. But be careful: some of the local or regional sites I visited in researching this book at that point had adult content right on the home page. If you are worried about that, stick to the national and international sites that do not allow adult content. Put in the zip code or geographic area that you are searching for.

38. CYBERSEARCH.

Use a basic search engine, such as Google™, and enter a key word for the kind of person you're looking for, or even a specific eligible person you've read about in the newspapers or magazines, and see what websites come up. You might also find write-ups on singles who are comfortable publicizing their search for a mate.

39. CREATE YOUR OWN WEBSITE.

Develop a website for the search or, if you create a website for your career, mention in your biography that you are single. You may hear from old classmates, former work colleagues or strangers who want to find out more about you. As with any stranger situation, exercise caution and care to protect yourself as you sort out e-mails or information to make sure you want to find out more about someone.

40. TRY OTHER TYPES OF ADVERTISING.

Katy McLaughlin printed up business cards that she calls a 'call-me card' with her picture, voicemail and an e-mail address that she distributed to her friends to hand out on her behalf.

Four single men in Texas reportedly rented a billboard at a cost of $2500, which is said to have led to 800 women contacting them for dates.

chapter 10

TRIPS, TRAVEL AND VACATIONS

Have you ever noticed how much friendlier most everyone is when you are traveling? Whether standing in line at the airport, or sitting next to you on a train or an airplane, especially in a foreign land, it is far more common to chat with others than in familiar surroundings when you are rushing from one appointment to another.

Whether you go on a trip just for singles to a foreign destination, like Paris, Fiji, Kyoto or Sydney, or you go to visit a friend or family member who lives in another city or state, getting out of your day-to-day routine by traveling is a way to broaden your world and meet new people who might become friends or the love of your life.

Should you travel alone or bring a friend along? Traveling alone can be scary and lonely but it may also increase the likelihood of talking to others besides the friend you brought along. It is, however, considerably more dangerous than traveling with a companion so be extra careful about your safety if you decide to travel alone. If you are traveling to an unknown city or country, make sure you inquire about any places you should be careful not to frequent especially at night. If you travel with a companion, you could work out a way of socializing together that might not detract from your goals of meeting new friends or eligible singles.

When you go on a trip or vacation, whether you set the trip up on your own, through a travel agent, or you are part of a tour organized by marital status, such as a singles trip, or by area of interest, like Charles Dickens enthusiasts traveling together to his home town or places he wrote about in England, of course you have to exercise caution, especially if you are traveling alone.

Before you commit to a destination, and certainly before you leave on your trip, find out how a single person traveling alone will be viewed, especially a single woman. If traveling alone will put you in a vulnerable position, either from a safety point of view or if you might be ostracized or viewed with contempt, you might want to travel with a friend, in a structured group setting or, if you are traveling for a business trip, asking another co-worker or even a family member, such as a cousin or sibling, to join you. As noted below, also check if there are any travel advisories in effect for any foreign locations due to local civil unrest or even healthcare concerns. Information is available at the United States government website: http://www.travel.state.gov

Apply all the commonsense suggestions in Chapter 4, 'Staying Safe During Your Search', with some additional precautions such as the following:

- Never leave your pocketbook or luggage unattended.

- Keep your passport with you at all times.

- Use traveler's checks or a credit card for purchases so you don't have to take an excessively large amount of cash with you.

- Provide contact information for every aspect of your trip for family members or close or best friends.

- Find out the customs in the foreign towns or cities you'll be visiting, such as whether or not a hotel is closed after a certain hour at night so it would be hard for you to check in or return after that time.

- Check that there have not been any recent health or travel warnings issued about a location that you want to visit. The United States government provides up-to-date information about travel at the website http://www.travel.state.gov. Travel warnings are posted at: http://travel.state.gov/travel_warnings.html.

- Know enough about the customs of any foreign places you are traveling to so you will not unwittingly offend anyone or, worse, cause your detention or even arrest.

- Have a plan for storing your expensive camera or video recorder, or even your passport, pocketbook or wallet, while you are swimming or unable to visually scrutinize your equipment or your key documents, money or personal possessions.

- If you do not have a contact number for each part of your trip, try to call home or check in at a cybercafe for e-mail messages so your family always knows your whereabouts.

- Do not wander off alone in questionable areas in faraway places. If you want to explore remote places alone, hire a reliable guide or ask a group from your tour to accompany you.

Travel and Vacation Ways to Meet

41. Go on a trip for singles.

There are so many trips now for singles that it is challenging to pick the group and the trip that might be right for you. There are trips or cruises organized for singles. Singlescruise.com is a company that has been booking cruises for singles since 1991. Some of the online dating sites organize trips for singles, as do the paid-membership social clubs, such as Social Circles in the tri-State (New York, New Jersey, and Connecticut) area, described in Chapter 12, 'Commercial Social Settings Including Bars, Clubs, and Restaurants'.

A well-established leader in vacations for singles is Club Med, which started in 1950. Club Med offers vacations for singles in locations that they call villages in spots around the world including Mexico, the Caribbean, the United States, Europe and Asia. Winter and summer vacations are available, depending on location and time of year, with an all-inclusive package covering housing, meals and activities.

Associations that you belong to may have trips organized for members. Unless it's a singles association, the trips will be open to all members although, depending on the destination and the time of year for the trip – when school is in session versus over a school vacation – you may find that singles or couples without childcare responsibilities are more likely to participate. One of the benefits of participating in such a trip is that those who go on the trip have membership in the same association in common; you start off with a greater probability that you will have some shared interests, such as film, television, running a company, medicine or writing, depending upon what association has organized the tour.

42. Traveling alone.

For some, being on a trip for singles, where everyone knows that everyone is considering everyone as a potential date, creates too much pressure. If you plan to travel alone, you can also plan your own itinerary or contact a travel agent for help. Any reputable travel agency would be helpful but there are also travel agencies geared to singles, such as Singles Travel International.

Airline stewardess Sharon Wingler has written a book about traveling alone, *Travel Alone & Love It*. At her website, Wingler includes a place where solo traveler visitors to the website share their recommendations for specific hotels, travel agents and destinations.

43. Visit friends or relatives in another city, state or country.

Ask them to have a party in your honor to commemorate your visit and encourage them to invite any eligible singles that they know. This will open your friend or relative's network to you and expand your universe of possible dates or mates to another city, state or country.

44. Join a travel club.

For those who prefer to travel in a group, rather than alone, travel clubs or organized and sponsored trips may provide enough structure while offering a chance to meet new people and see fresh places. One such company, Exotic Journeys Inc., in business since 1979, specializes in trips to India, Nepal, Bhutan, Sikkim, Tibet, Sri Lanka, Myanmar and Korea. Since 1993, the New York City-based Theatre

Development Fund (TDF) has been organizing trips, originating from New York City, to destinations throughout the United States and around the world. A sample of upcoming trips included China, Russia and Thailand, as well as theatre in Connecticut and Philadelphia.

45. Explore walking or bus tours, at home or out-of-town.

Walking or bus tours are an opportunity to explore your own city or a far-away destination. You will usually find people on the tours, as well as the tour guide, are quite friendly.

The advantage to a walking tour for meeting people is that, especially in the nice weather, you will have time as you walk to chat a bit in-between the times that you are quietly listening to your tour guide's explanations. Starting a conversation may be easier since you have the walking tour in common.

Whether you live in, or are visiting, a major city, such as Boston, New York City, Chicago, San Francisco or London, walking or bus tours are another way to meet new people. For walking tours, check your local newspaper, city magazine, such as *New York* magazine, the weekly local guide provided by your hotel, or search for listings on the Internet by visiting an online guide to a particular city. For bus tours, check the local phone book or the Internet listings for a particular city.

46. If you are over 50, check out the trips for older singles.

Trips and vacations for singles over 50 is an expanding field. Elderhostel, a non-profit organization headquartered in Boston but with members all over the world, organizes educational trips throughout the United States and internationally as well as outdoor adventure travel for those over 55. Not just for singles, you could go alone and room by yourself or ask them to match you up with a roommate.

47. Go on a singles weekend.

There is a heritage of weekends for singles going back decades to the Concord and Grossingers, two hotels located in the Catskills of New

Tips, Travel and Vacations

York State that are no more. Television documentary writer Barbara Gordon began her autobiography with this inscription: 'I have a favorite joke. A man and a woman meet at a singles resort in the Catskills. They are dancing together on a Saturday night. He says, "I'm only here for the weekend". She replies, "I'm dancing as fast as I can".'

Today, singles weekends remain a way to meet other singles even if events have spread out to a four-day weekend requiring a plane ride to another city or even another country.

Make sure you do your homework and check out any upcoming singles weekend thoroughly before you commit money and time to the experience. Ask all the questions you would ask about any new travel experience and, if possible, check out testimonials from past attendees. Find out the cancellation policy. Especially ask what activities are offered and how many singles they expect and in what age groups and from what types of background.

You can find out about available singles weekends by phoning a hotel that interests you and asking, visiting their website, or checking the newspapers, including the Sunday *The New York Times* travel section ads.

You might also contact local or national singles organizations or clubs and see what singles weekends they have scheduled. (Also see Chapter 12, 'Commercial Social Settings Including Bars, Clubs and Restaurants'.)

48. Take a business trip.

Traveling on your own or with others for business meetings or to attend a trade show or conference opens up people-meeting possibilities. You will be busy working during the day, but nights and weekends, if you are away for an extended period of time, is usually your time. Do research in advance about the best places to meet singles in the city you are traveling to.

You might also want to check out what business networking events are scheduled during your business trip, such as a breakfast meeting of the local Chamber of Commerce or an evening event organized by the local Company of Friends (CoF) group, for business executives and entrepreneurs, or mediabistro.com, for media professionals.

If this is a business trip for which you have to plan your own itinerary, consider booking at a hotel that is known to attract singles in your particular age and socioeconomic group, and stay there. If there is a health club or workout room, check it out instead of staying in your room.

49. Go on vacation right in your hometown or city.

If you lack the time, money or incentive to travel, still take your vacation and use it meet new people. Explore your own hometown as if you are traveling to a foreign city for the very first time. Get out of doing the same things and explore new places and events. Check out the local newspaper, city magazine or Internet listings and explore local or nearby restaurants, museums, concerts or clubs.

Do all the fun day and evening activities that you often lack the time to get to when you are working or rushing around. Since you are on vacation, even though it is in your own hometown or a city nearby, you may especially receptive to meeting new people since you have temporarily removed yourself from the day-to-day pressures, and routine or work.

chapter 11

Cultural, Educational or Volunteer Activities and Singles Associations

I met a single man in his late thirties who organized a lecture series on themes ranging from city architecture to food and nutrition. For each event he charged four dollars per person. He told me that over a three-year period, 10,000 singles participated in his lecture events. He explained his philosophy: 'If you met someone, it was a side benefit'. Attending cultural or educational activities, volunteering or joining a singles associations with a purpose you care about, may prove to be the way that you achieve that 'side benefit'.

Meeting Through Activities, Volunteering or through Singles Associations

50. Join a theater group.

Go to shows with the group. You could also get involved in putting on a show. Besides acting there are administrative jobs as well as marketing positions or even being an usher.

51. Go to the movies.

Join a singles group that organizes movie nights. For example, Australia's My Friends in Brisbane, Queensland, organizes Tuesday nights at the movies for its members although non-members are invited to attend as well.

Find out what movie theaters in your community are more conducive to socializing. Some cinemas have restaurants as well as video game arcades right at the duplex. 'When I was 33, I met my girlfriend at the movies', said a 54-year-old consultant. 'She was sitting next to me with her girlfriend and we sort of looked at each other at the same time and she said, "How do you like it so far?" and I answered, "I think it will do well oversea". After the movie we talked some more and decided to exchange numbers. I called her the next day, we went out to a party, and we dated and ended up living together.'

If you enjoy learning about movies as well as watching them, you could take a movie class with screenings and discussion.

52. Browse and shop at a local book or record store.

Go to a bookstore and buy a book, newspaper or magazine. If they have a coffee bar area, sit and read there. Bookstores tend to be very friendly places. If you frequent the same bookstore often enough, you may become known to the manager or booksellers as well as to other patrons who may introduce you to others.

53. Become part of a reading group.

Whether through a bookstore, friends, libraries or an association, participate in a reading group. As part of the activities, you could also attend bookstore lectures and author signings, both of which offer opportunities to meet fellow booklovers.

54. Coordinate a special event at a bookstore or library.

Ask the local bookstore if you could help them coordinate a singles-related event in the community for meeting, especially around Valentine's Day.

Putting together an event, such as an author event related to Valentine's Day geared to meeting a date or mate, might be a way to come in contact with the eligible singles in your community.

55. Meet people at your local library.

Investigate what your local library has to offer in terms of book sales, author events, movie screenings, or even training on computers. Find out about volunteer opportunities that would open up your chance to meet people taking out books or videos that you also enjoy.

In keeping with the philosophy that being visible is one of the first ways that a single person increases the likelihood that he or she might find a partner, you could go to the library and read instead of staying in your living room.

Check out what discussion groups the library offers. There is usually a time for socializing before or after the event so try to arrive a little early and stay after it ends rather than rushing out the door.

56. Join a self-help group for an issue you care about.

For listings of self-help groups, go to the in-depth website Selfgrowth.com. There are countless worthwhile self-help groups or causes to choose from that would welcome your participation. For other listings, visit the website of the American Self-Help Group Clearinghouse or the National Self-Help Clearinghouse.

57. Get involved in your religious group or community association.

Caring about others and strengthening your community ties may lead to introductions to eligible singles.

58. Become involved in various social, educational or cultural events of organizations that you already belong to.

Singles need to be present – not just sending in their membership dues. Attend as many meetings as possible of organizations that interest you since the other members you meet will probably share your interests. If you are unsure about how right a fit there is between you and a particular organization, attend as a guest until you are sure.

59. Take an all-day seminar or a workshop.

Whether you want to study acting, writing, cooking or a foreign language, people are friendlier when you have a common reference point, such as taking a seminar together. Pick topics that are interesting to you so if you do meet someone there, you will start off with a shared interest.

60. Go to a museum.

Whether it's over the weekend when single parents or singles without weekend plans want to be out and around people and art, or an evening concert or lecture that you attend, museums are wonderful places to meet others as well as places to go once you are dating. In addition to looking at the art or dinosaur collection, if it's a science museum, check out the cafeteria. If you are a single parent, you may find other single parents at museums on the weekends.

Becoming a member in a museum that reflects your interests, such as the Museum of Television and Broadcasting in Manhattan, also will open you up to 'members only' invitations for openings of new exhibits as well as social events.

61. Attend a dog or cat show.

Dog or cat shows are a shared activity that will definitely give you an opportunity to meet other dog and cat owners who feel enormous pride in their pets. (And don't forget the old standby of walking your dog as a way to meet people.)

62. Go to a concert.

Rego Park, New York-based Classical Music Lovers' Exchange, founded in 1980, now has more than 15,000 members. Members are both single and looking for a partner, or are classical music lovers who want to meet other classical music enthusiasts. Members post profiles and, if there is mutual interest, contact may be initiated online.

If you enjoy going to concerts, including rock concerts, consider buying two tickets and asking someone along instead of going alone. It might be the perfect icebreaker.

If you go to a concert for your favorite recording artist or band, you will know that those you meet are likely to share your taste in music.

63. Take a course in how to be a happy single.

At least you'll meet people in the course who are into self-improvement and accepting their singleness as a state to be enjoyed rather than a time to be dreaded. When I was single, I took two courses on that theme: 'Alone Again' and 'Living Alone and Loving It'. Both courses were informative; all the participants were single.

64. Attend or organize a singles expo.

Check out the singles clubs or organizations in your town or city and see if they have a Singles Expo coming up that you could attend. Some of the expos are put on by the commercial singles industry; there are exhibits demonstrating the latest products that singles might want to purchase.

If you wanted to organize a singles expo as a business venture, you might meet a lot of people who are single as well as others in the singles industry.

65. Attend music or film festivals.

Get together a group of friends and go to a marathon music festival, at the park or the beach, or a film festival open to the public. Ask your friends to invite eligible singles along. Be appropriately friendly to others that you meet at the festival. The film festival may have parties before or after the movie screenings that you might be able to get invited to, either as part of your admission or for an extra fee.

66. Attend consumer product shows.

At an annual product show, whether it is the yearly automobile or boat show in Manhattan, or a consumer electronics show, you are likely to meet others who are interested in those products. Get the schedule for the show since there may be networking opportunities in addition to the exhibitions.

67. Post a message or chat online on a subject of interest to you.

Once again, be very careful to maintain your anonymity and avoid making yourself vulnerable until you feel confident about exactly who you are dealing with when you meet someone through an online discussion group.

There are success stories of such online discussions that have led to romance and marriage. Fifty-two-year-old Barry, a technology specialist who used to live in England, met his second wife five years ago through an Internet chat room. That led him to 'leaving all and everything to move to the US'. They now have two young children and live in Connecticut in addition to their older children from previous marriages.

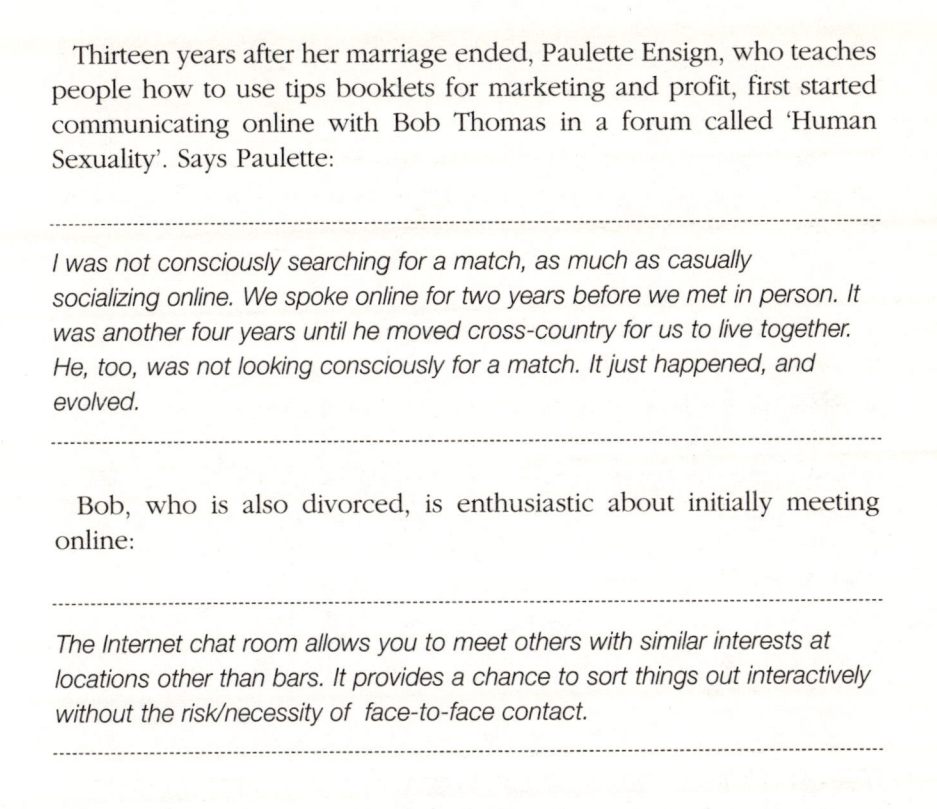

Thirteen years after her marriage ended, Paulette Ensign, who teaches people how to use tips booklets for marketing and profit, first started communicating online with Bob Thomas in a forum called 'Human Sexuality'. Says Paulette:

I was not consciously searching for a match, as much as casually socializing online. We spoke online for two years before we met in person. It was another four years until he moved cross-country for us to live together. He, too, was not looking consciously for a match. It just happened, and evolved.

Bob, who is also divorced, is enthusiastic about initially meeting online:

The Internet chat room allows you to meet others with similar interests at locations other than bars. It provides a chance to sort things out interactively without the risk/necessity of face-to-face contact.

68. Take a course to improve your networking and conversational skills.

There are courses in these topics available through adult education programs, such as the Learning Annex. Online communication courses are also a possibility today if you find it difficult to attend a class. A class in improvisation might also be useful as a way to loosen up.

69. Attend community events.

Block parties or neighborhood get-togethers offer opportunities to meet. Many towns, suburbs or cities offer open-air concerts in the summer or caroling at the holidays. Be prudent about your safety if you attend events in the park, especially at night; consider going with the company of at least one friend.

70. Read about eligible singles or offer to be in the article.

Locally or nationally, there are often round-up articles about eligible singles. Contact the participants or find out how to be considered if you want to be included.

71. Cultivate a new hobby.

If you are excited about your life and that includes your job and what you do in your spare time, such as your hobbies, you will seem much more positive and interesting to those you meet. Bored and desperate people usually push away new potential dates. Being involved in learning something new, from painting or playing the drums to photography or carpentry, will give you something to focus on besides your search or your job. At the class, you might meet another hobbyist or even when you go shopping for supplies for the hobby, you may meet someone.

72. Go to a poetry festival or a writer's conference.

You need not be a poet or a writer to benefit from the social and cultural atmosphere of literary festivals. For example, the annual Bouchercon is for mystery fans and writers. Held in a different US city each year, there are scores of panels, author events and social activities over several days.

73. Volunteer.

By doing volunteer work for a disadvantaged group or joining a local coed service organization you will be providing a worthwhile service to those in need. Check your telephone directory or read your local newspaper and see if there is a 'Volunteer Help Wanted' section announcing associations or groups that need your help.

74. Become politically active.

If you get involved in a political organization, including a local, state or national campaign, you will start off knowing that those you meet share your support of the same party or candidate. Volunteer to work at campaign headquarters for a candidate you believe in for the next election. You could answer phones, hand out flyers or buttons or place phone calls. If possible, go to headquarters to 'work the phones' rather than making phone calls on your cell phone or from home.

75. Join an organization or association that is for singles or is likely to attract single members.

Consider joining a local or national organization, such as one of the chapters in Australia of the international organization Partners Without Partners. The American Australian Association, established in 1948, has social and cultural programs for Australia and New Zealand expatriates. Find out if the activities and member benefits fit your needs and interests. Visit the association's website and read through the posted material, including any testimonials. Or you could phone or write for a sample newsletter (or read the newsletter online if it is posted there) or magazine available to members; attend one or more meetings or social functions, talk to other members, and find out if this group has what you're looking for in other members.

76. If you're a single parent, join a single parent association.

As mentioned above, with chapters throughout the United States and internationally, Parents Without Partners offers day, evening and weekend activities for its members. A man I spoke with who is married now and in his late twenties remembers the meetings for single parents that his newly divorced father took him to as a child. He confided: 'I knew we were there mainly so my Dad could meet women who were in his situation'.

77. IF YOU ARE INTO FARMING, JOIN AN ORGANIZATION FOR SINGLES IN AGRICULTURE.

Singles in Agriculture, a national association with chapters in Kansas, Iowa, Missouri, Nebraska, Illinois, Oklahoma, Texas, Indiana, Ohio, Wisconsin, the Rocky Mountains and the Northern Great Plains, is a membership organization for singles ages 18 and older who are in agriculture or an agriculture-related business. There are more than 1000 members in 41 states; social activities, such as dances, are offered through the local chapters.

78. JOIN ADVOCACY GROUPS.

The American Association for Single People (AASP) is an advocacy association for unmarried Americans; as long as you're single you may want to consider joining to advance the rights of singles as well as a way of meeting other singles.

There are also advocacy groups for singles issues to join for a wide range of concerns such as divorce and widowhood. Attending meetings, local, national or international, provides opportunities to meet like-minded singles.

chapter 12

COMMERCIAL SOCIAL SETTINGS

(BARS, CLUBS AND RESTAURANTS)*

Some refer to these types of meeting places, in addition to paying for a personal ad or a dating service, as the singles industry. Some have contempt for the bars and social clubs that cater to singles as if they are gouging singles out of their hard-earned money and not providing anything in return.

I asked someone who works at a major online dating service how she'd met her husband nine years ago. She replied, 'At a bar, the old-fashioned way'. I know two other couples who met at a bar and gotten married or are living together, both just within a few years. Thirty-seven-year-old Gloria, who has been married for three years and is manager of a law firm in Queensland, Australia, met her husband at a bar. So meeting at a bar is, for some, still the way to find the love of your life.

The singles bars and the social clubs catering to singles exist and are flourishing because they are filling a very real need, a need to meet new people. After a long day at the office, or working at a school or

---

* In the United States, the minimum age for entry to bars or clubs where alcoholic beverages are served is 21 and in Australia the minimum age is 18, but check each establishment's policies.

111

in a factory, there are still singles who do not want to go home to an empty apartment and boot up a computer to read and send e-mails.

There are those who prefer to be out and about, interacting face to face with others, whether at a bar or at an event organized by a social club.

Some see a definite distinction between the 'singles bar' and 'a bar'. The singles bar's function is to provide a venue for meeting other singles; there are hordes of unattached singles milling around; the emphasis is more on meeting other singles than on the drinking. Many may even be drinking just bottled water (out of a glass) or diet soda but they will still be meeting the minimum age requirements. Some bars offer free food as well as recorded music or live entertainers.

Mingling and meeting at a singles bar is what it's all about. The more people packed into the bar, the better. Although Thursday and Friday tend to be busy nights, some bars are crowded every day of the week.

Discos are another big part of the singles bar scene. Some places are institutions for meeting people. Roseland Danceland in New York City, a decades-old establishment for meeting, eating and dancing, has even added bands so that countless youths stand around listening to music, elbow to elbow. One woman who met her first husband at Roseland returned, 30 years later, after a successful 23-year-marriage ended by her husband's death, to find her new husband there. Lately Roseland has had standing-room-only concerts catering to younger singles.

Many singles, however, frequent neighborhood bars near their apartments who would never venture into a singles bar. A 40-year-old divorced woman who lives in Philadelphia told me that 'I only go to one bar alone where I know the owner and all of the staff'.

The first rule in being comfortable going into a neighborhood bar is: befriend the owner and the waiters or waitresses (or bartenders). You are no longer a single 'on the make' but someone from the neighborhood, stopping in for a friendly chat and drink.

In every community, bars develop reputations for providing a desirable atmosphere, good music, excellent food or all three. Where the 'in' singles bars are for meeting people changes from generation to generation and even from year to year. You want to network with other singles to find out where the 'in' bars are and also where people most like you are likely to congregate. You want to spend your time hanging out where you're most likely to meet someone who has the interests, traits and attributes that you're seeking.

Commercial Social Settings for Singles to Meet

79. GO TO A SINGLES BAR.

Select a singles bar that has been recommended by reliable sources as the kind of place that attracts the type of men or women you are interested in meeting.

Do your homework so you know what singles bars you might want to frequent. When you arrive, look around and see if your first impression is that you want to be part of that crowd. If it helps to bring a friend or two along, especially the first time, definitely consider doing that.

Make sure the music isn't so loud that you can't hear conversations.

80. JOIN A SINGLES CLUB.

Singles clubs have cropped up with just that goal in mind: to offer a multiplicity of activities that opens up the opportunity to meet new eligible single men and women.

Some singles clubs revolve around a theme or one particular type of activity, such as eating out at restaurants, attending movies, or sports activities. Other clubs have a wider range of offerings such as Social Circles, based in Manhattan, with more than 2000 men and women members in the Tri-State (New York, New Jersey, Connecticut) area offers at least one event per day, sometimes two or three a day on the weekends. They also arrange trips for singles to places like Fiji, Paris and Cancun. Dues are discussed when you meet in person since there are a number of available membership packages from which to choose. New York City-based Social Circles is associated with social clubs, mainly catering to singles, in Seattle, Portland, Chicago, Minneapolis, Denver and Tucson.

81. GO DANCING.

Alone or with a friend, go dancing if you like to dance. Don't wait for a date to ask you. By going to a club that offers dancing, you are not just focused on meeting someone but on the fun, exercise and creative expression that dancing provides. Since it is still acceptable for a stranger at a club with dancing to ask someone to dance, it can be an easier icebreaker for some than trying to think of the perfect opening line to say when you meet someone at a party or at a bar.

82. Write an article on your town's nightlife for singles.

Through the research you will find out where to go and expand your universe. It is an excellent way to find out about the 'in' spots in your community as well as interviewing single men and women on what is working for them.

83. Go to a sports bar.

At a sports bar, like ESPN in Manhattan, there is a lot of activity and moving around, much more than in a typical restaurant. Since there is a games room on the top floor where you can go before or after you have your meal, it is possible to meet people who are also playing the various games. The atmosphere at a sports bar is very convivial and open to socializing and meeting.

84. Frequent the 'in' restaurants, clubs or parties for singles.

In practically every community, a restaurant or bar starts to get a reputation for attracting single people who are looking to meet others. Find out what those places are and stop by to see if you feel comfortable spending time there.

Some bookstores offer free music for Sunday brunch in their café areas; you may find singles there, reading their Sunday newspaper, and enjoying the music. If they're out early enough on a Sunday, it may be an indication that they did not stay over at someone's apartment or home the night before; they might be available and 'looking'.

An alternative to noisy bars started in 2002. Known as The Quiet Party™, singles meet there by exchanging notes. Parties are being offered in several cities in the United States as well as in Beijing, China.

85. Go to a coffee bar or cafe.

Starbucks® and similar upscale coffee bars are very conducive to striking up a conversation with other single patrons. You can even work on your laptop so you don't look as obvious in your social pursuit.

86. Go to a cyberspace café.

Whether you're traveling and need to send e-mails to your friends and family from Dublin, London, Paris or Tokyo, or you're a New Yorker and you want to stop into the cyberspace café in Times Square, these places tend to be jumping with activity as well as with the friendliness you find on a plane or at the airport. It's so easy to start a conversation in a cyberspace café since so many who go there are from far away. 'Where are you from?' is an obvious and non-threatening initial question.

87. Consider a cooking class or a private dining club.

Adult education programs have cooking courses geared to a type of cooking, such as Italian or Indian. Take a cooking course in Italy or France. Start a progressive dinner event whereby you and other singles invite each other to your apartments or houses for one course of a six-course meal.

Six in the City is a membership group based in Brisbane that brings together six members – three men and three women – who are over age 30, who have dinner together at a restaurant on a Saturday night.

A well-established private dining club is The Single Gourmet, founded in 1982, with chapters in cities throughout the United States and Canada including New York, Atlanta, Boston, Toronto and New Orleans. Memberships are available for just three months or for the year. Events consist of dinners with 40 to 80 diners, or a monthly dinner dance with as many as 200 participants.

88. Casinos.

You have to be at least 21 to go to a casino in the US but, if you are above the minimum age and do not have a gambling problem, casinos and the surrounding bars, cabarets and restaurants are conducive to mingling. Also consider frequenting the art and artifact museums that some of the casinos have founded in or near their casinos. You could also go shopping at the nearby stores or use the health club facilities if you are staying overnight and the casino hotel offers that as an option.

chapter 13

SPORTS ACTIVITIES

One of the best side benefits of participating in a sports activity as a way to meet the love of your life is that it is also a healthy, positive activity for reducing stress, keeping your weight under control or even losing weight, if necessary, while at the same time you are socializing. Be careful not to get in over your head by trying to do a sport for which you just do not have the stamina or the ability, or committing to a sport for a prolonged period of time if you actually dislike it. Instead, try to seek out the sports activities that you are proficient in, or can become competent at, as well as a sport that you like and want to stick with.

Whether it's tennis, rock climbing, running, walking, swimming, volley ball, bike riding or skiing, do the activity first because you like it and second because you want to meet people. Then, when you do meet someone, you can continue that sport activity together.

89. TAKE UP A NEW SPORT.

There is an enthusiasm and a sense of wonder when you are learning a new sport. Also, if you learn the new sport in a class, you may meet others who are starting at the same point with the sport. They may be more open to conversation and socializing as you all learn the new sport together. In addition to learning the sport, consider joining a club for enthusiasts of that sport. If the sport is tennis or squash, add your name to their 'partners wanted' list.

90. Take a bicycle trip for singles.

You can seek out a company that arranges trips just for singles, or you can contact a travel agency and ask them if they have trips with a majority of singles or that are exclusively single. The World Outdoors, founded in 1988 and based in Boulder, Colorado, organizes such trips, including bike trips. Elderhostel, catering to men and women over 55, including singles, also offers bike trips.

91. Join a health or athletic club and attend regularly.

Increase your visibility by working out at a health club. In addition to health clubs, there is the local YMCA or YWCA.

92. Take an exercise class.

Take an exercise class, with or without a friend. If you have a fulltime job, consider a lunchtime class. You will be more likely to meet others who are also working and in proximity to your job.

93. Join a tennis or squash club.

Let them know that you are open to being matched up for singles or doubles for games. Tennis is a popular way to meet since many play doubles requiring a player to fill in on a regular basis or if someone has a scheduling conflict and needs to be replaced temporarily. If you belong to a tennis club, you could let them know that you are available to fill in if someone needs an extra for doubles.

94. Go bowling.

This is a sport that is conducive to chatting and socializing. See if there is a bowling league you want to join but try to check out that you will be comfortable with the bowlers before committing to a weekly game.

Take bowling lessons if your game could use some help. If you get good enough, you could enter tournaments, another way to meet other single bowlers.

95. Ice skate, ski or snowboard.

Whether outdoors in the winter at a rink in Manhattan, or at an indoor rink in the spring, ice skating is a sport that may lead to meeting another skater.

Skiing is a sport that has a lot of opportunities to meet others built into the experience. Whether you go to a nearby ski resort for a day, or you go away for a weekend or a week, skiing is an ideal sport for meeting people (but it definitely requires skill to master the skiing). If you are planning to go on an organized ski trip, find out about planned activities off the slopes.

96. Go roller skating.

Like ice skating, roller skating is a sport that requires skill and the chance to meet someone who shares your ability and interest in this sport. Inquire if a particular roller skating rink has any events or sessions just for singles.

97. Take a yoga class.

This is another opportunity for meeting like-minded singles while getting in shape and reducing stress at the same time. You might want to sample a class before you commit to four or eight sessions to see if you like the instructor and also if the participants are in the age group or gender ratio that fits in with your goal of meeting eligible singles.

98. GO TO A FOOTBALL, BASEBALL, HOCKEY OR BASKETBALL GAME.

Alone or with some friends, go to spectator sports events that attract those who share your enthusiasm for a particular team and sport.

99. GO RUNNING.

If you are careful about your safety, running, especially if you are near a popular spot for regular runners, such as around the reservoir in New York City's Central Park, is a healthy and a potentially social sport. Join a club for runners such as the New York Road Runners. The national association, the Road Runners Club of America, has over 600 clubs and 130,00 members.

Also consider entering a race; it need not be a marathon. There are much shorter races to take part in, either for fun or to support a cause. Running for a cause is a way to combine exercise with making a contribution to a worthy charity and with socializing.

chapter 14

SEASONAL OPPORTUNITIES: HOLIDAYS AND SUMMER

There are holiday get-togethers for singles, in the cities and at resorts, for Christmas, New Year's Eve and Valentine's Day, as well as summertime camps and trips over the summer just for singles. These get-togethers could be excellent opportunities to meet new people especially if your family lives far away, or you want to take a break from a family get-together for one or more holidays.

Summer is a prime time for meeting. Everyone is outside and going to beaches and concerts. It is light longer so there are more hours for activities that would be more difficult in the dark. Those who are uncomfortable driving at night, especially alone, have more hours during the day and into the early evening to socialize.

There are also summer traditions that have evolved in different parts of the country and in various parts of the world that encourage meeting and dating and finding the love of your life. For example, Fire Island in New York has been a mecca for singles for decades. It was in 1966 that Fran Silverman, author of the guidebook *Catskills Alive*, met her future husband, Ronald. Fran shares about her meeting:

We were each sharing houses on Ocean Bay Park in Fire Island. I was rooming with ten roommates, two of them male. He was one of four guys [in a neighboring house].

One day Ron and some of his buddies came over to our house on Fire Island and sat in front chatting with us. I remember thinking about Ron, 'He has a kind face'.

They were married two years later and have one grown daughter.

Seasonal Holiday Where-to-Meet Ideas

100. USE TIME OFF FOR NEW EXPERIENCES.

When you're not working, as well as on weekends, holidays and vacations, engage in completely new experiences. Sometimes all it takes to find the right one is breaking out of a routine or a rut that narrows the chances of meeting someone new with whom you might be a match.

By going to a new community over the weekends in the summer, or during a vacation, suddenly you're the new girl or guy in town.

101. ATTEND A SINGLES CAMP.

You could go to a camp on holidays or summer weekends, or during your vacation. Even if a camp is not exclusively geared to singles, such as Club Getaway, an adult camp which has been around for more than two decades and also has family weekends, you could inquire if there are special single events. You might want to bring a friend along (but don't stay glued to each other).

Also, if you have a job that enables you to take time off over the summer for a couple of weeks or months, consider getting a job at a summer camp. Quite often the majority of counselors are single.

102. Let Valentine's Day work to your advantage.

Although traditionally Valentine's Day is for couples, it has also become an opportunity for singles to meet through organized singles' events. Go alone or with a friend to a Valentine's Day singles' dinner or dance. Singlescruise.com organizes an annual Valentine's Day cruise departing from Miami.

103. Attend religious services catering to singles.

Check the local or religious newspapers or magazines, as well as the daily paper, for announcements about services for singles. For example, if you are Jewish, you might attend a service for singles for the High Holy Days or a Passover Seder. If you are Christian, there may be a Christmas Mass for singles that you could attend.

104. Participate in a holiday dinner for singles.

Check out listings in your local newspaper about upcoming Thanksgiving or Christmas dinners for singles. You could also host your own Thanksgiving or Christmas celebration; ask your single friends to bring along other singles. For holidays that are traditionally spent with family members, consider attending a program like the 'Thanksgiving for Single People', sponsored by Rowe Conference Center in Rowe, Massachusetts. It runs from Wednesday to Saturday. Single parents may bring their children.

105. Use the holidays to volunteer.

When many singles are looking for places to go at the holidays, especially Christmas or New Year's Eve, volunteer in soup kitchens, hospitals, prisons or at homeless shelters. Check out your local newspaper or the Internet for a list of volunteer activities especially for singles. Sometimes the volunteer association might even have a social event at the holidays. For example, New York Cares in New York has hosted a party at a nightclub to support its New York Cares Coat Drive.

106. Join in your friend's holiday celebrations.

If you have a friend who celebrates religious or patriotic holidays throughout the year, ask to be included with her or his family or other friends. Some couples with children, especially if they do not have a large family or a nearby extended family, and single parents may welcome the opportunity to invite their single friends to celebrate the holidays.

107. Organize a holiday party at work.

Organizing the event helps you to meet others. Holiday parties are also a time when it may seem easier to start a conversation with new men or women. If you are an entrepreneur or a freelancer, invite those you know through your business.

108. Attend a New Year's celebration for singles.

You need not be alone on New Year's Eve or New Year's Day just because you are single. Today it is much more common for singles to celebrate by going to a dinner or a dance. Check out nearby singles activities that you could attend alone or with a group of friends. Singlescruises.com finds their New Year's Day cruise, departing from Miami, to be a very popular one.

chapter 15

MISCELLANEOUS 'HOW TO MEET' IDEAS

There are also some zany ways or unusual ways to find the love of your life that are not easily categorized. I know one single woman who, when the elevator operators in New York City went on strike, volunteered to help out just to meet new people. I know another single woman who stood all day at the baked goods table of her block association's street fair in order to make herself more visible so she might meet someone.

An Assortment of Ways to Meet

109. SET A TARGET DATE FOR GETTING ENGAGED OR MARRIED AND WORK BACK FROM THERE.

Commit to that date and motivate yourself to keep meeting new people to try to meet that deadline. This is of course a dramatic suggestion, but for those who feel that their approach to meeting an eligible mate is too lackadaisical, having that kind of deadline and pressure might be just what's needed.

110. Conduct a survey on singles or write a column on the topic for your local newspaper.

You could survey everything from what singles are looking for in a date or mate to favorite places to meet others, to the three things someone likes or dislikes about being single. By doing interviews and observations for the survey you will increase your knowledge of the single experience as you also meet new people.

If you write a column about singles, your name will get out there as a single and you might find readers of your column start suggesting friends, relatives or co-workers who might want to meet you.

111. Move to a building or development with lots of singles.

Whether it's Boca Raton, Los Angeles, Manhattan, Austin or London, being in a building with lots of single tenants increases the likelihood that there will be activities geared to meeting people. Moving into a singles housing complex can be beneficial to your social life whatever your age. Living with men and women who are in the same age group will increase the likelihood that you will all have friends that you could introduce to each other.

112. Make a video on how to meet singles.

Interview others about how and where to meet new people, including any especially 'in' nightspots. Unlike the survey on singles previously suggested, this is more targeted at how to meet singles and it's on video. In doing the research, you will of course be meeting lots of new people. Use a camcorder and ask them to share what ways are working for them.

When the movie is done, have a screening. Invite everyone in the cast and ask them to invite their single friends along.

113. WEAR CLOTHING WITH A CATCHY SAYING OR A LOGO.

A T-shirt, sweatshirt or cap with an attention-getting saying could be a conversation starter. But be prepared to talk about your T-shirt, and what the saying means, if asked. Remember how cheerleader Angel Rivera shared in a previous chapter that wearing a University of Connecticut Huskies cheerleading sweatshirt is an icebreaker at a party. He is often asked, 'Are you a UConn cheerleader?'

114. CHECK OUT YOUR LOCAL FLEA MARKET OR GARAGE SALE.

Whether it's an urban flea market or a suburban garage sale, browsing through someone else's treasures may lead to a priceless romantic connection. For example, Sheila Gray, 40, and Jason Bagdad, 35, met at the Chelsea flea market in Manhattan according to Marcelle S. Fischler's 'Vows' story in *The New York Times* about the couple's romantic meeting. Sheila shopped there weekly; Jason went there just that one time, searching for a couch and a desk. A year and a half later, they were married. At the wedding, in his toast, Fischler notes that the groom told the guests: 'Little did I know that in looking to furnish my studio apartment, I would end up furnishing my heart and my soul.'

115. CARRY SOMETHING UNUSUAL.

A book with an intriguing title might be a conversation starter. Read in public – at a library or a local coffee shop – and let the title of the book you are reading be visible as a chat ice-breaker. Buy a monkey, chimpanzee or parrot and walk around with it on your shoulder. You will certainly be noticed. But only do this if you are truly committed to taking care of this pet and if it is permissible to have any of those creatures in your community.

116. Arrive half an hour early for appointments.

You never know whom you might meet in the waiting room at the office of the dentist, doctor, optician or lawyer.

117. Go on a TV show that matches up couples.

Certainly a lot of dating and mating shows have come and gone over the years, from the old-time *The Dating Game* to more recent entries including *The Bachelor* and *The Bachelorette*. In one of the most-watched shows of 2003, the couple who met through *The Bachelorette* got married on network TV.

Casting information may be posted at the website, Realitydatingshows.com. There may also be information about dating shows at the websites for the various TV networks, such as CBS, NBC, ABC and Fox. Industry trade publications, *Variety* or *The Hollywood Reporter*, may post casting call notices. But a cautionary note: these shows can be tough on contestants. Make sure you have the stamina for this type of an experience, whether or not you get the date or win any prizes.

118. Shop at stores where you are likely to meet someone.

Need to upgrade your TV, videocassette recorder, or DVD player to a state-of-the-art home theatre? That could be another way to meet a man as you shop at the electronic store or the electronics department for the right components. Men might shop at the perfume or jewelry counters at the department store. Perhaps there is a food court at the mall or a particular store where singles tend to congregate.

119. Offer a reward.

Instead of paying a commercial matchmaker, as long as your offer does not offend your friends or acquaintances, offer a gift as an incentive for an introduction to the love of your life.

120. Do your laundry at a laundromat.

Even if you have a washer and dryer at home, use the laundromat. If you have a place in the apartment house where you can do laundry, bring along something to read so you can wait for your wash to finish, rather than racing back and forth, diminishing the possibility of getting into conversations.

121. Keep up with the new 'in' places to meet singles in your community or nearby cities.

Although some places with always be associated with singles, some 'in' spots do change. Keep learning about new and innovative ways and places in your hometown or in the places where you are traveling to, by word-of-mouth, reading the local newspaper or magazines, or online listings.

If you have moved to a new town or city, whether it is for a short period of time or permanently, find out if there is an association with planned events as well as a website with forums where you can communicate about yourself that might offer meeting opportunities. For example, if you have moved to America from Australia or New Zealand you might want to join the American Australian Association which offers local cultural and social programs, often with discounts to members, providing opportunities to meet those who may share your background.

122. Move to one of the best places for singles.

Based on the number of singles, job growth, nightlife and cost of living, in 'Best International Cities for Singles' by Christina Valhouli's posted at Forbes.com, the following cities are listed: Sydney, London, Dublin, Bombay, Barcelona, Stockholm, Reykjavik, Paris, London and Ljubljana. Here are the top cities for singles in the United States, according to 'Best Cities for Singles' archived at the website for *Forbes* magazine: Austin, Denver, Boulder, Boston, Washington, D.C., Baltimore and Atlanta.

123. Shop at the local hardware store.

Kimberly Stevens reports in her article, 'When a Redo Leads to "I Do", Tales of love and romance are surfacing from Home Depots all over the country'. Readers of *Delaware Today* magazine selected the Wilmington Home Depot® hardware store one of 10 best ways to meet men.

124. Read accounts of how couples meet.

True stories of courtship and marriage may inspire you as well as detail additional ways to meet that you might want to consider. For example, each 'Vows' column in the wedding announcement section of Sunday's *The New York Times* profiles one couple from their meeting through their wedding. It is always a tale of romance and wonder, a reminder that love unfolds in mysterious and unique ways.

125. Positive image.

Imagine you and the love of your life giving to each other all the love you've dreamed of sharing. See yourself opening up a wonderful present from your beloved, for your birthday or for Valentine's Day. Envision yourself having the relationship you've always wanted that works on every level. Fantasize about your own wedding written up next to a photograph of you and the love of your life. Positive image about you and your spouse spending your honeymoon in Hawaii, Broome, in Western Australia, Fiji, Queensland islands or the Greek islands.

Just remember as you search for a romantic partner that all you need is one person who is right for you and who feels the same way. Finally, finding the love of your life will definitely make the time, effort and energy that it takes all worthwhile.

part 3
THE NEXT STEPS

chapter 16

CONTINUING THE SEARCH

For most, it is a convoluted path till you find the love of your life. Relationships begin and end, sometimes you end it, sometimes the other person ends it, sometimes fate cruelly ends it and you find yourself single again even if you thought you would never again be alone. Some take the ups and downs of dating easily and some find it tough to deal with the disappointments and go back to searching again. This chapter offers help with some of the predictable challenges in dating.

Eight Ways to Cope with Rejection

Whether you are the one who tells a date that you do not want to go out a second time, or you are the one who waits for the phone to ring and it never does, for most, dating is fraught with rejection. You can learn to cope with rejection, and pick yourself up, dust yourself off, and get back out there and date again, or you can take it personally and let it devastate you so much that you are fearful of trying again to meet new dates.

Rejection is a fact of life – especially of the life of a single looking for love. Probably the only rejection even harder to take than being passed over for a job or a promotion is being rejected by a date or a potential date when you liked him or her and wanted it to lead somewhere.

Understanding the process of rejection could help soften the inevitable emotional blow to your ego when you say 'no,' or he or she says 'it's just not working'.

Searching for the love of your life is somewhat like a writing career. When a manuscript or a proposal is accepted, you instantly no longer think about the dozens or even hundreds of rejections you may have received. You just think about the successful outcome.

Here are some suggestions to help you cope with rejection.

1. Be pragmatic.

Consider rejection in a practical way as a learning experience rather than reacting emotionally to it. Ask if there is a pattern to your rejections so you might modify your search accordingly.

For example, between my first and second personal ads, I changed the wording of the ad because the men I was meeting through the first ad were more interested in a date than a mate. Therefore, in my second ad, I spelled out that I was looking to get married. Adding that detail led to a very different type of response and expectation. My future husband Fred responded to that detail in my second ad, among other attributes and traits, because marriage and a family was what he was also looking to find.

2. Depersonalize the rejection.

View the rejection as a learning experience that will help you increase the likelihood of finding what you want.

3. Learn how to reject.

It's as challenging to become competent and comfortable at rejecting others as it is to learn to cope with being rejected. It is an art to reject someone in a way that is kind, sincere, honest and ego boosting. Rule of thumb: say to someone else what you would want to hear in a similar circumstance.

4. Avoid suggesting someone else as a more likely choice unless asked to do so.

It may be tempting to minimize the rejection by saying, 'Although we don't seem to be right for each other, I have a friend who I think you might want to meet'. Unless you're asked to recommend someone else, it can sound self-serving and condescending to offer to introduce someone to someone else.

Unless you can frame the suggestion in such a positive way that it is seen as a triumph, it could be interpreted as trying to ask someone to be satisfied with winning the second prize or even runner-up when they really want the first prize. Rather than getting a 'thank you for the suggestion', you may find someone saying, 'No, thanks. I don't need you to help me find a date.' Some, however, if it is handled correctly, may actually thank you for minimizing the rejection by suggesting a new possibility.

5. Clarify your goals.

Welcome rejection as a chance to realize what you do not want, and as a way of getting closer to what you do need in a romantic partner.

6. Be assertive.

Avoid perpetuating a relationship because you are afraid to hurt someone's feelings and cut it off. Even if you still care about someone but you feel he or she does not share your feelings, you may have to be the one to point out that it is time to end the relationship.

7. Take a long-term perspective.

Dating and a romantic relationship is such a powerful experience that it can be difficult to think about a time when the pain of rejection will subside and you will look back more kindly on a failed relationship or feel more positive about dating again. But you will recover from being rejected or rejecting another. If you get comfortable enough with rejection to continue the process of dating, eventually you will hopefully find that special someone.

8. Rejection is usually better than a 'maybe'.

At least a 'no' clarifies where you stand. A 'maybe' is ambiguous and it may lead to weeks, months or years of not really getting who you want, or what you want, but being too involved with someone to give a new relationship a chance.

Things to Do When a Romantic Relationship Ends

Here are 14 things you can do when a relationship breaks up to help you get on with your life.

1 Call up everyone you know and share the news about your break up. Let him or her know that you're open to blind dates or introductions.

2 Keep a breaking up journal. It could provide release and a catharsis from keeping all the angst and feelings inside. You might also read some of the breaking up date-bashing literature that some consider a catharsis for the 'getting over him or her' process.

3 Go to a support group for those who have had a romantic breakup. Although most groups are for those who separate from a marriage, or get divorced, any type of romantic breakup would qualify you for participation.

4 Make a list of 25 benefits of being alone, such as the chance to travel alone, go to bed and wake up anytime you want, do anything you want, see your friends without finding out what his plans are, and so forth.

5 Take the time to grieve over your romantic breakup and to get ready to get back into dating. Let yourself weep.

6 Try to analyze what happened in this relationship that it did not work out that could be useful when you begin dating again. Consider the relationship on your own or with professional help.

7 If you're a female, and you're used to waiting for a man to ask you out, try taking the initiative to ask out an eligible single man.

8 Go into an upscale store and buy $20 worth of your favorite frivolous things.

9 Join a health club and work out daily. Try to commit to at least one or two classes a week at a specific time and day.

10 Begin keeping a daily journal writing down your activities, thoughts, feelings, goals, desires and ideas.

11 Make a schedule for the next two months in which you plan the times you will see the people and do the things that you did not have time for before, and carry out your plans.

12 Make the most of your job as a way of having the social contact that you suddenly lack. Be friendlier while you are commuting, becoming part of a carpool, if appropriate, or arranging to commute with neighbors or fellow workers.

13 Force yourself to meet with someone and make conversation during your lunch hour.

14 If you have a pet, show it more attention. If you don't, consider getting one. Being able to give attention to others after a relationship's ended can be as important as getting it.

Reinforcing Your Goal

Revisiting the theme of applying time management principles to the search for the love of your life, reapply goal setting as a way to keep yourself committed to your search.

Dating and courtship is the rite of passage, the route one usually takes on the road to finding the love of your life and cultivating that relationship. Like looking for a job, it is not a question of how many resumés you send out, or job interviews you go on, but the achievement of the goal: getting a job.

Recommit to your romantic relationship goal, whatever that is for you, until you achieve it.

chapter 17

WHEN YOU FIND 'THE ONE'

How Do You Know

Here's a question posed to me when I told a single in her late twenties about this new book: 'But how do you know if someone's "the one"?'

Of course since each man and woman is unique, as is each relationship, answers to that question will vary widely. However, reading the range of responses to that question might be reassuring to those who have the misconception that there's only one answer or explanation – that it feels like you've been hit by lightning.

For me, I definitely felt something powerful when I first read Fred's letter in response to my second personal ad, and I really enjoyed talking to him during that first phone conversation. Then I kept calling back and nervously changing the time and place where we would meet later that night, and he was fine with that, and I distinctively recall being amazed and pleased that he was that easygoing and understanding. When I saw him for the first time at the bar where we initially met, I lost my breath. I guess they call that chemistry, a reaction to Fred that's as strong almost two decades later as it was that first night.

When I posed the 'How did you know?' question to my husband Fred, he replied:

Well, it was a series of things. First I obviously liked what I saw and then after spending a night talking to each other I realized that I wanted it to continue. It was a whole bunch of things. And then when you quit smoking for me and after living with you for three days after you quit smoking, I had already seen you at your best and now I was seeing you at your worst, I realized that you were the person I wanted to spend the rest of my life with.

On Christmas Day, after we met each other's parents, I pulled off the road after a couple of miles from my parents' home and asked you to marry me. We got married five days later and I still feel the same way today that I felt then.

Michelle Grady, who got married in 2003 to Sean, confides that she really felt 'weak in the knees' the first time Sean kissed her. Michelle and Sean had known each other for eight years, having met while students at Fairfield University. Michelle explains:

After we had been dating for about three months, I told him I loved him. However, he explained that he was not ready to say it back. We went shopping together the weekend after Thanksgiving. Sean led me into a jewelry store – I think to get some hints for Christmas presents is what he said.

When we walked past the engagement ring display case, he asked me what shape diamond I liked. My heart immediately started racing – the question was so unexpected. I casually explained that I liked emerald-cut diamonds and walked over to the next display case. I took it as a very big hint that our relationship was headed in a very positive direction.

If I recall correctly, the following weekend he told me he loved me.

Ironically, jealousy, often viewed as a negative emotion, as long as it is not excessive or unreasonable, is often actually a sign that one or both are feeling something distinctive and unique. It is often that emotion that leads to the exclusivity that is associated with a long-term committed relationship or marriage in many cultures and countries.

Starting to have jealous feelings, for example, was a sign to Kristen and her husband, Matt, that their friendship was transforming into something more. As Kristen notes:

After we were dating a while, looking back, Matt remembers a time in college when we were just friends, but he was 'oddly bothered', as he puts it, when I told him about a guy I'd met at a party the night before. I remember a time before we were dating that Matt and I were at a party with a bunch of friends and I was disappointed when he left though I wasn't sure why.

Jody Jaffe, who previously recalled how she met her second husband, shares how this relationship differs from previous ones. Jody says: 'For the first time, I feel like my mate and I are on the same team. Not only that, he's my biggest champion. That's a new and wonderful development.'

Tips for Becoming – and Remaining – a Happy Couple

Great! You've found Mr or Ms Right, or your soulmate, paramour, the love of your life, a mate, or just someone to date whose company you enjoy. What are some ways to increase the likelihood that your relationship will flourish and bring out the best in the two of you? This section offers some suggestions that you might find useful.

Ways to Help the Love Grow In Your Relationship

Here are ten suggestions – based on years of research into relationships – that will nurture the love between you.

1. Make sex a priority and find time for it, no matter how tired or preoccupied you are.

2. Eat dinner together and continue to go out on 'dates' with each other on a steady basis, even once you have children.

3. Get off the phone as soon as your mate walks in the door, not because you are talking about something he or she should not hear but because it is polite and shows that you care.

4 Don't badmouth your spouse to your friends or relatives. If you're having problems, deal with them in a constructive way, first with each other. If you need outside help, turn to someone you trust such as a religious or marriage counselor, psychologist or psychiatrist.

5 Compromise, compromise, compromise.

6 Keep your sense of humor and the fun and romance in your relationship and life together as you continue to be each other's best friend.

7 Divide up the necessary domestic chores so neither one feels the burden unfairly falls on her or his shoulders.

8 Make time for what you care about individually, as well as each other, such as hobbies, spending time with a special friend, developing new interests, or sports activities.

9 Be positive and supportive. Don't criticize. If you have to be critical, offer what you say as feedback and say it in the most gentle, nurturing way possible.

10 Actively work to keep the excitement in your relationship by keeping communication open between you and your mate, remembering and making a fuss over birthdays and anniversaries, planning and going on weekends away, excursions and trips together.

Put the Emphasis on Loving Your Partner

To be a happy couple, focus on being a more loving partner and on loving your partner first and being exactly your ideal of a loved one.

By focusing on accepting who your loved one is, not dwelling on what he or she is not, your relationship will improve as your mate feels the love your acceptance of him or her inspires. As your mate feels more acceptable and accepted, he or she will be able to give more love to you. You have become more lovable by focusing on giving love rather than on 'What has he done for me lately?'

Being Friends with the Love of Your Life

When I was researching *Single in America*, I also interviewed married couples. I wanted to know why those couples were happy. At the time I did those interviews, I was single, between marriages, and still had not yet figured out what might be the key to a happy marriage, so I was eager to hear from the masters.

All the couples I interviewed who proclaimed they were happy shared with me the reasons except one couple. They were silent or they said they couldn't explain what it was that made their relationship work.

That bothered me for years. If they couldn't explain why their relationship worked, how could I search for something that elusive?

Alas, a few years later, I heard through the grapevine that this couple whom so many others and I considered the ideal couple were actually quite miserable and now were separated by thousands of miles and, soon after that, divorced and living very separate lives.

My late father, William Barkas, D.D.S., was very articulate about why he loved my mother, Gladys, so much. When I asked him about their marriage and why they had been so happy for 54 years, my Dad said, as quoted in my book *Friendshifts*®: 'In my happiest days, my wife is my best friend. In my saddest days, my wife is my best friend. She's the one I can share all my thoughts with.'

Happily married couples often use one or all of these words to describe their relationship: best friends, lovers, respect, soulmate, exciting, passionate.

Sexual Intimacy Also Counts

Yes, you want to be best friends with your spouse, but for most, love and marriage also means sexual intimacy. Is passion possible even in a long-term relationship or marriage? In general, happy couples will answer a resounding 'yes.'

Sexual intimacy requires time and effort just like working on verbal communication. For example, couples need to continue dating, getting outside of the day-to-date routine so they can renew their relationship.

Varying lovemaking routine and sharing sexual fantasies may also help as well as giving sexual intimacy time and not rushing it in between other responsibilities.

Be Realistic About How Love Changes

'Familiarity breeds contempt' is a household expression. But you could also quote from poet Shelley's *Prometheus Unbound:* 'Familiar acts are beautiful through love'. So many people today dos-'a-dos their partners that long-term relationships are becoming objects of fascination and even bewilderment. Of course irreconcilable differences may necessitate severing a union, but how often is the reason for the change an unrealistic attitude about how love and romance may change over time?

There is a psychological, sexual and emotional ebb and flow to love. Just as Erik Erikson expanded the stages of life to include the entire life cycle beyond Sigmund Freud's focus on the earliest stages and years, couples need to understand the stages that marriages usually go through once the courtship and honeymoon phases are over.

Keep the Relationship Fresh and Exciting

Whether it's a trip together or buying a new negligee, it's important to keep your relationship novel and exciting. As book publicist Joanne McCall, happily married for seven years, puts it: 'It's important to keep the mystery alive in your relationship. One way to do this is to be spontaneous and fun – try new and different activities together.'

Improving Your Listening Skills

Two useful feedback techniques to see if someone is listening to you is for your listener to paraphrase your major points in his or her own words and for you to question him or her to find out if he or she understood what you said. Ask for feelings and reactions to what you have said from time to time rather than waiting till you finish speaking to request feedback.

Use verbal or nonverbal feedback as you speak. Remember that interpersonal communication is a two-way process; the speaker, and the listener, have a mutual effect on each other.

Dealing with Anger

Avoid letting your anger fester; deal with the issues that are gnawing at you. This is not a friend you see every couple of months so that it may be possible to let some annoyances slide. This is your lifemate, the person with whom you spend the most time. Not only will he or she probably know that you are harboring angry feelings, but living together may become difficult or even intolerable if there is the strain of holding back on feelings or grievances that you need to address.

Los Angeles-based relationships columnist, Susan K. Perry, Ph.D., author of *Loving in Flow*, advises couples to 'Assume good will.' Perry continues:

Always give your partner the benefit of the doubt. Assume he or she is behaving with honestly good intentions toward you, even if at the moment you're feeling hurt or confused. Remember that you love one another, and whatever is being done or said (short of real abuse!) is not intended to hurt you.

Pay Attention to Your Non-verbal Communication

Since less than 10 per cent of how we communicate is verbal, it pays to study the remaining nonverbal cues including: facial expressions, eye contact, voice (tone, quality, and speed), oral expressions or sounds (sighs, laughing, crying), posture (body stance), physical appearance (clothing, accessories, skin, hair, make up), gestures, stance, distance from listener or speaker, demeanor, pauses and silences, and body mirroring (if you mirror each other's stances and movements, which generally indicates greater rapport).

Three Tips for Couple Contentment

Matt Wilson, a computer systems engineer married to Kristen Finello, whose story of their meeting and courtship is retold at the beginning of Chapter 8, shares what has helped them to remain a contented couple:

1. Keep dating each other.
Make sure you enjoy your time with each other – even if you don't have any 'big' plans. For example, every December, Kristen and I order in food and watch the Chevy Chase National Lampoon's Christmas Vacation movie. It always makes us laugh and puts us in the holiday spirit. We also go out on movie and dinner dates and have done activities together like taking cooking classes and traveling.

2. Include your spouse in decisions.
We make all of our important decisions together. We have a system to discuss pros/cons and reach a conclusion. Spouses may not always agree with each other, but they can agree to disagree and move forward.

3. Enjoy the journey.
People, organizations and marriages have goals, deadlines and setbacks. Take the time to celebrate events with each other. Enjoy going through life together.

Write and Exchange Love Vows

When Fred and I married, we wrote our own vows (in addition to the traditional ones that we spoke as well). Whether or not you get married, writing a vow to your beloved is a way of starting off your relationship as a couple on a note of shared commitment, articulating your feelings and what is important to you. You are concretizing and clarifying what you are promising to each other. Reading those vows aloud in front of friends and family is also a powerful experience as you announce to the world what you have declared to each other.

Even the Happiest Couples Need Friends

As long as your friendships do not make unreasonable demands on your time or emotions, friends – those you have individually or the friends you share as a couple – add to your relationship. Developing or maintaining separate friends need not be a problem as long as those friends, especially if they are work-related, do not come between you and your spouse and you also have friends that you share, including other couples.

Embrace the Singleness within All Relationships

Even the most connected couples maintain their own identities and interests. Being a contented couple means that you each celebrate what is unique about each of you.

Taking an occasional trip alone or with friends also helps to renew and invigorate each of you as long as it is a reasonable period of time. That old adage, 'Absence makes the heart grow fonder', is oft repeated because it rings true. But a cautionary note: too much absence can make the heart grow cold.

Strive for interdependence as a couple. Happy couples report that their relationship helps them to grow and flourish as individuals as well as a couple and family.

As 47-year-old William, a married business coach living in Sussex, England, put it: 'Think source, not outcome. Make a space in your life and yourself for another person. Open yourself to possibilities. Yearn to learn. Be prepared to shift yourself. You are the only thing over which you have any control so don't expect to shift others.'

'Stay independent,' recommends 30-year-old Beth, who has been married for eight years. Beth continues: 'Have your own life, even though you are in a relationship. Don't let the relationship define you.'

BIBLIOGRAPHY

ABIX via COMTEX. 'Women go for their home alone'. *Australasian Business Intelligence,* July 7, 2002.

Amatenstein, Sherry. *Love Lessons from Bad Breakups.* NY: Perigee, 2002.

Baker, Michael. 'South Korea Ends a Taboo, Strikes Blow for True Love; Court Rules that Couples with Same Names Can Now Get Married.' *Christian Science Monitor,* August 4, 1997.

Barkas, J.L. (Janet Lee). See Yager, Jan.

Blake, Tom. *Finding Love After 50.* Dana Point, CA: Tooter's Publishing, 2003.

Brown, R.A. 'Romantic Love and the Spouse Selection Criteria and Female Korean College Students.' *Journal of Social Psychology,* April 1, 1994.

Business Wire. 'Love & Relationship Poll 2003.' February 4, 2003.

Darnay, Melissa and Zella Case. *Dating 101.* Plano, TX: Splash of Ink Corporation, 2002.

BIBLIOGRAPHY

De Vaus, David, Lixia Qu, and Ruth Weston. 'Changing Patterns of Partnering.' *Family Matters*, Autumn 2003.

Deyo, Yaacov and Sue Deyo. *SpeedDating™*. NY: HarperResource, 2003.

Egan, Ted. *The Land Downunder*. Norwich, UK: Grice Chapman Publishing, 2003.

Fischler, Marcelle S. 'Vows: Sheila Gray and Jason Bagdade.' *The New York Times*, January 27, 2002, page 8 (Weddings).

Fuchs, Marek. 'Scholar, Matchmaker and Convention Presence.' *New York Times*, August 31, 2004, p. B2.

Gabor, Don. *How to Start a Conversation and Make Friends*. Second edition. NY: Fireside Books, 2002.

Godek, Gregory J.P. *1001 Ways to Be Romantic*. Revised. Naperville, IL: Sourcebooks, 1999.

Gordon, Barbara. *I'm Dancing as Fast as I Can*. NY: HarperCollins, 1989.

Gordon, Phyllis A. 'The Decision to Remain Single: Implications for Women Across Cultures.' *Journal of Mental Health Counseling*, January 1, 2003.

Gray, John. *Men are From Mars, Women are From Venus*. NY: HarperCollins, 2004.

Halpern, Howard. *How to Break Your Addiction to a Person*. NY: Bantam, 1983.

Haynes, Cyndi and Dale Edwards. *2002 Ways to Find, Attract and Keep a Mate*. Adams Media, 1999.

Hellmich, Nanci. 'Playing the Personals for Love.' *USA Today*, March 11, 1985, pages 1–2.

Irizarry, Lisa. 'Love by the Book.' *Newark Star-Ledger*, April 16, 1999, pages 49, 54.

Jacobs, Andrew. 'After Telephone Courtship, A First Date Ends in Death.' *The New York Times*, August 17, 2002, pages B1, B5.

Jaffe, John. *Thief of Words*. NY: Warner Books, 2003.

Kim, Stella. 'Wired for Life.' *Time International* (Spanish edition), December 11, 2000.

Kuby, Joy. *The Fortunate Four: Other Journeys of the Heart*. Edina, MN: Beaver's Pond Press, Inc., 2003.

Larson, Zippy. *How to Find a Fella in the Want Ads*. Long Green, MD: Zippy Books, 1998.

Levey, Bob. 'Q&A With Bob Levey.' Interview with Tommy Curtis, February 11, 2003. Archived at http://www.discuss.washingtontpost.com/wp-srv/zforum/03/r_metro_levey021103.htm.

McLaughlin, Katy. 'How Far Would You Go To Meet a Man?' *Glamour*, May 2002, page 144+.

Newman, Robin. *How to Meet a Mensch in New York*. NY: City & Co., 1994.

Nierenberg, Gerald I. and Henry H. Calero. *How to Read a Person Like a Book*. NY: Simon & Schuster, 1973.

Perry, Susan K. *Loving in Flow*. Naperville, IL: Sourcebooks, 2003.

Roane, Susan. *How to Work a Room*. Revised. NY: HarperCollins, 2000.

Seattle Post-Intelligencer. 'Forget True Love: South Koreans Turn to Dating Services, 1997.' (Posted at elibrary.com)

Silverman, Francine. *Catskills Alive*. Hobe Sound, FL: Hunter Publishing, 2003.

Stevens, Kimberly. 'When a Redo Leads to "I Do".' *The New York Times,* February 10, 2000, pages F1, F10.

Tannen, Deborah. *You Just Don't Understand*. NY: Ballantine Books, 1990.

Valhouli, Christina, Best International Cities for Singles, posted at www.Forbes.com, June 2003.

Walster, Elaine and G. William Walster. *A New Look at Love*. Reading, MA: Addison-Wesley, 1978.

Warren, Neil Clark. *Finding the Love of Your Life*. NY: Pocket Books, 1994.

Wheelis, Allen. *How People Change*. NY: Harper & Row, 1973.

Yager, Jan. (a/k/a J.L. Barkas) '15 Ways to Meet Boys.' *Seventeen,* October 1980.

———. *Creative Time Management.* Englewood Cliffs, NJ: Prentice Hall, 1984.

———. *Creative Time Management for the New Millennium.* Stamford, CT: Hannacroix Creek Books, Inc., 1999.

———. 'Do You Abandon Your Life When He Comes Along?' Scripps-Howard News Service (Independent News Alliance), 31 January, 1984.

———. *Friendshifts®: The Power of Friendship and How It Shapes Our Lives.* Stamford, CT: Hannacroix Creek Books, Inc., 1997, 2nd edition, 1999.

———. 'How Well Do You Handle Change?' *Seventeen,* August, 1980.

———. 'Maintain Speed: Love Zone Ahead.' *Newsday,* 20 September, 1984.

———. 'On Being Single.' *Newsday,* October 1980.

———. 'The Power of "No!"' *National Business Employment Weekly,* Managing Your Career, College Edition, Fall 1988, pages 40, 43.

———. 'Precaution Best Defense Against Crime.' *Newsday,* 15 March, 1988.

———. 'Sex Habits of Indians.' *The Illustrated Weekly of India,* 21 October, 1973, pages 19–23.

———. *Single in America.* NY: Atheneum, 1980.

———. 'Twenty Ways to Meet Your Lover.' *Houston Post,* 31 January, 1990.

———. *Victims.* NY: Scribner's, 1978.

———. 'What Type of Woman Advertises for Love? Here's One Who Did.' *Cleo,* April 1989.

———. *When Friendship Hurts.* NY: Simon & Schuster, Inc., 2002.

——— with Fred Yager. 'Her Ad Brought Love and Marriage,' NEA Syndicate, 7 February, 1985.

Yager, Scott. 'Friends with Benefits: Are There Any?' *Westword,* February 2003, page 36.

Wingler, Sharon. *Travel Alone & Love It.* Chicago, IL: Chicago Spectrum Press, 1996.

Zaslow, Jeffrey. '"Have I Got a Girl for You": Helping Your Friends Dump the Dating Service.' *The Wall Street Journal*, 9 December, 2003, page D1.

Appendix

Resources

(Associations, Organizations and Companies)

> *Please note:* Inclusion in this resource section does not imply an endorsement of any service, company, association or product by the author or publisher. Websites or addresses may change, companies may go out of business or merge; therefore, the accuracy of any listing cannot be guaranteed. The companies, associations or individuals offering information or services for singles (or couples seeking relationship advice) is vast and ever-changing. The list that follows is not meant to be definitive or comprehensive; it is just a sample of available options. Any suggested additions to these resources, as well as any changes or deletions, should be sent by regular mail to: Dr Jan Yager, P.O. Box 8038, Stamford, CT 06905-8038, USA or by e-mail (without attached files): jyager@aol.com.

Websites with links to multiple services

The sites listed below, organized by geographic location, provide links to a multiplicity of singles services including online dating, social clubs, and introduction agencies.

http://www.singlesites.com/
Multiple sites including links to sites by region and religion. A dating directory of services for singles as well as international sites for Australia, New Zealand, the United Kingdom, Africa and Canada.

http://datingport.8bit.co.uk/australia.htm
Dating Port (Australia)

http://datingport.8bit.co.uk/nz.htm
Dating Port (New Zealand)

http://datingport.8bit.co.uk/uk.htm
Dating Port (United Kingdom)

Singlesonthego.com
http://www.singlesonthego.com/nationallinks.html
Directory of links to a variety of singles activities and resources including books on dating (www.datinglibrary.com), online dating, and advice for singles.

Social or Activity Clubs or Events for Singles

8Minute Dating
http://www.8minutedating.com
Variation on fast dating available throughout the United States; check the website for up-to-date information about events in other countries including Australia and England.

Speed Dating Sites
http://www.speeddatingsites.com
Provides links to speed dating events for singles in Australia as well as major US cities, Canada, Europe and the UK.

AUSTRALIA

Blink Speed Dating
Suite 15
361 Victoria Place
Drummoyne, NSW 2046
http://www.blinkdating.com.au

Singles dating events with one flat fee for the event held in Syndey, Perth, Melbourne, and Brisbane whereby ten men and women meet over drinks for one hour with each meeting lasting seven minutes before switching to another new person.

The Dinner Club
P.O. Box 756, Applecross
Western Australia 6153
http://www.dinnerclub.com.au
Established in 1985, a membership club, with annual dues, offering dinners and other events such as sailing, movies, and wine tastings. Non-members are also invited to attend some activities.

Six in the City
P.O. Box 2171
Milton, Qld 4064 Australia
http://www.sixinthecity.com.au
Membership (3 month minimum) for 30+ singles with dinner parties of three women and three men at restaurants in and around Brisbane, usually on a Saturday night.

My Friends
P.O. Box 1060
Stafford City, Qld 4053 Australia
http://www.myfriends.com.au
Membership (may pay by the month) offering dinners over the weekend and movies on Tuesday nights as well as other activities operating in Brisbane.

RSVP
http://www.rsvp.com.au
Although primarily an online dating site, RSVP also organizes speed dating and special events.

Speed Dating Sites
http://www.speeddatingsites.com/australia
Site with brief descriptions and links to a variety of speed dating sites and events in Australia and New Zealand.

New Zealand

The Company Company Ltd
P.O. Box 25304
St Heliers
Auckland, NZ
http://www.thecompanycompany.co.nz
Established by Alan Reeves in 1975, a membership club offering events for meeting people such as parties, cruises, musicals, fishing, and parties including a New Year's Eve party.

Speed Dating
Speed Date Ltd.
P.O. Box 33059
Takapuna
Auckland, NZ
http://www.speeddate.co.nz
Offers speed date events, organized by three age groups, from early twenties to late forties.

Also see *Speed Dating Sites* listed above.

United Kingdom

Original Dating
http://www.originaldating.com
Fast dating events in the UK.

Slow Dating
The Love Suite
Bridge View
Abingdon on Thames
OX14 3HN
UK
http://www.slowdating.com
A variation on the concept of speed dating by offering a 4-minute per date event rather than the more typical 3-minute per date. Sponsors events through the UK including London, Birmingham, Bath, Southampton, Nottingham and Bournemouth.

Singles on the Go
http://www.singlesonthego.com/london
Directory of links to a variety of activities in London and throughout the UK for singles including wine tastings, parties and charity functions.

South Africa

SpeedDater
P.O. Box 60643
High Cape
Devil's Peak 8001
South Africa
http://www.speeddater.co.za
Provides a calendar of events offered in Cape Town and other locations, organized by age group.

Travel or Vacations

Business Tr@veler Info Network
http://www.business-trip.com
Site developed by Michael Steinberg on various aspects of business travel, including a guide to selected American and international cities.

Club Med
GPO Box 1632
Sydney NSW 2001
http://www.clubmed.com
http://www.clubmed.com.au
Club Med has travel destinations around the world with some locations for singles only.

BudgetTravel.com
http://www.budgettravel.com
Site with information on inexpensive trips.

Exotic Journeys
http://www.exoticjourneys.com
Established in 1979, travel agency based in Chicago, with other offices internationally, that organizes trips to India, Nepal, and other locations.

Travel Alone and Love It
http://www.travelaloneandloveit.com
Informative website for the solo traveler created and maintained by flight attendant Sharon Wingler, author of *Travel Alone & Love It*.

Online Dating

> *Please note:* No one under the age of 18 is allowed to participate in an online dating site. Read the rules and regulations at each site. Know what you are agreeing to. Protect your privacy and identity. Be careful and keep yourself safe. Review the safety tips in Chapter 4, 'Staying Safe During Your Search.'

These sites vary widely in terms of membership costs, if any, as well as the kinds of men and women who frequent the site based on age, socioeconomic status, profession, and other factors. Make sure you check each one out to see which ones might be for you reading through the testimonials and sample profiles, calling the customer service representative, if there is one, as well as checking out if there are instructions for removing your profile if you wish to cease your affiliation with a particular site.

Australia

MatchMaker Internet Dating Services
c/- Trading Net Australia Pty Ltd
P.O. Box 98 Capalaba, Qld 4157 Australia,
http://www.Matchmaker.com.au
Australian version of the international site, www.match.com

UB Love
http://www.Ublove.com
An international site that has participants from Australia and New Zealand posting profiles at the main site, searchable by country among other factors.

http://www.datingdirect.com
On-line dating site for Australia as well as UK, Ireland, US and Canada.

Yahoo® Personals
http://au.personals.yahoo.com
Online dating site for Australia and New Zealand.

RSVP
http://www.rsvp.com
Site with more than 340,000 members that sells stamps in order to have a two-way search. The site also sponsors singles events including speed dating. There are interesting related articles about the site posted at the Press Centre.

New Zealand

http://nz.match.com
New Zealand version of the international site, www.match.com

NZ Dating.com
http://www.nzdating.com

United Kingdom

U date
www.udate.com or www.udate./co.uk
Site for finding friends as well as romantic partners. Although free to register, membership dues enable you to communicate with other site participants.

Dating Direct
http://www.datingdirect.com

Friend Finder Inc.
http://www.friendfinderinc.com

Yahoo! ® UK & Ireland
http://uk.personals.yahoo.com
Online dating site for United Kingdom and Ireland.

Friends Reunited Dating
http://www.friendsreunited.co.uk
Allows you to search for old friends by place or by name. Available for several countries including the United Kingdom, Australia, South Africa, Italy, New Zealand and the Netherlands.

Loopylove.com
http://www.loopylove.com

Pearmatch
http://www.pearmatch.co.uk

South Africa

South African Singles
http://www.southafrican.singlescrowd.com

Matchmaker
http://www.matchmaker.co.za

Ireland

Making Friends One
http://www.makingfriendsonline.com
You can search by country at this online dating and friendship site established in 2001.

Personal Ad Writing Services

Match.com
http://www.match.com
Editing or ghosting service available for a fee to members posting personal profiles who want help with the wording of their profiles.

Personals Work!
http://www.personalswork.com
Personal ad writing service based in Boston started by Susan Fox who met her husband through a personal ad that she placed.

Professional Introduction Agency (Dating Services) or Matchmakers

Find a professional dating service or matchmaker through referrals by satisfied customers or check out ads in magazines or newspapers.

Australia

Friends First
P.O. Box 8659
Perth Business Centre WA 6849
http://www.friendsfirst.com.au

Yvonne Allen & Associates
P.O. Box 657
Carlton, VIC 3053
http://www.yvonneallen.com.au
e-mail: melbourne@yvonneallen.com.au
Melbourne-area mailing address for this introduction service founded and run by psychologist Yvonne Allen.

Yvonne Allen & Associates
P.O. Box Q1464
QVB Post Office
Sydney NSW 1230
http://www.yvonneallen.com.au
sydney@yvonneallen.com.au
Sydney-based office contact information for this introduction agency.

Entre Nous
173 Victoria Parade
Fitzroy 3065, Victoria
http://www.entrenous.com.au
Founded by Rosalind Neville. Uses questionnaires that assess personality type to help with the matching. Offers seminars and relationship coaching.

New Zealand

Two's Company Ltd.
http://homepages.ihug.co.nz/~hkay/Sasha/index.html
Joining fee includes three introductions. Age range is 27 to 75.

On-line matchmaking

Australia

Find My Australian Soul Mate
http://www.findmymate.com
http://www.findmymate.com/Australia
Provides a list of questions, based on the works of Nathaniel Branden. Based on your responses, subscribers are matched to other subscribers.

United Kingdom

http://www.singlesearch.com
International site of Singlesearch.com, founded by Lisa and Robert Bentsen in the United States.

Divorce

Divorce Magazine
392 Parliament Street
Toronto, Ontario
Canada M5A 2Z7
http://www.divorcemagazine.com
Print and online magazine on divorce and related topics including referrals to professionals.

Relationships Coaching or Counseling

Roz Burkitt
The Ex Factor
http://www.theexfactor.co.nz
Burkitt offers workshops and seminars in New Zealand for the suddenly single.

Gottman Institute
P.O. Box 15644
Seattle, WA 98115-0644
http://www.gottman.com
Workshops and seminars for couples offered by couples researchers John Gottman, Ph.D. and Julie Schwart Gottman, Ph.D.

Don Gabor
http://www.dongabor.com
New York-based workshop leader teaches conversational skills; he is also the author of *How to Start a Conversation and Make Friends*.

Gregory J.K. Godek
http://www.1001waystoberomantic.com
This Los Angeles-based relationships expert is the author of *1001 Ways to Be Romantic*, and 12 additional related titles.

John Gray, Ph.D.
http://www.marsvenus.com
California-based author (*Men are From Mars, Women are From Venus*) conducts seminars on communication skills and relationships and also trains consultants in his methods.

Robin Newman
http://www.Lovecoach.com
Love coach Robin Newman is the author of *How to Meet a Mensch in New York*.

Allie Ochs
http://www.fit2love.com
Relationship coach based near Toronto, Canada, who offers workshops.

Susan Page
http://www.susanpage.com
Author of several books for singles and couples including *If I'm So Wonderful Why am I Still Single?* who offers coaching by phone.

Nancy White
LoveLifeU@aol.com
Coach for women on relationships and self-esteem issues; New York City-based.

Jan Yager, Ph.D.
http://www.janyager.com
jyager@aol.com
Sociologist and author of *Meet the Love of Your Life, Friendshifts®*, and *When Friendship Hurts*, who offers individual coaching by phone or in person as well as relationship workshops and seminars.

Major Internet Search Engines/Directories

http://www.google.com
http://www.yahoo.com
http://www.hotbot.com
http://www.lycos.com
http://www.search.aol.com
http://www.search.msn.com

Miscellaneous related sites

Homesick.com.au
P.O. Box 1959
Bondi Junction, NSW 2022
Australia
http://www.homesick.com.au
Networking and informative site for Australians who are living throughout the world. The Homesick Forums allow site visitors to post or answer forums on a variety of topics as well as offering a chance to develop new friendships or romantic social relationships. Global gatherings are posted at www.homesick.com.au/gatherings.html including New York City, Toronto, Athens, Copenhagen, Hong Kong, etc.

Associations

American Australian Association
http://www.americanaustralian.org
Established in 1948, this New York City-based association sponsors social and cultural programs with Australian or New Zealand performers and sports activities as well as social programs for Australia and New Zealand expatriates and American friends.

Parents Without Partners
http://www.pwp.freeyellow.com
Site for Australian Parents Without Partners association with chapters throughout Australia. Sponsors social activities and also offer information on being a single parent.

Finding New Friends, Old Friends or Former Classmates or Co-workers

Old Friends or Former Classmates or Co-Workers

http://www.schoolfriends.com.au (Australia)
http://www.schoolfriends.com/uk (United Kingdom)

http://www.batchmates.com (Offers the option of selecting a country, including Australia, New Zealand, United Kingdom, South Africa, Canada and Ireland)
http://www.alumni.net
http://www.gradfinder.com

New Friends

http://www.entertainmates.com
http://www.friendster.com

Index

A

ads, *See* personal ads or online dating
advertising, 82–93
    personal ads, 82–93
Allen, Yvonne, 163–164
Allin, Bill, 88–89
alone, 9, 10, 14, 20, 24, 28, 29, 44, 79 *See also* traveling alone
alumni, 17, 79, 168
American Australian Association, 167
American Library Association (ALA), 80
Americansingles.com 71
anger, 145, 165–166
appearance, 30–31, 37, 42, 56, 145
Asia, 92, 96

associations, 104, 109, 123, 125, 155–156, 167
attraction, 11, 12, 14, 28, 65, 139, 140
Australia, 17, 33–34, 91, 156–157, 160–161, 163–164, 167

B

bachelor, 4
background check, 34, 59, 60, 92
bar, 14, 24, 64, 76, 107, 111–114, 116
    coffee, 115
    minimum drinking age, 111–112
    neighborhood, 112
    singles, 10, 14, 112
    sports, 114

Barkas, J.L. (Janet Lee), *See* Jan Yager
Barkas, Gladys, 143
Barkas, William, 143
Bartlett's Familiar Quotations, 43
Bashmashnikov, Stan, 76
Beijing (China), 5, 17, 114
Bentsen, Lisa, 70, 82–83, 85
Bentsen, Robert, 70, 82, 83
biological clock, 9, 10, 16, 21
Blake, Tom, 77
blind date, 6, 10, 17, 29, 51–52
blind date protocol, 51–57
BookExpo, 80
bookstore, 102–103, 115
breaking up, *See also* divorce
14 things to do, 136–137
Bryson, Karen, 90–91
Bryson, Tony, 91
business trips, 94, 99–100

C

Calero, Henry H. (*How to Read a Person Like a Book*), 29
camp, 66, 121, 122, 159–160
Canada, 33, 65, 69, 88, 92, 115, 167–168
cards, *See* greeting cards
Caribbean, 92, 96
casinos, 115–116
cat show, 105
Catskills Alive, 121
Ceren, Sandra Levy, 57–58
change, 33, 37, 39, 75, 79, 80
charity events, 67, 120
Chicago, 78, 98, 113
China, 5, 17, 98, 114
Cicero, 10
Classical Music Lovers' Exchange, 105

Classmates.com, 68, 78
clothing, 31, 127, 145
Club Med, 96, 159
college, 5, 8, 28, 36, 62, 66, 72, 74
Columbia Book of Quotations, 43
commercial social settings, 26, 96, 111–116
communication skills, 16, 28, 29, 107, 144–145
Company of Friends (CoF), 78, 99
compatibility, 17, 38, 44, 70
questions, 44–48
Concerned Singles, 69
concert, 54, 100, 104, 105, 107, 112, 121
conversation, 61, 89, 98, 106
See also communication skills
courtship, 5, 6, 39, 52, 58, 130, 137
creative time management, 16–17
applied to romantic search, 17–22
Creative Time Management for the New Millennium (Yager), 16
cultural activities, 101–110
Curtis, Tommy, 64

D

dancing, 47, 61, 99, 113–114
date.com, 92
dating
8minutedating.com, 156
online, 91–93
speeddating, 156, 158, 159
datingdirect.com, 92, 162
Dayhoff, Signe, 24, 59

Dickens, Charles, 95
diet, 31, 36–37
Distefano, Amy, 58
divorce, 3, 4, 5, 27, 36, 44, 52, 57, 59, 64, 68, 77, 82, 107, 109, 112, 136, 143, 165
dog show, 105
dog walking, 105
dress, 30–31, 127, 145

E

8minutedating.com, 65, 156
eHarmony.com, 59
Elderhostel, 98, 118
Ensign, Paulette, 107
Erik Erikson, 144
exercise, 113, 118, 120
Exotic Journeys, 97, 160

F

Fairfield University, 72, 76, 140
Falzone, Paul, 19, 58
family, 4, 8, 9, 11, 12, 14, 15, 16, 21, 22, 35, 36, 43, 46, 47, 49, 53, 55, 56, 60–61, 63–64, 84, 94, 95, 124, 141, 146
film festival, 106
Finding Love After 50 (Tom Blake), 77
Finello, Kristen, 79, 145
first date, 38, 44, 56, 61, 76
first kiss, 76
The Fortunate Four and Other Journeys of the Heart (Joy Kuby), 63
flea market, 127
Freud, Sigmund, 144
Friendshifts® (Jan Yager), 74, 143
friend, 9, 12, 18, 22, 25, 27, 28, 29–30, 31, 32, 39, 45, 46, 47, 49, 51–58, 60–61, 62, 66, 68, 70–71, 84, 93, 94, 95, 97, 103, 106, 108, 113, 118, 122, 123, 124, 126, 128, 135, 136, 142, 143, 147
friendship, necessity of, 147
friendfinder.com, 71, 92, 162
friendster.com, 67
Fuchs, Marek, 'Scholar, Matchmaker and Convention Presence'. *New York Times*, 64

G

Gabor, Don, 165
goals, 6, 16, 18–19, 135, 137–138
Gordon, Barbara, 99
Grady, Michelle, 76, 140
Grady, Sean, 76, 140
Greatboyfriends.com, 70
Great Expectations®, 69
greeting cards, 61
grief, 36, 136

H

happy couples, 141–147
hardware store, 130
health, 95
HIV+, 25
holidays, 26, 107, 121–124
Home Depot®, 130
How to Read a Person Like a Book (Nierenberg and Calero), 28–29
How to Start a Conversation and Make Friends (Don Gabor), 165

I

India, 33, 42, 97
IndianFriendfinder.com, 92

interdependence, 147
Internet, *See* online chat, online dating, or online matching
intimacy, 30, 37 *See also* sexual intimacy
introduction agency, 163
introductions, 51–71
    by friends or family members, 60–61
Ireland, 162

J

Jaffe, Jody, 52
Jaffee, Cathy, 62
Jaffee, Tom, 62
Jdate.com, 71, 92
Jewish singles, 66, 71, 92
job, 76–81
    part-time, 79

K

Korea, 34, 97
Kuby, Joy, 63–64
Kuby, Keith, 63–64

L

Las Vegas, 80–92
laundry, 129
laundromat, 129
lavalife.com, 92
Leap Year Day, 61
Levey, Bob, 64
library, 75, 80, 103, 127
living together, 4, 111
London, 158–159
loneliness, 9, 94
love, 4, 8–14, 16, 18, 28, 30, 31–33, 34, 53, 62, 89, 130, 139–141, 141–142, 144
love.com, 92

Loving in Flow (Susan K. Perry), 145
lunch, 10, 12, 32, 52, 54, 57, 79, 118, 137

M

marriage, 3, 4, 14, 34, 37, 42, 45, 64, 67, 73, 76, 92, 130, 134, 141–142
match.com, 43, 70, 59
matchmaker.com, 71, 162,
matchmaking, 51–60, 64, 65
matchnet.com, 59, 71
McCall, Joanne, 4–5, 73–74
McLaughlin, Katy, 93
mediabistro.com, 78, 89, 99
Melbourne, 157
Millionairematch.com, 70
movies, 10, 45, 63, 102
moving, 81, 126
museum, 14, 62, 100, 116

N

networking, 12, 14, 18, 78, 99
A New Look at Love (E & G Walster), 28
New Year's Eve, 26, 47, 92, 121, 132
New York magazine, 9–10, 14, 89, 98
New York Road Runners Club, 120
The New York Times, 23, 99, 127, 130
New Zealand, 158, 161–162, 164
never-marrieds, *See* singles
Nierenberg, Gerald (*How to Read a Person Like a Book*), 28
non-verbal communication, 29, 30–31, 144, 145
NYU, 62

O

office romance, 73–75, 77–78, 79
  protocol, 74–75
Oneandonly.com, 70
online dating, 33, 43, 59, 60, 70, 71, 89–93
online matching, 70–71
Originaldating.com, 65
Oxford Dictionary of Quotations, 43

P

Parents Without Partners, 167,
Paris, 94, 113, 115, 129
parties, 61, 62, 63, 114
perfectionism, 37
Perfectmatch.com, 60, 70
Perry, Susan K., 145
personal ads, 9–14, 20, 42–43, 82–86
personals@yahoo.com, 90–91, 161, 162
politics, 47
Prometheus Unbound, 144

Q

The Quiet Party™, 114

R

reading group, 103
reality TV shows for finding a mate, 128
record store, 102
rejection, 13, 133–136
relaxation, 22, 28, 53
restaurants, 12, 28–29, 46, 55, 59, 73, 100, 102, 114, 115, 116
reunion, 47, 63, 66, 78
reward, 128

The Right One®, 58
Rivera, Angel, 27, 62, 127
romance, 4, 27, 37, 56, 78, 130, 141–142, 144 *See also* office romance
Rowe Conference Center, 123

S

Sadie Hawkins Day, 61
safety tips during the search, 94–96
  traveling, 94–96
school, 75–77
Schwartz, Pepper, 70
seasonal activities, 121–124
searching for the love of your life
  125 ways to find, 49-130
  continuing the search, 133–138
  finding the one, 139–147
  getting ready, 27–40
  more productive search, 15–22
self-confidence, 30
self-help groups, 103–104
seminars, 104
SeniorFriendFinder.com, 92
sexual intimacy, 4, 25, 141–142, 143
Shelley, Percy Bysshe, 144
shopping, 47, 116, 130, 140
shyness, 12, 14, 18, 72
Silverman, Fran, 121–122
Silverman, Ronald, 121–122
Single Booklovers, 69
The Single Gourmet, 115
Single in America (Jan Yager), 3, 5, 8, 143
single parent, 4, 36, 124

INDEX

singles
  clubs, 96, 113
  reasons for increase, 3–4
  study of, 8
Singlescruise.com, 96, 124
Singlesearch.com, 70, 82
Social Circles, 96, 113
South Africa, 159
South Korea, 34
sports, 117–120
Speed Dating™, 66
sports activities, 117–120
Stevens, Kimberly, 130
studying, 75–77
Sydney, 94, 129

T

theater group, 102
Theatre Development Fund, 97–98
time management, 6, 15, 16, 35, 137
  applied to romantic search, 16–22, 137
Together Dating®, 19, 58
Toronto Star, 88
Touby, Laurel, 78
trade shows, 80
travel, 94–100, 147
trips *See* travel
tsm.com/dating (Singles Resource Network), 91, 92–93

U

ublove.com, 92, 161
UConn *See* University of Connecticut
udate.co.uk, 92, 161
uk.match.com, 91
University of Connecticut, 27, 127

V

vacations, 94–100
  at home, 100
Valentine's Day, 123, 130
Victims (J.L. Barkas/a/k/a Jan Yager), 23
The Village Voice, 9, 14
volunteer, 18, 36, 47, 67, 80, 123–124
vows, 146
'Vows' column (*The New York Times*), 127, 130

W

Walster, Elaine (*A New Look at Love*), 28
Walster, G. William (*A New Look at Love*), 28
Warren, Neil Clark, 70
website creation, 93
wedding, 12, 58, 63, 64, 76, 127
widowhood, 68
Wilson, Matt, 72–73, 79, 145–146
wine tasting party, 66
Wingler, Sharon, 97
writing, 12, 14, 43
  articles about singles, 82, 126
  personal ads, 20, 43, 83–84

Y

Yager, Fred, 6, 8, 11–14, 139–140
Yager, Jan, 8–13, 15–16, 139–140, 166
Yager, Jeffrey, 47
Yahoo.com, 90

Z

Zaslow, Jeffrey, 67

Please Share Your 'How We Met' Stories With Me!

Thanks for sharing about any of the annotated 125 ways that are especially effective to you in achieving your relationship goals. Let me know what information or ideas in the introductory or concluding chapters were especially useful as well.

I look forward to receiving a newspaper clipping of your wedding announcement and any other news you wish to share. (And let me know if I have your permission to tell the world, or if you prefer me to keep your story confidential.)

I also appreciate receiving information about any new resources as well as being informed about any possible corrections to any current listings that are either outdated or defunct.

Here's my contact information:

Dr. Jan Yager
P.O. Box 8038,
Stamford, CT 06905-8038, USA
e-mail: jyager@aol.com
www.janyager.com

About The Author

Dr Jan Yager is the author of numerous highly-acclaimed books including *Single in America*, *When Friendship Hurts*, *Friendshifts*®, *Who's That Sitting at My Desk?* and *Creative Time Management for the New Millennium*. Her books have been translated into more than a dozen foreign languages.

The author has a Ph.D. in sociology (City University of New York), a masters in criminal justice, and she did graduate work in art therapy. She has appeared on major talk shows and is regularly quoted in newspapers, magazines and online publications.

Dr Yager has taught at the University of Connecticut and Penn State. A member of the National Speakers Association (NSA), she conducts workshops or delivers keynote addresses throughout the United States as well as internationally on relationship and business issues.

She lives in Connecticut with her husband Fred, a communications executive and writer, and their two teenage sons.

How Jan met Fred: when she was 35, Jan decided to take a more active role in her love life by applying the time management principles she had developed through researching and writing her book *Creative Time Management*. Through a personal ad that she placed in *New York* magazine, she met Fred. They married 23 days later and have been enjoying a wonderful marriage ever since as well as collaborating on two suspense novels, *Untimely Death* and *Just Your Everyday People*, screenplays, and non-fiction titles including *Career Opportunities in the Film Industry*.

For more information, visit www.janyager.com and www.fredandjanyager.com.
To book Dr Jan Yager for speaking engagements, contact your favorite speaker bureau or send an e-mail to: yagerinquiries2@aol.com.

THE NATURE OF HEALING

The Modern Practice of Medicine

Eric J. Cassell

OXFORD
UNIVERSITY PRESS

OXFORD
UNIVERSITY PRESS

Oxford University Press is a department of the University of Oxford.
It furthers the University's objective of excellence in research, scholarship,
and education by publishing worldwide.

Oxford   New York
Auckland   Cape Town   Dar es Salaam   Hong Kong   Karachi
Kuala Lumpur   Madrid   Melbourne   Mexico City   Nairobi
New Delhi   Shanghai   Taipei   Toronto

With offices in
Argentina   Austria   Brazil   Chile   Czech Republic   France   Greece
Guatemala   Hungary   Italy   Japan   Poland   Portugal   Singapore
South Korea   Switzerland   Thailand   Turkey   Ukraine   Vietnam

Oxford is a registered trademark of Oxford University Press in the UK and certain other countries.

Published in the United States of America by
Oxford University Press
198 Madison Avenue, New York, NY 10016

© Eric J. Cassell 2013

All rights reserved. No part of this publication may be reproduced, stored in a retrieval system, or transmitted, in any form or by any means, without the prior permission in writing of Oxford University Press, or as expressly permitted by law, by license, or under terms agreed with the appropriate reproduction rights organization. Inquiries concerning reproduction outside the scope of the above should be sent to the Rights Department, Oxford University Press, at the address above.

You must not circulate this work in any other form
and you must impose this same condition on any acquirer.

Library of Congress Cataloging-in-Publication Data
Cassell, Eric J., 1928–
The nature of healing: the modern practice of medicine/Eric J. Cassell.
p. ; cm.
Includes bibliographical references and index.
ISBN 978–0–19–536905–2 (hardback)
I. Title.
[DNLM: 1. Physician-Patient Relations.   2. Holistic Health. W 62]
610.69'6—dc23   2012022299

Portions of this book first appeared in Cassell, Eric J. "Suffering, whole person care, and the goals of medicine" and "Appendix: The nature of persons and clinical medicine." In: Hutchinson, Tom, Ed. *Whole Person Care: A New Paradigm for the 21st Century*, 1st ed. New York, NY: Springer, 2011.

1 3 5 7 9 8 6 4 2
Printed in the United States of America on acid-free paper

Dedicated to
Donald Boudreau
Colleague and friend
Were it not for Don and later his associates on the
Faculty of Medicine at McGill University
and our continuing conversations about developing and teaching
a new curriculum
I would never have have been encouraged and aided in the development
of the ideas that grew to become this book
...
and
For Patsy, always

Contents

Preface — ix

Acknowledgments — xxi

Prologue — xxv

1. Sickness — 1

2. The Person, Sick or Well — 25

3. Functioning — 51

4. What Is Healing? — 81

5. Listening: The Foundation of the Healing Relationship of Patient and Clinician — 95

6. The Evaluation of the Patient — 115

7. Knowing the Patient — 141

8. The Patient's Reaction to Illness — 163

9. The State of Illness — 175

10. Healing the Sick Patient — 195

11. Healing the Suffering Patient	219
12. Respect for Persons and Autonomy	231
13. Purposes, Goals, and Well-Being	243
Index	257

Preface

THE HEALING TRADITION in Western medicine goes back to its origins. Asclepius was a legendary Greek physician—the son of Apollo and Coronis (a human). His first teacher and foster parent was the wise centaur Chiron. When Asclepius became so skillful in healing that he could revive the dead (considered a crime against the natural order), Zeus killed him. Even though most physicians have no idea why Apollo and Asclepius are mentioned when they take whatever variant of the Hippocratic Oath is used in their medical school, their presence in the oath affirms a tradition of physician-healers of more than 2500 years.

During my fellowship, Walsh McDermott, the Chair of the Department, said that the chance that a patient entering a physician's office would be decisively affected by the visit dated to only 1925 (the discovery of insulin). Despite my endless respect for McDermott, I thought that improbable. Any system of medicine that lasts 2500 years must be doing something, and that something is probably more than merely an unlettered placebo effect. (As though we actually know how the placebo effect works.) On the other hand, we have little knowledge of what physicians have been doing all this time that might have been effective. (Some clues are offered in Chapter 5.)

In the twentieth century in the United States the words healer and healing acquired a negative connotation starting in the 1920s, largely, at least in the beginning, as a result of the crusade by Morris Fishbein, the aggressive editor of *The Journal of the American Medical Association* from 1924 to 1949. Fishbein labeled anything that was not strictly scientific medicine as quackery, and healing fell under that heading. That attitude became quite general. As the twentieth century advanced, science and technology took over medicine. Science also entered and became influential in the intellectual life of Western society. The power of science to answer humankind's important questions (sickness and disease fit in here) was reinforced by Positivism, which started in the mid-nineteenth century. For positivists, "every rationally justifiable assertion can be scientifically verified or is capable of logical or mathematical proof" (*Oxford English Dictionary*, 2nd ed., electronic). As the hold of positivism weakened in the late twentieth century, that strict, and practically ideological, hold on intellectual and scientific life diminished. It has not diminished in medicine, however, where the scientific viewpoint that the only information of value is the verifiably objective has gotten stronger. This has paid off in the hugely successful enterprise of medical science in its pursuit of knowledge about body function and disease.

Unfortunately, between Morris Fishbein's successful crusade and the growth of medical science, aspects of sickness having to do with the sick person and not just body parts got pushed aside. Dealing with, for example, the impact of disease on the patients' personal life and psychological, social, and spiritual disruptions depended on how much the clinician knew or cared about such things. Clinicians early in the scientific era learned about and focused on such human problems because they grew up in a medicine not yet heavily scientific. Their students—the students of the last generation of powerful chiefs of medicine right after World War II—were also trained to pay attention to these "humanistic" (not then called such) concerns, although in a somewhat attenuated manner. From later in the twentieth century to the present the idea of medicine as a healing profession looked good in slogans written by the laity but was not part of scientific medicine's self-image. Clinicians' concern with the effects of illness on sick persons apart from what happened to the body was essentially ended by the increasing power of medical science, despite its unquestionable blessings. The same scientific hegemony, which has decreased attention on the humane aspects of medicine, has interfered with the *growth* of clinical medicine (known since antiquity as the healing arts), which is concerned with the care of one individual particular patient at a time. As long as the care of the sick is *only* about defeating acute diseases (characterized by a sudden onset, a sharp rise, and a short course) or traumatic injuries, only applying medical science (if that were possible) might be justified. Contemporary medicine is overwhelmingly occupied by chronic diseases with often uncertain onset and a course that frequently ends with the patient's death. Here, success depends on a variably sick patient's continuing interest, understanding, motivation, and application to an unending regimen that is often unpleasant, sick-making, and of uncertain outcome. Included among contemporary chronic diseases are many cancers, HIV/AIDS, many major incapacities (posttraumatic as well as disease generated), as well as the better known diseases such as asthma, diabetes, chronic obstructive lung disease, heart failure, epilepsy, coronary artery disease, chronic renal disease, multiple sclerosis, amyotrophic lateral sclerosis, and on and on. The application of medical science to these is often critical, but long-term success depends not only on the essential knowledge of disease and pathophysiology, but on the clinician's judgment, mastery of relationships with the patients, communication skills, mastery of the clinical method, knowing intimately the behavior of patients and other clinicians, continuing interest and compassion as much in the middle of the night as in the morning, and on and on. In the past these efforts would have been included in the unwritten curriculum of medical training and lumped together as the "art of medicine"[1] to be contrasted with medical science. Many of these essential clinical skills are still not part of formal medical training in the majority of medical schools. In recent years communication skills have received attention in most medical schools. They are taught, however, primarily as having to do with, for example, taking the patient's history, breaking bad news, dealing with the angry patient, and negotiating mutually endorsed treatment plans. Although much better than in the past, this is a restricted understanding of communication—especially medical communication. It is the use of the spoken language in general that must be taught. I have said in the past, the spoken language is the most important tool in medicine, almost nothing happens in its absence (Cassell 1985). More than 20 years ago I wrote the following (Cassell 1991):

> For more than two generations remedies for medicine's dehumanization and impersonality have been a failure. Great teachers have tried, wonderful books have been written, innovative medical school courses and curricula have been established, and even new medical schools have been founded on ideas believed to offer solutions. For the most part, all these attempts, large and small, have been disappointments. Over these decades there have been many great teachers, more wonderful physicians, and nothing less than superb medical care to be found. But these islands of excellence remain just that, islands separated from the mainland.

I believed that when the sick person became central in medicine, the problem would be solved. This was wrong. In step with many social changes occurring in North American society following World War II, the patient has gradually become the central subject and object of clinical medicine. More recently, in keeping with the vast social changes during the same period—the civil rights movement, the women's movement, disability rights, and gay rights, in which full social personhood was achieved—the patient has become a person. Patients in the past did not fit the full social category of personhood. For example, they were not considered able to decide or act for themselves. By becoming persons, patients gained equal

---

1. Art is used here in the sense of the exercise of knowledgeable and practiced skills in the pursuit of a craft as in the art of cabinet making or weaving. It is distinctly not art in the aesthetic sense. In this book no distinction is made between the "art" of medicine and other clinical knowledge, it is all clinical medicine.

status with all other competent adults. There have been many important steps on the way. Carl Rogers, a well-known psychologist, wrote about "client-centered" therapy in 1951. Michael Balint, who wrote about the doctor–patient relationship in 1970, described patient-centered medicine and the idea and name caught on (Balint 1970). In 1977 George Engel published his paper on the biopsychosocial nature of medicine, which was a very influential concept but did not translate into practice as he had wished (Engel 1977). In 1980 Moira Stewart and others from the University of Western Ontario published perhaps the best book on patient-centered medicine (Stewart et al. 1995). By now almost every medical school, teaching center, and hospital flies the flag of "Patient-Centered" medicine. As noted, I was wrong. The medicine practiced on the floors of those institutions remains stubbornly disease centered.

Why is this so, and what has it got to do with healing? First, the definitions of patient-centered medicine vary considerably. One definition seems to me to be focused principally on polite, well-mannered, and customized care that meets the patient's needs, desires, concerns, and wants. (The Institute of Medicine's definition is of this sort.) Another definition by Donald Berwick is primarily politically egalitarian: "The experience (to the extent the informed, individual patient desires it) of transparency, individualization, recognition, respect, dignity, and choice in all matters, without exception, related to one's person, circumstances, and relationships in health care" (Berwick 2009). Because both express the idea of respect for persons, there can be no question of the need for both true politeness and true political egalitarianism. Although they may be necessary expressions of the patient's status as a person, neither responds to the inherently medical concern with the patient as a person—in the sense of related to the occurrences of sickness requiring a doctor—or to the recognition that a person has a body. Two key ideas about this have become clear in these past 50 years or so. First, that sickness occurs in the whole person because whatever happens to one part of a person happens to the whole and thus every other part (it could not be otherwise). Second, that the nature of the particular patient has an influence on the expression, presentation, diagnosis, treatment, course, and outcome of disease in that patient. Because of these two facts alone medical care should undeniably be patient centered.

There are other reasons. In recent times clinical medicine has increased markedly in technical and technologic sophistication and attractiveness to both doctors and patients. Simply put, we can do more for more patients than ever before and our patients are knowledgeable and demanding consumers. Unfortunately, we also do more for more patients that is unnecessary, technology driven, too expensive, and not productive of gains in individual or statistical measures of health. Despite widespread concern over these excesses and cost, no one knows quite how to solve the problem of cost and unnecessary care. So, there we have it, a major change in direction of medicine—putting the patient, the sick person, in the center as the major focus of clinical medicine—which has been gestating for decades and yet stays unborn. Clinical medicine itself struggles to get free of problems of excess—excess cost, excess utilization of technology, and excess treatment, as well as increased patient and physician dissatisfaction.

I believe that clinicians, no matter how much they want to be patient centered or focus on healing, do not really know how to do it. Good experienced clinicians know how to put the patients' needs, concerns, desires, and choices into their decision-making process. They know how to *not do* things that the patient does not need. They know how to stop diagnostic efforts when they are not productive. They know how to keep the patients' best interests in the center of their decision-making process. Even the best clinicians, however, are most often focused on the disease and afflicted body parts, still largely controlled in their actions by disease imperatives. How could they not be; all the valid, reliable, and reproducible information clinicians get is about the disease or diseased functions not about the patient. Even the best who may be able to do it do not know how to teach it.

There are medical schools whose curricula, trying to solve the problem of contemporary dehumanizing, teach approaches to patient-centered medicine. Descriptions of patient-centered programs routinely identify a need to integrate the science of medicine with a focus on the patient. One describes a weaving back and forth between science and its pathophysiologic perspective on disease, and patients in their human complexities. Another describes a dialogue between the patient's experience of illness and its alleviation and the doctor's diagnosis of disease and its treatment. Yet another suggests a so-called Double Helix Curriculum between the sciences and clinical concerns (University of Rochester 2011). These various approaches to patient-centered care perpetuate a *fundamental error*—the problem they are trying to solve is not that there are two kinds of knowledge—medical science and knowledge of patients—but rather that there are two explicitly separate goals. The first goal is focused on the scientific knowledge of disease—the prevalent perspective of the past two centuries. The second goal is focused on the human problems of the patient(s) (Boudreau et al. 2007).

These curricula are not the solution because their premise is incorrect. There are not two goals. *There is only one goal: the well-being of the patient.* Well-being? If we are successful in our care of patients they should have a sense of well-being. "The state of being or doing well in life" (*Oxford English Dictionary*, 2nd ed., electronic). The patient was sick and now well-being has returned. Well-being is separate from ideas of disease; a patient can be diseased and yet have a sense of well-being. Well-being is multidimensional, it is not just physical or emotional. This quotation from a study of the attitudes of people to complementary and alternative medical practices makes the point. "The goal of health then is well-being, not simply the absence of disease. Many [respondents] used the term 'balance' to describe what they meant by well-being. They strive for balance in their lives even when disease is not present. Others explained well-being by distinguishing between healing and curing. Even when people have a disease that cannot be cured, they can improve their lives spiritually, emotionally, mentally and socially. They experience healing. The focus on holism and well-being requires a different relationship between the practitioner and patient" (Easthope et al. 2003). Well-being is a patient goal—only the patient can know whether he or she has a sense of well-being. We can think the patient is better—disease indices say things are good—but the patient does not have a sense of well-being. The patient had angina and a successful angioplasty or bypass produced a return of good coronary blood flow, but the patient is not better—has not returned to work, or the previous place in the family, or has not resumed sexual function—the patient has not returned to a state of well-being. The patient had a malignancy and was successfully treated into remission. Unfortunately, the person fears and waits only for the recurrence. The person has not had a return of well-being. The patient has chronic obstructive pulmonary disease (COPD) and his life is occupied and preoccupied by the disease and its treatment. Life has become organized around the disease—medications, treatments, and visits to physicians—and despite what clinicians would think was reasonable lung function, there is no sense of a life returned or a sense of well-being.

Well-being is not just quality of life. Psychologists, who have been studying the subject in recent years, write of well-being in many contexts such as job related, in relationships, environmental, and economic. They measure it on scales of pleasure, satisfaction, affect, happiness, and their opposites (Eid and Larsen 2008; Kahneman et al. 1999). In general, well-being is related to feelings of being oneself (with oneself and in relation to others), being able to live life as desired, and feeling able to accomplish what is considered important. Put another way, patients have a sense of well-being when they are able to pursue their purposes and achieve their goals in life's various dimensions. A goal is a point, place, or activity a person wishes to achieve. Purpose is the underlying reason the person wants or aims to achieve that goal. Purposes, such as devotion to family, a profession, music, business, or something of large dimension, are often an integral part of the person that cannot be removed without diminishing the person. Well-being is the state of being that accompanies doing well in life. It is always relative to the person's situation. For patients to return to a sense of well-being requires help (unless the illness is trivial). It is equally important to realize that medical care wrongly directed may destroy well-being or keep it from returning. Well-being clearly should be a goal of care. Well-being in itself, however, is simply not a recognizable medical goal. Yes, it is an ultimate goal; when the patients' sense of well-being has returned they will say thank you. How will I, as a clinician, know I am on the right track or that I am getting there? Clinicians need goals they can conceptualize in medical terms. We clinicians are pragmatic animals, we have to have something we can smell, hear, see, feel, measure—even measure with a questionnaire. I like a smile on a patient's face as much as anyone, but we need more. With all this as a background it becomes possible to reconceptualize what sickness is and look anew at medical care—the care of the sick.

In medicine over the centuries doctors have understood sickness as an affliction of the body or its parts. Doctors and patients have long believed that when people became sick it was because they had a disease. That definition means that relieving sickness involves defeating disease. The history of medicine is the story of the gradual unfolding of an understanding of the body and a search for the root of disease. What diseases were, however, and what caused them have remained elusive in the millennia since the Hippocratic era when medicine became a rational (not religious) enterprise. The history of medicine is too often written as though all the steps along the way were on the path toward the medicine of today. The actual story is one of good steps and missteps this way and that, of unconnected discoveries and theories that gradually produced an accretion of knowledge about sickness and the body and its parts. In every era doctors have believed that (to one extent or another) they understood what was happening and what caused disease and death, and that they had remedies for what ailed their patients. The idea of cure, however, remained out of reach. Doctors did not believe that there were cures for the most serious afflictions. Always, however, doctors have taken care of the sick and sat with them as most got better, although many died. Then, with the discovery of antibiotics, all that changed. A different medicine showed itself after World War II, a medicine of cure. Optimism began to pervade the profession and its appreciative public.

A new understanding of diseases emerged as the scientific establishment in the United States and then the world grew in size and in its incredible ability to answer questions—as long as the questions were of the right sort and open to the classical methods of science. In medicine the right kinds of questions are about specific parts of the body, agents that might afflict it, and primarily pharmacologic solutions to what is uncovered. They must also be amenable to reductionist methodologies.

Our prevalent problems of sickness and disease have outgrown the abilities of those methodologies to solve all the problems. It has been true throughout the history of medicine that as one set of problems was solved another kind was uncovered. The near defeat of infectious diseases, the marked increase in the reach and success of surgery, and pharmacologic solutions to many previously stubborn problems have resulted in large populations of persons living with chronic illness, incapacities, and the afflictions of aging. These persons, most of whom have impairments of function, may not be able to pursue important purposes, achieve their favored goals, or have a sense of well-being. They cannot live their lives the way they wish to. Medicine's definition of sickness fails this large population because disease or individual afflicted body parts alone do not explain the difficulties. Their problems are not confined to classical definitions of disease. Yes, the problems of our patients are rooted in the body, but they reach out into every one of life's dimensions. They are problems of function and all human functions start in the body, but the patients have difficulty working, sleeping, with relationships, with transcendent (spiritual) issues, or they find it impossible to participate in all of life's multitudinous activities. The trouble may start with a neuromuscular defect, as in amyotrophic lateral sclerosis, but their solution lies in the resolution of problems of living in the world. The same is true of heart failure, advanced COPD, and any other chronic disease you can name. A definition of sickness that is not based exclusively on disease is needed; it must be appropriate to our contemporary medical problems and guide the medical care of our times. The definition must lead to *a medicine that can be taught*. The definition must be something that meets the needs of clinician-healers in caring for patients. The definition must lead to a medicine that returns patients to well-being—even patients who are dying. Here is a definition derived from the developments in medicine over the past decades.

A person is sick who cannot achieve his or her purposes and goals because of impairments of function that are believed to be in the domain of medicine.

The definition does not mention disease. The most common reason that persons are sick and consequently cannot achieve their purposes and goals is that they are diseased. Diseases can be present without sickness and sickness without diseases. This definition is about sick persons. The term sick person includes the body. A body always includes its person. Purposes and goals are inherently person-centered because only the person knows what purposes and what goals are important. Because they are person-centered, purposes and goals are not reductionist. Function is a unifying term covering all body functions, human activities, and participation. Functioning is necessary to the achievement of purposes and goals. People who achieve their purposes and goals have a sense of well-being. Action in the service of the patient's well-being is healing. To borrow from an epigraph quoting Donald Boudreau at the beginning of Chapter 4: What is Healing: "All the therapeutic interventions of physicians are exercises in healing." Every skill, every modality, every technology, and all the knowledge of the clinician are in the service of healing.

The mission of this book is to show what must be done so that healing can be achieved. However, before that can be described some concepts that are omnipresent in medicine and that are important to healing must be adequately defined and clarified. Sickness is central to medicine and describing it in the terms of the contemporary patient is the topic of Chapter 1. It is persons who are sick and persons who are at the center of contemporary medicine so Chapter 2 is about persons, sick or well. The chapter is also necessary because despite the emphasis in contemporary medical schools on person-centered medicine, there are no courses about what persons are. Academic psychology may generally be about aspects of mental or nervous system function but not about persons. Psychiatrists are trained primarily to deal with mental illness and emotional disorders. Clinicians must come to know about everyday persons. Physicians accustomed to physiology and pathophysiology, both of which are about function, need to learn how to see and understand human function in a more global fashion. The purpose of Chapter 3 on functioning is to begin to fill that need. The contents of these earliest chapters are in support of healing, which is the subject of Chapter 4. In this book, healers is an inclusive term used interchangeably with clinicians. Not all clinicians in contemporary medical care are physicians, and for those who are not the same knowledge and skills of healing apply.

Chapters 5, 6, and 7 are all concerned with learning about the patient—the person who is sick and has come for help with his or her health. The focus in these chapters is not as much on technology as is usual in contemporary medicine. Appropriate technology, if available, is always important—sometimes vitally so. There is, however, no substitute for the person who is the healer because healing occurs in the relationship—it is interpersonal—between the healer and the patient. Learning to listen, not just listen, but listen attentively, is the fundamental skill of healing. It is part of learning to observe every detail—said and unsaid—and register as much as possible that is present (or not present). Evaluating patients as part of healing is more comprehensive than in contemporary medicine because it is not only the bodily signs of disease (although they are always important) but functional capacities not often evaluated and generally considered as everyday abilities that require attention. Some of these turn out to be signs of future troubles (or success) and thus have become important. Coming to know patients as the persons they are is the province of Chapter 7. Healers who have been active as healers for many years come to really know about persons. Sometimes impairments of function and some diseases are less exciting with increasing experience. Persons never lose their fascination.

Chapters 8 through 11 are about healing sick persons. Clinicians may remember when they were in school and could not wait to get to actual patients. These chapters are about actual healing and actual patients.

The care of patients is a moral undertaking or perhaps a moral-technical one. That is because what is done must be in the best interests of the patients—what is good and right for patients—as they know them. Good and right are words in the moral world, they are not technical issues even though technical knowledge may be required for their achievement. In the medicine of our times patients are persons and as such have the right to self-determination and the freedom to make their own choices. We know those words as describing patient autonomy. I believe that patient autonomy is a much richer concept than that and that autonomy usually cannot be achieved alone—all by oneself. As that is true of the healthy it is all the more the case for sick persons. The two fundamental principles of ethics in clinical medicine are benevolence and respect for persons—one aspect of which is respect for the autonomy of persons. Chapter 12 is an in-depth discussion of these concepts.

Chapter 13 is a discussion of goals and purposes. This is a new topic for clinicians to pursue. I mention in the Prologue the problem that reductionism—a key to the success of experimental science—presents to the rest of medicine and to to society as a whole. It is one thing to talk about whole patients—the patient of patient-centered medicine is a whole patient—but quite another thing to keep that person in mind while taking care of the patient. Reductionism is always calling—like the Sirens singing Ulysses to the rocks—and soon we have lost sight of the patient while pursuing an impaired function to ever smaller domains. For example, the patient with spina bifida cannot keep pushing her wheelchair to the place where she is a professor of philosophy because of elbow pain. Her professorship represents a lifelong fight for achievement despite her considerable congenital impairments. Soon the elbow joint is the clinician's sole concern and the professorship and the pursuit of its purposes that keep her going in the world have dropped from sight. How much better to recognize her purposes, acknowledge them, and keep them in sight while treating her. This chapter describes how the questions are asked, what the answers mean, and how to use the information. Chapter 13 also advances the concept that has been gaining substance throughout the book, that the person of the patient, as a person, offers a new arena for active therapeutic intervention and a description of such actions. This is in addition to clinicians' abilities to intervene in pathophysiology and in the body.

The approach to patients described in this book—careful listening, observing, evaluating sick persons and their illnesses, finding out their goals and purposes, and focusing on function, and the person of the patient—takes time. Kenneth Ludmerer, who writes so well about the education and evolution of physicians in the twentieth century, once voiced the doctor's most common complaint particularly well: "the time has been wrung out of the system." Almost 40 years in the solo practice of medicine taught me that my most valuable asset, like yours, was time. (I am certainly not advocating for solo practice—those days are gone.) How can I put forth an understanding of healing that may move the healer's eyes away from the computer or medical app (at least briefly) and that takes time to learn and to practice? It is, simply put, better medicine. The more skillful you get the more satisfying this kind of medicine is and the less time it takes. It actually saves time—fewer wasted words, less wasted effort, fewer unnecessary tests and treatments, and fewer wasted visits. It is extremely satisfying to see your proficiency grow and to see yourself grow along with it.

Healers who are more knowledgeable and skillful are more effective with patients. It is my hope that this book is a step in that direction. Since knowledge and skill continue to grow through the years of practicing, studying, and thinking as a healer you will not be as effective this year as next year or the year after that. Now, however, is when this patient needs you and needs all you know and can do. This is no different than throughout the history of medicine. That is why you always want to be better tomorrow. That is why knowledge of healing is learned throughout a lifetime. It is an active process; you have to dig, turn over what is on the surface, and look behind what is obvious and what is not said as much as what is said throughout a lifetime of healing the sick. And you must also read and think. No matter how much you know and learn there is endlessly more. See what Hippocrates said as his first statement of this basic truth: "Life is short, and the art is long, the moment quickly passed, experience perilous, and decision difficult. Healers must not only be prepared to do what is right themselves, but also make the patient, the attendants, and the externals cooperate."

References

Balint, M. (1970). Treatment or diagnosis; a study of repeat prescriptions in general practice. In: *Mind & Medicine Monographs, 20. Series Treatment or Diagnosis; a Study of Repeat Prescriptions in General Practice*. London, Philadelphia, Tavistock Publications, J. B. Lippincott, p. xviii.

Berwick, D. M. (2009). What patient-centered should mean: Confessions of an extremist. *Health Affairs 28*: w555–w565.

Boudreau, J. D., Cassell, E. J., and Fuks, A. (2007). A healing curriculum. *Medical Education* 41: 1193–1201.

Cassell, E. J. (1985). *Talking with Patients: The Theory of Doctor-Patient Communication*. Cambridge, MA, MIT Press.

Cassell, E. J. (1991). *The Nature of Suffering and the Goals of Medicine*. New York, Oxford University Press.

Easthope, G., Adams, J., and Tovey, P. (2003). *The Mainstreaming of Complementary and Alternative Medicine: Studies in Social Context*. New York, Routledge.

Eid, M., and Larsen, R. J., Eds. (2008). *The Science of Subjective Well-Being*. New York, Guilford Press.

Engel, G. L. (1997). The need for a new medical model: A challenge for biomedicine. *Science 196*(4286): 129–136.

Kahneman, D., Diener, E., and Schwarz, N., Eds. (1999). *Well-Being: The Foundations of Hedonic Psychology*. New York, Russell Sage Foundation.

Stewart, M., Brown, J. B., Weston, W. W., et al. (1995). *Patient Centered Medicine: Transforming the Clinical Method*, 2nd ed. Abingdon, UK, Radcliffe Medical Press.

University of Rochester School of Medicine and Dentistry. http://www.urmc.rochester.edu/education/md/prospective-students/curriculum/. Accessed September 3, 2011.

Acknowledgments

FUNDAMENTAL CHANGE IN medicine is a very slow process. In 1969, in an article "Death and the Physician" published in *Commentary,* then a liberal publication, I said that "As the culture changes and the nature of disease changes, the functions of the healer must also change." At the time I did not know what that meant, but the comment (which I think the editor inserted) started me thinking about healing, what it is, how it comes about, and what it does for the sick. I have been thinking, reading, and talking about healing (and trying to do it) ever since. In *The Healer's Art,* which was published in 1976 [Cassell, E. J. (1976). *The Healer's Art.* Philadelphia, Lippincott], the topic comes up again. At the end of Chapter 1, where the world of the sick and sickness itself are described, it says that "Ostensibly, the physician deals only with disease elements of the illness. His manifest function is the cure of disease, but his latent function, healing, which involves restoring the sick to the world of the healthy, is a secret even to himself." This book is part of an increasing literature devoted to unveiling the secret.

The quotation from the *Healer's Art* of 1976 makes another point. It was written in what we now call sexist language. I no longer write that way as part of the large social change that took place in the United States and other Western countries not long after. As part of that change the bioethics movement was born and patients became persons—not just patients. Bioethics has had a large impact on medicine and a very large impact on me. I am a Fellow of the Hastings Center and was a member of the Board of Directors for decades. Even though this book is written since I became less active at the Hastings Center, the influence of my colleagues, what I learned, and what I continue to learn because of them is unabated and pervades everything I write. As a result of a talk I delivered at the Center about the care of the dying in 1971, I became interested in that subject. From then on caring for dying patients increasingly occupied my interest. There were no hospices, physicians, or nurses specializing in the problem at the time so my learning curve was very steep. The care of the dying began to reteach me medicine.

I was fortunate because most of the patients in my general internal medicine practice were not dying and I discovered that the basic lesson I was learning applied to them as well. The lesson then (and now) is that attention to the person of the patient is as vital as attention to the nature of the sickness.

In 1982 "The Nature of Suffering and Goals of Medicine" was published by me in *The New England Journal of Medicine*. The central fact that suffering has to teach medicine is that bodies do not suffer, only persons do. Because of the paper on suffering, however, and my work with the dying, Dr. Balfour Mount of The Faculty of Medicine at McGill University invited me to give a talk on the subject to his Fifth International Seminar on Terminal Care, October 3, 1984, in Montreal, Canada. Balfour Mount is an extraordinary and inspiring person whose thinking and humanity are consistently ahead of everybody. He founded the first hospice in North America at the Royal Victoria Hospital in Montreal, Canada. He has been a driving force behind the establishment of Palliative Care (he invented the name) as a recognized medical specialty. He would tell me that I should give a lecture about some impossible subject, which I would reject out of hand, but soon find myself writing. That is how, for example, I came to give the talk on "Love and Intimacy in Medicine" at the Fifth International Congress on the Care of the Terminally Ill in September 1994 in Montreal, Canada. [This lecture became the epilogue of Cassell, E. J. (1997). *The Nature of Primary Care Medicine*. New York, Oxford University Press.]

The importance of treating suffering and of the centrality of the sick person have been slow to enter contemporary practice. I came to understand that changing medicine requires basic changes in the education of physicians. I was fortunate to be asked to talk to the Curriculum Committee of the Faculty of Medicine at McGill in 2002 and that increased the intensity of my thinking about medical education. More interactions followed. Then in February 2005 I began meeting with Dr. Donald Boudreau who *really* knows about medical education *and* clinical medicine. We were in agreement from the beginning that if there was to be a real change in medical education it had to begin in the earliest weeks of medical school, and it had to involve at the start the most basic tools of physicians: observation, clinical thinking, description, communication, and others that together form the clinical method on which all clinical medicine is based. (How can you, for a start, put patients in the center of your thoughts if you cannot really see, hear, talk to, think about, or describe them?) Don knew everybody else at McGill and, it seems, in North American medical education, and could gently (and effectively) make his way through the shoals of medical school statecraft. All his knowledge and rare acumen are hidden behind genuine modesty. McGill was where the basic form of contemporary medical education began with William Osler in the 1870s and early 1880s so it seemed reasonable that McGill should be where the next real change started. Abraham Fuks was very supportive of our effort when Dean of the Faculty of Medicine at McGill. Now retired from the Deanship, he is a basic member of the trio (and friend) whose special interest in the language of medicine and medical thinking is so congenial. Many others on the faculty too numerous to name have supported our work as colleagues but also as friends. All of this made McGill an unusual and nourishing environment for me that kept new thinking and ideas bubbling up.

I have been fortunate these past several years to be asked to teach at the Harvard Medical School Program on Education and Practice in Palliative Care Developed by Dr. Susan Block and Dr. J. Andrew Billing. It is the best adult educational experience I know. I have had nothing but pleasure teaching with Dr. Susan Block, a psychiatrist, who as physician and teacher is the best of the best. The course has also given me the opportunity to present in lecture form several of the chapters in this book and to work through ideas with its students who come to the program as already experienced clinicians. In many lectures and presentations throughout the United States and other countries, the concepts that form the basis of this book have been presented and I have learned from comments and criticism. Janet Abrahm, a fine clinician and professor of medicine at Harvard and a leader of the Palliative Care Service at Dana Farber Cancer Institute, has read through and helped straighten out parts of this book. Dr. Mary Brooksbank, an excellent palliative care physician in Adelaide, Australia has also been a great help in this regard. I comment on several occasions in the book about the negative effects of reductionism, but as large as that problem is, the difficulty of developing a more productive approach to holism seems especially stubborn. Richard Zaner, always insightful and especially savvy philosophically, has helped me once again in phenomenologic approaches to this problem. A new colleague, Geoff Riley, Winthrop Professor and Head of the Rural Clinical School of Western Australia, has parallel interests in solving the problems of holism. This emphasizes the fact, commented on by Sir William Osler in *Aequanimitas* a century ago, that any physician can find brethren in any part of the world whose language, methods, and aims are identical.

The problem, late in a long life, of acknowledging the many people who have helped over the years is that there are so many to whom I am grateful but might fail to mention. In the formation of ideas, the discussion of issues, reading and commenting on what I have written, and in general helping in my development as a person, a physician, and an author there are so many who have had an influence. It is like a bouquet of beautiful roses from long ago the pleasure of which never entirely leaves your memory but whose exact source is mystifying. There is one large group to whom I know I owe a special debt—my patients going back more than half a century. I loved practicing medicine because I loved taking care of people. I think that I was put on earth to do that. Their influence on a book such as this is immense. Many specific cases discussed here are about people that I cared for in the past.

I am grateful to Joan Bossert, who was my first editor at Oxford University Press, for her faith that if I wrote what I knew about medicine, sickness, and the human condition, and said it clearly enough (certainly not the case initially), it would be understood. Joan and Oxford have continued to be supportive over the years. Now I am happy to be under the guiding hand of Abby Gross because there is still more to do.

These days, retired from active practice, I most often write while sitting in the second floor of a barn, surrounded by books and looking out into the woods and watching wildlife go by. The computer gives access to the library at McGill University and other vast resources. These idyllic circumstances unfortunately do not put the thoughts into words or the words into a manuscript any faster than in the much more hectic past when I was practicing medicine. An important (and difficult) goal when I am writing is to make ideas logically coherent and transparent (thank you, Joan Bossert). That desire has been pushed into consciousness repeatedly by how beautiful and clear the music of Ludwig van Beethoven is. There is a big difference, of course, between musical ideas, melodic development, and the development of ideas in a book. Nonetheless, I come away from listening to the piano sonatas (and his other music) moved to make clarity happen.

My mother and father, Anne and Hyman (Hy) Goldstein, were supposed to be in the dedication of the book *The Nature of Suffering*, but that somehow got lost. They were wonderful parents. My father was a wise man and insistent on the importance of building ideas from their fundamentals. I would be so unhappy at the length of time my physics homework took when he required that I start always with $F = MA$, but he turned out to be right about that general principle also. My children, Justine and Stephen, are both successful and productive and my granddaughter Julia seems headed in the same direction. Stephen's loving wife, Alexa, talented and creative, is the source of this book's cover. Now the task is to stay alive and well enough to further cultivate and grow the ideas that have been gestating through my life and get them into print. I am blessed, nothing less, by being able to share these ideas and thoughts as well as finished pages with my beloved wife, Patricia Owens, and her acute sensibility. In addition, because she knows more than anyone about the world of disability policy, I have learned and learned from her about the impact of impairments on their lives of persons with disabilities.

I have come to know the answer, finally, to the question, what is it all about? It is all about love. (And luck.)

Prologue

THIS BOOK ABOUT the care of patients is centered on sick persons and their inability to live their chosen lives. Here, the interest of clinicians includes diseases, but goes beyond this to focus on patients' themselves, their purposes and goals, and the impairments of functions from the molecular to the spiritual that interfere with their achievement. Directly obtaining information from patients and knowing about patients are central.

This prologue comes before anything else because it is about appreciating and maintaining in awareness two basic and automatic influences on thought—**meaning** and the role of **science** in clinical medicine—that get in the way of understanding the ideas here as well as the accurate assessment and appreciation of patients.

The assignment of meaning to percepts is a cognitive function that is almost instantaneous, invisible, precise, accurate, fundamental—and *individual*. Look into the woods and you see a bunch of trees. Yes and no. You actually see a bunch of colors and shapes, but the meaning, *trees, leaves, etc.* immediately comes to mind. In the clinic you see an old man with yellow skin and sclera and a big abdomen. In a flash you register a jaundiced old man with ascites (probably). The assignment of meaning even made a probabilistic statement in the same instant. For trees as well as the jaundiced man, although we assign the same label, you and I mean something different because our experiences that shape the labels we assign have been necessarily different. Maybe they are just a tiny bit different or perhaps even greatly dissimilar. Unless we sit together to study the issue (very unlikely) we will not know our differences of meaning.

If meaning was only the assignment of labels with various complexities of content it would merely be an admirable (and very helpful) function of thought. Meaning is much more than that. Because the word itself has many meanings, let me clarify what I am talking about. The identification and labeling of perceptions involve an assigning of meaning. We look out and see an angry appearing bunch of people coming and we say "that is an angry mob." We have assigned a meaning to what we see. This is the most common kind of meaning because it is the *labeling of experience.* The two examples that I gave—the trees and the jaundiced old man—are that kind of meaning. Labeling experience is a judgment in that it could, after all, be wrong. That labeling experience is a judgment also implies that two people may assign different **meanings** to the same experience. They can both be correct because the same experience may have different **meanings** for different persons—sufficiently unlike to require different labeling. Or one can be correct and the other incorrect, yet they will have been exposed to the same external experience. We would expect that in the two examples given people would agree, but that is not necessarily true. You look out and see trees; I see the same scene and say, "Isn't Spring wonderful." I look at the jaundiced old man and I say, "Look at that abdomen. He probably has a belly full of tumor."

The opposite face of the labeling of experience is the one most commonly associated with the idea of meaning, the meaning of words and symbols. The dictionary definition of trees, for example, uses other words to define the symbol. More important in everyday life, however, is the connotation of a word. The connotation of a word is the sum of the properties, attributes, or implications of the word apart from its strict definition. In everyday speech, those attributes of words—their emotional loadings and other **meanings,** as in a house is a home with all the ideas associated with home—are why language can be used to communicate so much. Of course, strictly speaking, the attributes are not of the word, but of what the word symbolizes. Much of the impact of the word on the person comes from its connotation. I have previously shown[2] that the many attributes of meaning include almost every level of the human condition. There is, of course, the cognitive content—the stuff we use when we reason from one idea to the next—as well as images, where the word brings to mind what something looks like. This is why we can label visual experience. And the sound of things allow the labeling of auditory experience—in fact, all the senses, major and minor, that track both the outside world and inside the body from joints to viscera. Perhaps you think I have gone too far, that I included too much as part of meaning. But if not, how will you label the experience of certain foods and beverages and the pleasurable feel of them going down or label the feeling that foretells the onset of diarrhea (the cramps)?

Experiences evoke feelings—emotions—from love and ecstasy to despair and rage and so also do the words that label those feelings—these feelings are part of the meaning. Feelings are not just things that happen in your head, they have effects on the body. Think of the physical feelings that are part of love, sorrow, joy,

---

2. See Chapter 13 in Cassell, E. J. (2004). *The Nature of Suffering.* New York, Oxford University Press.

anger, and amusement. Notice that I said that they are "are part of" the emotions. The emotions *do not cause* the physical reaction; the physical reaction is *part of the meaning*. The smile is a constituent of amusement, the heavy feeling in the chest is a part of sorrow, and scared feelings are an aspect of fear, and so on. We know that the flow of catecholamine, hormones, endorphins, and so on accompany these physical sensations; these are also part of the meaning.

There is ample evidence that some aspects of meaning are hidden from conscious recall or awareness because of their association with painful or even forbidden (usually childhood) memories. As a consequence, the experience that is labeled by a word or phrase may include not only cognitive content, but body sensations, images, sensory information, and emotions whose origins are inaccessible to consciousness. It is also clear that the assignment of meaning, manipulation of the content included in meaning, and thought employing meaning can operate out of awareness. Sometimes it stays behind your eyes, so to speak, and at other times it presents its conclusions to consciousness. However and wherever, meaning is part of the processes of thought.[3]

Another element of the meaning of experiences (and their descriptive vocabulary) is importance. The importance of something is always importance to someone. To say something is more or less important is another way of saying that it has greater or lesser value to that person. In ordinary conversation adjectives and adverbs modify nouns and verbs so as to make their meaning more explicit. They also, however, intensify or diminish the meanings of the words that are modified, as in a beautiful, lovely, nice-looking, ordinary, spavined, or useless horse, or, for a person, elated, happy, even-tempered, angry, sad, or depressed. Someone runs speedily, swiftly, or clumsily. By so modifying they add a dimension of value or importance to the nouns or verbs. Feelings, as we have seen, are an element in meaning. They can be of variable intensity. The word *cancer* can strike terror into the heart of one person, merely frighten another, or arouse interest in someone else (the oncologist). The emotional response to the sensory component of meaning may also be variable, thus introducing a variable element of importance. In general terms, therefore, we can say that there is always an importance or value aspect of meaning, which is contributed by all of its components.[4]

The complexity of meaning, its individuality as well as commonality, and especially its widespread—but almost invisible—effects on the person emphasize why I have put this description in the front of the book. A physician seeing a patient,

---

3. For a more complete description of the phenomenon of meaning, see Cassell, E. J. (2004). *The Nature of Suffering*. New York, Oxford University Press, 2nd ed., Chapter 13.

4. *Ibid.*, p. 239.

hearing about an illness, or examining the patient is having experiences that evoke meanings that may be all right for the task of disease hunting, but might bring up, though out of awareness, impersonal or even negative responses to the patient. These reactions in which the clinician's task is healing and the relationship to the patient is most important might not be helpful (or worse). The solution is straightforward but difficult. From the first contact with the patient, the healer has to be consciously and actively aware of the response the patient is evoking so that it is under the clinician's control. This means thinking about the patient *and* thinking about what you are thinking about the patient. This is not simple. It is particularly difficult because clinical thinking is in part very sophisticated pattern recognition. When a pattern is grasped, the next step is assigning a label, which puts the clinician back into the problem of meanings, which may begin invisibly to guide thought. A patient who has lived much longer than expected and who cries as she talks about it may make the label "Survivor guilt" come to mind. The next thought should be, "What do I actually know about survivor guilt?" The answer should be, very little. This again opens the clinician to careful thought about what the patient is saying.

The place of **science** in clinical medicine must also be clarified before starting out. The promise of science when it entered medicine in force before World War II was that medicine would be based solely on scientific fact. The statistical methods that have been so crucial in the development of new medical knowledge have smoothed out the differences between individuals rather than emphasizing them. Scientific medicine, then, would be freed of the problems raised by individuality, subjectivity, opinion, and the weight of authority. This is the way people speak of evidence-based medicine now. We hear this currently in the often expressed belief that the only evidence that is valuable is objective evidence and only what can be measured truly meets the standard. This means that patients' reports of their illnesses and their symptoms, which can only be subjective, and the reactions of the clinician in response to the patient, which are also necessarily subjective, will always be suspect and can never be granted full citizenship in scientific medicine. The specter of failing the test of scientific adequacy always seems to be present. In this book and the definition of sickness on which it is based, subjective reports from patients about their goals and purposes and the functions required for their achievement can never be scientific, yet they are essential. In fact, the sick-person-in-full who is our major concern (each of whom is distinctively particular) is not and cannot be an object of science. This is neither bad nor good, it simply is. On the other hand, many aspects of sickness, particularly those in body parts, can fit within the canons of science and should be held to such rules.

Persons' meanings, whose cardinal importance I just discussed, *cannot* ever be anything except subjective. What of other dimensions of sickness? What of goals and purposes, or desires and concerns, or affective responses to illness, or pain, dyspnea, or other symptoms? For that matter what of utterances and opinions and anything else about sickness including prognostic statements by physicians? None of these is measurable, but that does not mean the information cannot be accurate. The information can be exact, precise, and replicable when obtained with care. It can also be valid, correct, and point to the truth. Bemoaning the subjective nature of all these things or complaining about the lack of science when it comes to meaning and what patients say is like deploring the fact that patients are human.

The problem is not that so many aspects of clinical medicine cannot be dealt with scientifically. Rather, the romantic but *impossible* idea that science was going to create a clinical medicine from which subjectivity, opinion, and the greater inherent authority of some rather than others would be banished is not now and never was helpful. Look at what did happen, however, in these 70 or so years. The contemporary quality of scientific evidence is one of the great advances of medicine, scientific ideals permeate aspects of medicine in which they are appropriate, and there have been untold achievements in knowledge and technology all of which are a consequence of science. The central fact of the science of medicine is that it achieves its goals because the goals have been made small enough to accomplish with the scientific method. This is called reductionism. What price has medicine and the society paid for the reductionism necessary to makes medicine's leaps forward? We have lost our appreciation of wholes—whole persons, whole societies, and even the country as a whole. This is also true for readers in countries other than the United States. Now the task is to accept the undeniable fact that all persons (patients) are wholes in themselves and each is different from another. Then it is necessary to include the flood of subjective information that is obtained from patients systematically with rigor and discipline so that we meet the ideal laid down by Alvan Feinstein for a science (in the original sense of knowing through study and mastery of knowledge) of patient care where $N = 1$ [Feinstein, A. (1967). *Clinical Judgment*. Baltimore, Williams & Wilkins Co.] We must keep in mind, while doing this, that we are caring for whole persons— kept as wholes in our thoughts because it is their ability to pursue their purposes and achieve their goals that is the North Star that guides our actions.

The Nature of Healing

I

Sickness

PEOPLE GO TO doctors and become patients when they cannot pursue their purposes or goals because of impairments that they believe are in the province of a physician. They also see doctors when they know they are ill, believe sickness[1] looms, fear illness or disability, or wish to prevent sickness or its consequences.

The dominant theory of sickness for the past two centuries is that someone is sick because of disease or injury. As a consequence, the focus of physicians and patients alike has been on the disease or injury—what it is, what it is doing to the patient's body, and what must be done for it. In the past 50 years attention has shifted toward the patient—the sick person—but the perceived cause of the illness, the disease, has continued to be the primary interest of medicine.

It is a consequence of history, the dominant theory of disease, and the development of science that the physical manifestations of sickness are best known. They are also the most thoroughly explained and most prominent in the thoughts of sick persons and their clinicians. Sickness is not restricted to the physical derangements of disease, however, nor does it include only the psychological or social phenomenon that may accompany it. Because humans are of a piece and *whatever happens to or is done to one part affects the whole*, sickness inevitably involves the entire person, every single part. If the source of the disorder is personal, psychological, social, or spiritual it follows that there will *necessarily* be physical manifestations as well. Because pride of place has conventionally been given to the physical domain—the whole array of diagnostic methods is focused here—this will be prominent in the eyes of the clinician (and the patient). That priority, however, may not be true to the patient's experience. Nor are the physical aspects necessarily true to the origin or impact of the sickness. If the disorder has its source or impact elsewhere (e.g., terror), that is where attention should ideally concentrate. It is, therefore, equally important to understand what has happened in the other areas of the patient's life aside from the body because these may provide healers with the opportunity to influence the illness decisively. To go further, sickness makes itself known by interference in functioning. The impairments of

---

1. In this book, the words sickness and illness are synonymous.

functioning that characterize illness involve all aspects of the human condition—physical, personal, psychological, social, and spiritual. Which impairments are actually most intrusive or important in any instance (if we could have something like a bird's eye view) will follow from the nature of the disorder, the particular person, and the context.[2] Knowing this and moving past a solely physical understanding of sickness are important because healing is directed toward maintaining or restoring functioning——any function that is impaired but important. This removes or modifies the impact of the sickness on the person's life and permits the return of the state of well-being that comes from the pursuit of goals and purpose.

Sickness and its manifestations are inextricably bound up with the phenomenon of meaning. Everything that happens to people—events, relationships, every sight and sound, everything that befalls the body—is given meaning. Meaning has cognitive, physical, emotional, and spiritual dimensions. Thus, meanings have an impact on every aspect and dimension of persons. Meaning is the medium, the intervening agency, that unites all aspects of sickness and its impairments with the sick person (Cassell 2004). In other words, people do not do things because of events, objects, circumstances, or relationships; they act because of their meanings.

Sickness is thus personal and individual. It is related to the characteristics of the sick person and is influenced by the particular individual whose sickness it is. It changes patients; it may affect their body, actions, thinking, behaviors, and response to others and to the world around them. These changes may occur without the patient's awareness. The actions of healers must also be personal to be true to the illness. They are directed toward what is making someone sick, the effects of sickness, and sick persons themselves. As a consequence, healers must learn as much about persons as they do about illness itself. This knowledge should equip them with the skills to understand this particular sick person. When someone is seriously ill, that person's being includes the illness.

The Causes of Sickness

From its beginnings the search for the cause of human illness has been concentrated on the body. Afflictions of the human heart—love, grief, melancholy, and such—were believed to be at the root of some sickness, as was sin, but from early on doctors sought the roots of disease in the body. The advances of medicine, particularly in France in the late eighteenth and early nineteenth century, found

---

2. Context refers to the external social, political, technological, religious, and physical environment.

diseases in the body largely as a result of connecting the findings at autopsy with the symptoms of illness borne by sick people.[3] The manifestations of disease in those early years of the modern invention of disease were dramatic. Patients did not come to the attention of doctors or enter hospitals until their afflictions were advanced. Why were psychological or emotional factors not considered in the search for cause? Because they were not yet "invented" and would not be for almost a century. (René Theophile Laennec, on the other hand, the inventor of the stethoscope and prominent among the French physicians who gave birth to modern concepts of disease, thought that the sadness of failed love contributed to tuberculosis.) Why were social factors not considered in the search for cause? They too had not been invented then in the sense in which we use the term.[4] The discovery of the germ theory of disease later in the nineteenth century strengthened the idea that the seat of disease was in the body. The definition of disease that emerged from the nineteenth century included unique causes as well as unique alterations of body structure. In the early decades of the twentieth century the belief that human illness might also be caused by psychological factors—psychosomatic illness—gained increasing influence (Dunbar, Wolfe et al. 1936; Dunbar 1938; Groddeck 1977).

In earlier times it was believed that symptoms were the expression of the mental or physical phenomena of the disease process—things that happened to people who were so afflicted. It was well known that some people were more aware of their symptoms than others, as though they were more attuned to their bodies. Others were considered more stoical, indifferent to the discomforts and pains of their bodies. From this perspective there were bodily disorders giving rise to symptoms—the symptoms were there—but the degree of their recognition varied from one person to another. Sick persons were considered unwitting hosts to the events causing their distress; it was thought that they played little part in the process by which they came to be sick, analogous to the ways persons are affected by weather, although they cannot be said to influence it.

In the 1980s behavioral scientists became interested in illness and symptoms. Study after study demonstrated that determinants other than physical distress also played a part—even a major part—in people's symptoms and in their decisions as to whether they should consider themselves sick, that psychological,

---

3. Giovanni Battiste Morgagni published an extensive atlas of pathologic anatomy in 1761 (French edition 1765). Although well known and universally praised, it did not become the basis of a system of medicine in the same manner as the findings of the French school.

4. Rudolf Virchow, the great German pathologist and the discoverer of the cellular basis of disease, was sent by the Prussian government in 1848 to investigate the outbreak of typhus in Silesia. His report blamed the social conditions of the workers for their disease and ever after he campaigned for bettering the social conditions of workers.

cultural, social, and personal factors, in addition to physical phenomena, determine the person's response to symptoms (Davis and Horobin 1977; Eisenberg and Kleinman 1981; Pennebaker 1982; Rachman 1982; Sanders and Suls 1982; Fitzpatrick, Newman et al. 1984; McHugh and Vallis 1985; Morse and Johnson 1991). All this attention and research led to the general acceptance of the idea that patients are involved in their sicknesses at every level of the human condition. However, as medical science grew increasingly sophisticated and molecular, technology increased in power, and the number of effective medications grew, ideas about psychological and social factors in causation lost power in medicine (if not in the popular mind).

It is interesting that in recent decades even the concept that diseases may be multi-determined has fallen from the front of people's minds. This in the face of examples such as the fact that many people are infected with the tubercle bacillus but do not develop tuberculosis, suggesting that the disease has determinants other than the presence of mycobacterium. Similarly, since the 1950s it was firmly believed that psychogenic factors played a part in the development of duodenal ulcers; it was not until the 1980s when the role of *Helicobacter pylori* in its etiology was established that this belief declined (Marshall and Warren 1984). However, *Helicobacter* is found in many people who do not have duodenal ulcer and duodenal ulcer occasionally occurs in the absence of the bacterium. In times past, this would have prompted a search for other influences in the development of peptic ulcer. Perhaps just as the freely available H_2 blockers have relieved the hyperacidity that is believed to have a role in ulcer disease, the potency of other contemporary pharmacologic agents has diminished interest in the search for additional causes of illness. Belief in the molecular (and genetic) determinants of disease has so firmly captured medicine that acceptance of any other causes seems to have fallen by the wayside

At this time, then, faced with a sick person, physicians understandably search for the cause of the illness in some disturbance of pathophysiology, which should in theory be traceable down to the level of genetic change.[5] It is believed in Western medicine that the discovery of such abnormalities should ultimately lead to effective therapy. The search for other elements of causation, sadly, seems not to be essentially interesting or of real importance to medicine or its practice. Patients who are interested in other perspectives on illness look to systems of treatment such as herbal medicine, the chiropractic, psychological modalities, and other forms of healing that are currently grouped under the title "complementary and alternative

---

5. It is amusing that the name "personalized medicine" has been attached to the search for genetic causes of disease because most people—probably including the scientists who named it—think that their personhood is more than merely their genetic makeup.

medicine." In fact, these alternatives have gotten so much interest from patients that some mainline institutions offer complementary and alternative therapies in addition to standard practice under the umbrella of "integrative" medicine.

Because the dominant theory of sickness in our culture is that when you are sick you have a disease, when someone experiences bodily dysfunction, it is natural that the person should wonder what it means in terms of disease. It is an inevitable part of any experience of impairment that it is given meaning, seen as this or that and interpreted in the light of what a person knows or has experienced. The experience is influenced by ideas about how the body works and the things that happen to it. Cause is intrinsic to meaning; therefore, it is human nature to attribute to every happening—every experience—a cause (Billings 1985). Causes are sought in the world around and the world within. It is also common for people to confuse experience with its cause. For example, people may feel pain in a joint and believe the pain is caused by arthritis, after which they may speak of their arthritis and not the pain. As a part of an experience attributed to sickness a name is generally assigned—some specific malady, ailment, or disease—and with that attribution ideas of cause, seriousness, possible outcomes, or danger come into being. It is the impact of attributions, which vary among persons, that result in seeking medical care.

All of this suggests a confusion of ideas about what is wrong with the person. There are actually three different "entities" that describe what is wrong with the patient:

1. The disorder: A characteristic of the patient that is made up of all of the disturbances or derangements of function in any system of the human condition that actually exist. *The disorder is what patients actually have, independent of any assigned meaning—"a derangement or abnormality of function"* (Dorland 2011). The disorder is the out-there-in-nature actual abnormal thing(s) or morbid process that the patient experiences. The disorder is made up of every aspect of altered function whether the patient or the doctor is aware of it or not. It is the total and complete phenomenon associated with the patient's illness.
2. The sickness: How the patient experiences and thinks about the disorder; the patient's subjective attribution of a name for, a description of, or a belief about the manifestations of the disorder as the patient experiences them. Patients may not actually experience all the impairments of functioning associated with the meaning(s) ascribed by the patient to the sickness. If, however, they are part of the meaning they are part of the sickness.
3. The disease: The name or pathologic process to which the physician or the diagnostic process attributes the patient's disorder. The diagnosis is the

physician's response to the patient's sickness. Helen Chmura Kraemer, an often honored biostatistician writing about diagnostic tests and measurements, said that the diagnosis "represents an attribute, not of the patient, but, rather, of the diagnostician or the diagnostic process in response to the patient. In many cases the diagnosis expresses a physician's subjective belief that the patient has [the disease], a belief that may or may not be warranted. Succinctly stated, a disorder is what the patient has; a diagnosis is what the physician gives him" (Kraemer 1992).

It is as if the disorder is a text about which the patient makes one reading and the physician another. It is common for physicians (and most others) to focus on the diagnosis (the disease) and lose sight of the disorder and the sickness. This is an error. It is true that they are different, but all three are about the patient, and each will have its own unique impact on the patient and contribute to the total effect of the disorder. The healer, therefore, should focus on the whole picture. The picture includes the actual derangements or abnormalities of functioning that the patient experiences and how meaning was assigned to these that led to the person's belief that help was necessary. Also included is the pathophysiology—all the derangements or abnormalities that doctors uncover—the meaning that the doctor assigns to these is the name of the disease that is believed to be the basis for the abnormalities of which the person has become aware.

It would seem that I left something out in describing the three different entities that characterize what is wrong with the patient. The disorder and the disease seem clear enough, but describing the sickness as "the patient's subjective attribution of a name for, a description of, or a belief about the manifestations of the disorder as the patient *experiences* them" hides more than it reveals. The problem is the word experience; experience is a word that stands for very large possible consequences. Generally an experience is an event or condition that someone is consciously affected by; something that happens to a person and the subjective impact of that something. When important things such as sickness happen to people they reverberate throughout the whole person. Things that happen enter the train of thought. The thoughts pull up other thoughts, ideas, emotions, and meanings. Memories are recruited that are related to the ideas stirred up and these ideas, emotions, meanings, and memories immediately begin to shape the response to the experience. The nature of the response depends on the experience, but it involves not only thought and emotion, but also overt actions, and bodily responses all the way down to the molecular and occurring over time.

All of this response changes the experience—not what is happening, but its impact. The more serious the sickness, the more all-encompassing is the response. It is well known that different people experience sickness differently; and behave differently when sick. This means that their response to the happening that is sickness will vary and the fact of that variation is well known. Three questions are raised, however. The first question is why in the face of the fact that some people behave differently most people seem to respond to sickness in a similar fashion. The second is why if all the things that I have described above occur we do not know more about what happens in persons because of the experience of sickness. The third question is what this all means to the healer.

The similarity of most people's responses to sickness reflects the power of dailiness[6] to determine behavior. For all our differences in many things, at least on the surface, we are remarkably similar. It is a mistake to believe that we are equally the same below the surface, in our inmost thoughts, emotions, and ideas. This implies that things may be going on beneath the surface in response to the person's experience of illness that will have an impact on the sickness but will not be known to clinicians unless they go looking. The answer to the second question is related to the fact that we still generally believe that when someone is sick it is because of a disease and physicians are generally more interested in the disease than in the someone. As a result, physicians are not taught about the normal mental life of persons; what they know they have to learn for themselves. This is a pity because the answer to the question of what all this means to healers is that the importance of what I have described as the patient's experience is that *experience can be changed*. Perhaps the disorder cannot be altered, but the experience of the patient is open to alteration by changing the patient's thinking, meaning, and emotions. Transform the experience, the description above suggests, and perhaps the patient can be helped to be better; and that after all, is the point of healing.

Sickness Has an Impact on the Whole Person: Tumor versus Terror

People have good reason to fear sickness. It is an experience that can impact any aspect of a person's life. The knowledge that nothing can happen to a part without far-reaching effects on the whole is not the everyday worldview of most people, so that their experience of *illness*—once they have decided that is what their impairments of functioning mean—will usually be confined to the *body*. Persons

---

6. Dailiness is the world in which we all live our everyday life. Of course everybody's everyday life is different to one degree or another—or so it seems. In terms of the meanings of things, the overriding values, beliefs, what people believe in, and meanings of the society in which we live and that determine our everyday life, which are quite the same in any period of time from months to years. We do not perceive small changes to daily life as they occur, which is why pictures of people from even 20 or so years ago look different; clothing, hairstyles, everyday slang, and language use are different. And so on. Dailiness is, given the possibilities, quite uniform.

deciding that they are sick because of a set of physical symptoms will then see other occurrences as something that happens *because* they are sick; sickness is the primary event and other disturbances such as fear, avoiding other people, or difficulty thinking or experiencing emotion flow from the sickness. That is not the case. The *sickness is all of the disturbances of functioning in toto* in whatever part of the person they occur.

Experienced clinicians are aware that characteristics of patients themselves—past experiences, personality, religiousness, physical fitness, and many others—seem to have an impact on patients' prognoses. If that is the case, are they not also part of the patient? Of course, but not all aspects of the patient have equal weight. Furthermore, some have an impact in the beginning of the case and others later on; some enter the determination of treatment and other help decide what to do when help from others is needed, and so on. When clinicians were primarily focused on the disease, life was simpler; it was only the disease that counted (officially, anyway). We do not have that luxury.

Maintaining a view of the total patient who is sick is more difficult in contemporary medicine because of the division into specialties and subspecialties. Oncologists, gastroenterologists, cardiologists, and the many other specialists deal with a part of the patient. This book is written from the point of view that a healer is responsible for the whole patient. This does not require that the healer know everything about everything because that is impossible. Nor does it suggest that every narrow specialist will be knowledgeable about the role of the healer because that will not happen. Healers should remain responsible for the care of the sick person even though they may obtain the help and advice of others. In the text that follows I use the word clinician to mean someone responsible for the medical care of the patient. In contemporary medicine, not all clinicians are physicians.

An example will help.

Victoria (Tori) Williams was 67 years old when she was found to have metastatic disease in her liver from carcinoma of the ascending colon. The diagnosis was made because she had been complaining of a persistent right upper quadrant ache. Unfortunately, the oncologist and his nurse were unable to start treatment because she was fearful to the point of terror. During frequent unfruitful visits to the oncologist she acted as though she had never heard what he had told her repeatedly about her disease. The nurses were, she thought, cold and impatient with her, but they were unable to make any appointments because she kept changing them. Weeks after the surgery, she had not yet started chemotherapy. The oncologist and his staff assumed that she was afraid of dying. Her internist had cared for her for many years and was surprised by the patient's terror because she had previously seemed to be a straightforward sensible woman with an active sense of humor. She was a working attorney, although no longer very busy. She had two grown daughters and several grandchildren. Although she had been divorced for many years, she had longstanding active close male friendships. She was socially very busy in the small wealthy community in which she had been born and still lived and was clearly someone whom people found attractive. She saw her daughters relatively often but regretted not being closer to them. She had not told her daughters about her cancer and had not seen them in many weeks.

Nobody had asked her what she was afraid of. It took only a few questions to discover that it was not dying that frightened her; her terror was that she would be ostracized and abandoned, even by her daughters, when people discovered her diagnosis. Her mother had died of cancer and she took care of her until her death. She believed that when her mother was sick nobody wanted to come near the sick woman—or her. She also believed that even her mother had hated her because she was sick, even though she cared for her.[7]

In this dramatic instance the fear of social ostracism is part of the diagnosis in this patient with adenocarcinoma of the colon metastatic to the liver. We have to clarify the various meanings that a disease diagnosis has in individual patients. It is generally believed that, for example, the diagnosis of adenocarcinoma of the colon refers to an invasive tumor characterized by an identifiable unique cellular pattern that behaves in a generally specifiable manner but whose behavior is altered by cellular and molecular attributes that may vary from tumor to tumor. The attributes of her tumor are considered important because they (and similar characteristics of other tumors) have an impact on treatment and the predicted outcome. Many clinicians would be worried that Tori Williams's belief that she will be ostracized would reduce her chance or duration of survival. Her terror, then, is a significant aspect of her sickness in the same way that characteristics of the tumor are important. Other physicians might disagree because they are usually taught that the tumor is an objective entity that can be understood apart from the patient in whom it occurs. In contrast, the terror is subjective and cannot be thought of the same way or given the same weight as the tumor. This is a common error. Correcting it will clarify the important distinction between what clinicians have to think about and the focus of others—pathologists, investigators, and maybe even surgeons. For those of us caring for her, the tumor is an

---

7. We will read about this woman again briefly in Chapter 11 on the suffering patient.

objective thing but so also is her terror. For the patient the terror is subjective because she feels it. For us it is a *thing* to think about just like the tumor.[8] Other physicians may focus primarily on the tumor, but the healer's central concern is the patient. Adenocarcinoma of the colon is part of the patient and terror is part of the patient. In terms of what must be done for and what will happen to *this* patient, the consequences of terror are perhaps as great as characteristics of the tumor. That is why I say that her terror is part of the diagnosis. Much more is known about the impact of the tumor than about the impact of terror, but that is only because of the old prejudice that favors tumors over terrors as objective things for study. What is terror? Is it social, psychological, spiritual, or personal (something that arises primarily from the person that she is)? It would seem to be a psychological state induced by a social phenomenon (ostracism), with spiritual meanings (having to do with things that transcend her as an individual), and personal because it arises from her personal history.

I am emphasizing the point that just as sickness is rarely confined to only one part of a person, the various aspects of an individual's self (social, psychological, etc.) are rarely clearly delineated from one another. Still, almost everyone knows that terror is uniformly awful and damaging. That depth of knowledge about terror is inadequate in the sense that an equivalent level of knowledge about adenocarcinoma of the colon would be insufficient. The knowledge base necessary for healing is broader than for medical specialties in general. I have used the dramatic example of Tori Williams to illustrate how important it is to see how wide the impact of the disease on the person is — and how the altered patient in turn alters the sickness and the dynamics of the disease. I could use other less dramatic illustrations and they would make the same point.

To solve Tori Williams's difficulty—to alleviate the terror—it was necessary to resolve the fear of ostracism. Simple reassurance was insufficient (as is often the case). The first step was to convince her to allow her daughters to know what was wrong with her and how serious it was. She permitted that because of her physician's convincing assurance that he would be with her when she told them and that if she wished, he would speak to them first. She wanted to tell them herself, but she wanted the physician to see all three of them together on the same day. The visit took place and it was clear at the time that not only would they not abandon her, they would all be closer. As her illness unfolded, her relationship with the daughters strengthened and became more loving. She also grew much closer to her grandchildren. By the time she died the intensity and constancy of

---

8. In medicine, the definition of objective has almost become synonymous with measurable. That is not what the rest of the world thinks. For most, something is objective if it is an object of thought, feeling, or action. It is something presented to consciousness as opposed to the actions or reactions of consciousness itself. Objective as what is measurable is too restrictive.

the love that she experienced for and from her daughters and grandchildren were the basis for her belief that the cancer was "one of the best things that ever happened to me." The whole process of her care took a lot of time and many visits, but her clinicians thought the outcome was worth the effort.

Let me go further with the category of the social self. The history of American culture—Western culture in general—is the story of the progressive development of individualism. As a consequence we tend to think more about ourselves and our patients as individuals and less about the social dimensions of existence. These two—individual and social—are frequently considered in tension, as though society can diminish our individuality and individuality may be antisocial. To some extent this is true, but a more accurate image is their continuing dynamic equilibrium. In medicine, the recent advances in individuality have expressed themselves in person-centered medicine but with diminished public importance of the doctor–patient relationship. The increasing strength of the general social bond is expressed in our awareness that society needs to provide medical care for all and perhaps a sense that "we're in it together." Politically, this is certainly apparent; as this book is written, a large part of American society seems to have a lesser belief in the social bond and the responsibility of society for its weaker members. In society in general there is a generally diminished belief in authority, particularly the authority of physicians.

What we see when observing social groups large or small does not make clear the extent of the interconnectivity of humans. An analogy to mushrooms and mycelial growth may seem strange, but it is useful. Mushrooms can be seen growing on the ground, one here, another there, several more scattered around. In fact they are not separate but are all connected beneath the surface by a web of mycelia that stretches over large areas and on which they are dependent. Human beings are like that although instead of mycelia they have a number of forms of contact that are essential and keep them not only connected, but nourished and continuing as seemingly independent beings. Various kinds of communities exist—brief or lasting, or large and small (e.g., professional, geographic, demographic, or experiential) in which language, shared meaning, and largely verbal (and now digital media) communication with others are the prime mode of connection, but body language, clothing, manners of walking and moving, and other human characteristics bind people together into a community. Sickness may change—sometimes dramatically—the social connectedness of patients. From ostracism (as in Tori Williams) or shunning, to diminished or attenuated contact, the sick person is in different social relationships than when well. It is not clear what impact this has on patients, but clinicians usually have examples in which the effects have had a negative impact on the patient's outcome. Occasionally the opposite is noted. For example, a woman who was 32 years old had a mastectomy. The house staff empathized with her and were extremely attentive. In retrospect, she thought the mastectomy experience was wonderful. It was the first time in her life that she felt that people cared about her and took care of her.

If little is written about these social phenomena, especially in the context of medicine and healing, how is the clinician to know about them? This occurs by listening carefully to what patients say, asking careful questions, and trying to understand their experience of illness. After a few years, attentive clinicians will begin to understand sick humans and what makes their behavior different from the healthy (about whom they will also have learned a lot). That learning will pay off in better management of the sick and patients who do better. For example, in this instance it was not difficult to relieve Tori Williams's terror and fear of ostracism and with that regain a cooperative patient willing to start her treatment and work with her doctors. This is just one instance of what will be many examples in this book of the value of understanding sickness in all of its personal dimensions by uncovering the basis of patients' fears, apparently aberrant behavior, lack of cooperation, or other problems in caring for them. This example also shows that patients influence the outcome of their disease in many ways and it is not necessary to look for arcane mind-over-body phenomena (although there may be such). Failure to cooperate with medication, diet, exercise, appointment schedules, and many more will just as surely have an influence on outcome. These behaviors are a part of sickness just as was Ms. William's terror.

Sickness Makes Itself Known by Interference in Functioning

Human functioning is the overriding, all-encompassing, ever present activity that involves the entire range of capacities from the cellular to the spiritual. It is inseparable from every aspect of human beings as agents willing and doing, in thought and emotion, in the special senses and sensation in general including pain. Directed functioning is necessary for the achievement of purposes. The workings of the social world, large and small, require individuals to maintain many functions. Values, desires, needs, concerns, and purposes require the ability to function. The abnormal states and pathophysiology that underlie sickness make themselves known by interferences in functioning. This is further evidence that sickness involves the whole person. The primacy of functioning demands healing that is directed at the whole person.

It is difficult for healers to focus on impairments of functioning as the crucial fact of sickness because of the long habit of thinking about diseases and only their physical manifestations as revealed by history, physical examination, laboratory tests, X-rays, special studies, and so forth. Healers, however, must determine therapeutic action in relation to their patients' impaired functioning so these persons can once again pursue their purposes and achieve goals. The knowledge of disease, medical science, and the technology of medicine remain crucial but *not central*. Persons are central, as are knowledge of persons and their functioning and knowledge of what is required to restore them to agency given whatever impairments remain.

Two patients will help clarify the distinctions. Tori Williams is already known to us. Sickness announced itself to her as to so many by pain. Questioning her to get a history of her illness should initially focus not on the disease diagnosis, but on what the pain is doing to her, what it gets in the way of, what she cannot do, and what it means to her. The shift in emphasis in this kind of history and the detail of the questions are all focused on functioning. When the questioning is complete there will emerge a picture of a person: her activities, the life she leads, what matters to her, and her social participation. Against this background, the genesis of her terror will become obvious. Also obvious is that relieving the terror is initially as important as treating the tumor because of its impact on her functioning. It should continue to be throughout her care. Survival will not be the ultimate goal because long-term survival is not possible; a maximally functioning Tori Williams is the point.

Here is the other patient:

Gloria Harrington is an 86-year-old widow who recently returned from an arduous trip to Israel. Prior to the travel she exercised regularly and vigorously, was careful about her diet, and in general took care of herself. Visiting Jerusalem and religious sites awoke long-repressed but profoundly upsetting memories of her escape from the Holocaust at age 16 and the many family deaths that occurred around that time. While in Israel, she became sick with exhaustion, weakness, poor appetite, and some cough. She was happy to get home but surprised to discover she had lost 14 of her 135 pounds. The doctor in her small town discovered that she had a slightly elevated creatinine and was anemic. She was referred to a hematologist and a nephrologist. She had an anemia of chronic disease and three renal cysts. Surgery was planned for the kidney when she refused further intervention. The hematologist considered multiple myeloma but studies were negative. Meanwhile her appetite, weight, and energy gradually returned, her laboratory values improved, and she resumed her previous activities slowly. She was able to stay out of bed for longer intervals and felt stronger and less emotionally upset.

The story of her travel, the emotional trauma, the onset of the illness, its nonspecific nature, and especially the evidence of improvement should make a healer cautious about potentially injurious intervention. Geriatricians know this and they are, as a specialty, more focused on functioning as it is discussed here.

All sick persons share features with these two patients—they all have impairments of functioning in all aspects of their being. In Williams the initial problems were physical; psychological malfunctioning and self-perceived difficulties in social participation followed. In Harrington the initial abnormality of functioning was psychological—brought on by the recovery of profoundly disturbing memories from adolescence. Loss of appetite, weight loss, loss of energy, and weakness appeared almost immediately and laboratory abnormalities were discovered on a first visit to a doctor. It is important to see these cases as wholes rather than as a causal series of events; *functioning is a process, not an event*. The physical manifestations of Harrington's sickness were not *caused* by the psychological trauma; they were part of the sickness of which the terrible memories were the initiating event. Intervention in her physical manifestations would likely cause more damage than good.

Sickness Is Inextricably Bound Up with Meaning

Victoria William's sickness did not start with the growth of her tumor or even with its spread to the liver. Adenocarcinoma of the bowel is her disease, but not her sickness. Her sickness began when she first had pain in her abdomen but it became substantially different—and worse—when she was told the diagnosis and the meaning to her of impending death like that of the mother unfolded, being ostracized, and abandoned. Gloria Harrington's sickness also starts with meaning, the meaning of the events that were recovered from her past during the trip to Jerusalem. It is essential to understand that meaning is not merely a cognitive event, nor even a cognitive and affective process. *All meaning* has physical, emotional, spiritual, and cognitive dimensions. Not just the meaning of events such as the Holocaust, but even the meaning of trivial things such as paper clips or snowflakes (Cassell 2004). Meaning is dynamic; it includes what things come from and what they become; it always predicts a future. If the future implied by the meaning threatens pain, for example, then the diagnosis of cancer will include the forecast of pain. The person will begin to respond to the diagnosis as if pain was already part of the problem. Worry about the pain of cancer may start before the person is aware of the actual presence of the malignancy.

Meanings always include emotional feelings. Feelings are rarely unique to one object or event and so the emotion evoked by the meaning will bring into thought other events or memories in which the same emotion was present. Meanings evoke other meanings—for example, "cancer" may include "doctor" and the meanings associated with "doctor" are recruited. For this reason and others, meanings are connected to one another forming a web of related meanings. Once a meaning is evoked with its many ramifications it is tenacious and rarely easily dismissed, which is why the words "don't worry," or even superficial explanations or reassurance are usually ineffective. The same persistence explains why once a bad thing has been suggested it leaves the mind slowly—if at all. This is aggravated by the tendency for bad news to be stickier than good news. Suggest that something bad might happen—no matter how remote the possibility—and it never seems to leave the mind.

It is important to reiterate the key point that people act on the basis of meanings—the ideas people have about things—not on the things themselves. Whatever we perceive is a something or another thing. Primary qualities with no meanings attached are things of science, not of daily life. The fact that, by and large, in the same circumstances different people perceive the same things only demonstrates how many meanings we share in common. Not all meanings, however, are shared and not in all circumstances. Sickness is one of the situations in which people may sometimes see things differently than others because they do not share the same sickness experiences or changes in functioning. Sickness is also a time when meanings are not necessarily fixed—the patient and her cancer for example. With treatment, reading, discussions with doctors, the internet, and much more the meaning of the cancer may change, and as the meanings change, the person changes. The meaning and the thing are in a back-and-forth relationship. It is only a sign that we are in the infant beginnings of a medicine of persons that the impact of that relationship and its potential for good or bad still elude us.

It is also in sickness that persons may experience what they do not understand or recognize. Acute symptoms such as pain, vomiting, or diarrhea may suddenly appear and the person cannot understand their presence. People try and figure out what is happening. Perhaps they initially try innocuous explanations, but if severity, associated symptoms, or duration deny simple answers they begin to think of more serious reasons for their symptoms. "Thinking of reasons" is another way of saying looking for the meaning of the events. Rather than remain quiet, or dismiss questions, healers should be explaining what is happening. (This will be discussed in other chapters of this book.) The explanations do not have to be correct (for most of the history of medicine our explanations have been wrong) but they should be sincere, based on best judgment, complete but brief, and understandable. The explanations for the symptoms should not contain all the maybes that are occurring to the healer—the healer is not meant to be sharing doubts or fears but instead providing pathophysiologic explanations that allow the patient to make sense of events. If we had some meter that showed the catecholamine cascade, tightening skeletal muscles, constriction of smooth muscles, glandular dysfunctions, and the consequences of these physiologic responses when fear is elicited and unrelieved, healers would pay more attention to the danger of unexplained meanings. Thus, one reason for healers to understand the place of meaning is that meanings can do damage. The other reason is that meanings can be changed. Because they are linked to each other in a web of meanings, because bad news hangs on more stubbornly than good, and because the meanings a person assigns are part of that person, changing the meaning of things is not easy. The first step is to find what the patient thinks is happening and why. Patiently, in jargon-free language, offer alternative explanations that make sense to the patient and should be acceptable.

An example of what changing the meaning can accomplish may be helpful. A young man had an osteogenic sarcoma and following treatment had a total knee replacement. Two years later with no evidence of recurrent tumor, he began to have escalating pain in the leg. He was told that the knee would have to be "revised." Subsequently, pain relief could not be achieved with increasingly large doses of opioids. It turned out that the patient thought that his leg was going to be amputated—that was *his* meaning for "revised." When that misapprehension was cleared up, his pain was controlled on relatively small doses of analgesics. This issue of meaning will arise repeatedly throughout the book.

All Sickness Is Personal

Sickness is always *individual and particular*. Each person's illness is different from that of another even if they share the same pathophysiology or impairment of functioning. There are several reasons for this. Different people assign different meanings to similar events and thus will act differently in response to their occurrence. As they act they change the situation and the illnesses diverge. Genetic makeup, body habitus, diet, exercise, habits (smoking, alcohol, etc.), other diseases, habitual medications, kind of work, intelligence, knowledge and education, illness behaviors and other behaviors, cultural background, social status, income, medical care, attitudes toward physicians, and much more all have an influence on the onset, course, diagnosis, treatment, and outcome of disease. These features of persons impact their functioning from the physiologic functions of their body systems, through their execution of tasks as they go through their lives, to their participation in relationships and life situations (WHO 2001). This impact is found to some degree in acute diseases and accidents, but it is prominent in the vastly more common chronic diseases that afflict contemporary patients. Sickness is personal in other, deeper senses that provide the basis for the importance of the relationship between patient and healer. Earlier I suggested that the basis for the mostly invisible web of social relationships is largely hidden from view. Certainly, cognitive and emotional factors play a part in the way humans relate to each other. In serious illness there are impairments in cognitive function (Cassell 2001) and executive function ("the ability to plan, initiate sequence, monitor, and inhibit complex goal directed behaviors") (Schillerstrom 2005). Emotional responsivity and emotion-based behaviors are also altered by sickness and these changes have an impact on the social presentation of patients. Many of these changes occur out of consciousness and apart from conscious control. Whether visible or not or known to the patient or not they can be an important part of serious illness. Experienced healers act on these changes whether they are aware of them or not, but in order to do so they must be sufficiently connected to the patient. There are good reasons that the healer–patient relationship has been a focus of attention since the beginnings of Western medicine.

Physicians have always known this but the belief that it is medical science that makes the diagnosis and treats disease has concealed the facts. This knowing is part of the tacit knowledge of physicians and has been included in the "art of medicine." It is usually disregarded in medical fashions like the current evidence-based medicine, but if it is disregarded in the course of the clinical care of patients, their care quickly becomes inadequate. If medical care is directed at returning functioning to patients, where functioning includes individual personal activities and participation in society, disregard of the meaning of the impairments of functioning and of the personal nature of sickness would be disregard of the sickness itself.

The personal nature of sickness requires that healers know their patients as persons and relate to them as persons. The aim of care—that patients be able to pursue their purposes and goals—makes medical care personal and requires greater personal involvement by their healers.

This case shows the interrelationship of disease, disorder, and sickness.

> Sonia Martinez is an attractive 54-year-old computer technician and mother of three grown children. She has had pain in the right shoulder of 8 weeks duration. She had a skin and nipple-sparing right mastectomy for stage II (large) in situ ductal breast cancer discovered by routine mammography two years ago. She did not proceed with a planned reconstruction procedure. Three months after surgery she developed severe pain in the subscapular area on the right radiating into the right arm. She could hardly lift her arm or use her right hand and she stopped working, sure she had recurrent disease. Her work-up revealed no tumor and physical therapy to the supraspinatus and infraspinatus stopped the pain. However, she did not return to work and only cared for her older daughter's two young children. She stopped cooking, letting her younger daughter take over the house. Previously socially active and involved in church activities, she now

stayed at home. She stopped praying. She no longer completely removed her clothing in front of her husband or daughters. She stopped having sexual intercourse and became alienated from her husband.

Eight weeks ago she developed deep aching pain in the top of her right shoulder going down onto the chest wall. She went to a local physical therapist but after two weeks of worsening pain she stopped. She withdrew into herself and did not listen to her family's pleas that she see the doctor. Five weeks after the onset of pain she saw the oncologist who assured her that it was muscular. Because her pain became worse she returned and again the oncologist found nothing. X-rays of the shoulder were normal as was amagnetic resonance imaging (MRI) of the shoulder. By this time she was no longer playing with the grandchildren, had stopped bathing and attending to her appearance, and seldom spoke. She was again taken to the physician who found nothing, although he could not get her to use her hand or arm and the shoulder seemed frozen. A bone scan revealed metastatic disease in the humerus and humeral head on the right. A complete work-up revealed no other evidence of disease. A biopsy revealed a tumor with HER2 tumor marker and she was started on Herceptin. The shoulder was radiated. Review of function revealed a severe generalized disorder of function that had started almost immediately after her mastectomy and had gotten worse after the initial episode of pain; she was now almost completely disabled. She was physically capable of most activities except those involving her right shoulder arm complex, but she did almost nothing. She was withdrawn from the community, did not work, and did not perform her roles as wife, mother, and grandmother. She did not perform marital functions. She was profoundly depressed; in fact, she was positive that she was soon to be dead. She could not think and no longer read newspapers or books. She had been convinced after the first episode of pain, even after it was gone, that she would never again be healthy. She slept poorly and always felt exhausted. Even when her pain was severe she steadfastly refused pain medications.

This is a case in which the disorder and sickness are as important as the disease even though the disease is life-threatening. Furthermore, the disorder dysfunction in almost all spheres started early in the course of her disease and should have been looked for after she did not proceed with breast reconstruction. Her sickness, the belief that death from her cancer is inevitable, became progressively worse, intensified by the occurrence of shoulder pain. It would be common to say that she had developed a second disease—depression—and that this was her diagnosis. It is true that depression is the disease diagnosis attached to her psychological dysfunction, but it is secondary to her sickness. The case illustrates the interaction between the three entities—disorder, disease, and sickness—and the importance of treating all three. The disease diagnosis was made and her cancer was treated. She developed some evidence of disorder after her surgery that became much worse after the initial subscapular pain. If looked for she would have been found to be sick—the belief in impending death. This increased her dysfunction to the point at which it was almost global and the sickness became totally disabling. Further disease was diagnosed as recurrent cancer and depression. Although the prognosis for her malignant disease is good, treating her sickness will be very difficult. Unless treatment of the sickness is attempted, her future is bleak, and treating her depression in itself will be inadequate. Functional recovery represents a challenge. The case also exemplifies how suffering develops, because by the time this patient was well into the recurrent shoulder pain she was not merely disordered, sick, and diseased she was suffering.

In malignant disease it is common to attend to the disease and neglect the subsequent disorder and the sickness. As this case illustrates, that is an error. Healing is directed against all three manifestations and requires skills as varied as the highly technical, psychologically insightful, and personally empathic. I do not believe it is an exaggeration to say that acquiring the skills and the knowledge on which they are based will go a long way toward making a good doctor of someone.

Segmentation of cases into discrete and almost separate parts is another barrier to understanding the importance of addressing derangements of function that define the sick person. This case helps illustrate that problem:

> A 72-year-old man with progressive multiple myeloma first diagnosed two years earlier was admitted to the hematopoietic cell transplantation unit of a well-known cancer center. He had tolerated his high-dose chemotherapy reasonably well and achieved a near-complete response. During the 7-day period of the actual transplant he was predictably sick but did well, watched over carefully by the transplant team. His physicians saw him daily (although they did not examine him) and his nursing care was superb. The transplant unit followed the preestablished protocol to the letter responding appropriately to changes in his hematologic status. He did not develop infection. When it became possible, he was strongly urged to walk the corridors a calibrated distance daily.

How would the shift in perspective that I have described be useful with this patient? His abnormalities of function are primarily hematologic and the weakness expected of patients in his situation. He has the disease for which disease theory is unsurpassed. We cannot see how a healer would do anything different than his physicians. This is true only as long as you restrict the view of the case to the period of transplantation. That perspective is common but incomplete. His case starts two years earlier and continues through the transplantation and may go a number more years (if he does not die of something else). Because of the multiple causes of functional derangements from hematopoietic to social that can be expected to interfere with the pursuit of his purposes in life over the course of his sickness, his case is the example *par excellence* of the need for healing.

Caring for patients by slicing the case into segments as though each is separate from the others is common. For patients, a sickness is a whole no matter how it is seen in medicine. Partitioning care is difficult to avoid in the contemporary climate in which there are hospitalists, multiple other specialists, as well as delivery systems and payment methods that encourage division. In a way, seeing patients in this fashion is similar to the problem of language previously cited. The usual language of pathophysiology encountered is the language of events rather than the language of an ongoing (and flowing) process. Here the patient is divided into a series of apparently discontinuous events rather than the continuous process that is life sick or well. Physicians tend to see patients as though each office visit was separate from the one that came before and the ones that follow, like stops on a subway line where the interest is in the stations, not the subway line. We ask the patients how they are and whether anything of note has happened, attentive to the possibility of specific details or complications of the disease. It is an unusual physician who goes back to replay the unfolding story of function and changes in activities that may have occurred prior to this particular visit and then fits current events into that story. Physicians are alert for the symptoms or signs of trouble that occur in the particular disease process afflicting the patient. They are, however, not equally alert for evidence of trouble in the patient's functioning apart from the disease. For this reason it is common to read medical charts that detail patients' visits and medical care for years without any information about their unfolding life and function in the everyday world or how their disease is affecting their life. Actually, patients frequently tell their doctors what is happening in their lives, but except for how it describes a disease-related symptom that information does not get entered into their record. The medical record is generally a collection of information—facts about a disease, not usually about a person or a person's disorder or sickness. Remember, the disease is an interpretation of or an explanation of the disorder, it is not the disorder. In contemporary medicine the amount of information can be considerable, while explicit knowledge or understanding of the patient or the patient's disorder remains almost nonexistent.

Patients may experience functional impairments—and have a disorder—for which no disease is found. Much recent literature attests to the fact that functional impairments in asymptomatic adults such as diminished grip strength, quadriceps strength, walking speed, and balance predict disability many years later in patients with no diagnosed diseases (Rantanen et al. 1999). When disease is found, the functional impairment may not be generally considered as part of the disease. Frailty in patients with congestive heart failure is an example. Here the prognosis of the disease may be determined by the "incidental" finding rather than the disease itself. Furthermore, correction of these problems changes the patient's prognosis even if the disease is not improved (Fiatarone et al. 1994). This is discussed at greater length in the next chapter. Important here is the understanding that disease is by no means the only source of impairments of function that are improved by being found and corrected. Patients recognizing their functional losses may be sick, but patients may also have a disorder with its functional losses without disease or sickness.

This next case illustrates much of this.

Joan Planterof is an 82-year-old woman who developed polio at age 20. She was left with severe impairment in her back and leg muscles. With appropriate rehabilitation and braces, she was able to live her life, have children and a stable marriage, and work outside the home. A dozen years ago, in common with other patients who had polio many years earlier, she began noticing a diminution in her hard-won function. Some physicians dealing with these patients believed that they had developed a postpolio syndrome due to a recrudescence of the virus. There was no solid evidence for this and it seemed more likely that the explanation for increased weakness and impairment was wear and tear on the overburdened residual musculature. Currently the patient is no longer able to walk more than a short distance outside the home and uses a mobility device. In the house with canes, a walker, or helping hands she is able to lead an active social life, work at the computer, and generally meet her activity needs. She is sure she will soon be totally disabled, homebound, and dependent. She bases her prediction on the rapidity with which she believes she is losing mobility and other muscular function. Careful questioning fails to support her belief about rapid and increasingly severe functional loss. There is no question that over the past several years she has been able to do less and has been less active outside the home. The progression appears to be no faster than in previous years. The aging process also seems to be playing a part.

Despite the attempt in the early years after its appearance to attribute postpolio syndrome to a recrudescence of the polio virus and make it part of a disease entity, evidence for this has not been forthcoming. In this patient as in others, there has been new muscle weakness and atrophy in the limbs, excessive muscle fatigue, and diminished physical endurance without evidence of other diseases that could explain the new symptoms. The cause of postpolio syndrome remains unclear, but is likely due to a distal degeneration of enlarged postpoliomyelitis motor units. Contributing factors to postpolio syndrome may be aging (with motor neuron loss), overuse, and disuse. Postpolio syndrome is usually only slowly progressive (Trojan et al. 1994). It is difficult to distinguish her present state from the modest but progressive decline in function and muscle strength experienced by most survivors over many years (Sorenson et al. 2005).

Joan Planterof has a disorder characterized by muscle weakness characteristic of patients who have had polio. It seems to have worsened, since her ability to walk and get around has deteriorated. She considers herself sick as she is no longer able to pursue the social and personal activities that are important to her. However, a considerable part of her current problem is that she has decided that she has postpolio syndrome that is worsening rapidly. As is common in patients who have made a disease attribution, she sees evidence everywhere for the bleak future of rapid decline she predicts for herself. Careful questioning about her past and current function, her activities, and her living situation does not support her dire predictions and her belief that her present circumstance is bad and deteriorating. Further evaluation and treatment by her long-term physical therapist are warranted; occupational therapy evaluation may also be helpful. Patients such as this have won their independence and their full lives by hard work and struggle since their initial polio. The personal characteristics that made all this possible are usually still present to be called back into action to help her at this time. Concentrating primarily on her neuromuscular status will be insufficient. Her functional losses at this time start at the motor unit and extend to her social existence. These are all within the ken of the healer, although others may be asked to join in her care.

In this chapter I have shown how sickness appears when viewed through the lens of altered function and inability to pursue usual activities. This understanding of sickness has many implications for what healers do to evaluate patients and plan their treatment. For healers, our patients are the people who occupy our working hours and much of our thoughts. They were interesting when it was all about disease and the way this book describes their care makes patients even more interesting. I must confess that I *love disease*. I use to practically adore pneumococcal pneumonia—it is difficult, sadly, to find a good case anymore. Students would always laugh when I said that; I think they just did not understand. But disease is nature speaking. Years ago, as I started to become more experienced and as I learned the skills with which to see deeper, I discovered that the real thrill involved the sick persons. They would not have been the way they were without the disease, but it became increasing apparent that the sicknesses—the beasts

I actually confronted—would not have been the way *they* were if the patients were different.

Sickness is nature and human nature irrevocably entwined. You see some manageable diseases so often that they become less interesting. But sick patients never are.

References

Billings, J. A. (1985). *Outpatient Management of Advanced Cancer: Symptom Control, Support, and Hospice-in-the-Home*. Philadelphia, JB Lippincott.

Cassell, E.J., Leon, A.C, Kaufman, S.G. (2001) Preliminary evidence of impaired thinking in sick patients. *Ann Intern Med*.134:1120–1123.

Cassell, E. J. (2004). *The Nature of Suffering and the Goals of Medicine*, 2nd ed. New York, Oxford University Press.

Davis, A., and Horobin, G., Eds. (1977). *Medical Encounters: The Experience of Illness and Treatment*. New York, St. Martin's Press.

Dorland. (2011). *Dorland's Illustrated Medical Dictionary*. Philadelphia, W.B. Saunders Co.

Dunbar, F. H. (1938). *Emotions and Bodily Changes*. New York, Columbia University Press.

Dunbar, F. H., Wolfe, T., et al. (1936). The psychic component of the disease process in cardiac, diabetic, and fracture patients. *American Journal of Psychiatry 93*: 649.

Eisenberg, L., and Kleinman, A. (1981). *The Relevance of Social Science for Medicine*. Boston, Dordrecht.

Fitzpatrick, R., Newman, S., et al., Eds. (1984). *The Experience of Illness*. New York, Tavistock Publications.

Fiatarone, MA et al. (1994). Exercise training and nutritional supplementation for physical frailty in very elderly people. *N Eng J Med* 330:1769–1775.

Groddeck, G. (1977). *The Meaning of Illness*. New York, International Universities Press, Inc. (original publication date 1925).

Kraemer, H. C. (1992). *Evaluating Medical Tests: Objective and Quantitative Guidelines*. Newbury Park, CA, Sage Publications.

Marshall, B. J., and Warren, J. R. (1984). Unidentified curved bacilli in the stomach of patients with gastritis and peptic ulceration. *Lancet 1*(8390): 1311–1315.

McHugh, S., and Vallis, T. M., Eds. (1985). *Illness Behavior: A Multidisciplinary Model*. New York, Plenum.

Morse, J. M., and Johnson, J. L., Eds. (1991). *The Illness Experience: Dimensions of Suffering*. Newbury Park, CA, Sage Publications.

Pennebaker, J. W. (1982). *The Psychology of Physical Symptoms*. New York, Springer-Verlag.

Rachman, S., Ed. (1982). *Contributions to Medical Psychology*. New York, Pergamon.

Rantanen, T et al. (1999) Midlife hand grip strength as a predictor of old age disability. *JAMA.* 281:558–560.

Sanders, G. S., and Suls, J., Eds. (1982). *Social Psychology of Health and Illness.* Hillsdale, NJ, Lawrence Erlbaum Associates.

Schillerstrom, J E, Horton, MS, Royall, DR. (2005). Impact of Medical Illness on Executive Function. *Psychosomatics,* 46:508–516.

Sorenson, EJ, Daube, JR, Windebank (2005). A 15-year follow-up of neuromuscular function in patients with prior poliomyelitis. *Neurology* 64:1070–1072.

Trojan, DA et al. (1994). Predictive factors for post-poliomyelitis syndrome. *Arch Phys Med Rehabil.* 75:770–777.

WHO. (2001) ICF: International Classification of Functioning, Disability, and Health. Geneva, WHO.

2

The Person, Sick or Well

THE DISCUSSIONS OF healing, sickness, function, and almost everything else in this book are centered on the person. It is time for us to understand better what a person is, sick or well. Physicians would not speak about the liver, a gangrenous foot, or an abscess without specifying in detail what they are talking about. The same holds true of persons—especially sick persons. It is not unusual to read discussions about sick patients in bioethics, their rights, and our obligations toward them as though they were just like any other person but they happened to be sick, as though the sickness was like a knapsack they carried around—dispensable. Every clinician knows this is not correct; sickness has an impact on people. On the other hand, because everybody is a person and lives among and has constant contact with other persons, it is certain that everybody has ideas that may well be different about what persons are. So faced with a particular sick person two clinicians, for example, might have very different ideas about them. Clinicians might also have different criteria by which they judge people and are often unaware of the standards or ideas that enter their judgments.

It is difficult to comprehend how little sustained systematic study the topic of person has received in psychology, the natural home for such inquiry. The word self is the term that many in the human sciences use instead of person. But a self is not a person, if for no other reason than (as we shall see) most people have more than one self. Selves do not seem to be understood as having bodies—and certainly not intestinal gas. And nobody would say, "He's a really swell self." Rather, the idea of self represents the depersonalization of the person as it is subjected to the same reductionist mode of study as other objects of science. The person has become the subject and object of contemporary medicine. This chapter is about persons. More specifically, it is about persons in relation to sickness and medicine

Sickness changes people, as we shall see, and there have been calls to abandon the word patient, which is seen by some as demeaning and the result of paternalistic practices. This seems to me to be misguided. In the end we come back to calling them patients because a patient is a person who is in relationship with a doctor or medical care.[1] Something happens when a person comes to see a doctor or, to keep in tune with contemporary medicine, enters into the medical care world because of sickness, its prevention, or concern about it. Being a person who is a patient, then, has to do both with sickness and a relationship with a doctor. The relationship can be with others such as nurse practitioners, physician's assistants, or people who function in many respects like physicians. They occupy a social role associated in the past with physicians and much of the power and the set of socially expected behaviors go with the role. When I use the word clinician I am talking about individuals who take care of patients on the model of doctors. Both clinician and patient in the therapeutic relationship occupy reciprocal roles and a set of socially expected behaviors that go far back in history.

Medicine and physicians have been primarily concerned with what were called diseases ("a morbid physical condition") since the beginnings of Western medicine in Greece *circa* 450 BCE. Doctors diagnosed and treated diseases while the main ethical goals were to do good and avoid harm in the process of treating the morbid conditions. Diseases in the modern sense of the term were first described somewhat more than 200 years ago. For physicians and their primary interests, however, the patient remained subsidiary to the disease. This system of priorities first began to change in the 1950s with the rise of the slogan, "Treat the patient as a person." The phrase literally means treat the patient *as if* the patient were a person. That seems amusing to some, because what else would a patient be if not a person? The patient would be a patient, of course. Until the late 1960s a patient was not a person. Personhood, the subject of considerable philosophical debate, is a confusing topic because it can be the basis for determining moral status, legal status, and social status, and these are not necessarily the same. Some people believe that personhood is conferred at conception, or shortly after, whereas others have more demanding criteria. Conflicting positions on this issue are matters of belief that cannot be settled by argument or empirical evidence, which is why there is no way to end debates about abortion or assisted death. In discussing medical care, however, personhood, like patienthood, is a social status.[2] Even that does

---

1. Here is the first mention of relationships, which are so important to understanding persons. In this chapter I am going to be discussing various aspects and dimensions of persons—relationships, the mental life, and emotions—to mention a few. Because of the complexity of persons it is difficult to divide the text into exclusive categories. I am sorry for any confusion, but please bear with me.

2. Society grants such individuals the full status of persons in our society (or its local variant) and as such they are entitled to all the rights, privileges, responsibilities, and duties of adults in that society. As we all know or quickly discover as we grow up and move around the world, the rules for such things are mostly unwritten, changeable, vary from place to place, and are sensitive to socioeconomic and other disparities. Personhood is the status that contains those things however defined. In the United States since World War II egalitarianism has increased and the change in the status of patients is part of that change.

not end problems of definition. To those raised in the present era it is difficult to conceive of a time, only decades past, when full membership in American society was not extended to all adults. (As minors, children under the age of 18 do not have full adult legal or social status.) Ours is an egalitarian society, so if a group was not treated on the same terms as the majority culture, we would have to say that its members did not enjoy full personhood. By that definition, in the past, full personhood was not accorded to women in public (and to some extent even in the family), ethnic groups such as blacks and Asians, Jews and Catholics, persons with disabilities, and especially important for this discussion, patients. All of this changed after World War II with the civil rights movement, the women's movement, the drive for patients' rights, the American's with Disabilities Act, and the celebration of ethnic differences—all following the late 1950s and increasingly into the late 1960s and following.

What did it mean to be a patient and, as a consequence, not a person? Patients were considered not to have agency that means not to have power or direct influence in the world of medicine into which their illness put them. They were not expected to make decisions about their care (although many did); decisions were made for them by their physicians. Physicians (it was believed) had the knowledge and were not affected by sickness so they could make rational clear-headed judgments (it was thought) in the best interests of their patients (who because of sickness were unable to do these things). Nowadays we call that paternalism. It was a different era then.

Having now achieved full status, patients are persons like the rest of us. As a consequence of the bioethics movement and current legal standards, patients have the moral and legal right to self-determination; they have a right to full information about their condition and any other information necessary for them to make informed decisions about their treatment and their care. If they are considered to have decisional capacity (and whatever their state the prejudice is in favor of considering them able) they have the right to refuse or terminate care and to mostly determine their treatment. We still call them patients, however, because that status causes physicians to think about them differently than non-patients. The difference in status allows physicians to compartmentalize patients so that they can think about them dispassionately; this is necessary for both physicians and patients.

There is something else that complicates the issue of changing the focus of medicine to the person rather than the disease and that is the fact that diseases are considered to be physical things that affect the body. They are not simply physical, but objects of science like the body itself. Why are social determinants not considered a part of diseases? Because when diseases in the modern sense were discovered in the late eighteenth and early nineteenth century, social determinants of individual diseases were not given thought. The same was true of psychological determinants of sickness, which were also not considered. It would be more than another century before the influence of either social or psychological variables on sickness in individuals was an important part of mainstream medical thought.

In the 1930s social and cultural aspects of persons began to be considered important as part of the social medicine movement. That is when the social history became an accepted part of the patient's medical history. Because of their influence on individual sickness and patterns of illness, socioeconomic status, family history, ethnicity, work history, personal habits, and exposure to tobacco, alcohol, and other drugs or toxic substances became an accepted part of the physician's knowledge about the patient.

On the basis of beliefs about the physical nature of diseases a person is believed to be sick because he or she has a disease. If no disease—no affliction of the body—can be found in a sick person, the fact of sickness is put in doubt. Similarly, the causes of sickness (and the diseases that cause them) are to be found in the body, and in contemporary medicine the hunt for cause extends all the way down to the molecular and genetic level.

Increasing attention to the sick person and the movement for person-centered medicine (even though presently focused on relatively superficial aspects of the person) require more consideration in medical education and practice. The definition of sickness used in this book is heavily dependent on a deep understanding of persons because only sick persons can know what purposes and goals are important to them and what functions are impaired and in what manner. It does not matter that the sick person may not spontaneously know these things; it may take careful history taking and verbal interaction with the healer before they are clear enough to guide clinical action.

Before considering the impact of sickness on persons, we have to examine the nature of persons.

To understand sick persons we have to start with a general description of persons. As you read this discussion bring to mind the seriously ill in order to be aware that sickness has an impact on almost all facets of personhood.

A person is an embodied, purposeful, thinking, feeling, emotional, reflective, relational very complex human individual of a certain personality and temperament, existing through time in a narrative sense, whose life in all spheres points both outward and inward and who does things. Each of these terms is a dynamic function, constantly changing, and requiring action on the part of the person to be maintained—although generally the maintenance is habitual and unmediated by thought.

Persons are always in action and never quiescent in the manner of inanimate objects. Persons are complex and can support contradictory thoughts and actions simultaneously, which, however, produce new thoughts and actions. Although basically stable in personality and overall psychological and social being, persons are always changing perceptions, thoughts, and actions in a continuous manner. Thus, for example, a thought or an action evokes new information, which modifies the original thought or action; the modified thought or action now further evokes new information, which further modifies the thoughts and actions, and so on for a time. If these changes are thought of as individually very small in scope and very short in time then a picture emerges of persons as dynamically and interactively responsive to their inner and outer environment.

Almost all of a person's actions—volitional, habitual, instinctual, or automatic—are in response to meanings. The actions and behavior are primarily reactions to ideas and beliefs about things rather than to the things themselves. This should not be surprising since perception itself is an *act of thought,* not merely the registration of sensation.

A human being in all its facets interacts simultaneously outwardly into the world and with others, as well as inwardly in emotions, thoughts, and the body. Generally speaking, despite the multiplicity of actions, behaviors, and responses, all of the parts and actions are consistent and are harmoniously accordant. In contrast, suffering, in which all the parts of a person are affected, variously destroys the coherence, cohesiveness, and consistency of the whole. The person's experience of this is of no longer being in accord and "whole," but rather of "being in pieces," of not being able to "hold themselves together." It is in this sense that suffering threatens or destroys the integrity or intactness of the person.

In this and following sections I am going to start dealing with the vitally important topic of human relationships because persons live at all times in a context of ever present relationships. Some relationships are as close as glue while others are formal. Close or formal, we are all separate beings (except in intense love where two people may feel like one). A variable degree of trust in both the self and others is necessary for the initiation and maintenance of relationships. Persons seek power and in relationships there is always a contextual power differential. That human life is overwhelmingly communal by nature has been partially obscured by the importance of individuality and individualism developed and growing over the past number of centuries in Western European and American societies. On the other hand, in every thought, feeling, and action and in almost every idea about yourself and in every dream, fantasy, and fear, the presence of others is reflected. In normal life, physical appearance, dress, walking and other bodily movements and actions, language, speech, and gesture, everything is tuned to others in everyday life (even facial expression is a social construction). The same is true of ideas and beliefs—even ideas about how the world works. Humanity is not one homogeneous mass of people; it is divided up into cultures, subcultures, and ever smaller groups—but always groups. The same is true and is well known about language groups consisting of shared language and meanings from large ones like national groups to small individual groups such as airline pilots, golfers, or doctors. Where there is common language there are common beliefs and prevalent sentiments. Part of the molding of individuals to each other must necessarily be physiological, although the extent of such conforming is unknown.

People want to be accepted and valued by others and admired by others (and themselves) and they want to be like those that they admire. Vanity to a greater or lesser extent is present in all and is a part of the relationship of persons to others and to themselves. It is not surprising, given all of this, that among the first acts of a person in a new grouping of individuals is the reading of the nature of the congregate and its individual members—at which people can be amazingly fast and surprisingly accurate. By contrast, as they want to know about others—to read them accurately—they have a personal interest in not being transparent. They want to be seen as they would like others to as see them, not necessarily as they are (or believe themselves to be). Robert Burns' line strikes true: "Oh wad some power the giftie gie us, to see oursel's as others see us!"

Imagine, if you can, being a person in an environment in which he or she was absolutely and completely unnoticed. No one turned around or turned aside, no one looked up, no one spoke (or answered), all acted as if we were nonexistent beings no matter what we tried. Rage and impotent despair would soon well up. What if we were lying for hours on our back, covered with a sheet except for our face, on a gurney in an emergency ward or in the hallway outside an operating room. No one looked at us; no one answered a question or responded to our speech. No one recognized our existence except occasionally to bump into the gurney without a word. Or suppose we were in a hospital bed and no one seemed to see us *as us*. Suppose when we were spoken to we felt like the person on the gurney outside the operating room or, worse, the unrecognized person. No one spoke personally to us only coldly or impersonally or used only our first name and perhaps the wrong name at that. Then when things were done to our body even if it was unexplained, uncomfortable, or painful we might be grateful for the attention. If you can bring these painful scenes to mind you will understand the almost animal gratitude such persons would have for personal voices, little pleasantries, answered questions, and a reassuring touch even from total strangers.

As fundamentally true as the communal nature of human life is the fact that ***all persons are different in virtually every feature of their existence**—biological, physical, psychological, and spiritual.* As a result of differences or even conflict between the life someone *must* live in a family, group, or community in order to thrive or survive and that person's individual inborn nature and behaviors, all persons have one or more public, private, and sometimes secret selves that are different and distinct to a greater or lesser degree. Selves also appear in response to relatively enduring circumstances, or even to crises, in life that require a different set of behaviors or traits. There are usually only a few such selves, each emerging in situations similar to those that originally evoked them, usually in childhood. This implies, correctly, I believe, that whatever other selves a person has, if any, all persons have an original self (perhaps authentic would be a better word)—an inborn and lifetime enduring constellation of personality and physical characteristics—whether it ever reveals itself fully or not. These different selves are characterized by consistent, cohesive, and coherent traits and have a disposition to behave in certain relatively distinct ways. They are even sometimes marked by differences in appearance, stance, gait, and speech from other selves of the same person. Even though selves are different one from one another, no one would confuse them with being a different person; executive control remains with the dominant self. (This distinguishes the phenomenon of different selves from the pathologic entity multiple personality disorder.) Despite the occurrence of different selves I do not believe we should question the general belief, supported by good evidence, that personality is enduring over a lifetime.

Although **there may be more than one self**, the empirical self—the self I experience now, that I experienced a few minutes and more time ago, that might emerge in different circumstances and that I expect (without awareness of the expectation) to experience as time unrolls in front of me is what I call me. I will not be aware, usually, that I am behaving like a different self than I was (say) in the doctor's office that I just left. This me has a frame of mind and a bodily state of feelings, both of which I am more or less aware, and is involved in some purposeful activity with some subsidiary goal in mind. For example, I am more or less aware and involved in what I am wearing and largely influenced by my surrounding environment physically as well as cognitively, socially, and morally. The importance of this is that where all around me people are talking from a specific frame of reference—for example, the oncology care environment in which patient survival and response to chemotherapy are the dominant frame of reference—that is the set that will also frame my response to the actions and words of others as well as my own. If I am in such a context I may experience myself in such terms. Doing so may be against my interests as I know them, but I will probably be unaware of the impact of the frame of reference or even, perhaps, of its presence. In some circumstances, we call this peer pressure and recognize its power. It is also true that I can be so influenced by the context I am in (the physical setting, circumstances, other participants) that I find myself reacting in ways that are really inappropriate to my general circumstances. For example, we often employ "standardized patients" in teaching. They have generally been taught what part they are to play as well as the setting and situation—the medical circumstances—of the patient they are portraying. These "patients" are actually healthy. However, when playing their part—e.g., a patient being told bad news—they will react as though they truly are being told bad news. They get frightened, they may start crying, and they may be anxious and experience the physical sensations that go with those responses. They are, in these circumstances, truly existential beings. This is why professional actors can so often *really be* the person they are portraying; they make it happen by acting *as if* they *are* that character. The point is that the self that I experience, the me of a particular circumstance, is not generated solely from within me. Usually I will not know this; I will probably not be aware of the impact of the ideas, meanings, and behaviors of others on my ideas, meanings, and behaviors. Usually (but not always) I will think these things came from within me—that they are me. This is the explanation for the participation of a person in group behaviors that may be difficult to square with the person as you know him or her. Or it even may be difficult for the person to understand. The fact that circumstances may have such an impact is yet another reason for doctors to be so careful about what they do and say when with patients. They may be creating the very thing (e.g., fear) they are trying to alleviate.

How do we know ourselves? Persons know themselves as themselves by their thoughts, the sound of their own voice, and what they look like in the mirror. They know themselves by beliefs they hold about themselves and the world they live in. I am a man, a doctor, a husband, a father, a friend, an American, and a liberal Democrat, and every one of those features of my identity—of me—has an influence on every aspect of my ideas, thoughts, and behaviors. A large library of ideas and behaviors past and present emerges from this identity and may easily be brought to mind. Some are more hidden in memory or are otherwise obscure. But me is not just what you see as you behold me in this minute. These other features just mentioned, which may come from the past or an anticipated future, even though you cannot see them, are also me.

Persons also know themselves to be truly themselves by their aptitudes, skills, and accomplishments and by their ability to make things, do things, and write things. The philosopher Hegel was correct when he said that when people create something—a piece of furniture, a cake, a lecture, or give voice to song—they also create themselves. Persons recreate themselves every day. What they did yesterday or last week is not sufficient; it is what they can do today that is also important—sometimes most important. This means that **persons are partially existential creatures**; it is today that matters much more than most people realize. (This is not to minimize the influence of the past or an expected future.) Children are probably wholly existential; the big picture does not concern them as it does adults. But that allows them to tolerate the distress of today without dragging into it what happened yesterday or what is anticipated for tomorrow.

The empirical self includes an awareness of the body and many of its functions. The functions of the special senses and the somatic senses are generally within the awareness of the individual so that if they develop abnormalities, the functional loss reaches awareness. Muscle strength, walking speed, pulmonary capacity, bowel and bladder function, and others are part of what persons know of themselves. This is true of healthy as well as sick persons, although persons will adapt to slow loss of function and sometimes be unaware of significant impairment until it is pointed out to them. This same adaptiveness allows persons to change the way they carry out tasks or the manner in which certain actions are performed so that they can do things despite major losses in function in almost every system from the cognitive to the hand and other extremities. On the other hand, as impairments in function develop, particularly in systems such as bowel and bladder control, that have an impact on social function, persons may change their habitual behavior to avoid embarrassment. It is not uncommon to find older individuals who will not willingly leave their homes or travel because they do not wish to use a strange toilet.

A central feature of persons is that they are adaptive. This varies in degree among individuals (partially in relation to age). Starting in very young childhood, the necessity is that persons must "get along"—conform to a greater or lesser degree to the demands of their physical, emotional, and social circumstances and to the significant persons who are part of their context. Different selves are a manifestation of that adaptability. Children must accommodate to or attune themselves to the family of their birth (or developing years) even if they are, by nature, different. The original inborn self that may not fit in the family then fades into the background and may not show up except in congenial environments, if at all. A frequent event that underlines this is the common experience of adults who find that they revert to childhood behaviors when they return as adults to the home of their parents.

An important element of the situations in which selves emerge is the behavior of other persons—often those in authority. Are the authority figures kind and loving, domineering and imperious, authoritarian and demanding, or do they show other attributes. Sickness is one of the situations that may bring on the emergence of one of the selves different than that found in everyday life. In part, this is less the impact of the sickness itself than the environment of care, and the behavior of those within it—nurse, doctors, and others—is important. It can be startling to see someone who is an authority figure in her own right but who has had long-term serious disease revert to behaving like a dependent child in a surgeon's office. How the healer deals with the sickness and the sick person can evoke a dependent, anxious, frightened, and uncertain patient. Or the behavior of the healer can bring forth a more original less "sick" self who deals well with serious illness and even dying. It is the phenomenon of different selves that causes people to say of someone in a specific stressful situation (such as sickness) that they would not have recognized him or her. It is important to understand that these different selves, which sometimes manifest themselves as different voices within the person and with different—and sometimes directly opposite—opinions about what behavior is appropriate to a situation, are each acting in the best interest of the patient—as they understand those interests.

This once led to a strange situation with a patient whom I knew well in the waiting area of the hospital admitting office. The patient was coming into the hospital for what she knew was risky but necessary surgery. Agitation and conflict were written all over her face. "Listen, you two," I said loudly and forcefully apparently talking right past her eyes, "Stop fighting right now. It is doing her damage and she cannot afford conflict and argument right now. She really needs this operation and she cannot afford to be so upset. After this is all over you can get back to fighting, for all I care!" Calm and peacefulness spread over her face. I have no idea what the other people in the admitting office thought. The hospitalization went well.

The inner negative voice—sometimes called the inner naysayer—is another similar phenomenon. It may well be present in everyone, but I do not think it is like a different self. It is the voice of caution, of damping down expectations, suggesting that given the positive or negative possibilities, the negative will win out: so be prepared. It seems to serve the purpose of keeping the person from taking chances or going out on a limb. It also prepares the person for a negative result. If we could ask it what purpose it serves it might say that it is the voice of safety, of the safe course of action.

The inner naysayer is not the same as optimistic versus pessimistic personality profiles. The problem for the person is that the naysayer points out evidence in support of its position. For the patient wondering about his heart, the same pattern of activity and breathing thought to be innocuous can be reinterpreted by the naysayer as evidence of cardiac limitation. The presence of this negative voice is a reason why physicians should be careful about their cautionary language.

"Careful now, until your surgery, you should really take it easy."

"Because of the disease in your bones, you should really try not to fall. We don't want a fracture."

"Don't let yourself get tired, it is important to save your energy."

These are typical examples of what physicians say. Unfortunately, their net effect is to frighten the patient into inactivity. Mostly people do not need help getting scared; they can do it all too well on their own. Such statements from the doctor can change a patient from someone who is trying hard to get better and is acting as though healthy into a timid, fearful patient. This phenomenon underlies the fact that when physicians speak to a patient what they say will be given meaning based not only on the physician's language, but on what experience or attitudes or the part of the patient is interpreting the utterance. It is more difficult to change a negative interpretation into a positive one than to prevent the negative perspective in the first place.

More about relationships. Eudora Welty said, "Relationship is a pervading and changing mystery ... brutal or lovely, the mystery waits for people, whatever extreme they run to" (Welty 2002). Nowhere is that mystery more important than in clinical medicine, where relationships abound, waiting to provide information and aids or barriers to the attentive clinician. How odd is this? A person can go to see a physician who is a stranger and within minutes the physician has a finger in the patient's rectum. And the person (now a patient) says "thank you." What made that otherwise inexplicable event possible? We know it was the doctor–patient relationship, but the name does not explain it. What happened was guided by a complex set of rules and entitlements that applied to both patient and physician. We might guess that the doctor learned those rules and entitlements (not called such) during long years of training. For all we know, this exact situation has never happened to the doctor (or the person) before, yet we expect the physician's behavior to be as described. Why did the patient undress, much less bend over to expose the reluctant anus to the finger's penetration, something almost universally abhorrent? Perhaps the patient contains the same rules and entitlements (or their mirror image). This suggests that role behavior (for they were playing the parts required by their respective roles) resides in both of them. It would not take much to show that each of us has a whole library of roles that we follow throughout daily life and that are quite detailed. They make daily life possible. But they also imply that even when we are complete strangers our behaviors are not strange. The degree to which our daily behaviors are rule guided is startling since we generally believe our behaviors are spontaneous and responsive to our chosen purposes. They are spontaneous, but well within our cultural guidelines.

When the light changes on a busy corner of a city street, the crowd surges across. It appears like chaotic movement until you see a moving picture of the scene where you realize that the motion of people is an orderly ballet. In New York City during a busy rush hour, eight lanes of traffic merge quickly and smoothly into two lanes to enter the tunnel under the Hudson River—a wonderful demonstration of the power of unwritten social rules. The rules are different in different cultures—witness Paris traffic—but they are never absent except in catastrophes.

We all know these rules, at least tacitly (or they would not work), which makes it possible for us to take a history from a patient and use daily living as a test of function. Knowledge of the rules of daily living is a crucial part of our *clinical knowledge* from which comes the saying that everything a healer learns is medicine. Knowledge of persons then is knowledge of people in the complicated web of relationships in which life is conducted. In every facet of life the person is functioning in a largely rule-guided manner—as a pedestrian on the street, elevator passenger, moviegoer, TV viewer, restaurant guest, casual acquaintance, classmate, friend, close friend, lover, hospital patient, spouse, parent, child, grandparent, soldier, employer, employee (and every job is different), and so on. Spend some time observing people in their daily lives but stop and dwell on the different situations for sufficient time to see how similarly persons in each situation behave. Of course you can look closely at each individual in these situations to also see how differently each acts and how different each is from the others. This is each person's own perception, as an individual acting individualistically. I have spelled it out in such detail to make clear how much most people, usually without awareness, already know of clinical utility and how much there is to be known. So when the patient says, "I felt so funny and faint that on the corner I fell to the ground but held onto the streetlight. I made it look like I had dropped my coat, but really what happened was that I, like, fainted for a second." We know that nobody does that without a reason because such a display is intensely embarrassing—and some people would rather die than be embarrassed. We take the symptom seriously.

All persons have a capacity to love to a greater or lesser extent. Everybody seems to be captivated by the idea of love. Thousands of books have been written and many thousands of songs, but love remains a mystery. Ella Fitzgerald sings, "What Is This Thing Called Love," but she does not tell us. Even when we are in love or are sure of our loving and being loved, it is wonderment. On the other hand, except for the most unfortunate, love—flowing in both directions—is a fact of infancy and young childhood. From that young experience we get the basic characteristic of the feeling of love; it is a merging of two people. Of course, under even the best of circumstances the merging of loving persons (or at least the feeling of merging) is of relatively short duration, but their belief in their love may be enduring. The feeling of merging, attachment, or connection can occur in the absence of recognition of the feeling of love and it is usually pleasant, but sometimes threatening as it may be accompanied by a frightening awareness of vulnerability.

The *capacity* to merge with others seems to be accompanied by a *desire* to merge that is greater in some people than others, occasionally being extreme. When people are sick, especially very sick, their ability to connect to others—particularly caregivers—is greater than at other times. This seems to me to be the source of the sometimes very strong attachment of the very sick to their clinicians. Here is one of the situations when the fact and the manner of the attachment of sick persons to their caregivers are reminiscent of the attachment of these persons to their mothers in infancy. Psychoanalysts generally believe that these attachments by the sick are similar to the phenomenon of transference in general in which the patients react to the psychiatrists as they reacted to their mother or father. Not surprisingly, persons who care for the sick also seem to have more than the usual ability to form connections. With these strong connections goes the ability to be more aware of the feelings of the other person. In general, the loving attachment seems to be a conduit to the feelings, thoughts, and even the body of the merged persons. We know so little of this because it is so difficult to study and because it shares in the disbelief in such things in dailiness. Nonetheless, a study of tape-recorded verbal communication in families had to be suspended because nobody ever finished a sentence; the family members seemed to be able to know what their spouse or siblings were about to say. The recordings seemed to be evidence of everyday telepathy. However, everyday belief says there is no such thing.

There really is little doubt, judging from ordinary experience, that some degree of knowing what others are thinking is commonplace. It is certainly possible to feel the feelings of another person and that capacity is not uncommon among experienced clinicians, especially psychiatrists and psychotherapists. Learning to do this requires being able to distinguish what you are feeling as coming from the other person rather than arising within you. A student and I were making rounds and we came into the private room of a depressed man with severe end-stage complications from diabetes. The student said, as we left the room, "That is certainly a hopeless case." It was not a "hopeless case," but the student had picked up and could feel the patient's feeling of hopelessness. This is what psychiatrists mean when they tell you to use your feelings.

All persons are sexual to one degree or another. In the past, physicians in general were often not good at taking a sexual history from patients because they were often embarrassed by the subject. When the HIV/AIDS epidemic came along a sexual history became very important and clinicians learned that it was not difficult; you just had to know how. Very sick patients usually lose sexual desire and do not have sexual thoughts until they start to recover. It is one of the functions, like reading the newspaper, lost in serious illness but a good sign of recovery when it returns. On the other hand, patients who are chronically ill, even if dying, may experience sexual thoughts and sexual desire. For that reason, questions about sexuality should be part of taking a history, even in a dying patient. Sexuality is not simply about physical desire and orgasm even in healthy persons; intimacy is an integral part of the human experience and may be vitally important to a patient even in the absence of normal erectile or vaginal function. Because people may be embarrassed to ask for help in these circumstances, clinicians should remain aware of the possibility. Clinicians show their recognition of these and other intimate problems by asking simple and unembarrassed questions.

All persons have a past, present, and a future. The neurobiology of memory is turning out to be complex—more than one kind of memory and more than one perspective on past events. The past, as remembered, is a lived series of events and when they are spontaneously recounted it is in terms of the things that matter personally: events, relationships, primarily, but sometimes circumstances such as the weather. However, persons are capable of great detail if prompted or otherwise helped to remember. Not surprisingly, as they go further into the past, unsupported memory becomes less reliable—particularly for unpleasant or unhappy events or circumstances. Traumatic events in the past, however, may stand out in memory or, if they were sufficiently painful, they may be selectively forgotten. Persons generally see the present and themselves in the present as an unremarkable extension of that past—the past merely unrolling to the present. In questioning people about the past it may be portrayed as a series of discrete events that represent what is important to the questioner or it may be sought and described as a narrative, a story about the person in which events are embedded in the more general story and tied to other events, such as holidays or anniversaries. In doing this, the narrative prepares the person for its extension into the future as the future is continuing to unroll.

The future is always uncertain; it cannot be otherwise. People tend to have enduring ideas about what the future will bring and how they will make it happen. Everybody indulges in hoping and their hopes are part of their construction of the future. The future is the canvas on which the optimists and the pessimists paint different pictures. Not too many decades past, very little was written about hope outside of a theological framework. Currently, it is a growth industry and of concern to medicine where people speak of its importance and of the dangers of losing hope and of hopelessness. Hope seems to be constructed of both desire and expectations. It is a process of thought arising in part from personality and the contributions of others—particularly physicians. For the very sick, maintaining or restoring hope is an important function of physicians. I believe that hope is the expression of the desire to remain the person we are as long as possible. This idea of hope can be supported and made true in the worst circumstances. It allows patients to regain purpose, motivation, expectations, and goals even in the face of death.

A person is more than a spatial object, or something you can see and touch. A person is also a temporal object, like a piece of music that extends through time. As such, **persons have an aesthetic dimension** in which it is possible to judge whether the seeing or knowing about the person through time presents a harmonious aspect to consideration. I have to stop a moment to explain what I mean by saying that persons have an aesthetic dimension (beyond whether they are pretty to look at).[3] This understanding of the aesthetics of a life over time fits nicely with the use of the narrative to describe a person over time. One part of the story of a life or a part of a lived life fits with the preceding and the following parts of the narrative. This is like reading a book in which its parts hang together, or conversely, where its parts are in discord or unbalanced. Or it is like looking at a picture and seeing that one element "goes" nicely in relation to the other parts of the picture or, conversely, it is jarring. There can be no objective measurement of this idea of "fit," but it is not usually idiosyncratic; there will mostly be agreement among observers. Reflect on what you know of the lives of different people and you will see that in some, life is lived in a harmonious fashion whereas in others the parts—lasting days, weeks, months, or years—are discordant, out of balance, or do not fit together. It is almost as if parts of the life were lived by different persons. The belief that the life as lived should be concordant allows us to say that what happened to someone does not seem to fit their life as lived.

Illness may represent an unpleasant shift in the narrative, a disruption of the preceding story, a bump in the pattern—sometimes of major dimensions. Little can be done about this because it is in the impersonal nature of sickness. The process of care, however, can be carried out with active thought given to fitting into the aesthetic balance of the person's story and thereby reducing the ugliness of the illness and its care. I have little doubt that there will be greater acceptance

---

3. Generally, the word aesthetic is considered to have to do with the beautiful and may be dismissed from serious consideration in our context with the phrase, "beauty is in the eye of the beholder." First, that is not true. The aesthetic dimension of things is stable; you do not get filled up and finished with it like, say, an appetite. It is relevant to the thing being considered. The feeling that is the response to the aesthetics of an object is about *that* object—it is evoked by *that* object. It is not idiosyncratic, it is a common feeling shared by others; more than one person will also find the thing pleasing (or ugly). Although it is true that aesthetic appreciation, like the taste for wine, can be educated, we can learn to appreciate the form of something that previously made little impression. The aesthetic feeling evoked by something usually does not change over time. It is probably also true that once educated, aesthetic appreciation does not deteriorate any more than people lose their ability to read words. The aesthetic is classically associated with the beautiful and although it is probably the case that a whole life can be beautiful, generally speaking we will want a word that is true of what is beautiful but is not in itself beauty. I think we can substitute the word harmony to say that the aesthetics of temporal objects deals with harmony in terms of the form of the life or part of a life lived by a person. Harmony, says the OED, is a "Combination or adaptation of parts, elements, or related things, so as to form a consistent and orderly whole; agreement, accord, congruity" (*Oxford English Dictionary*, 2nd ed., electronic). Thus, the aesthetic dimension of a life as lived, of a temporal object like a person over time, is the aesthetics of harmony.

of care that fits a person's life narrative than of treatment given without regard for such balance. This requires that clinicians acquire an aesthetic viewpoint of their patient's life and that requires conscious effort. Most of us have practice in taking an aesthetic perspective because that is what allows us to know about the coherency and accordance of characters in movies or fiction. This is innate because all persons have an aesthetic sense, a sense of order, harmony, and beauty (as they know it). This does not mean, as Benedetto Croce explained almost a hundred years ago, that they can paint or make a poem that will bring tears to your eyes. Those are the artistic expression of an aesthetic impulse, not the aesthetic thought itself that comes prior to its expression.

Persons act on the basis of the meanings of things, as I pointed out repeatedly, not on things themselves. Many of our meanings acquired in the past are often beyond recall so that we may not know why we act the way we do. This will be discussed in greater detail below.

Persons are thinking all the time. Your mind is almost certainly and almost constantly occupied by a stream of thought varying from moment to moment as your focus, interests, occupations, and preoccupations shift. Content of the stream of thought, which is mostly like silent speech, also arises from memory as the information from the world evokes ideas and associations that have been stored in both distant and recent memory. These thoughts are *personal*. Mine are mine and yours are yours, and as far as we know or have thus far discovered (despite clues to the contrary), yours do not become mine, nor mine yours. My mental life is not a machine—it is personal—so that as all this activity goes on material is provided for further thought. That thought influences the focus of the subsequent mental activity, which may change what is of interest and further change the direction of thought, and so on. As I have suggested, the train of thought is also a commentary on your activities so that as you are occupied—for example, while exercising—the train of thought will offer a meaning to explain something that happens, such as some difficulty lifting a weight. Sometimes the focus of thought becomes captured by one subject—for example, a fear or love so that all these aspects of thought are in the service of what can become monomania. Actually, what is provided by all this mental activity are ideas in the form of words and their meanings, and it is the meaning that we dwell on when thoughts become concrete. So the love-struck person interprets everything in terms of the love and its object. The fearful person sees only further support for fear.

The same thing can happen when sickness occupies the person. Then all the facts generated by the various modalities of thought are interpreted in light of the sickness. For example, shortness of breath previously interpreted as an indication that the stairs are steep now becomes evidence suggesting heart disease, and fatigue become evidence of escalating weakness; gradually, a case is built that further supports the idea that the person is sick. It matters little (in the short run) whether the individual *actually is* sick, what matters is the evidence arising from the inevitable flow of thought. If the person *is* sick the evidence can be ignored or denied (in the short run) and then the facts that a disinterested observer might find proof of sickness can be disregarded.

If you train yourself (which may take months), all this thought, which is like lip reading a book in your head, will disappear from consciousness and your mind will seem to be quiet.[4] The thought does not stop; it simply disappears from view. There is much evidence that problem solving may also proceed out of consciousness, so that suddenly the solution to a problem that has been of interest will appear in consciousness. Anxiety or worry will bring back the conscious train of thought even in those best able to reduce its intrusiveness.

Also continuous and in part feeding the stream of thought and fed by it is the **unending assessment of its world by the mind**—mostly out of awareness. Sensation—the major senses and the minor—are joined to perception, and to mood, which are also constant. Each of these is a different mode of appraisal and together or separately they provide constant intelligence about the world—both inner and outer—that may or may not become part of the flow of thought. The output of the mind's continuous activity of appraisal is a flow of meaning. I do not know whether the flow of meanings that arises from all this activity is primary or whether meaning is assigned only when attention is focused on the assessment—prior to which there is only the flow of sensation. The moment something comes to mind whether a gurgle in the lower intestines or something we perceive visually, it comes as or with meaning. You may feel the gurgle, but the assignment of meaning (unless it is an ordinary gurgle in which case that is the meaning) is almost instantaneous. Meaning has an impact in almost every dimension of the person from the molecular to the spiritual. That is to say that meanings are not merely ideas in a dictionary but are also body sensations, feelings, and spiritual expressions. Meanings are both social—the meanings of words and many other things—held in common in social groups, and also personal—supported by a private glossary. That is to say that the word peach is the common meaning applied to the round, downy skinned, highly flavored, pulpy sweet fruit with a roughly furrowed stone of the *Amygdalus persica* tree that comes in different varieties, and that makes sense in the phrase, "She's a peach." But peach also has personal

---

4. It is not difficult. While walking on the street many years ago I would push thoughts from my mind while staying focused on a fire hydrant about a block away. When thoughts returned in 15 or 20 seconds, I would push them out of mind again. When thoughts came back I pushed them away again. I kept that up for a few minutes every day. Gradually thoughts stayed away for longer and longer periods. After about 3 months I discovered that my mind was quiet. From time to time, but rarely, I have to practice again.

meanings to you—taste, the feel in your mouth, etc.—which may be different than to me, and so on. Similarly, you know that certain clinical facts mean that the patient has pneumonia, an infection of the alveoli, but pneumonia has some special meaning to you because of the cases you have seen.

Persons understand their world primarily, it is generally believed, by two kinds of thought, reasoning and emotiveness. Reasoning is based on facts (or what are believed to be facts) and is able to follow ideas to their ends, take them apart, combine them to form new ideas, and generally go beyond the information given. Truth is thought to come from correct reasoning, but logical thought produces truth only if the ideas on which it is based are true. It is not uncommon to hear reason denigrated as irrational if the ideas on which it operates are about subjects such as mysticism, religion, or those that are considered irrational because they are not based on facts. This is not correct. Reason is a method of thinking that can be used to understand and follow any set of ideas whatever their subject. If the ideas are faulty—internally incoherent, or such as cannot be logically connected with other ideas—then the reasoning will be faulty, but its subject will not have been irrational. The mind also employs intuition to know things from objects or events apparently without the intermediary of reasoning. Intuition has a bad name because it appears to be magical knowing. It does not deserve its negative reputation because it is often correct and it is open to confirmation by other, more logical processes. Much is being written now about intuition, so that it is gaining the reputation it should have for its speed, accuracy, and acuteness. Experienced physicians acquire dependable intuitions about sickness and patients but know to check their accuracy before they make crucial decisions. Conventional ideas about intelligence are now also being challenged. The combination of new technologies for investigating the brain and increased attention by psychologists to the operations of thought are leading to a reappraisal of older concepts about thinking. Ideas are probably generally in the form of words, but artistic, sculptural, or musical ideas (which may be called motifs) are in the form of the art in which they occur—sketches or musical notes, for example.

Emotive thought also operates on content from perception and memory producing specific instantaneous evaluations that are felt as emotions. Emotions are feelings, affections such as pain, pleasure, love, amusement, amazement, anger, sadness, dejection, or joy. Much less is known about emotion and emotiveness than about ideas and reasoning because from antiquity emotions (which were called the passions) were thought to contaminate thinking and interfere with reasoning. Sometimes, even in contemporary writing about cognition, emotions are dismissed as lesser than or contaminations of thought. They are not; they are a central and essential element of the mental life. Certainly the emotions that sick patients have about their sickness are as much a part of the sickness as are the symptoms. Sometimes, when patients tell us about something we ask, "How do you feel about that?" That is really a request for their emotional reactions, but the phrase has come to mean both thinking and feeling. There is certainly no thinking about sickness that is free of emotion if you are the one who is sick.

Emotion is as primitive as the existence of animals. Motion, the sine qua non of animality from paramecium to man, requires at least two feelings (however they are characterized in other organisms) to explain why the animal goes here rather than there: desire and fear. Just as there is a flow of thought in which ideas seem to be central, there is a stream of thought in which mood is the content. The list of human emotions is well over a hundred in number. Emotion may be experienced as transitory, where one brief experience of emotion may follow another as the emotional reactions to thoughts and experiences. One emotion may last for hours. For example, if someone steps on your foot you might have a flash of anger that in its onset occurred too rapidly for you to identify a thought that preceded it or of which it is a component. The anger is the primary result of the emotive response to being stepped on; no thought beyond that is a necessary response. After being stepped on, perhaps it happens that the anger lasts all day long and you are still talking about the incident hours later. Then we think that the original flash of anger, a response to being stepped on, has been coopted by another, more lasting idea, the idea that you are (say) commonly abused by other people. As noted above, emotion can take over the stream of thought, and you might be thinking about abuses and the things that have happened that reinforce that idea for hours to come.

Finally, an emotion such as anger may become the dominant mood. Then we might not say that the person is angry but that the person is an angry person. The dominant mood could as well be joy, despair, sadness, or love. It is not difficult to see how persons who are sick may be taken over by a dominant mood as suggested above. It seems to be the case, however, that sick persons' emotiveness is blunted, just as their cognition is impaired and executive control is diminished. Although there is experimental evidence of the impairments of cognition and executive control, the evidence for the impact of sickness on emotiveness is anecdotal. Patients report, for example, that although they know they should feel love for a family member visiting and they say the words, they do not feel the emotion.

People generally seem to consider themselves unitary beings. If you ask them if they are more than one "I" they usually don't think so. "Who are you?" "I am me." "Are you more than one me?" "No, just me." "Okay, if you are just one, who writes your dreams?" "I do." "So, why don't you understand them?" "I don't know."

It appears to be the case, however, that below the surface of consciousness there are other entities that in certain circumstances (for example, in hypnotic states) can openly voice opinions that are not necessarily the same as those expressed in ordinary everyday conscious states. This has been known for at least 150 years, demonstrated in the famous French neurology clinics of Jean Martin Charcot and Pierre Janet. The importance of highlighting ordinary everyday consciousness is that in the everyday setting, persons are strongly influenced by rules of everyday life. The rules are not merely precepts that apply in daily society, but also by beliefs, acceptable behaviors, and conventional modes of dress, patterns of speech, and other guidelines for living in the world of dailiness. These **other, inner, voices** are not ruled by dailiness. On the other hand, they are usually shy and hesitant. They are easily dismissed and they are overridden by doubt and/or anxiety. (You have an unspoken idea or something inside you voices an idea and your daily self denies the idea or the thought and you go along with the dailiness.) Doubt is the everyday mind's pronouncement that these inner thoughts and ideas should certainly not be heeded and are perhaps nonsense. Actually, however, when doubt arises it means the inner voice is suggesting something that would be denied as impossible in the everyday world. By the time you have finished reading this section, many of you may experience this aspect of doubt for yourselves. On the other hand, it is a common experience for people to decide to do something chancy and hear an inner voice saying no! I do not think this voice is the same as the naysayer, but I really do not know. More than one inner voice, however, is not uncommon. These voices rarely speak in full sentences or paragraphs, instead they are cryptic. This inner world and the inner voices come to consciousness and are not what is usually meant by reference to the unconscious, or the Freudian unconscious (see below).

There is little systematic knowledge of these phenomena because they have not been studied. Clinicians who use hypnosis may be familiar with them because they make themselves known from time to time. They are described in prescientific books of psychology such as William James' famous text from the end of the nineteenth century. After that period, psychology was eager to be "scientific" like physics so that only phenomena that could be studied in the laboratory were considered acceptable. That may be why we know so little about the will (also discussed at length by James)—the action of willing or choosing to do something—even though the word is used all the time and the thing is part of common experience. And that is why we know so much about aspects of behaviorism, now discredited, that lent itself to laboratory study in part because behaviorists dismissed the idea that there was a mind. (Fine for pigeons, not so good for understanding humans.) I raise these issues because these phenomena are important to clinicians taking care of the sick. In the emotionally stressful world of the sick, other voices—if they make themselves known—are important to heed because they may be expressing authentic and even helpful aspects of the sick person. Conversely, conflicts otherwise unapparent may manifest themselves in this fashion.

The other reason to point up this phenomenon is to make it clear that the inner life of the mind is more likely to be complex than simplistic. If these inner voices are persistent and not so affected by dailiness, they are more likely to be voicing authentic inner opinions that quite reliably represent the person's "true" thoughts. They deserve attention.

It is also evident that the experiences of sick persons, their reactions to their illnesses and care, and their behaviors may in part be responses to events, feelings, and experiences of early or later childhood that are lost to conscious recall. Some offer their past experiences back to early childhood as an explanation for what they think now, or what is happening now. Memory of the past is quite clear for some and variable for others. The accuracy of these early memories may, however, be open to question. It has been said that unhappy or negative memories are shorter lived than happy ones, but traumatic memories back to childhood may be selectively remembered in considerable detail. There can be no doubt, on the other hand, that there can be selective rejection of information from awareness. This means that although past memories may be quite clear, what reaches awareness may not be the whole memory. It is also the case that the past can be rewritten to serve the purposes of the present.

Person can **dissociate** themselves partly or completely from events, experiences, memories, or bodily sensations. Dissociation is different from simply not remembering or forgetting, where a memory can be jogged back into existence by a clue or someone actively helping. **Dissociation** is an active process that selectively bans the dissociated material from consciousness or conscious recall. The memory of traumatic events may be hidden by dissociation, as may dreams, unpleasant conversations, or things people have been told that they did not want to know. Clinicians learn this when they give a patient bad news and shortly the person behaves as if, or even says that they have never been told. People are also able to dissociate themselves from the experience of physical pain as though they cannot feel the sensation. One self may dissociate itself from other selves as though they or their behaviors did not exist. In its most extreme form this is found in the pathologic entity of multiple personality disorder. However, dissociation in everyday life is a normal protective mechanism of the mental life.

It cannot be disputed that events in childhood back to infancy may form the basis for an adult pattern of behavior and that these events, even though they have this impact, may not come to awareness. Events in this sense are not restricted to brute facts but are also the person's emotional response to recall of early relationship with parents, siblings, caretakers, or others. These memories may not be merely forgotten in the sense that with a little jog from another person or a subsidiary recollection they will again come to mind, but may be actively repressed. Even actively repressed early memories or their emotional content—memories that are not and cannot be brought to consciousness—may have an impact on behaviors, including speech and bodily responses to stimuli (including sexual stimuli), which seem to come out of the blue or seem completely unexplainable. (This is what is usually meant by reference to the unconscious or "the Freudian Unconscious.") All of this may be particularly important in illness in which things happen, for example, complete dependency, which are in themselves reminiscent of childhood. When that happens, the door may be opened for the effect of childhood events and their emotional content, remembered, dissociated (incomprehensible and therefore shoved aside before even being remembered), or repressed (remembered but hidden from consciousness), to have an impact on the course of the illness. For example a woman was severely abused in early childhood, all the details of which she had forgotten beyond recall. She required a mastectomy and during her hospitalization bitterly fought—even biting—the doctors and nurses. This continued until, with help, the memory of the abuse was resurrected and she realized she was reacting to the mastectomy as she had to the earlier abuse. Another young woman (with assistance) remembered how she had been uncharacteristically pampered during a serious illness in young childhood. When serious sickness occurred in adulthood a demanding unrealistic (and uncharacteristic) desire for special treatment intruded into (and obstructed) her care and continued until the childhood events were uncovered. The intrusion of events and emotions from even the remote past into current illnesses is common.

Fear is an emotion as universal in animals as is desire. Generally fear is described as an aversive emotional response to a specific stimulus—persons know what, in the situation, they are afraid of. Sometimes the fear is momentary, perhaps in response to an impending needle-stick. Other times the fear is a pervasive emotion that invades everything—the fear of the hospital, for example. Fear of surgery is another example. Sometimes fears seem to be less specific such as about dying, unfamiliar situations, loss of control, or dependency. When that is the case it is often possible to track down what the patient is afraid of about hospitals or surgery, such as loss of control or dependency. If the exact details of the fear can be elicited it can often be laid to rest. It has become common, especially in specialized surgical settings such as cardiac surgery units, for the patient to be told in exquisite detail about what is going to happen. Well-prepared patients are less afraid, have less postoperative pain and other complications, and generally do better.

Fear is an emotion that can have bad consequences from the molecular to the spiritual level and the effort to resolve it is worth whatever times it takes. The most effective antidote to fear is information; however, to be useful, the information should be focused around the particular concerns of the patient, at a level the patient can understand. Too much information, or undesired information, can lead to more fear. Information is transmitted in the context of a therapeutic relationship and for the information to be accepted and to do its job the relationship must be trusting. Trust is not blind trust. That is why it is so important to be truthful and honest. If you say something will not hurt, that has to be true. It is much better to be honest about a painful procedure explaining in detail what you (or others) will do about the pain. Simple reassurances are rarely helpful and the words "Don't worry" are probably as useless as anything else that is useless in medicine.

People in strange and threatening settings such as, for some, hospitals or other medical situations, can be expected to be frightened. If they deny fear or fear is unapparent, it should be actively, but gently, sought; once understood, specific reassurance can be offered. Sometimes people have fears that seem understandable, but on further questioning the fear is not what it first appeared to be. The fear of death is very common, but often—perhaps most often—the real fears are not death but the fear of separation from others or from the group, or fear about the dying process. The importance of finding the true source of fear is that effective amelioration becomes possible.

Anxiety, like fear, is a normal response to certain kinds of threatening situations. Anxiety is, however, more complex than fear. It is important to distinguish the kind of anxiety that can occur in anybody as distinct from the psychological anxiety disorders such as generalized anxiety disorder, posttraumatic stress disorder, panic disorder, and social anxiety disorder. Whereas fear has an identifiable object, anxiety is vaguer and it is less easy to identify what is at the root of the anxiety. For example, persons may have distinct fears of death or of dying but they may also become anxious when they believe death threatens. When anxiety is present it is experienced as variable feelings of dread, tenseness or jumpiness, restlessness, and irritability. There may be an anticipation of bad things or a general apprehension. Restlessness, trouble concentrating, anticipating the worst, and waiting for the ax to drop are characteristic, as are nightmares and bad dreams. The anxious person's world threatens, but what is actually the source of the threat is not obvious. Physical manifestations are almost universal and can, at times, be quite extreme, such as heart palpitations, shortness of breath, and chest pains that may seem like a heart attack to the person, Fatigue, nausea, stomach aches, headaches, diarrhea, or other physical symptoms may make the anxious person sure that he or she is physically ill. Physiological manifestations are common, such as elevated blood pressure, increased heart rate, sweating, pallor, and dilated pupils. However, anxiety can make itself known by mild feelings of unease, irritability, and apprehension without obvious physical symptoms or go all the way to a full blown panic attack in which the person is sure that death is imminent.

Why all of this is present may be, often is, completely unknown to the person. Sometimes in a patient who is sick, threatened by serious possible consequences, or in a threatening (to the person) environment, the source seems obvious to an observer. But it is not obvious to the patient even as the cause is pursued. There are a number of reasons for the obscurity of the causes of anxiety in individuals. One is that the source is so scary to the person that it is repressed. That is, the person not only does not know the source of the anxiety, but cannot know because the idea is intolerable.

Here is a simple but illustrative example. A mother is anxious each time her child is on a trip—not fearful, anxious—but she does not know why. Everybody says that it is obvious that she is afraid something is going to happen to the child; she agrees that it must be that, but the anxiety persists. A physician asks whether she is afraid of a car crash in which the child will be killed. As she listens to the words, she is almost overwhelmed with palpable horror and all its physiologic accompaniments at the unacceptable thought, but finally and reluctantly agrees. The anxiety stops and now she is sometimes fearful when the child is away, but does her best to ensure that the child will travel safely and not be involved in an accident. The idea of a car crash was repressed because the thought of her child's death was impossible to bear. It may have been that a trusting relationship with the physician provided the safety that allowed her to confront and accept the fear, and not be so overwhelmed by it. That is an uncomplicated example, but many are not so simple. Even in this instance conflict is present between the apparent need to repress the danger to the child and the need to protect the child from the danger. Different voices, more than one self and myriad memories, some conscious, some forgotten, and some repressed, suggest a mental life below awareness that might be marked by more than one meaning and more than one emotion for the same events and relationships. Where there is more than one meaning, conflicting memories for the same event, and more than one way of responding to similar stimuli there is the potential for conflict. Where action to mitigate the threat is thought to be necessary but conflict exists whose nature is not available to consciousness anxiety follows. This is because persons cannot defend against a threat whose real nature is not known to them. The source of the conflict that is always present in anxiety may be as simple as in the instance noted above in which a fear is repressed, but situations in which the fear is evoked continue to occur.

The conflict may be more complex. For example, a person may seem to be very anxious in response to the threat of death, but it is really not death itself, but conflict about it that is evocative. A very sick person has come to terms with his impending death, but his wife is extremely upset at the idea of his death and he feels that his acceptance of death is a betrayal of his intense love and loyalty.

He is afraid of what will happen to his wife when he dies, but he is tired of fighting an illness when the inevitability of death seems to offer surcease. As a consequence of this conflict of which he is unaware he becomes anxious and his anxiety is wrongly interpreted by observers as evidence of his fear of death. There was a period in which great credence was given to something called "death anxiety," which was believed to be nearly universal. More careful recent research has failed to support the concept and its universality.

Anxiety is sometimes aroused in situations in which different selves in the same person come into conflict. An older woman found herself anxious in situations in which she kept asking herself, "which me am I supposed to be, the compliant, hard working, but resentful me, or the hardworking but interested and creative me?" Without being aware of such a conflict, anxiety is evoked that resolves when the conflict is made clear. Anxiety is extremely common, especially in the medical setting. There are effective antianxiety drugs, but they do not expose, clarify, or generate understanding of the conflict that always exists. It may not require sophisticated psychotherapy to uncover and resolve the conflict. That is preferable to medication but anything that works is better than allowing someone to endure chronic anxiety.

Some clinicians, particularly psychiatrists and psychotherapists, would use the word ambivalence to describe what I have noted as the conflict always found in anxiety. in serious illness, for example, wanting to live but not wanting to suffer, wanting to be cared for but feeling guilty about it, the person is of two minds, ambivalent and conflicted, and these feelings are commonly sources of anxiety. There may be partial awareness of these feelings of conflict, or even perhaps clarity about them, but the tension that creates the anxiety is not being able to have both desired outcomes even when they are known.

Every person has a body. This person's body is different from any other person's body because it is this person's body. Person and body are integrated and in constant interplay. They can never be separated except in death or (maybe) in special states of unconsciousness. The body can do some things and not others. People become habituated to their body's enormous range of abilities and incapacities. They generally know exactly what every part can do (of which they are or can be conscious). These capacities become accepted as a part of their person ("me"). This physical view of persons has been partly hidden by the cultural importance of and attention to individuality developed over the past number of centuries in Western European and American societies. Individuals presented as though they were not also bodies. It sometimes seems as though the body has its own intentions that are not the known intentions of the person. People also generally know when parts are not working properly and these impairments of function—if they come on quickly enough to be noticed and are lasting and important enough—become symptoms as they are joined to other incapacities. On the other hand, if impairments of function emerge only slowly, are easily accommodated, or are deemed unimportant, even quite impressive impairments will soon be adapted to or dismissed. This is why careful questioning is such an important part of the evaluation of a patient. This is particularly so because of the importance of impairments of social, psychological, and spiritual function that are part of the understanding of sickness at the heart of this book.

The truth about bodies is that things happen to them—they can be injured or get sick. Bodies sometimes bleed, smell bad, make embarrassing sounds, have embarrassing functions, make inopportune demands, create strong desires, sometimes look bad, and become old and slow, and sometimes ugly. (These facts are frequently denied or hidden in everyday life.) Persons grow up with profound ignorance about how the body works even though most people learn about it in school. Certain functions such as the bowels and urinary system are even less well known because of everyday stigmata about them. Sexual organs are also poorly understood although, in general, sex education has advanced greatly in recent years. Modesty keeps people from really knowing about their sexual function. It is interesting that when people look at pictures of nude persons they see very little. It is as though they hide sexually meaningful things from their own view.

Unfortunately, clinicians can have considerable knowledge about diverse diseases but be quite ignorant about the body's everyday functions. This limits their ability to ask questions in the hunt for impairments of patients' functions. It also reduces their ability to make things function better.

Everybody dies.

Conclusions

Almost nothing about persons that I have discussed in this chapter is unaffected by sickness. What sickness does is impair function, but the functions that it limits are found in every sphere of a person's life as it is lived. The knowledge of this provides an opportunity to understand sickness, but it also creates therapeutic opportunities that are far greater than are usually considered. The fundamental understanding that must not be forgotten diagnostically or therapeutically is that whatever happens to one part of a person happens to the entire person. Also, however, whatever is done for one part of a person has an impact on the whole person.

Reference

Welty, E. (*2002*). *On Writing.* New York, Modern Library.

3
Functioning

HUMAN FUNCTIONING IS the overriding, all encompassing activity that includes the entire range from the cellular to the spiritual. It is never entirely still or absent except in death. To think of sickness in terms of functioning implies consideration of living beings with minds, emotions, thoughts, intentions, choice, and agency—the ability to act—in other words, persons.[1] The reason for the complexity is that we cannot really know about functioning humans without knowing the state of the body and bodily functions and what the person is doing and for what reasons or intentions. Moreover, it is necessary to consider the person's context or environment because what persons do (even with the same purposes)—what functions they perform—may be different in different settings and may even be altered by possible hindrances or enhancements found in some environments. Functioning is personal because the execution of similar tasks or activities by different persons will involve a different employment of functions and different intentions.

The basic aim of healers must be the enabling or return of function so that patients may pursue or achieve their purposes and goals. This requires an understanding of sickness (discussed in Chapter 1) that is different than contemporary concepts of disease. Sometimes functional limitations are overcome by employing all the therapeutic power and technology medicine commands. Cure most often returns the functions lost or impaired by disease. On occasion, functional impairment is overcome by the rehabilitation of (say) the function of the shoulder–hand complex or similar actions, and on occasion by the intervention of other persons with special knowledge acting on various aspects of function or body structures. On occasion, interventions are necessary to facilitate interpersonal functioning in the workplace, community, home, or in the bedroom. In all these places the spoken language plays an essential part, so this aspect of functioning

---

1. There are some patients we treat who do not fulfill these criteria—they are either young children, patients on life support, or are in an altered state of consciousness. Without getting into the complexities that these states entail, for the purposes of their treatment we consider such patients to be members of the class of persons and to act as if they have (had or will have) intentions and choices.

or its impairment may require special attention. Speech is an activity requiring a number of functions (mental and physical) and body structures; impairments of speech may require intervention in the activity at any of the many functions involved. At times the patient is enabled to pursue his or her purposes and goals only by the healer's personal interaction with the patient that changes the patient's intentions or motivations. Achieving these aims requires an understanding of function that is different than merely something acting in the manner for which it was created or achieving its purpose. Here functioning is an "umbrella term covering body functions and structures, activities, and participation" (IOM 2007; WHO 2001).

It is imperative that I lay out a set of definitions because terms such as function, functional impairment, impediment, handicap, or disability are used differently in different sources and in the present as compared to the past. The need for a common understanding of these words is necessitated by the International Classification of Function (ICF)—a classification cannot succeed unless everyone understands its terms in the same manner. We are primarily speaking about the healing of the sick, and sickness is our umbrella term for all the impairments of function the patient experiences as a consequence of some pathophysiology in any of the body's systems that has befallen the sick person or that may on occasion occur for reasons apart from pathophysiology. The ICF uses the term "health condition" as its umbrella term to cover disease, disorder, injury, or trauma. Pregnancy, aging, stress, congenital anomaly, and genetic predisposition are also, for the ICF, health conditions. Clinicians do not heal aging or pregnancy, although they may act on functions that are affected by those health conditions. In a sense classifications and classifying are like map-making; they have a removed view of the terrain. Healing cannot be accomplished from a distant view, so we concentrate on the individual sick person. Nonetheless, definitions are essential; no field can move forward in the absence of a widely accepted terminology.

The definitions in this paragraph are taken from the ICF (pp. 10, 211–214) (WHO 2001). *Body function* is the physiologic functions of body systems including psychological functions. *Function* is both the noun and the verb of the action. Things function when they perform, move from one state to another, or exercise their properties. Functions can be a simple act of urination (although even urination, especially in males, is not simple and has several subsidiary functions), or contraction of one muscle group. It may be a complex set of operations that requires multiple subsidiary functions for its enactment, such as the movement of all of the limbs of the body in the activity of running. Persons must function in order to engage in activities or (say) participate in the running of a household (or the care of patients). All of these—*function, activity, and participation*—lie along the path leading to an individual's *achievement of goals or the realization of purposes*.

There may be *limitations of activities* or *restrictions in the person's participation* in life's necessary activities or performances. Finding the source of these limitations is a diagnostic act of clinicians and remediating them is part of therapeutic activity. Two words pose problems. The first is *impairment*. In contemporary medicine (and daily life in the disability community), the word impairment—the inability or limitation of an individual to perform activities or participate in life situations—is a broader term than the term used by the ICF to denote problems in body function or structure. I am going to continue to use the word impairment in its broader everyday contemporary sense as meaning both limitations in function (e.g., weakness of a limb) and activity (e.g., limitation in mobility in daily life). This usage is shared by the Institute of Medicine (IOM 2007). I will not be surprised if this wider usage is eventually accepted by the ICF. *Disability* is used by the ICF as an umbrella term for impairments, activity limitations, and participation restrictions. However, in the United States and, importantly, in The Americans with Disabilities Act (ADA) of 1990, the definition of disability has three parts. Persons are disabled if (1) they have a mental or physical impairment (2) that substantially limits (3) one or more major life activities (such as caring for oneself, performing manual tasks, seeing, hearing, speaking, learning, and working). Members of the disability community have made it clear that a limitation or impairment becomes a disability because of something in the social world that makes it impossible for the person to participate often because society does not offer accommodation for the impairment. The wheelchair-bound person cannot get around because the sidewalk curbs get in the way, a bus cannot be boarded, or the doorways are too narrow. The limitation(s) that requires the wheelchair is part of the person; the failure of other persons, workplaces, or society to accommodate the person is what makes the limitation a disability.

These various parts of the definitions underlying what is involved in functioning are the framework around which the structure of healing is built. They allow healers to see what they are trying to accomplish. They provide a more formal perspective on some of the things clinician-healers have been doing to make their patients better for a long time.

The function of something in human systems is always part of or somewhere within an increasingly complex hierarchy. One function is part of the next level, which goes on to the next level and so on. For example, the functioning of the contractile motor unit leads in the aggregate to the contraction of a muscle fiber, which leads in the aggregate to the contraction of the muscle, which leads in the aggregate (and is joined to other functions involved in the motion of the part) to the motion of the part (e.g., a limb), which leads in the aggregate (when joined to other functions) to the functioning of a part of the body, which, when joined to the functioning of other parts, leads to an activity of a person (e.g., walking), which when joined to other functions produces further activities and participation in life and leads to the accomplishment of purposes or goals. Goals and purposes are often parts of future goals and purposes and so on. Writing something requires, among many other things, an action of the intellect and psychological functions as well as the functioning of the shoulder–hand complex. If the text is to be spoken publicly that requires voice and speech functions. The speech may be part of an activity that leads to recognition of skills (or not) that may lead to social participation and a place in a community, and so on.

Considering that example it is obviously artificial to ignore functionings that extend past the boundaries of the body. On the other hand, all functioning up to and including the pursuit of purposes and goals involves the body. When persons are sick because they believe that they are unable to accomplish their purposes, that failure can usually be traced from the activity that is part of the pursuit of purpose all the way down to a physiologic or pathophysiologic mechanism.

Because of the complex nature of human functioning, functional loss is rarely all or none. Early in the course of many afflictions, nervous or muscular, characterized by muscle weakness, for example, all the motor units involved in the muscle's action are rarely impaired (compromised). Because of this, muscle strength will be only partially reduced. Again, because of the number of functional units initially involved in many diseases, compensatory mechanisms come into play that reduce the mechanical impact of the initial impairments (losses) of functioning. The degree to which functional impairment is apparent in a particular patient is related not only to the basic pathophysiology, but also to the context. Let us consider muscular dysfunction: it is more prominent in settings in which muscular activity plays a large part—for example, in athletes or in laborers—and is less prominent among the sedentary. If other symptoms are present, such as fever, functional impairment may be more intrusive. Functional limitation is also related to the individual patient; some persons are exquisitely aware of functional impairment whereas others do not notice impairment until it is advanced. The impact of functional impairment also depends on the importance of the functioning to its related purposes in the person's life—think of a lecturer who develops speech impediments. Because persons react not only to the change of physiologic functioning but to the meaning and fears for the future, small losses of functioning in a physiologic sense may cause profound losses of functioning in the activities and participation of the that person. As there are inhibitors of functioning, there are enhancements. The person's assessment of success or failure in the accomplishment of an activity may have an impact on the functions involved in its pursuit. We sometimes say of someone that he pulled back too soon. Or, conversely, that seeing the goal in sight, she doubled her efforts.

An organism must be alive and intact to function. It may be difficult to conceive, but medical science and the science taught to physicians are not based primarily on knowledge of intact living organisms—animals or persons; it could as well be about static non-living systems. Physicians, of all people, do not have to be reminded that patients are alive; physicians *know* that patients die—the fact is with them all the time. Despite that, their knowledge of medical science is generally not about living organisms. Anatomy as it has been taught right up to the present era is the anatomy of the dead. Only recently have textbooks of anatomy appeared that stress functioning—and these are mostly about muscles and joints. In fact, the earliest descriptions of losses in human function were about muscles and muscular disorders, not about the person's losses. When diseases were first described in the modern era they were known by their structural abnormalities—first those that could be seen at autopsy and later those visible microscopically. In contemporary medicine, pathophysiology has gained a strong foothold, starting about a hundred years ago, and with it have come ideas of function and the importance of thinking in those terms. The descriptions of the pathophysiology of rheumatoid arthritis that follows portray descriptions of events, not processes. The molecular and genetic descriptions of disease that mark medicine in the twenty-first century are similarly lifeless. The brilliance of contemporary medical science lies in its dissection of diseases down to their molecular fundamentals, but an exquisite understanding of disease cannot explain why the patient is sick any more than the formula H_2O can tell you why water is wet. It seems probable that if the language and structure in which medical science explained disease reflected patients' experiences of their disease, there would be no disparity between our understanding of medical science and of the person who is sick. Although historically understandable, both language and structure of explanation now stand in the way.

Rheumatoid arthritis is an excellent example of a chronic disease with the potential for inducing sickness and having a major impact on the well-being of the patient. Notice the language used in the following description of its pathogenesis. It is not my intention to describe rheumatoid arthritis or its pathogenesis fully, but only to remind clinicians of the kind of language that makes up the contemporary literature of pathogenesis:

> Rheumatoid arthritis is a systemic disease characterized by a chronic inflammatory reaction in the synovium of joints and is associated with degeneration of cartilage and erosion of juxtaarticular bone. Molecular investigations of rheumatoid arthritis have markedly changed the understanding of the pathogenesis, although the etiology remains unknown (Weyand et al. 1997). Many proinflammatory cytokines including TNF-α, chemokines, and growth factors are expressed in diseased joints. At the

present time the inflammatory (and destructive) joint response is believed to be the result of chemokines (which attract monocytes in chronic inflammation) and their receptors (Charo et al. 2006). As yet there have not been therapeutic agents arising from these findings. Earlier studies showing the role of tumor necrosis factor (TNF) in the pathogenesis resulted in an effective disease-modifying therapeutic approach using anti-TNF agents (Feldmann et al. 2001). These therapeutic agents increase the risk of serious infection and malignancy (Bongartz et al. 2006).

The language of pathophysiology is similar. This example is from the *Merck Manual*, 18th edition.

Prominent immunologic abnormalities include immune complexes produced by synovial lining cells and in inflamed blood vessels. Plasma cells produce antibodies [e.g., rheumatoid factor (RF)] that contribute to these complexes. Macrophages also migrate to diseased synovium in early disease; increased macrophage-derived lining cells are prominent along with vessel inflammation. Lymphocytes that infiltrate the synovial tissue are primarily $CD4^+$ T cells. Macrophages and lymphocytes produce proinflammatory cytokines and chemokines [e.g., tumor necrosis factors (TNF), granulocyte-macrophage colony-stimulating factor, various interleukins (IL), interferon-γ] in the synovium. Release of inflammatory mediators probably contributes to the systemic and joint manifestations of rheumatoid arthritis (RA).

In chronically affected joints, the normally thin, delicate synovium thickens and develops many villous folds. The synovial lining cells produce various materials, including collagenase and stromelysin, which contribute to cartilage destruction, and IL-1 and TNF-α, which stimulate cartilage destruction, osteoclast-mediated bone absorption, synovial inflammation, and prostaglandins (which potentiate inflammation). Fibrin deposition, fibrosis, and necrosis are also present. Through these inflammatory mediators, hyperplastic synovial tissue (pannus) erodes cartilage, subchondral bone, articular capsule, and ligaments. Polymorphonuclear neutrophils (PMNs) often predominate in the synovial fluid (Beers et al. 2006).

In contrast, here is an example from a description of the physiology of joints. This example, describing the role of the supraspinatus muscle, is abstracted from a description of the shoulder joint.

Supraspinatus initiates the process of abduction at the shoulder joint, being more important than later when the deltoid takes over.... It braces the head of the humerus firmly against the glenoid fossa to prevent an upward shearing of the humeral head (this has been likened to a "foot on the ladder" where a small force applied at one end will produce a rotary rather than a shearing action) while at the same time producing abduction. After the initial 20° of abduction, when the stronger deltoid takes over, supraspinatus acts to brace the humeral head (Palastanga et al. 1989).

Here is another description from a different source.

The supraspinatus is still an effective stabilizer of the glenohumeral joint, however, because its rotary component is proportionally larger than that of the other rotary cuff muscles. The more superior location of the supraspinatus results in an action line that lies farther from the glenohumeral joint axis than the action lines of the cuff muscles. The supraspinatus has a large enough moment arm that it is capable of independently producing a full or nearly full range of glenohumeral joint abduction while simultaneously stabilizing the joint (Levangie et al. 2005).

The latter two are *functional* descriptions of the muscle (and the joint); they tell us what the muscle *does* in the function of the abduction of the shoulder. From these accounts it is a short step to a description of the various motions of the shoulder joint and the shoulder in activities as varied as bed-making, arm-swing during walking, dressing, and eating. The structure of the explanation and the type of language would be similar even if we progressed to activities of the whole arm and then to the role that the pathology of the joint or its musculature plays in various impairments of the function of the shoulder and arm. We would also look for functional explanations of the compensatory mechanisms that allow these impairments to be overcome.

We would next come to the functional impairment imposed on the patient by the problem that rheumatoid arthritis causes in the physiology of the shoulder and its impact on the function of the arm. Step by step we would assess how the change in function of a muscle impinged on the personal, social, emotional, and spiritual function of the whole person. It is not difficult to see how, on the bases of these descriptions, we can move from the function of parts to the function of the whole and then to how these affect the accomplishment of goals. There is no barrier at the interface of body and person, or person and social being, to impede the healer's overall understanding of why the person needs healing and where to intervene. There is no separation between the scientific and personal knowledge of function. The conceptual voyage from function to goal or purpose and from functional impairment to interference in the person's purposes and goals is logically coherent; it makes sense. It is but another short step to establishing desired outcomes of healing.

This relatively smooth, incremental transition from the description of the physiology of the joint to its relation to the purposes and goals of the person is crucial to understanding what makes diseased people sick and how to make them better. If other features of rheumatoid arthritis—fever, malaise, and weakness—were added to this description, the reason for sickness would be obvious. Then we could tell the story, step by step, of how the patient progresses from malfunction of the joint and other constitutional elements of rheumatoid arthritis to malfunction of the whole person. We could also infer the wide range of interventions (in addition to specific treatment of the arthritis) that a healer might make to restore the person's ability to pursue his or her goals despite progression of the disease.

Before these excursions into pathogenesis, pathophysiology, and physiology I suggested that if the language and structure of the description of a disease in medical science were similar in form to the patient's experience of its associated dysfunctions and impairments, there would be no disjunction between the understanding of a person with sickness and the perspective of medical science. Traditionally we do not discuss a sick person in terms of pathophysiology. This poses an important problem: The language used to describe the pathogenesis and pathophysiology of the joints in rheumatoid arthritis cannot be used to relate experiences of affected persons; it is a language of static isolated events. *This happens and that happens and that happens and because of that the other thing happens. And these other things are also found.* As a consequence the cartilage degenerates and the bone erodes. Lacking is the next step—"Then what happens? When? How fast?"—the description of persons and their experiences, usually in narrative form.[2] Required is a history, a tale, or a story of something that occurs over time.

Pathophysiology also describes a process; it tells a story of events occurring over time to produce something that is a consequence of the events. However, the language of contemporary pathophysiology does not use the narrative form. If there is to be a narrative, *you* must construct it; *you* must create the story, because *as given* it is not there. Narratives require an element of time passing *sequentially* that is not part of the pathophysiologic description. Unlike the language of pathogenesis and pathophysiology, however, the language of physiology and

---

2. Narrative. Concepts and uses of narrative have become prominent in contemporary medicine, primarily in relation to describing patients' illnesses and understanding their relationships to their illnesses. Interest in narrative in medicine goes back many decades, but its recent importance is largely the work of Rita Charon. [Charon, R. (2007). *Narrative Medicine: Honoring the Stories of Illness*. New York, Oxford University Press.]

descriptions of impairments of motion is a language of function. The description above of how a joint moves creates a story with a beginning and stages along the way that lead to an outcome: abduction; the arm moves away from the body (and the humeral head does not dislocate in the process). We can go from that part of the story to the function of the whole arm, the whole body, and the whole person, continuing in the language of narrative, of related things happening over time, each leading to the next related thing. Like the current language of pathophysiology, telling the story of the unfolding of events over time is also the language of process.

I have a friend, an oncologist, who says that when she was a student and learning things in "science-speak" she was poor at memorizing things like the pathogenesis and pathophysiology of a disease, so she would construct a narrative about what happened that she could then remember as a story. Here is an example of a story that reveals the pathophysiology of rheumatoid arthritis:

> Rheumatoid arthritis is a chronic inflammatory disease of the joints of unknown etiology. Over weeks and months the inflammatory process produces an effusion in the joint and the normally thin, smooth synovium of the joints becomes thickened and distorted by the inflammatory process. The altered synovium with its abnormal cellular structure and many active chemical soluble substances (cytokines) destroys cartilage and ultimately, after many more months, distorts the bony architecture of the joint. Without its normal cartilage, the rheumatoid joint now consists of bone against bone, a structure that impairs joint motion and produces pain. The joint inflammation also leads to tightening of the periarticular musculature and encompassing fascia that further decreases joint motion, causes more pain, and ultimately results in wasting of these muscles. In its acute flares, rheumatoid arthritis is also associated with fever and other systemic manifestations, so the patient is sick, in pain, and has diminished joint function.

Rheumatoid arthritis provides a good example of the importance of narrative—of constructing a story—because there is a natural progression from the events in pathogenesis and pathophysiology to the story of impaired joint function, then impaired limb function, and then the impaired person's function. *The narrative is complete when the healer becomes the storyteller because it is his or her job to change the outcome of the story.* Narrative is important in healing because it allows the healer to construct a story that goes all the way from basic impairments of function to the well-being of the patient—the healer's goal—in a coherent manner that helps direct the healer's actions.

The story of rheumatoid arthritis is not only about a joint, multiple joints, or even an entire body. A story about just a body might read as follows: "I have a 15-year-old female body with a swollen, warm, and reddened left elbow, right knee, and fingers of both hands. These joint changes began about 3 months ago and were accompanied by constitutional symptoms...." None of us would start a clinical narrative that way. Instead, we might say, "I have a 15-year-old female high-school student with a swollen, warm, and reddened left elbow, right knee, and fingers of both hands. These joint changes began about 3 months ago and were accompanied by constitutional symptoms. She has been unable to go to school for the past 2 months because of..." This is usually the end of the story as told, but is it really the end? It is merely a convention that clinician healers' narratives end at this point, a convention based on the body–person dichotomy and the language problem within science that keeps us from focusing on the narrative nature of function—the *true* narrative. Our traditional static language perpetuates the dichotomy.

A real narrative would continue with more about the functional impact of the disease on her life. We would read that its greatest influences were both the omnipresence of her mother, who had become her primary caregiver, and her sense, from the rheumatologist's description of the disease, that she was now "different." She has begun to withdraw from her previous activities and lose contact with her friends. She may feel the typical teenage rebellion against her parents, but expressing it is difficult because of her reliance on her mother. Her feeling of difference may produce an increasing sense of isolation that has variously severe negative consequences for teenagers. For clinicians, for healers, her story—every patient's story—provides the details that will form the basis for decisions about what must be done for the story to end well. We can certainly help her deal with her feelings of being different. By having her meet others of her age with rheumatoid arthritis, we can increase her activities and participation. When her socialization, which is such an important human function, is enhanced, her devastating feeling of isolation will decrease. We can treat her as the individual she is rather than merely her mother's child, and we can work with her and her mother together to help her find a safe environment in which to express her individuality. Clearly, treatment of the arthritis is necessary, but that alone will not be sufficient to help this now socially impaired teenage girl to well-being.

Rehabilitation physicians and therapists have been oriented to function mostly in terms of parts of the body, and their field is only 60 years old. In the past 40 years the heart has been studied clinically—functionally—using treadmills, stress-echocardiography, cardiac catheterization, and other techniques, which had evolved along with cardiac surgery. It is safe to say that thinking in terms of functioning is not yet a habit with most clinicians. Conceiving of living organisms is thinking not only of the functioning of parts, but the activity of the whole, because except in rare pathologic instances parts do not act autonomously more than momentarily. It is also, more fundamentally, thinking in terms of change—change over time and change through space.

To think of the activity of the whole organism presupposes intentions that presuppose mind. When human beings are involved in activities or participating in life situations we call it behavior, and human behavior always presupposes intention. Approaching sickness then from the point of view of functioning inevitably ends in the same two places, being alive—living a life—and mind (Jonas 1966). Where there are intentions, there is choice. Emotions are as fundamental as function—we choose because of desire or fear or any of the other multitude of emotions that exist on the spectrum from desire to fear. Bodies in isolation do not exhibit choice, intentions, or mind—these are characteristic of persons. Thinking of sickness (or health) in these terms always involves the person, in a context, an environment—the world in which persons live and to which they react.

Functioning is *always a process* that takes place over time. That means that it is necessary for healers to see and think about patients, sickness, and relationships as being in motion and always changing. Wherever we are in the course of the functioning from the first moment to the last, there is a *was* and a *will be*—a past and a future. This is true of sickness itself. Of course they cannot actually be seen in any moment because they are either past or future. The past and the future are important to healers so healers have to get used to hypothesizing about the relevant past and future and in time they will be quite good at it. This means that in looking at failures of functioning it is not sufficient to look at an incident or an aspect of the impaired functioning; it is as important to know what happened before and what happened or is expected to happen after. What is the impairment doing to the person living her life, why is it important or not important (in terms of daily living), and what is the person's response to it? We often say, "What is the story of what is happening?" These questions are part of the *initial evaluation* of a functional impairment but they remain relevant. Thinking this way requires a habit of mind, something that must be consciously practiced. Within a number of months (it takes at least that long even actively practicing) it will be habit.

The concern with functioning has been growing since World War II, perhaps in part because of the need at that time and in subsequent wars to return wounded servicemen to an active role in their world. It is not yet a habit widespread in medicine, however, and the fact that it is intertwined with thinking about persons suggests that it is a difficult habit to acquire. Why should that be? Thinking medically about whole persons seems to present difficulties. The basic concepts of suffering, which were published in 1982 (Cassel 1982), took a long time to find general acceptance. The central idea in thinking about or caring for suffering is that bodies do not suffer; persons do. Suffering is an affliction of persons. Clinicians with extensive experience in the care of the dying do not seem to have trouble with the idea. Others would agree with the concept but fail to treat suffering per se, focusing instead on pain or other symptoms. Why were many experienced clinicians able to think in terms of the person but not others, and why were inexperienced clinicians generally unable to think and act in terms of persons? That there are these questions leads to the expectation that dealing with functioning will also encounter difficulties because it too is directly associated with process, persons, minds, context, and environment.

Perhaps the problem to be solved is reductionism itself. Functioning appears at first glance to be the kind of medical issue that is most easily understood in the classical reductionist mode in which all medical personnel are trained. It is common for complex clinical problems to be reduced to straightforward issues of the function of body parts. For example, if a mill worker cannot work because of a chronically painful back we understand that the problem is the back. The man has trouble getting on and off an examining table, he says that he cannot stand without pain except for short periods of time, and he is unable to lift or carry heavy loads. Treatment is directed at the back and the problem is further reduced (currently) so that treatment is usually focused on the back muscles. Until a few years ago the problem of the failed back was reduced to pathology of the lumbar spine and many surgical procedures were carried out that generally did not relieve the pain. The current approach also produces limited results. Physicians may be troubled when they discover that another individual with a seemingly identical back impairment continues working in the mill. They tend to blame the nonworking man for personal failures—after all, the other man is working. It is now well known, however, that two individuals with identical physical impairments doing the same work may have very different employment histories depending on factors such as their education, family situation, the social situation at work, supervisors, and motivation. One may be unable to participate in a specific role while the other, though impaired, continues to participate. In other words, reducing the problem of a mill worker's failed back to a problem of muscles may produce some pain relief but does not return the patient to functioning. Neither does it provide an adequate basis for determining who should receive disability benefits in lieu of earnings. This is where reductionism brings us. It leads away from a more person-oriented view that is possibly more successful therapeutically. Reductionism has, however, been essential to the progress of science and reductionist thinking, for all the problems it raises, is *very difficult to avoid.* It *can be done,* however, as we learn how to think in terms of wholes, of persons and patients in their world.

The treatment of cancer in its later stages provides further examples in which the clinical problem continues to be reduced to a disease—cancer—and is not seen in the larger context of what to do with a person who cannot achieve his or her purposes and goals but who is still living in the world. Even in palliative care, initially oriented toward body, mind, and spirit, there has been a recent trend toward focusing on the patent's pain as though that is the crucial issue rather than the problem of functional impairment associated with dying or severely symptomatic chronic disease. The mill worker has a painful back, the patient with end-stage cancer has cancer, and the palliative care patient has pain. There can be no doubt that in these examples the specific problems exist—back pain, cancer, unrelieved pain. If these are disregarded the patients will be poorly treated (or worse). On the other hand, the back problems of individuals such as the mill worker are notoriously resistant to treatment; how could they not be, that back has been repeatedly injured in a lifetime of arduous labor. The patient's cancer may only get worse, and the dying or severely chronically ill patient whose pain alone is treated will go on to unrelieved suffering.

If the mill worker, without rehabilitation, is paid disability benefits because he can no longer do his current job, experience has shown that he will sometimes experience emotional difficulties such as depression, his family life may be disrupted, and other skills he could use are often ignored. This may occur because people do not realize that loss of the purpose of which working was a part is the loss of a vital part of the patient. The lives of patients with end stage cancer revolve around the cancer and its treatment and they usually do not resume normal existence in whatever time they have to live. Normal existence includes important underlying purposes that are lost as a consequence. The severely chronically ill or dying patients cannot achieve the purposes or goals that are important to them. These patients have things to do, intentions and goals—such as relationships to repair or unfinished work to do—with which they can be assisted. Too often the phrase quality of life is inserted as a goal. Aside from the fact that there is *nothing* that does not have to do with their quality of life, the phrase says very little. What does this patient want to accomplish? What underlying purposes have been disrupted that could, with understanding care, be resumed? What does he or she think is still important to get done, and how do clinicians help them achieve these goals? The answers to these questions, vital to the patients' well-being, involve maximizing function to the degree possible. In these terms much can be accomplished by the clinician.

Janet Abrahm, an experienced oncologist and now a palliative care clinician, has pointed out that in discussions about whether a patient with late stage malignancy wants third or fourth level chemotherapy the wrong question is usually asked. The issue is not whether the tumor might shrink 10% or something similar, but what the patient wants to accomplish that the treatment and a physician focused on function might make possible.

There are other advantages to the focus on functioning as compared to the usual concentration on the disease process. Focusing on loss of and restoration of functioning emphasizes what the sick person experiences. Impact on the lives of the sick persons depends on the lives they led before becoming sick, their ages, occupations, their expected future, their values, and their social existence—almost everything that makes them who they are. Understanding the effect of a particular functional alteration in a patient brings together knowledge of physiology, pathophysiology, human activities and participation, society, culture, and almost every facet of a person. It is difficult to think of complex human functioning in its totality that does not involve and require knowledge of the person. *A medicine that is focused on functioning is inescapably patient centered.* It could not be otherwise. The sick who require crutches to walk do not despair only of the incompetence of a contractile unit or neuronal stimulation of the muscle bundle or even the weakness of an individual muscle. They will, at least initially, consider *themselves* diminished; their confidence in themselves and their abilities will be reduced. For example, they may consider themselves sick in part because they have difficulty walking in public, are acutely aware of how slowly they move, or are fearful of heretofore conquerable challenges such as stairs. They despair that they will ever not be stared at by others. On the other hand, with appropriate help they may feel themselves, in their newfound ability to walk with crutches, to have conquered the impairment that made them sedentary. Others with diseases in which gradual deterioration is the rule, such as progressive multiple sclerosis, will require help at many levels from adapting to wheelchairs or scooters to continuing to live their lives. Physicians, because of their training, have the capacity to see that from the incompetent neuromuscular or contractile unit to stares of others or (conversely) the sense of achievement is *one functional complex*—a mosaic of elements that make up the whole. They are also able to understand the achievement of the person who, through using crutches or scooters, returns to increased functioning in the world of activities and participation with others. Physicians should not merely have empathy for the embarrassment of the crutch walker (although that also); they have knowledge of the functional whole that starts at the pathophysiology of the neuromuscular or contractile unit and finishes at the patient's difficulty walking with crutches and the attendant social distress. It is the case, however, that clinicians may concentrate on the disease and not see it as their basic responsibility to follow the patient through all the ramifications involved in the loss of functions that underlie the inability to fulfill goals. The great advantage physicians have, however, is that they have the ability and knowledge to understand impairments from (say) the contractile or neuromuscular unit to the fulfillment of purpose because that gives them the potential ability to *intervene at any point in that process.* The focus on functioning addresses the lived life of the patient that stretches from sickness to the patient's experience (definition) of health. *The role of healer extends from the fundamentals of disease to the activities and participation necessary for patients to pursue their purposes and know themselves as healthy* (Drum et al. 2008).

There is no actual conflict between attending to impairments in functioning and paying attention to diseases. The advantage of the added focus on functioning is that it brings the clinician's interest and action from the basic pathophysiology all the way up to the patient's purposes in the social world. Patients—in fact, all of us—know ourselves, in large part, because of the pursuit and accomplishment of our purposes; we participate in the activities and do the things that are necessary and important to us. The achievement of our purposes requires individual and collective functional competency in human systems. The list is large: cognitive functions, emotional functions, transcendent functions, sensory functions and pain, voice and speech functions, cardiovascular function, respiratory functions, hematologic and immunologic functions, digestive, metabolic, and endocrine functions, genitourinary and reproductive functions, neuromusculoskeletal and movement-related functions, functions of the fascia, and functions of the skin and related structures. Patients believe themselves sick because of the impairments of functioning and the threats of further loss that might occur, at least in part, because of disease per se. When patients are asymptomatic—for example, when they have asymptomatic hypertension—physicians cause them to do what is necessary to lower their blood pressure by threatening future loss of functioning, a stroke. By this time the dangers of future functional impairments when asymptomatic disease is neglected are part of the culture's knowledge. In addition, there is now effective and easily achievable treatment. It is no longer necessary for the threat to be emphasized by the physician. When we attend primarily to functioning we are in the arena of the patient's problem. Considering disease in relation to its impact on functioning, on activities and participation, rather than for itself gives the clinician three things: an increased understanding of the patient's disorder, an extension of therapeutic power because of the wider arena for possible intervention, and a greater appreciation by the patient.

Persons lose functioning over time not only because of disease, however, but as part of daily life, when no disease is diagnosed, and often without awareness. This is exemplified in the process of aging in which functioning in almost every system noted above is diminished or changed. Loss of visual acuity and loss of hearing are frequently corrected, but many other losses occur without awareness. Verbrugge and Jette (1994) called this the *disablement process* as the person progresses from limitations in functioning to impairments of functioning to disability, where environmental and social demands can no longer be met. Guralnik and his colleagues, extending the value of these observations, show how diminished lower extremity strength for whatever reason predicted disability and even death rates years later. These impairments may occur in the course of chronic diseases such as congestive heart failure, where activity is restricted (with consequent weakening of less used muscle groups) or in persons with no diagnosed disease (Guralnik et al. 1995). These findings and the fact that some declines in functioning that accompany aging or are nonspecific effects of chronic diseases can be reversed suggest the further importance of focusing on functioning and its limitations in situations in addition to the setting of specific diseases. These facts emphasize that functional impairment and the inability to pursue goals is a *process;* it always has a history and careful questioning brings out the story. The process nature will become apparent in hearing the patient tell what he or she could do as a young person and then how the functioning waned over time—all the while the patient is attributing these increasing impairments to the "normal" process of aging. What is not made clear by asking questions may be revealed by careful physical examination. This emphasizes again how the physical examination is different when functioning is the focus of attention.

The recognition of functioning or its impairments as determinants of health or illness increased markedly, as I noted above, after World War II and even more so in the past several decades. In 1980 the first trial editions of the World Health Organization's *International Classification of Functioning, Disability, and Health* (the ICF) began to appear. They aimed to change the focus on health and illness from disease to the patient's experience of health-related impairments. By the mid-1990s the ICF system of classification was sufficiently robust to form a basis for the measurement of the state of individuals and populations. Started in the 1980s, the *Medical Outcomes Study* was a large-scale study measuring clinical status, functioning, and well-being in persons with different medical and psychiatric conditions. Its focus is functioning and the impact of impairment on the health of individuals. As the ICF is an extremely detailed classification of functioning and its impairments, the *Medical Outcomes Study* is a careful and comprehensive evaluation of questionnaire methods for determining functioning and its impairments (Stewart and Ware 1992). Initially there was considerable confusion over the definition of terms, but the terms and their definitions set out early in this chapter are now generally accepted.

The intense efforts to study and understand functioning and well-being and the acceptance of these terms in the field of rehabilitation and in population studies of health have not found parallel acceptance in day-to-day medical practice. The research that has been done and the measures that have been developed, however, provide a solid intellectual and clinical basis for adopting this understanding of sickness in everyday medical care. For healers, a way to understand sickness and health as it is lived has been systematically developed; it has only to be adapted to clinical practice (Stewart and Ware 1992; WHO 2001). Reading the ICF and the *Medical Outcome Study*, on the other hand, can be an intimidating experience. My feeling was almost despair at the extent of the ICF and its description of functioning and its impairments to a level of minute detail beyond any clinician's ability to put it into practice. In its present form, the *Medical Outcomes Study* is not applicable to contemporary clinical practice. The material in the *Medical Outcomes Study* especially, however, should be adapted to medical practice because it provides the basis for questions that can be used to track down functional losses.

A focus on functional loss has generally not been an important aspect of the usual methods by which physicians evaluate patients. As I have stated previously, there is no conflict between attending to impairments of function and attending to disease. It is often said that given a patient's symptoms physicians take a history and do a physical examination in an attempt to find a disease diagnosis that fits the pattern and seriousness of the symptoms and physical findings. The diagnostic efforts including laboratory tests, imaging studies, and other special studies are in the service of a search for a disease. The intention of finding a disease diagnosis is even more prominent in the contemporary era of extensive diagnostic technologies and widely effective therapies. If the symptoms and physical findings do not seem serious, or a diagnosis is not forthcoming, the goal will change to finding a treatment to relieve the symptoms.

For example, if a patient has chest pain that suggests heart disease, tests will be done to demonstrate that heart disease is present or to diminish its probability. The intensity of the search may depend on the presence or absence of other factors that bear on the probability of the diagnosis—risk factors such as diabetes or hypertension, patient age, family history—matters that do not reflect what the patient is experiencing. In the absence of such factors the diagnosis may be dismissed without regard to the patient's experience. The diagnosis becomes, "no evidence of heart disease."

As another example, if the symptoms, no matter how mild, point to the possibility of malignancy the diagnosis will be pursued relentlessly until it can be put aside. In that case the patient may receive symptomatic relief if treated at all. On the other hand, if a cancer is found, the tumor will likely become the single-minded focus of diagnostic and therapeutic effort perhaps with little regard to the patients' actual impairments of functioning. The language of survival— chances of survival, length of survival, and quality of survival—will rule the world the patient has entered often without concern for the actual impact of the disease or its treatment on patients or their functioning. From then on the patient's cancer has center stage even after there is no residual cancer. Its prognosis and expected course will form the basis of medical actions. In recent years the emotional and social distress that accompany cancer have received considerably more attention as clinicians are more aware of the widespread impact of cancer and its treatment. I believe it is fair to say that these consequences of the malignancy are seen as things that "happen to" the cancer patient rather than an inescapable part of cancer. Cancer is generally not considered by clinicians as a process that starts with the tumor's origins and continues on with its influence increasing throughout the body and on into every aspect of the person over time, but rather a "thing." The language of functioning is generally not a part of the cancer scene.

As I noted above with cancer, diseases are still considered by many clinicians to be things rather than processes. I showed above that the problem is one of language. I used rheumatoid arthritis to illustrate that diseases are generally described as static phenomenon. Descriptions of joint function, on the other hand, are descriptions of process—events occurring over time. Reading about cancer of the breast does not tell you why the patient is sick. I am not sure that is how clinicians actually think, but that is the language they use. If we listen to them talking to patients, talking to each other while making rounds, and talking to medical colleagues, they will use the same language of events. The liver chemistries are this and this number, the blood sugar is this number, the EKG shows this, a chest X-rays shows that. Experienced physicians may put all this information together in their head and make a *process* of the disease in their thought. But the everyday language around them keeps them thinking in disease terms as an automatic and natural consequence of the data they are considering. Equally unfortunately, disease thinking stops at the body's edge in denial of the "biopsychosocial" verities. You may wonder how else they might speak. There is no reason not to say, for example, "the last alk[aline] phos[phatase] was 54 and today's is 176," rather than simply the alk phos is 176. Or "The hemoglobin A_{1C} last month was 6.8 but yesterday's is 8.4," rather than simply the hemoglobin A_{1C} is 8.4. In both instances the report of a laboratory value is given more meaning when given as a process—in terms of change. A trend is a report of functioning unfolding.

From function and disease to person. This next example reminds us that it is not the functions per se that are important, but the persons whose functions they are. It is a lesson in the problems of clinical reductionism.

> A 48-year-old intelligent successful single business woman developed a type II decompression illness after scuba diving in Mexico. She was in severe lower body pain and was unable to move her legs when pulled from the water. She was in a decompression chamber within 5 hours, but was left with severe weakness and almost constant pain in her legs. Many months of physical therapy taught her how to walk with crutches and to care for herself, but she could not return to work. She decided to go to law school (she wanted to work on the legal problems of the disabled) and

she managed, with considerable physical difficulty, to graduate. However, she has been unable to manage the jobs she entered after law school. She believes it is because her legs are worse and her pain is more debilitating. Examination failed to confirm increasing difficulty. She refused to take pain medication or to return to physical therapy because she believed she should be able to continue without medication or further help. She is considered strong-willed by many (and stubborn by others) and she agrees with both of which characterizations.

She clearly needs help, but where is the healer to act; what and where is the problem(s)? Effective physical therapy made it possible for her to walk with crutches and care for herself and even go to law school. She had excellent psychotherapy for the recent period of worsening difficulties. Yet her overall impairment continues and is, perhaps, worse. The usual approach to this patient would divide her problem into its neurologic, rehabilitation, and psychological elements with different people for each. What is needed at this time is an understanding of the patient's impairment(s), but there is no substitute for talking to her to find out. We might say that we have to take a history. Although that is true, it is a different kind of a history because the object is not to make a diagnosis, but to find out what the matter is. Why is she unable to walk and what has worsened? When, precisely, did it worsen—what was happening to her then and to her life? What kind of pain does she have, where and when and how? Why it is worse and when did that happen? What is her objection to pain medication, behavioral methods of pain relief, and hypnotic methods of symptom control? We are trying to obtain information about her impairment from the ground up, so to speak. We need to find out about her lived day, particularly what, when, and how she does things (and what she does not do), in addition to determining her wishes, desires, and goals. Looking at her various functional impairments—legs, pain, difficulties with specific aspects of daily life, and so forth—would be the usual approach. It is not, however, just the parts of her in which the impairment lies. This is one problem with reductionism—classifications are inherently reductionist. The difficulty seems to lie in her failure to understand that *she is impaired*—that it is not just pain or functional difficulties with her legs. As we hold onto our knowledge about her neuromuscular functioning and her pain while we look at the whole tapestry of her current life in which her impaired functions are imbedded, we see someone who is doing the same things as the doctors—seeing her obstacles as, for example, pain and impaired legs. The problem is not her parts, it is her as the person she is that is impaired. Is she stubborn and strong willed? Temperament and personality are real things but they are not usually considered life goals. The problem to be solved is not her legs, which have been corrected to the extent currently possible. Her physician or other clinicians need to help her understand that *she is impaired* and that what is keeping her from functioning better is not a part, it is her whole person refusing to be an impaired person. After that has been accomplished, if she will *be* an impaired person, she may well do anything—even take pain medication—to improve her functioning. If seeing sickness in functional terms is fundamentally patient-centered, then the focus of treatment is that person not just her parts. After all, we are all impaired from the point of view of Superman who can "leap the tallest buildings." Because all of us are "impaired" in the same fashion we do not call it impaired, we call it normal, and we accept our limitation (which we do not see as a limitation). This patient's problem, at this time, is impaired perception. If she cannot change her perception of herself (as difficult as that may be) she will continue to be unable to return to living her life in an optimal manner. As an example of this, in the deaf world there is a movement on behalf of the idea that the deaf are not impaired, but are in fact a unique culture.

Usually, when clinicians take a history they are looking for the telltale signs and clues to a diagnosis. Once they have a diagnosis, they generally understand the patient's problem in terms of the disease. If a diabetic stumbles a lot and is unsteady on his feet, the idea of diabetic neuropathy comes to the clinician's mind and informs both further questions and further examinations. The inference may well be correct and will help the clinician decide on treatment. That conclusion says little about the patient's actual functional loss and what should be done to minimize its impact. Here is another example of changing self-perception in which the outcome was successful. A public figure developed diabetic neuropathy and stumbled so often in public that damaging rumors got about that alcohol was affecting his gait "and who knows what else." The functional problem was addressed by convincing him to use a cane. He resisted the idea but his clinician persuaded him by arguing that people stumbling because of alcohol do not use canes—they try to hide the problem. Using a cane in public, as predicted, changed the public focus on his impairment.

The problem in this kind of functionally oriented history-taking is to avoid premature conclusions about the diseased physical state, psychological makeup, or personality characterization. This is difficult because conclusions about physical aspects of an illness are called a diagnosis (probably not useful here), conclusions about psychological elements are often also diagnostic (and of not much value), but conclusions about personality are the stuff of social life and also get in the way of knowing where to act.

Going back to the previous example, our lawyer, why doesn't she take pain medication? She stubbornly refuses. Is it because she is stubborn or because of something else into which the stubbornness fits? Remember, she is intelligent.

There will be a reason and when we hear it, it will make sense. *She* is impaired. Stubborness and fixed ideas about medication were fine for her unimpaired self. If she wants to once again be the unimpaired person she was in the past, part of getting back there is that the impaired person takes analgesics. A story of sickness and impairment is being told and the task is to understand how to change the story so that it comes out better by intervening in functional terms: But which functionings and how? We are interpreters of the story in terms of our interests in sickness, functioning, and healing. These are similar to but different from our interests in the diagnosis and treatment of disease. What gets in the way of successful interpretations of a story are, most of all, the prejudices of the interpreter. It is not a question of ridding ourselves of all prejudice, because that cannot be done. Prejudice occurs simply because we have preexisting interests and foreknowledge that push us to premature conclusions. The task is being aware of our biases and prejudices so that we can be aware, to the degree possible, of their influence. It is in listening to the story being told that we become aware of the patient's interpretation of events, behaviors, and interpretation of knowledge that, added to the physical problems, produce or exacerbate the impairments of functioning.

I could not figure out, once, what was wrong that a patient with normal weight who believed that her perceived weight problem was that she was constantly eating. (The maintenance of weight is a function, and eating is a subsidiary function.) Recounting her food intake did not clarify the issue because it suggested a large intake of calories inconsistent with her normal weight. Asking her to describe her day in minute detail—no detail left out—revealed the difficulty. It was not eating too much; the problem was that she compulsively stole food that she did not actually eat! It is like examining the body with great care and really seeing and feeling what is there as opposed to just looking for evidence of a disease or a diagnosis. What ties all the details of a case—a patient's story—together? Each will logically fit with the others. Nonpsychotic human beings (she was not psychotic) in thought and action are almost always logically coherent and when it appears that they are not, it is because the premises that would make the logic apparent have not yet been found. In other words, when you cannot understand someone's behavior or thoughts it is most often because the basic premise is not apparent and must be sought. In this instance the functional impairment was in her eating pattern (and in the disturbed thinking behind the behavior).

Here is another example. A busy man in his fifties had an automobile accident. He entered the intersection and was struck by a car coming from the side. Although his injuries were minor he could not get over the idea that he had had an accident. Nothing like that had ever happened to him before. He wanted to be examined because he was sure that there must be something wrong. Nothing was found. Three weeks later he had another similar accident. Again the examination was negative. Again he was not reassured. He insisted that he had not seen the incoming vehicle. He was sent to the ophthalmologist who found that he had homonymous hemianopsia on the basis of a brain tumor. Sometimes the functional impairment is straightforward, but the problem is that the physician is not listening (or looking) for the source of the functional loss.

Functional impairment and the inability to pursue goals are a personal *process;* it always has a history and careful questioning brings out the story. In a disease such as chronic obstructive pulmonary disease, as the patient's global functioning becomes increasingly impaired, goals and purposes change—there is no choice but to adapt. The history of the patient's functioning not only changes over time, but so also does the patient's adaptation and response. The fact of our interest and the questions we ask are themselves stimuli for changes in the patients' perceptions of and attitudes toward their impairments. Patients with advanced pulmonary diseases are in their state because of the gradual progressive failure of the functions of respiration. From the changes in the structure of small airways and alveoli, to narrowing of their airways probably secondary to inflammation and smooth muscle spasm, to the flattening of their diaphragms, and the changes in the structural configuration of their chests they cannot maintain normal gas exchange in the face of this complex set of (usually worsening) impairments of functioning. Because of this they do not have sufficient oxygen to maintain normal activities. These patients are gradually forced first to change the manner by which they pursue their purposes and then to alter the purposes themselves.

This example illustrates how focusing on the disease may obscure what is happening to the functioning of the person.

> A 74-year-old man with no living family and few friends developed congestive heart failure on the basis of ischemic cardiomyopathy. There was difficulty adjusting his medication and getting him to follow his regimen. He soon returned to the hospital in congestive heart failure. Three weeks elapsed before he could be discharged. He received "Meals on Wheels" and the visiting nurse made a weekly visit to take his blood pressure. Within 6 weeks he was readmitted because of congestive heart failure. On this admission he was thought to have cognitive failure and difficulty engaging with the staff and other patients because of brain failure. Discharge to a residential nursing home was planned because it was believed that because of his dementia he was unable to live independently and maintain his medical regimen and that was why he went back into congestive heart failure each time.

In longer hospitalizations, and especially in the elderly, the therapeutic focus on the disease is understandable, but inadequate. During the time that these patients are hospitalized or in other institutions, the functioning of other body systems is decreasing. The slogan, "use it or lose it," is crude but accurate. Cognitive, emotional function, sensory function (particularly visual and auditory), muscular loss, and loss of balance, among other things, diminish unless they are actively maintained. In patients such as the one I cited, physical therapy would be common. An occupational therapist should also evaluate this patient and start working on his cognitive and other losses. It would not be a surprise to find a functional person reemerging in this apparently failed old man, who might again become reliable about his own care in an assisted living environment in which he could interact with others in an active social community.

The Care of the Dying and Palliative Care

There are special lessons to be learned from the care of the dying, and palliative care. The "big advantage" in these settings is that disease-oriented care has failed or is inappropriate. Why is this an advantage? When we cannot focus primarily on the disease because it is useless, we must shift our attention to the enhancement of the person through the improvement or maintenance of function. In these settings in general, impairments in many systems are the norm. Too often this decreased or deteriorating function is accepted as inevitable and the patient's inability to pursue goals and purposes is seen as a natural consequence of the dying state. There is nothing inevitable about quadriceps muscles that become so weak because of bed rest that the patient cannot walk or rise from a sitting position. An inability to walk or move around because of the failures of balance resulting from prolonged bed rest is not a necessary consequence of being in the process of dying. When patients get out of bed, it would be in the patients' interests to have the bed automatically fold into the wall until they have to go to sleep. Because that will not happen soon, try and keep patients out of bed. Recliner chairs will do fine for most rest and care needs and do much less damage than a bed.

It is vitally important to clarify what the patient wants to accomplish—what goals and purposes are important—and then work with the sick person to maintain or enable the functions necessary for their achievement. This kind of care will change the patient's experience of sickness and probably change the trajectory toward death or recovery. Sometimes I tell patients that "Just because you are dying is no reason to be sick." Is what the patient says now consonant with what you know of the patient and the patient's family? Are there family problems that may have come up in previous conversations, or that other clinicians—the social worker or nurse, for example—have elicited or know about that would help in decision making? Is there work that the patient believes must be finished and, if so, is it a reasonable goal? Are there other purposes and goals that have been stated previously or that you can elicit now? Clinicians are not there to say no or yes, but rather to facilitate. You want to help patients reach conclusions that are consistent with both their goals and their capacities. Whatever the goal is, success is important. Occasionally, however, dying patients will seize on a goal that simply cannot be achieved, as though by doing that they can put off death. This deserves some conversation. Sometimes patients want to do things that at first seem impossible but excess caution may not serve the patient well. One of my dying patients (in New York City) desperately wanted to go to Paris for a week with his grown daughter. Carrying off the trip seemed to us to be improbable at best and certainly not a good idea. But we could not be sure he would *not* be able to go and make it back. It seemed so important to him that we thought we should try and help. The daughter was worried about the trip but she was willing. So with supplies and equipment necessary for his care and his symptoms well controlled, they set out. (I was not entirely forthcoming to the airline.) They made the trip successfully and both were truly happy that they had gone. He died only days after returning.

This way of relating goals and capabilities is also useful in other, nonpalliative situations.

Pain

Pain is included in the ICF with sensory functions. The ICF classification associates pain with potential or actual damage to a structural component of the body. That is not always possible to demonstrate. The control of pain and other symptoms may make it possible to rehabilitate the dying patient and slow or diminish other impairments, restoring function in different terms. For this reason, an accurate understanding of the patient's symptoms and the losses they represent is very important. There will be no test or measurement that can substitute for the discovery process of asking questions to elicit pain and other symptoms in sufficient detail to understand them. Pain and other symptoms, however, are not merely measures of structural damage or functional impairment. They all have meaning to the patient and that meaning is often indistinguishable from (say) the shortness of breath—meaning has an impact on function. Pain is always interpreted (as are other symptoms) and in that manner the patient personalizes the symptom. It is thus possible to say of lasting pain that the presentation of the pain—the way the patient experiences it—*is its interpretation.* Put another way, when the pain or the patient's behavior in regard to the pain seems strange, we should try to determine the following: "If that pain is trying to tell me something what would it be trying to say?" A woman had pain in the right iliac region for a period of time and finally saw her physician who found nothing. Within a week it was on both sides of her lower back and again the physician found no explanation. Less than a week later she had similar pain in her left upper back. A bone scan revealed a metastatic lesion in her right iliac bone. When she was started on adequate opioids the pain was gone from the left lower and right upper back and was mostly relieved in the right iliac region. The presentation of rapidly worsening and spreading pain was, at least, saying, "Pay attention to me, I might be dangerous." It also got the physician's attention. Sometimes the patient interprets the symptom as a sign of impending death correctly or incorrectly and sometimes of other serious implications. This is particularly important when you cannot control pain—you find yourself escalating the analgesic dose or making other drug manipulations day after day that should be effective but are not. Opioids, especially in the large doses commonly given currently, are effective analgesics (except, sometimes, in special circumstances such as neuropathic pain). (The most prominent symptoms to emerge in that setting often signal toxicity.) When that happens the pain seems to be saying that there is some other factor at play in addition to pain.[3] A common reason for pain that cannot be controlled is the dire interpretation the patient has attached to the pain. A man with an enlarging thigh and an expanding metastatic lesion in the right femur from non-small cell carcinoma of the lung had increasingly severe pain that did not respond to large and escalating doses of pain medication. It turned out that he believed that his leg was going to be amputated. When he was promised that amputation was definitely not being considered, his pain was relieved with considerably smaller doses of medication. In both these instances the presentation of the pain fit the patient's interpretation.

Mental Functions

Mental functions must also be attended to. These include global mental functions such as states and quality of consciousness, orientation functions, emotive functions, psychosocial functions that enable and maintain relationships, and temperamental and personality functions that initiate and maintain the manner in which the person interacts with the world. Confidence and optimism (or pessimism), agreeableness, trustworthiness (or their opposites), and others can contribute or interfere with achieving goals and purposes. Energy and drive are also mental functions. So too is maintaining attention. Memory is another mental function. Cognitive functions receive more attention from clinicians than these other mental functions. This is especially true of higher-level cognitive functions such as thinking and reasoning that are often measured as tests of mental functions in general.

---

3. I seem to be suggesting that the pain (or the body) has intentions. It is difficult to come to another conclusion.

All mental functions are vital and their appropriateness, regulation, and range are often impaired in serious illness. Emotions (whatever else they may do) serve in an evaluative capacity; they are like adjectives, commentators on the emotional meanings of things, persons, actions, losses of function, and events. Whatever happens to the patient has emotional importance—sadness, fearfulness, unhappiness, despair, anger, or perhaps positive emotions such as satisfaction, joy, or relief. The emotions occur as commentary on the *meaning* of the symptom—what it is believed to represent, signify, or foretell. Anxiety, fear, sadness, or even feelings of relief or optimism are not the meaning but a response to the meaning of the symptom. All of these functions are not only important in themselves but also for their contribution to how other impairments of functioning are understood. When patients are questioned about symptoms in a yes or no fashion or in a manner that seems to ask for direct fact on a surface level, their answers will not usually include the emotions evoked by the symptoms. The patient's replies to questions of this type can, however, reflect the social significance the patient believes will be attached to the answers, what the patient thinks the clinician wants to hear or the answer the patient might believe to be most socially acceptable in the current setting. The influence on the behavior of patients of social factors is further discovered by questions that go below the surface. ["What does that mean to you?" (Or one of my favorite questions) "And so…?" "What do you think…?" "How does that make you feel…?" "Does the (symptom) make you wonder…?"] The seeming vagueness of these questions and the unfinished sentences of which they are a part almost pull from the patient answers that better characterize the patient's deeper thought. This seems to imply that there is one set of answers at a superficial level and another set at a deeper level. In fact, this is most often true.

This also, like the emotional significance of functional loss, stresses the importance of questioning that goes deeper than merely the discovery of impairment or the patient's story. The emotions that are discovered by questioning more deeply have an impact not only on the meaning but on the experience of the symptoms. The pain itself is experienced differently if it has been changed to a sign of worsening disease and looming death. Thus, the answers to the questions about symptoms are influenced by the emotional response or loading of the symptoms. When clinicians elicited symptoms primarily to make a diagnosis, the fact that the symptom pointed to this or that disorder was what was important. In our understanding of sickness, the symptom as reported by the patient, and its meaning and emotional significance are important because of what they say about the sick person as well as about the nature of the sickness.

The emotional component of the meaning of a symptom (impairment or change of function) has a past and an anticipated future. The past is almost always acting on the symptom in the present and influencing its future. For example, a young woman developed multiple painful mouth ulcers from the medication for her rheumatoid arthritis. The mouth sores triggered a memory of pain and helplessness from a number of years earlier when she had a total knee replacement. As she was trying to fall asleep with her very painful mouth she developed severe resting pain in her left leg—very unusual for her. Then a sudden memory swept over her of being left on a gurney after surgery in a very cold hallway with excruciating pain in the operated (left) knee. There was no one present and no one answered her calls. She started crying and sobbing for what seemed a long time before a doctor came along and had her transported to her room. Now, trying to sleep, the memory of the experience came back so strongly that she found herself crying and sobbing again. The symptom, mouth sores, is also changed by the memory that provoked increasing tightness of her facial muscles and jaw, which aggravated the mouth pain. In this example the influence of the past is easy to demonstrate, but to some degree it is always present, although not often as evident. The emotional loading of the symptom also influences the future—just as in this young woman whose tightened facial muscles made the pain worse. Fear about a symptom may cause the patient not to report the discomfort, or not to follow the prescribed regimen, taking too little or too much medication.

Living in the present moment and *only* the present moment is never experienced without difficult effort. Being in this moment and not a moment before or a moment later requires considerable practice. There can be no fear in *only* this moment. There is in this moment and only this moment no dread of what has happened in the past and will happen again. Fear and dread require the past and the future, which will permit an assignment of meaning to the experience. For example, with pain there may be fear that the pain will keep getting worse or dread that some awful event that happened before will occur again. In this moment and only in this moment, there is neither past nor future. The way things are experienced in ordinary everyday life, however, is quite different. An experience always includes aspects of the past and expectations of the future. The past that the person's thought introduces into the present experiences is not a catalog or complete reading of the past, but traces that reinforce perhaps an ongoing interpretation of the present and expectations for the immediate future. These expectations for the future are not dispassionate probability statements. They are, instead, hopes (or fears) for the future that are intertwined with other immediate or contemporary events all of which together feed the dominant fears or hopes for the future. For this reason many hopes are for small things—e.g., I hope I will be able to eat again without pain. Because the experienced past and the expected future are often interpretations of the actual past or probable futures, they can be influenced by healers. Changing these ideas—fears as expressed are ideas—can change the patient's beliefs about the future (and, sometimes, even the past). This changes the experience of the sickness. These are interventions in the sick person's mental function.

Executive control is another mental function. It is involved in a loosely defined collection of brain processes responsible for planning, cognitive flexibility, initiating actions, and inhibiting other actions. It is impaired in illness and this often presents itself as patients who cannot initiate or take part in planning activities, whose capacity for trouble-shooting is poor or absent, and where new responses are required. These patients are easily confused by events requiring their participation, but which they have not previously faced.

Impairment of mental functions is very common in persons with serious illness and in the dying. Patients with many of these difficulties will pass a Mini-Mental Status Examination so that their clinicians consider them to be "cognitively intact." Unfortunately, knowing what day it is, the name of the president, and why you are in the hospital does not necessarily signify unimpaired mental functioning. On the other hand, unless the impairment is severe, these patients can know and express what is important to them when decisions are to be made and much else that requires intact mental function. Just as they may require support to walk in the hallway on their own legs, they may require support to think things through, express themselves, and express opinions on ideas and options presented to them. Because they have these mental difficulties does not mean they are mentally incompetent (although if these defects are severe they may indicate a serious lack of capacity).

It is important to say again that the enabling or return of function so that sick persons can pursue their purposes and achieve their goals is the basic aim of healers. Attention to function comes about because *patients have defined their sickness by the inability to pursue their purposes and goals because of impairments in functioning that they have defined as medical.* The longstanding habits of medicine may make clinicians look only for disease or difficulties in physical functioning in the sick person. That is not adequate to the current definition of illness. Perhaps the person is afraid to start a new career because of fears that he or she will not have the energy, stamina, or endurance to return for further schooling or because there are stigmas attached to being a diabetic (or some other disease or impairment) in certain environments. People who have health concerns that interfere with planning for the future have disturbances of function. Troubles with family relationships or marital difficulties are problems of function. Persons whose sickness is interfering with economic self-sufficiency have problems in function. In this view of sickness, our understanding of function is broader than it was in the past. Clinicians must look closely at these examples and take them apart to see what the actual functional disturbance is. The generalized reassurances so common in the past will not be sufficient from this perspective of illness. Instead, clinicians will find themselves becoming expert in such matters so that they can help the patient go past such fears.

Perhaps the problems are with cognition, emotional adaptation, or even perception. These are issues that many clinicians avoided in the past because they seemed *too psychological or marked by emotional illness*. A different perspective on the same problems removes them from the domain of psychotherapy—and thus some degree of mental illness—and sees them instead as problems of personal functioning that could well be within the expertise of physicians. From this point of view the body of knowledge presently called positive psychology—the psychology of normal life—falls within the ken of internists and primary care physicians. These issues and the many concerns of everyday life that may interfere with adequate functioning are also important in the care of dying patients where enabling them to achieve their goals and purposes can be crucial to their best interests as they define them.

As we come to the end of the discussion about functioning it seems reasonable to ask if there is any moment in which functioning is absent. Most healers have grown up with a biological perspective and for them functioning and life coexist. When healers say life and functioning are coexistent, they mean that every dimension of everyday life expresses itself in function—from the cellular to the spiritual is one throbbing being. Healers seek out those functions whose impairment robs humans of their reasons for being. They celebrate, encourage, and facilitate ways in which the patient escapes the burdens of impairment by enabling healing alterations in functioning or changes in behavior.

Healers caring for the sick focus their actions on function to facilitate the removal of impediments to the pursuit of purposes and the achievement of goals.

References

Beers, M. H., Porter, R. S., Jones, T. V. M., et al. (2006). *The Merck Manual of Diagnosis and Therapy*. Whitehouse Station, NJ, Merck Research Laboratories.

Bongartz, T., Sutton, A. J., Sweeting, M. J., et al. (2006). Anti-TNF antibody therapy in rheumatoid arthritis and the risk of serious infections and malignancies: Systematic review and meta-analysis of rare harmful effects in randomized controlled trials. *JAMA 925*(19): 2275–2285.

Cassel, E. J. (1982). The nature of suffering and the goals of medicine. *New England Journal of Medicine 306*(11): 639–645.

Charo, I. F., and Ransofhoff, R. M. (2006). The many roles of chemokines and chemokine receptors in inflammation. *New England Journal of Medicine 354*: 610–621.

Charon, R. (2007). *Narrative Medicine: Honoring the Stories of Illness*. New York, Oxford University Press.

Drum, C. E., Horner-Jonson, W., and Krahn, G. L. (2008). Self-rated health and healthy days: Examining the "disability paradox." *Disability and Health 1*(2): 71–78.

Feldmann, M., and Maini, R. N. (2001). Anti-TNFα therapy of rheumatoid arthritis: What have we learned? *Annual Review of Immunology 19*: 163–196.

Guralnik, J. M., Ferrucci, L., Simonsick, E. M., et al. (1995). Lower-extremity function in persons over the age of 70 years as a predictor of subsequent disability. *New England Journal of Medicine 332*: 556–562.

IOM. (2007). *The Future of Disability in America*. Washington, DC, Institute of Medicine of the National Academies of Science.

Jonas, H. (1996). *The Phenomenon of Life* (pp. 7–26). New York, Dell Publishing Co.

Levangie, P. K., and Norkin, C. C. (2005). *Joint Structure and Function: A Comprehensive Analysis*, 4th ed. Philadelphia, F.A. Davis Co.

Palastanga, N., Field, D., and Soames, R. (1989). *Anatomy and Human Movement: Structure and Function*. Oxford, Heinemann Medical Books.

Stewart, A. L., and Ware, J. E., Eds. (1992). *Measuring Functioning and Well-Being: The Medical Outcomes Study Approach*. Durham, NC, Duke University Press.

Verbrugge, L. M., and Jette, A. M. (1994). The disablement process. *Social Science Medicine 38*: 1–14.

Weyand, C. M., and Goronzy, J. J. (1997). The molecular basis of rheumatoid arthritis. *Journal of Molecular Medicine 75*: 772–785.

WHO. (2001). *ICF International Classification of Functioning*, Disability and Health. Geneva, World Health Organization.

4
What Is Healing?

"Although a clinician can be both a healer and a scientist, he cannot be an effective therapist if he merely joins these two roles in tandem by oscillating between them, adding laboratory science to bedside art. A clinician's objective in therapy is not just a conjunction, but a true synthesis, of art and science, fusing the parts into a whole that unifies his work and makes his two roles one: a scientific healer.... As a healer, the clinician's purpose is to treat the sick person, not merely the manifestation of disease...."

ALVAN FEINSTEIN (Feinstein 1967)

"All the therapeutic interventions of physicians are exercises in healing. There are some impairments of function where the technologies of medicine are most appropriate and some where the skill of healing is best employed; virtually always, however, both are in play and proper balance is the issue."

DONALD BOUDREAU (2006)

SO MUCH IS written about healing and yet what it is remains unclear. The experience of many laypersons and clinicians is that there are differences in the manner and rate at which different persons get better from severe as well as mild illnesses. Some people recover from an illness when there was no such expectation and others seem inextricably mired in what should be much less severe sickness. These differences seem in part due to the pathologic process, related also to the nature of the sick persons themselves, and also partly a function of who takes care of them. Some clinicians appear to be more successful at making their patients better than others, and again the reasons are often not apparent. On the basis of experiences like these and many, many others, it is widely believed that something called a *power of healing* exists. In cultures in which contemporary scientific medicine is not present there is always a class of people who are considered to be healers, believed to be able to make some sick persons better beyond ordinary expectations. There are widespread differences in the healing methods used in these cultures. This fact and others have led to the belief that what healers do is to allow or cause the body's own powers to heal itself to be expressed. They do this usually by acting through the person of the patient, as though the person could be more or less empowered to help the body heal itself.[1]

A patient of mine was operated on for carcinoma of the prostate and had a cardiac arrest during surgery. Consciousness never returned and the patient was maintained on life support. Within a few days the tumor had grown through the incision onto the abdominal wall. We watched in awe as the tumor grew appreciably from day to day, spreading on the abdominal wall and apparently throughout the abdomen. The patient died some 10 days postoperatively. At autopsy the abdomen was almost a sheet of tumor that had grown in that short time. I thought of it as an example of a tumor completely unopposed by the person.

The variety of healing methods described in the literature is great. In the United States at this time there are many types of active healers, including religious healers. Sometimes the goal of religious healers is to bring what they believe to be Christ's power to heal to bear on the person and in other instances they believe the task is to remove the demonic influences that are thought to be making the person sick. From all of this (and much more) we would have to conclude that it is not known what the basis of healing is, but also that there is little doubt that there really is something called healing. When the therapeutic (and scientific) revolution in medicine occurred in the United States in the 1930s the word healing began to have a bad name, because it was often equated with quackery. Morris Fishbein, the long-time editor of the *Journal of the American Medical Association* in that era, devoted himself to banishing anything that was not scientific medicine and relegating it to the domain of quackery. His influence was very effective, but the baby seems to have gone out with the bathwater. It became accepted wisdom that in treating sick (diseased) patients, it did not matter who

---

1. That sentence is written in a manner that implies that the body and the person are separate entities, although throughout this book I have emphasized that there is no such separation. I do not think it denies that thesis to point out the obvious fact that one part of a person can make things happen to other parts. Certainly, my hands can do things to other parts of me and my gastrointestinal tract can influence my state of mind. It is widely believed, with good reason, that fluctuations in our emotional state are accompanied by changes in bodily functions. It is also true that we can actively influence physiologic functions, with or without that intention, and furthermore, that skilled clinicians can have an influence on the bodily functions of their patients depending on how they work with them. No one doubts that a doctor—with just words and attitude—can scare a patient half to death or conversely bring peace and peacefulness to the patient and the patient's body with other words and a different attitude.

the doctor was, it was the knowledge of medical science that made the difference and that cured the patient. I believe that is incorrect. In this book, as you can see by the quotations that open the chapter, the generic word healing is used for all the actions of clinicians in treating patients. And more, the underlying assumption in the whole book is that the primary agent of treatment is the clinician. It follows that some clinicians will be better healers than others and that the differences are not merely their respective knowledge of medical science.[2] What healing is, what healing actually does, however, is not described in the healing literature in a manner that will allow us to say that "This is what healing does." For example, we are often told that healing makes sick patients better, that it makes them whole again. This sounds reasonable, but it is circular and does not answer the question.

One reason clinicians do not know what healing actually does to make patients better is that we have been led astray by misleading ideas about the goals of medicine. The goals of medicine have generally been divided into two categories: *treat the disease* and (especially as a result of the movement for patient-centered medicine) *care for the patient* focusing on the personal aspects of sickness. This is not right. There are not two goals. There is only one: *the well-being of the patient*. Well-being? If we are successful in our care of patients we want them to have a sense of well-being: "The state of doing or being well in life" (*Oxford English Dictionary*, 2nd ed., electronic). They were sick and now they are better; well-being has returned.

Well-being is separate from disease. Patients can have a disease and yet have a sense of well-being. Well-being is not just physical and not just emotional. Well-being is a patient's goal—only the patient knows whether he or she has a sense of well-being. We can think the patient is better—disease indices say things are good, but the patient does not have a sense of well-being. The patient had angina and a successful angioplasty or coronary artery bypass produced a return of good coronary blood flow, but the patient is not better—has not returned to work, or the previous place in the family, or has not resumed sexual function— the patient has not returned to a state of well-being. The patient had a malignancy and was successfully treated into remission. Unfortunately, the person fears and waits for the recurrence. The person has not had a return of well-being. The patient has chronic obstructive pulmonary disease and his life is occupied and preoccupied by the disease and its treatment—the parade of physician visits and the daily devotion to the correct medication at the right time. Life has become organized around the disease and despite what clinicians would think was reasonable lung function, there is no sense of a life returned, or sense of well-being.

---

2. In English there is a distinction between the words for curing and healing and most people in the medical professions have been trained in curative medicine. In French and Spanish, for example, there is no such distinction; the words for the two are the same.

What do patients have when they have a sense of well-being? They believe they can accomplish their purposes and goals. Put another way, they can do the things they need and want to do to live their lives the way they want to. Most persons are realistic. If they were sick and now better, they know they are not the same as before the stroke—but at least they can do the things that are important to them. If they are dying and cared for by a hospice unit is their life occupied and ruled by the process of dying, or are they doing what they believe needs to be done the best they can before they die? What is important to each person is individual, personal, and important to their lives and the way they want to live and be in the world—or to put it another way, what is important is patient-centered. In healer's terms, what do you need to have a sense of well-being; you *need to able to function well enough to pursue your purposes and goals.* Chapter 3 shows how function involves the whole person including, but not solely, the body. The definition of sickness used in this book meshes with the understanding that the goal of care is the well-being of the patient. Persons are sick (we say) when they cannot pursue their purposes or goals because of impairments of function that may occur from the molecular to the spiritual.

What does healing do? Healing returns a patient to well-being by improving impediments to function that impair the person's ability to pursue purposes and goals. That definition has a reductionist mechanical quality. In part that is because the word "function" seems to imply mechanism. I hope that after reading about function in Chapter 3, you have moved on from seeing it in mechanical terms. That does not yet solve the problem. I think we can understand healing better if we start with the fact that patients often say that they want to be treated like a person by their doctor, or that so and so is a good doctor because "He treats you like a person." What do those phrases mean—what does it mean to be treated like a person? Humans know that they are all much alike and live in groups, but also that each of us is an individual and different; we prize our individuality. As I discussed at length in Chapter 2, individuals want to be treated like persons with their own qualities, needs, desires, concerns, and values, but especially their own personal features.

Sickness is often seen as eroding the particularity of the patient, and when it is not the disease that does it, it is often the medical care. In times past, when (especially indigent) hospitalized patients were in big open wards with 30 to 40 or more beds cared for by impersonal physicians who were concerned more about the patient's disease than about the patient, patients did not expect but were very grateful for any personal attention from the staff.[3] The rise, following World War

---

3. As sociologists have shown, however, patients on these big impersonal wards created their own society in which they were persons who had identities, roles, and a culture of their own mostly unknown to the doctors and nurses. In those days hospital stays were of much longer duration than currently so that the societies of patients generated on the wards had stability and were important to the patients' self-image and well-being.

II, of an almost radical individuality and other social developments emphasizing the individual as separate and knowable apart from their group identities has changed all that. Patients, we are regularly (and properly) reminded, are persons now and patient-centered medicine emphasizes the particularity of patients. Effective healers, I believe, have always known the importance of recognizing the individual person. Patients first know that they are being treated as persons when clinicians *listen to them*. We believe that when people *listen to us, they hear who we are*. People know it even better when they are treated as the person they *see themselves* as being. Gary Larson published a cartoon in which penguins are crowded onto an island from one end to the other—an indistinguishable mass of penguins. In this gaggle you see one penguin with a balloon over its head that says "*I WANNA BE ME!*" We sympathize with the exceptional penguin, but we are not sure what he (or she) means. In the seventeenth century it was believed that all people wanted to be admired, to be like those they admired, and to be seen as exceptional. That sounds like our penguin. We also know that persons want to be acceptable, to be known as being *somebody*—a part of something larger than them, an organization, a profession, a person who knows the ropes, *somebody*: anything except nobody. Given those criteria, it is not so easy to be the person you believe you are when you are sick or when you are one among many. But those criteria also give us the path to knowing the person as the person wishes to be known.

How does this square with this earlier definition of healing? "Healing returns a patient to well-being by improving impediments to function that impair the person's ability to pursue purposes and goals." I wanted you to give up seeing human function as something mechanical. The presentation of the self in social situations (which is what I was talking about when I said what persons wanted) is a *function* and it is far from mechanical. In the chapter on function (Chapter 3) this was discussed at length, but here we can see that as with most complex human functions, many subsidiary functions are involved. For example, it is difficult to present yourself as *somebody* if you do not speak English (in the United States), your speech is impaired, or you have a bad tremor, if you look or smell bad, if you are lying on a gurney, or you are naked. We know that now, and we know what is important to persons, so no matter how much pain they are in, what their situation, or how they speak, look, or smell, we know to listen to them and to find a way to give them the status they have or need so they can know they are being seen as somebody.

When you know how to see someone as a person, have you made them "whole"? I wanted to abandon the definition of healing as making whole because I did not yet know what it meant. However, the definition has been around a long, long time and deserves respect for that reason alone. In the *Oxford English*

Dictionary (2nd ed., electronic) (whose quotations about this usage of whole go back to the eleventh and twelfth century), *whole* and *sound* are equated—like a boat with a sound hull: no holes or cracks. A sound boat can function like a boat; a sound person with a sound body and a sound mind is able to function as a person. Physicians considering this problem tend to separate the body from the person. The body is a distinct entity about whose functions they have a lot of knowledge. That is a medical way of seeing things because when doctors are trained the body is separate from the person. Doctors are educated in medical science that could as well apply to nonliving systems—nothing about it insists that it is about the living. Physicians, without thinking about it, visualize the body as lying down, just like their cadaver in medical schools.

That is not how you or I see our own body and it is not how patients (or physicians) see theirs. It is true that someone might say, "My body is in good shape," as though speaking about a separate object. But people know that their bodies are part *of them*. They do not doubt for a minute that the body is alive; in fact, people often speak as if the body had a mind of its own or its own intentions. I can look down at my leg and (maybe) conceive of it as separate from me, but I would never do that with my hands—which are even part of my spoken interactions with others.[4] In English we use the words somebody, nobody, and anybody to mean person. Originally and until the seventeenth to eighteenth centuries the two parts of each of those words were separate as in some body, no body, etc. The word body was equivalent, in English, to the person, just as in times past childhood was a period of life whose goal was adulthood, but now we grant children their own identity as persons (if not in law). Now equivalence has diminished and the body is an inseparable part of the central entity that is the person.

Depersonalized bodies do not function; functioning presupposes intentions. Intentions presuppose choices and choices bring us to minds. Mind brings us to persons because we do not conceive of bodies as having intentions or choices, only persons do. In the early days of disability determination the physical functions involved in working were assessed using objective measures. It soon became apparent that performance on these tests had as much do with the person's motivation as with the physical impairment. One person with a leg amputated above the knee retires to home, disabled. Another person with an identical impairment returns to work—more is involved in disability than physical impediments to function. How does this square with the question "What is healing?" and what has it got to do with being whole? It looks as if being healed is about being made whole *in the sense that* a whole person is a sound person like the sound boat that

---

4. In certain neurologic disease states persons *can* come to see a leg, arm, or hand as though it was separate from them. See Oliver Sacks' book, *A Leg to Stand On* (1984).

can function as a boat. To be whole is to be able to function like a person, but as we learned from the exceptional penguin, it is also to be acceptable, to be able to be like others, to be somebody, to be a part of something bigger than you, and to be admired. To be healed is not just about the body, but it is also not about some abstraction of a person—a person has a body or they are nobody. Clinicians cannot consider the body without its person and cannot consider persons without their bodies. That is a simple sentence, but not, I am afraid, a simple task.

Is this just another way of saying that contemporary changes in medicine are shifting medicine's focus from the disease to the sick (or well) person? Yes; but changing to the words healer and healing for what clinicians are and what they do carries with it an enlargement of the clinician's job. It remains absolutely necessary to treat the disease, but *the underlying reason for treatment is to return the patient to a functioning whole.* A functioning whole person not just a functioning body. It is for this reason that clinicians must understand that part of their role is to know the person.

We get into confusion about person versus disease, or illness versus disease. We are able to heal even the very diseased patient who is sick. Other patients with equivalent disease—as much pathology and pathophysiology—are not sick. Despite their diseases they function sufficiently to achieve their goals and pursue their purposes. They limited their expectations for what they were going to be able to do because the disease put a burden, sometimes a very heavy burden, on them. They had a sense of well-being, a belief that they had reason to be pleased with how well they were able to function because they were well aware that continuing as they were before in the face of their disease was an achievement. What does it mean to say that the disease was burdensome, but they were not sick? What is the burden if it is not sickness? In the modern era the word disease refers quite specifically to derangements of the functions of the body usually attributed to anatomic, biochemical, molecular, genetic, or equivalent abnormalities. Sickness, we have said in the past, is the patient's experience of the disease—in other words there is a distinction between disease and illness. This is not a new understanding; it was noted in Feinstein (1967), and the meaning of the difference was discussed at length in *The Healer's Art* (Cassell 1976). The distinction, however, as nice as it may sound, is really false. It is an artificial distinction that originally helped introduce the importance of the person of the patient. We know the person is important, so we should move on.

Suppose a sedentary writer has an osteosarcoma of the tibia. That is a disease by any definition. Suppose (further) that the person alters the little walking he does because of discomfort, or a woman runner with the same disease stops running because of pain. Are their alterations of gait part of an illness, but the tumor is disease? This is because gait changes are in the person but the disease is in the body. That does not work; gait is as physical as the tumor. However, the nature of the person was influential in how the gait change influenced their lives.

Osteosarcoma is a disease by classic definitions of disease and those definitions, arising in the early nineteenth century, are an invention of the time. They are artificial in the sense that the physicians of that era declared that a disease was something in the body, living, as they did, in an era in which the mind–body duality was almost universally accepted. Generally medicine—physicians—still want osteosarcoma to be defined by the changes in the tissues of the bone. For healers, clinicians in general, and for the widest understanding of the affliction, osteosarcoma is the whole spectrum in the person of all the personal, physical, psychological, social, and spiritual impairments of function that have become associated with and initiated by the pathology of the bone—including the treatment. What if someone wants to discuss the genetic changes that may be associated with the disease? This does not matter. Anyone can discuss any aspect and still be discussing osteosarcoma. Their language, goals, tools for achieving understanding, measurement methods, and so on may all be different, but it will still be osteosarcoma under discussion. Clinicians, healers, are meant to make people better so what they discuss about osteosarcoma will probably most often be those aspects in which their interventions can be affective. They should always be aware, however, that everything they know about the affliction flows from the characteristics of osteosarcoma of the bone.

It is difficult for physicians trained in Western medicine to leave behind their focus on the body as they learned about it in their medical training. The task is exemplified by considering what sickness does to persons. Exploring symptoms as part of making a diagnosis is something all doctors learn, but now we are interested in more than pain, cough, fever, and so on. We want to know to what extent the patient's sickness limits everyday activities—functions. For this information to have meaning it has to be in the context of the person's everyday life. "When you were well what was your day like?" "How has that changed?" "Do you have difficulty doing your work?" "How about the things you are used to doing around the house?" It is also important to inquire about social activities at home and with friends or family, including sex, spouse, family, friends, and/or community. "Is your illness getting in the way of your relationship with your wife?" "Has it affected your sex life?" "How are things this week compared to a week (or month) ago?" The "review-of-systems" that is part of classical history-taking was meant to discover what else the sickness was doing to the person's physical state; this series of questions is focused on what sickness is doing to the person. You also need to discover the extent to which the patient has been troubled by emotional distress because of sadness, anxiety, fear, or depression. These are impairments of function (and impair other functions) and need treatment.

It is important to discover what the patient's purposes and goals are and whether their pursuit is impeded. "What is the worst thing about your illness right now?" Sometimes when I think I am not getting at the real difficulties, I say (about a symptom or impediment to function) "if I could wave my hand and make that all better, would you be well again?" "No, then what is really bothering you about all this?" "Are there things that you feel are very important that you want to do now—like, say, seeing your sister again? Things that if you got those done or got started on them you would have a better sense of well-being?" Patients may not be accustomed to clinicians asking questions such as this so they may not initially answer directly and some probing may be required. I might say, "Lots of times when we're sick there are things we wanted to do but can't because of being sick and in bed—some are intimate or very personal, some about the family, or work, or almost anything that is important. Generally, you don't get a chance to talk about them or ask for help, but they are important. I can try and help with these problems or find someone who can." In general, this set of questions or their equivalent should be asked even if it is apparent that the patient would not be able to carry out the functions. What is important is that he or she *wants* to. The questions, which, as I noted, patients will find unusual from a healer establishes your interest in the patient and not just the disease or symptoms.

The whole task of discovering these things does not have be accomplished in one visit; parts of the task can be done now, some later that afternoon, and some the next day because not only does that help sustain the patient's strength but it shows that you have a continuing interest. Also find out what the patient would require to pursue or accomplish these purposes—and details matter. All of this may take some (gentle, but persistent) digging. These questions should not be asked with the team present; what the patient believes should be done may be private and involve secrets or the secret life. It may also be necessary to gently but firmly evict the family—"Would you excuse me, I'd like to talk to Delores alone for a few minutes." I can hear the objection; look at the time this would take! Yes, it takes time but with practice and increasing skill the time required will decrease.

This line of questioning is very important. *The answers to these questions help form the structure on which the whole plan of care for this patient will be based.* This is opposed to the past when the disease was the focus and care was designed only around the disease. It remains necessary to reiterate that this approach does not replace treatment of the disease. Treating the disease is an essential part of the healer's job, but the measures of success are not only better disease indices, but the return of function in the broad sense as it is discussed in this book.

One of the most important functions that healers serve is to clarify and work with patients' meanings. Often when nothing else can be done to make someone better it is possible to change the meanings that the patient has applied to the situation, or a symptom, or an anticipated procedure. It is difficult but necessary to remember that when the meaning of something has been changed, the thing is changed.

Healing does not end here. Think back to Chapter 2 in which we discussed what a person is, and remember that important illness has affects or alters almost every aspect of a person. Healing is directed at returning sick persons as closely as possible to their healthy selves. This was what clinicians strove for when they were treating disease, except that there it was to be accomplished by returning the body to health. That was not all, however, because every clinician knew—and it was universally acknowledged—that sickness had widespread dire effects from hopelessness and continued fears to residual muscle weakness and impaired gait. Good clinicians considered the repair of these problems to be a part of their job. Others, acknowledging their importance, called doing those things part of the art of medicine. How to carry out these tasks was rarely manifestly taught, however. This is also an essential aspect of the healer's job. Healers should have a deeper knowledge of the nature of persons and thus they should be better able to go after those personal features of sickness. In Chapter 9, where the state of illness is discussed, how healers deal with specific characteristics of the sick such as their disconnection from the world of the well or the loss of the feeling of indestructibility will be discussed at length. These problems, although almost universal in sick persons, are not a *necessary* feature of illness. When the problems are solved the patient remains diseased but does not behave "sick." Sometimes I say, "Just because you are dying is no reason to be sick." It is like the loss of muscle tone in bedridden patients. Somebody confined to bed will rapidly lose strength in the quadriceps no matter what is making them sick. Sick or not, however, quadriceps strength can be maintained by exercises.[5] This does not minimize the seriousness of a major illness. It is true that some things (like the loss of quadriceps strength) can be prevented or repaired, but that does not change the fact that it happens consistently. It also does not change the fact that the sick are different than the well. They are different, if for no other reason than they are probably lying down and you are standing up, they usually do not look like themselves, and they may not be able to do ordinary things like stand up and walk. You can do all of those things, and, in addition, you may be standing over them. They may be in pain or have other disabling symptoms and you probably are relatively symptom free. With your assistance, however, they can be a good working approximation of

---

5. Beds are dangerous. If I had my way, when a patient got out of bed, the bed would automatically fold into the wall and the patient would spend the day walking, sitting, or in a reclining chair.

themselves. Your aid is different from everyday help ("Here, let me help you over to your chair."). Your assistance starts with making a connection to the patient (see Chapter 5) so that you and the patient are a "we." Then any time you would normally say you, as in *you* can do…, *you* will be able to…, or *you* might need…it becomes *we* can do…, *we* will be able to…, or *we* might need…We, we, we.

To see what I mean, watch almost every clinical encounter in the hospital and you will see the clinicians explicitly distinguishing themselves from their patients. They are separate from the patient; they talk *to*, not *with*, the patient and the way they sit or stand in the patient's presence declares their separateness. When patients are being examined they do it from a position that emphasizes the separation. Of course, they are separate, that is not a stance it is a fact. Maybe the separateness is preferred and slightly or overtly emphasized because many clinicians do not want to be too connected to the sick; closeness is threatening. When a healer examines a patient his or her stance should declare closeness. Listening to the heart, the healer's position is almost alongside the patient and the hand without the stethoscope rests on the upper back lightly as though to pull the patient slightly closer. It takes some time to learn to do this and to understand that it does not represent a threat; instead it is clinically effective (and personally satisfying).

A cluster of lilies in my yard needs a supporting stilt when they bloom so their weight does not bend the stalk to the ground. They require the support to be their beautiful selves. The patient needs the supporting connection to be himself or herself. At that, it is only an approximation (the patient knows this), but the connection to the patient is not only important in itself but a statement of intentions. In the chapter on knowing the patient (Chapter 7) I discuss the problems and advantages associated with this way of being with patients. The personal and clinical advantages outweigh any difficulties. You will gradually discover how much better this approach to patients is. Of course, the healer will be going from patient to patient and forming a *we* with many of them and it soon becomes habitual. The major defense against any difficulties of this stance is that the healer is working. It is with the professional self that the healer is forming a *we* with the patient. The clinician's personal self; the one he or she takes home and who lives within the family, is different than the professional self. All of us are more than one self and that the doctor me is not identical with the family me. They are separate—the separation may be Mylar thin but it is real and protective.

I can illustrate what the healer does to maintain the personhood of the patient by discussing the cognitive impairment that is present in most patients sick enough to require care in bed. Such patients think like children of usually less than 10 years; they are very concrete in their thought. Some will say that they have regressed. They are *not children* and I do not believe regression applies. They are sick and they think and act like sick persons. They do not perform normally on a number of Piagetian tests of cognitive function (see Chapter 13). For example, put an identical amount of water in two urine cups and have the patient acknowledge that they are equal. Then, with the patient watching, pour the contents of one of the cups into a tall thin container (like a test tube or urinometer). Now ask the patient which has more water the other urine cup or the tall thin container. They have to contain the same amount of water, but (to your amazement the first time you do it) the patient will point to one, usually the tall thin container. The reason this happens is that with this impairment the patient cannot deal with transitions and sees only static states. Sick persons with this cognitive impairment cannot deal with abstractions, they cannot make a choice when presented with more than two options simultaneously, and they cannot take the point of view of a person other than themselves. These patients will perform normally on a Mini-Mental Status examination (unless they have other cognitive difficulties) so they will be considered to have the capacity to make autonomous decisions.

They will be believed to have the capacity to give informed consent for surgery, research participation, and other consents. Because they are considered to be autonomous, they will have to make their own decisions and choices. It is not fair to have them make such choices by themselves. With your assistance, however, they can make authentic decisions. Your job is not to tell them what they should do, or to make what are called substituted choices, but to find out what their decision would be if they were able to make autonomous choices. This is done by avoiding abstractions—or making abstract choices into a number of exemplified concrete choices—and gradually questioning so that you determine what would be in their best interests *as they know those interests*. It takes time, but as you get better it takes much less time with the next patient. In the same manner it is possible to deal with the disconnection of the sick from their world, the problems of uncertainty and inadequate knowledge, the emotional impairments of sickness, their feelings of being out of control, their feelings of helplessness, and their loss of hope and that awful state, hopelessness. The healer becomes the source of connection and knowledge and the healer becomes the patient's agent of control.

This is an important dimension of healing—helping restore the attributes of the sick person's life to characteristics that distinguish the healthy. Things such as safety and security are true of the healthy but gone from the sick person. Loneliness is common among the sick who also (and seemingly paradoxically) have lost the privacy we all value and instead are exposed to the probing of others. Healthy people usually have an orderly, coherent, and predictable world in which they can act on their purposes and in which they have a sense of self-worth and an established identity. These and other traits are true of the healthy and lost to the sick. The healer helps reestablish a meaningful and "healthy" world. Think, for a moment, of the effect on the sick person of all these characteristics of sickness (and suffering). Even without any other pathology to induce illness, a world of danger, insecurity, loneliness, disorder, uncertainty, helplessness, and even hopelessness would in itself be a source of illness. This is why it is safe to say that sickness makes sickness. It is not difficult to conceive of how often the person is made sick by things that happen to them not related to their disease, by the nature of their medical care, by changes not in the body but in the person's world, and by problems in the person's relationships with others brought on or exaggerated by illness. Reflect on these and you will see that persons with serious disease can be like the well or like the sick—what happens to them can be helped by others, by effective healers (see Chapter 13).

Because of the personal and individual nature of these things they are rarely made better by impersonal forces. They require instead a healer who has made a connection to the sick person and has reached within himself or herself for the resources that go out to the sick person or the suffering patient. The healer has to be present—in direct, unmediated relation—to the sick person. *It is the healer plus the patient that constitutes the healing entity.* Put another way, healing is personal and healing is individual in both healer and patient. As I said before, efforts by the healer to do those things that make intimate and interior demands on the healer are kept from injuring the healer because, at least in medicine, healing is professional. The healer is working.

But what wonderful work!

References

Boudreau, Donald. (2006). Unpublished document, "Basic Concepts," distributed to incoming medical students of the Faculty of Medicine, McGill University.
Feinstein, A. R. (1967). *Clinical Judgment*. Baltimore, Williams & Wilkins Co.
Cassell, E. J. (1976). *The Healer's Art*. Philadelphia, Lippincott.
Sacks, O. (1984). *A Leg to Stand On*. New York, Touchstone.
WHO. (2001) ICF: *International Classification of Function*. Geneva.

The primary tool of attentive listening is not the ear, it is the clinician. Although listening, at bottom, involves learning about the person of the patient and the illness, it is also about the development of the person of the physician. Clinicians who listen carefully to their patients year after year learn an incalculable amount about people, about what and how they do things, about illness and being sick, about how people deal with sickness, doctors, tests, surgery, hospitals, and their staff, about medications, about how the body works when well and when ill, and about how the world works (at least the social world). Listening to all this enables them to grow as individuals. Listening—attentive listening—is a learned skill at which some will be better than others because of differences in aptitude and the time it takes to become skilled. Differences in native ability are overcome by knowing the importance of listening, knowing what you are listening for, and working at it and practicing. Like all the skills of physicianhood, it is a satisfying pleasure when you know you are doing things well and getting better at them. It may seem strange that it requires effort to become good at listening, because all of us are listening all the time or we could not live our lives. Why, then, do we have to actively learn attentive listening? Listening, in this regard, is similar to learning to communicate in that it takes more than merely knowing the language and using it in speech. The reason, in both attentive listening and communicating, is that we are doing medicine. The requirements of the patient—the person—the doctor, and their relationship, and then the diagnostic, therapeutic, and interpersonal activities require special attention and attentive listening (and communicating) and that moves the endeavor forward.

When setting about listening, clinicians will want to be sure that they are listening to the authentic patient. What does that mean? If you have ever role-played and really gotten into the role you know that you began to act like that person—you will have feelings and responses appropriate to the role. If this were not true, teaching with simulated patients would not work. Actors are especially good at this—they do not just act like the character they are playing, they try to become that person. It is also not surprising that being in a scary situation, in the presence of a dominating person, or feeling uncertain, needy, or diminished might have an impact on how a person behaves or the persona projected. It is certainly true of clinicians. A doctor who does not feel doctory, or who is unsure, feels inadequate, or has no sense of medical authority, is going to have trouble speaking to a patient or taking a history. You only have to remind yourself of your early days in your first clinical clerkship to know how true that is. What this tells us is that the context, the circumstances in which a conversation takes place, has an effect on how the conversation will unfold, from how well the participants listen and talk, or even the words and ideas a speaker projects. We want our patients to be as much their authentic selves as possible as we listen to them because part of our task is to

5

Listening

THE FOUNDATION OF THE HEALING RELATIONSHIP OF PATIENT AND CLINICIAN

CLINICAL MEDICINE IS based on knowledge about individual patients. In the past I would have just added "and the diseases that afflict them." Now, *in addition*, clinicians are listening for impairments of function. It is not possible to listen for functional impairment, however, without hearing about function. The story of an illness is a tale of an individual unique life being lived in its quotidian detail, complex interpersonal activities—work, marriage, parenthood, aspirations, and purposes—and how a pathophysiology interferes. In the past clinicians avoided listening to this because it slowed them down and seemed irrelevant to their purposes and goals. Now we go out of our way to hear it (although selectively—time is still a concern) and become efficient in its pursuit. We try to hear what this patient's underlying or essential purpose is and what well-being is for this patient. The definition of well-being is necessarily patient-centered and because of that healers are also patient-centered.

This is a chapter about listening attentively. Gathering information from the patient through listening will be the basis for knowing who the patient is, knowing what the matter is, and starting toward the solution to the patient's problem.[1] In the process, the clinician should be coming closer to the patient, ideally making the kind of unique very close connection that is possible in the doctor–patient relationship. As clinicians become better and more adept at this special relationship, how it can lead to a kind of knowledge of another person becomes clearer. This knowledge is the basis for the precision in clinical medicine that allows us to speak of our work as clinical science. We become extensions of our patients as we try to discover what is impairing their levels of functioning and interfering with the pursuit of their goals and purposes. We are also trying to discover the

---

1. Chapter 6, on the Evaluation of the Patient, discusses what a diagnosis actually is and how it is arrived at.

meanings on which their actions are based. The secret of discovering this kind of knowledge is attentive listening.

In the technologic medicine of our time clinicians too often act as if finding the disease and making the patient better are the direct result of specific diagnostic and therapeutic activities. In contemporary terms, it is as if the technology does the job. Patients subscribe to the same fallacy. My new patient at her second visit, boasting in the waiting room about what a good doctor I am, said, "He ordered the colonoscopy which is how the diagnosis of Crohn's disease was made." I was peeved because I knew she had inflammatory bowel disease within a few minutes of listening to the history of her illness. This patient's vignette tells less than half the tale. The forgotten part is what makes the whole process work, but it is too often taken for granted or done poorly.

Think about what happened. This woman, an advertising executive, modest and distrustful, is a stranger (although the friend of a patient) who walked into the consulting room worried and in distress because of abdominal pain and loose bloody bowels that she had concealed for two weeks. There is more to it. During this symptomatic period she was frightened at what she thought meant cancer and she slept poorly. She ate little. She did not work well, experienced trouble concentrating, and lost her sense of confidence and power. Worry about abdominal cramps and impending bowel movements became her constant companion. She was irritable at home and afraid to tell her husband why. She avoided sexual activity, and did not want to be as social as she usually was and as her husband expected. He felt pushed aside and wondered what he had done.

Within 20 minutes of the start of the visit, chattering about a mutual friend, she went into an examining room and completely disrobed. Before another 20 minutes had passed, she had been fully examined, including having first a speculum and then two fingers inserted into her vagina and one finger in her rectum. She left the consulting room a short time later feeling much better with a tentative diagnosis, prognosis, and plans for a colonoscopy—another unwanted invasive act. She was ready to carry out the plan we had arrived at together.

The script for her visit and what ensued is primarily cultural tradition. It is a powerful custom. A patient goes to the doctor, relates the story about her illness, and tells the doctor the truth and the whole story (which she had previously hidden). Despite her modesty and distaste for the process, she undresses and permits an examination of her naked body including penetration of her vagina and rectum. The doctor, the recipient of her story and her temporary suspension of modesty, focuses his attention on her "medical" case and does not stray into unrelated "personal" matters. In the examining room he makes no comments and takes no physical actions that are not clearly related to the medical problem. Both the physician and the patient seem to understand the boundaries that circumscribed their conversation and their actions. Even the subjects of the physician's questions fit a traditional mold going back centuries.

Changing the definition of illness requires a different kind of history because it involves aspects of the patient's life and functions not usually part of a medical interview. Patients will, after perhaps an initial period of puzzlement, accept interest in function and well-being when it is explained. The traditional roles and permissible actions will, however, remain the same. The basic, generally invisible, skill that makes it all work now and for millennia past is listening—*attentive* listening. In this chapter I am going to describe in detail what it is that clinicians do when they are listening attentively. The discussion is in the service of becoming a more skillful and effective listener and a better healer. When I was a medical student I did not attend my second year lectures. Periodically I worried that the lecture that I missed would give away "the secret of all of medicine." Of course that was silly; the lectures, according to my friends and their notes, gave away no secrets. There seemed to be, in fact, no "secret of all of medicine." That is not true, there *is* a secret. The secret is *listen*! Of course, it is not really a secret, it is a quiet, in the background, skill too often taken for granted. Listen to what? Listen to the person, listen to what your patient says and how; listen to what the patient does not say (and how). Listen to the family. Listen to other physicians, to the nurses, social workers, the nurse's aides, and everyone else who has contact with the patient. Last, but by no means least, listen to the body. Actually, there is one more person to whom you must attend—listen to yourself, your words and your thoughts.

Listening is an active—not passive—skill. Hearing is a perceptual process using the ears for the reception of sound. Listening is a cognitive skill that at the minimum requires attention to the words (or sounds) and is usually immediately and automatically followed by the assignment of meaning to what has been heard. Just as seeing is a cognitive act in which we see a particular something rather than another thing, we listen to sounds and hear a particular thing and not another thing. When listening to speech, identification of the words in an utterance is almost instantly followed by assignment of meaning to the utterance.[2] Sometimes you do not quite hear what the other person said, but, as if hearing was delayed, a few moments later you know the words and understand the utterance. In the brief hiatus of incomprehension your mind has been decoding the sounds and coming up with an interpretation of the utterance that seems to work. That phenomenon, known to us all, is clear evidence of the active cognitive nature of listening.

---

2. What an utterance is does not have a precise linguistic definition. As used here it refers to a natural unit of speech bound by pause or silence. We tend to hear speech as one or a series of utterances. Sometimes it is used to denote linked phrases that together form what speakers say in their turn (perhaps followed by someone else's utterance).

know them as they truly are. In bringing that about we modify *our* behavior and act in such a manner as to encourage the patients to be themselves. I watched a friend of mind, a surgeon who was a tall, imposing man, taking a history from a small woman. As he spoke to her he unobtrusively slid down in his chair until his eyes and hers were at the same level. Somewhat further on I am going to discuss in more detail how we encourage patients to feel comfortably themselves.

Patients have an expectation that they will be relieved of their illness because of the doctor. They feel that expectation on their way to see a doctor and the expectation conditions their responsiveness to the physician's words and actions. It is important to understand that the openness to being made better pervades the patient—body, mind, and spirit. It is not "just psychological." Placebos can have a positive effect even when the patient knows beyond doubt that they are placebos if the doctor is strongly supportive of the effect.[3] For that expectation (which may not be conscious) to be fulfilled to the degree possible requires the development of a relationship between the two. It also requires physicians to be aware of its benefits and not throw them away by disregarding them. The doctor–patient relationship—the healer–patient relationship—is one of the special social constructions in our culture (and probably all cultures) with important consequences for the effectiveness of clinicians and the outcome for patients. In addition to its benefits, the relationship also imposes responsibilities and restrictions on the behavior of physicians. Unfortunately, the doctor–patient relationship has become iconic and of mythic proportions so that its realities are difficult to discuss. The relationship has also been attacked, vilified, made fun of, minimized, and interpreted as merely an unequal power relationship. What does it matter if on occasion negative things have been true—as reprehensible as that may be—it is not just any relationship, but one between doctor and patient. The relationship is present when there is a patient, a doctor, and an illness, and it exists whether you "believe in it" or not. Patients need doctors to be relieved of the burdens of sickness and doctors need patients to be doctors. Patienthood changes persons, depending in degree and form on the severity and length of illness, the personality, character, and demographics of the person of the patient, the context of the illness, and the interaction with a physician. The role of the physician and the fact of being a physician have an impact on both patient and physician and are also dependent on the circumstances, experience, specialty, personality, character, and attitude of the physician. Like it or not, in caring for the sick person, the doctor is not simply somebody with special knowledge and the patient is not merely

---

3. The placebo effect and the anticipation of improvement at the doctor's hands are positive. A small number of patients have a negative placebo effect and an anticipation of the doctor doing nothing salutary for them.

someone with a bodily affliction. Just as a sickness, whatever it may be is not only an affliction of body parts. The social construction of medicine and the actors and their roles are real and influential. The clinician has the choice of learning how to maximize the relationship with the patient and its impact on the clinical situation or not. Why would anyone choose ignorance?

Much of what has been written about the doctor–patient relationship was written in the light of acute illness and solo practitioners and did not make distinctions about the patients' illnesses or the various specialties of physicians. Acute severe illness or life-threatening injury can create an effective relationship between clinician and patient in less than minutes. In a few instants a person with devastating sickness or injury is converted into someone trusting and willing to follow even the most stringent directives of a stranger who is the clinician. Often forgotten is that in the same few moments the clinician has become intensely personally concerned, fearful, and linked to the fate of the stranger who is the patient. In such circumstances what does the nature of the clinician's employment matter? In the contemporary world, however, chronic illness is the rule, commonly requiring the care of one (or even several) clinician year after year. The exigencies of insurance plans, forms of doctors' practice organizations, and even the possible need for very special doctors, surgeons, or hospitals that may be in distant cities mean that a relationship with only a single clinician is the unusual circumstance.[4] Furthermore, contemporary patients with chronic diseases may have learned a great amount about their afflictions—thus earning the authority of knowledge. All this might make us wonder whether the doctor–patient relationship still has any meaning or usefulness. Perhaps even more so as doctor and patient have come to know and respect each other over (possibly many) years.[5] Even in these circumstances, however, because of their skill some clinicians will have much more access to patients and their bodies than will others. These clinicians can make their patients better (by whatever definition) while others fail. What makes the difference?

---

4. Many insurance plans or other payment mechanisms in the United States have made it difficult for the patient to keep the same physician over long periods of time. It is as if the patient's relationship with a doctor—contrary to long held belief—is really unimportant. In this view, medicine is about technology, the body, and disease and personal issues are not essential. This has been and still is the deep-rooted fallacy of medicine since the last quarter of the twentieth century.

5. The patient will come to know the doctor as a doctor and the doctor know the patient as a patient. Patients will sometimes comment about how little they really know about the doctor even after many years. Similarly, having taken care of a patient for many years, something surprising may happen in the patient's everyday life that reveals how little the doctor knows of the patient.

To understand this we have to look again at illness. Although we will be discussing this in detail in later chapters, it necessary to keep in mind some of the general effects of sickness before going further into what attentive listening entails. Fear, ignorance, uncertainty, and changes in purpose are always present in important sickness. Actually, ignorance, uncertainty, and interference with purpose occur in everyday life. What will the weather be this evening? Am I doing a good job? Does my boss (teacher, friend, relative, or anyone else) like me? Can I adapt to the circumstances of a shipboard cruise? Will I miss my flight? Is the plumber competent? Will I sleep well tonight; be able to eat dinner; do I smell bad; do I look good; did I accurately remember yesterday's events? The list of uncertainties is close to endless, but the form of the social structure and the rules of everyday life will generally provide acceptable answers to these uncertainties. That is, it will if you behave according to the rules—which, although unwritten, you have spent your life learning, mostly outside of awareness. Ignorance? No matter how much education, how much exposure to similar experiences, how much time on the job, or anything else you mention, there will be things you do not know. Who cares? Whatever you want or need to know you will probably learn about it soon enough or it (whatever it is) does not really matter. We commonly say Google it. You may notice, when you do use a computer and its search method to look something up on the internet, on the top of the page it will have some variation of the following: "1–10 of about **126,000** for **typhoid fever** with **Safesearch on**. (0.08 seconds)." You would not dream of looking at all 126,000, possibly relevant, entries. You probably found out enough on the first page or so to relieve your ignorance sufficiently. As for the really important things in life—what is in store for you in the future, what will happen to your children, your finances, and so forth, the questions may worry or even disturb you, but you know what you can know and fortunately are usually able to move on with your thoughts or actions.

How different serious illness is. The ordinary comprehension of daily life is inadequate when illness poses threats. Questions about the future and what is going to happen are vital and cannot be laid aside without help. Will the pain stop? Do you really have the best doctor? What can you do about it if you do not? Is the doctor trustworthy? Is the doctor being completely truthful? Will you live through this? Will you work again? How much impairment can you expect? What side effects can you anticipate? You read so much about medical errors, are they happening now to you? And this goes on and on, one question after another. In the contemporary world in which people often act as if they know everything, patients soon learn that they know nothing—or at least not enough to answer all the questions that arise. The internet is of little help (except to cause more fear) because "126,000 entries" basically means conflicting answers—or answers that raise more questions. For example, a young woman with rheumatoid arthritis finds that her anti-tumor necrosis factor (TNF) medication is not working any more. In the beginning it was effective but that has gradually diminished. Other drugs are available and her rheumatologist has offered two alternatives, which she looked up on the internet. "At this point," she says, "I have decided, through discussions with my dad and my rheumatologist, that I will try the Simponi first. It is a once monthly injection, as opposed to the Actemra, which is an infusion, like my Orencia." The rheumatologist offered her alternatives but did not discuss the technical issues that bear on the question, but in the contemporary manner left her to make the decision herself because she is an autonomous person. (This is a common, but I believe, mistaken, understanding of the concept of autonomy. See Chapter 13 for a full discussion of the ethical issues.) She is being asked to make a complex technical decision that is in the province of the rheumatologist. She was not, however, questioned about her personal values that bear on the decision and about which *no one* knows better than she. Together, she and the rheumatologist would make an appropriate decision-making unit. By herself and with her father, an optometrist, she is exposed to unnecessary uncertainties.

The previous case highlights the fact that sick people commonly do not understand what is happening to them. The questions are endless. "Will the bleeding stop and what will happen if it does not?" "Why is the pain getting worse when I was told that things are getting better?" "I saw my wound when the doctors were changing the dressing today and it looks awful—purple and swollen—is that the way it should be?" "I know from the newspapers that minutes count when you are having a heart attack and you are supposed to have a balloon thing, but nobody seems to be doing anything." "The doctors said that there was nothing more they could do for me, so what is going to happen now?" "They said that I am still having trouble after my heart operation because of pericarditis, but I don't know what that is, what it means, and what I am supposed to do about it?" What are the consequences of not understanding what is happening to you in serious illness or of not knowing the best thing to do? They cannot be good. In addition to uncertainty, sickness alters purpose. All of us go about our days filled with purposes large and small. As our definition of sickness makes clear, however, the impairments of function in sickness make the accomplishment of purpose difficult. Moreover, the central purpose of all of us is aimed at the being of ourselves. In sickness, purpose is diverted from that usual goal and directed to the relief of distress. Who is to help with ignorance, uncertainty, and diversions of purpose—and the many other questions and necessary actions that come with being sick? The doctor will help, if the illness is serious enough.

We do not usually think of ourselves as going to physicians to resolve such issues; we seek the aid of physicians to treat our disease, as people have done in Western cultures for more than two and a half millennium. It is only since 1925 (insulin) and 1937 (sulfa drugs) that physicians have been able to treat diseases decisively.[6] From the beginnings of medicine in ours and all other cultures medicine has had specific treatments for diseases, however defined, which people (including doctors) believed were effective. From our contemporary vantage point we know that those old treatments were almost always worthless—or worse.[7] As Oliver Wendell Holmes, Sr. said in 1883: "If the whole materia medica, as used, could be sunk to the bottom of the sea, it would be all the better for mankind and all the worst for the fishes."

Contemporary medicine is marked by the effectiveness of its treatments and the endless wonder of diagnostic and therapeutic technology. One medical specialty after another—cardiology, gastroenterology, nephrology, oncology, and pulmonology—is preoccupied with its technologies, instrumentalities, and its treatments, which are effective to a greater degree than ever. The current *materia medica* (and, more practically, the *Physicians' Desk Reference*) is filled with effective medications that would still be "worst for the fishes" but are very useful for humans. As noted many times in this book, this armamentarium and the physicians who direct it are focused primarily on diseases or their symptoms. The goal is the cure of disease. Chronic diseases, the problems of the disabled, and the infirmities and functional losses of aging are not amenable to cure. And everybody dies.

Were all doctors, in times past, worthless and did patients get no help from their physicians? Was every benefit merely "psychological" or a placebo response? Are the fear, ignorance, uncertainty, and obstruction of purpose that characterize sickness "only psychological"? If I could create in you a state dominated by fear, ignorance, uncertainty, and an inability to pursue your purposes, would not your being as you know yourself be profoundly altered? I believe that the impact of that state on your being would reach every aspect of you—physical, psychological, personal, social, and spiritual. "We are of a piece, what affects one part affects the whole and what affects the whole has an impact on every part." A vital aspect of healing is the effect of the healer on those characteristics of sickness. With this in mind, we can better understand the utility of the doctor–patient relationship that allows a sick person to reach out to a doctor, who may be a stranger, with the

---

6. Surgeons have been able to treat diseases decisively, but until anesthesia (1846) and the beginnings of antiseptic surgery in 1867, the results were often horrendous. It was probably not until the beginning of the twentieth century that surgery was routinely painless and infection uncommon.

7. One of the wonders of medicine is that in almost every era doctors have discovered that what went before was wrong, without the equivalent recognition that we must also be wrong-headed about some beliefs we hold dear.

expectation of relief. To the patient the doctor is knowledgeable, knows what to do, and is larger than the problem. The doctor is without fear in the face of the sickness, no matter how terrible, and is unafraid to act despite uncertainties.[8] That is, with reason, the cultural expectation of doctors. The error that gets in the way of understanding is to equate sicknesses with the diseases that are believed to be their cause. Late in my fourth year of medical school, I had what appeared to be a respiratory illness, although I was sicker than I expected to be. Still, like most of us, I paid little attention to it. I lived in a hospital then and I was talking with a friend in my room. Thirsty, I took a drink of Coke and it came right back out of my nose—soft palate paralysis. That really scared me and I started to look things up in my neurology textbook. One thing was worse than the next and they all seemed to be fatal. Panicky, I called my doctor who was attending at the hospital. He came, examined me, found my soft palate paralyzed as expected, and then discussed the problem, minimizing nothing. He thought we should go to Bellevue (where I was a student) because they had a respirator. (This was 1954, when a respirator was a Drinker respirator—the iron lung.) Despite the discussion I calmed down and the fear went away. The head of student health was alerted, and when we got to Bellevue and I saw how frightened he was, my fear returned. Again my physician calmed me down by talking about the problem, its seriousness, and what would be done.[9]

Relieving these universal burdens of sickness is, unquestionably, valuable in itself because it allows each patient again to be the person she knows herself to be. Then the person is able to do the things that she thinks are important to being herself. Of course serious illness modifies goals—so do aging, education, frustrations, and other exigencies of life. Persons sick or well know this, even if it sometimes takes them time to come to terms with these facts. (The following chapters will deal specifically with these tasks.)

If the generic doctor of the doctor–patient relationship can relieve some of the impact of sickness, it makes sense that a clinician who knows the patient can be more effective. This is because the general characteristics of sickness that

---

8. Of course doctors have fear, uncertainty, and ignorance. But they learn to hide these from patients no matter what the personal cost. Burdening the patient with the doctor's doubts or anxieties is not helpful. And doctors always have purpose in which patients share—the patient's well-being. These abilities are learned, sometimes at a high price. If clinicians cannot master these things, they simply should not care for the sick.

9. It turned out to be some unnamed encephalitis and over the next few weeks the illness resolved. This is not how we expect to learn in medical school, but I never forgot the lessons. My own physician telling me all the dangers did not frighten me; he demonstrated that he was knowing and able to act. The student health physician frightened me because his fear implied his ignorance, uncertainty, and inability to act, which implied that things were even worse than I thought (which would have been difficult).

I discussed may be different and show themselves in different degrees in different patients. We are not all ignorant to the same degree and about the same things; some tolerate uncertainty better than others; fear and its impact are variable, and our investment in our purposes differs. There is no better way to discover this about patients than to listen attentively to what they say and question them carefully. As the goal of healing has enlarged, more knowledge about the person of the patient is required. What it means to say that it "Allows each patient again to be the person he knows himself to be" requires questioning and listening—not just listening, but *attentive listening*. This, in company with observation, allows the construction of a narrative—inside and unspoken—so that the narrative's shortcomings urge further exploration. All of this is efficient and is done in limited time. In discussing the young woman with rheumatoid arthritis I suggested that she and her rheumatologist "together would make an appropriate decision-making unit." That would have been better than just turning the decision over to her, but I meant to imply something more than the two of them making the decision in consultation with each other. I wanted the rheumatologist—with his clinical skills—to create a close connection with her. As a consequence, her values, needs, and concerns as the person she is (with a chronic painful disease and as a psychology doctoral candidate) would become merged with his technical knowledge and knowledge of persons and issue forth as her autonomous decision, while he remained firmly within the boundaries of being her rheumatologist. Do I know how to go about all these techniques and goals? Yes, generally, but I, we, still have much to learn. Let's go on.

Each person in ordinary society is generally considered as a separate individual in his or her own space. Atomistic is the word for that idea. Members in a family are not thought of as atomistic; they are connected with one another; close connections between family members are common and commonly accepted. Connected individuals behave as though they share, to a variable degree, thoughts and feelings and frequently express this idea. It is not unusual for one family member to report awareness of or participation in the feelings of another. Sometimes each seems to know what the other is thinking. The same very close or intimate connectedness is common in very loving relationships, especially where sexual connections are present.

Sick persons need other people to help them, particularly their physicians. Their need may be so great—particularly in serious illness or injury—that they are willing to lower their boundaries (although outside of awareness)—to connect closely to others and to allow others to merge with them. The degree of connection between sick persons and clinicians is variable and is dependent on the needs of the patient and the characteristics of the clinician involved. This kind of interpersonal connection increases the ability of physicians to influence their patients' thinking, ideas, meanings, and also their bodies. Such connections facilitate care as the caregiver is also more cognizant of the needs of the sick person. Effective clinicians may or may not be more consciously aware of the need to make a connection to patients than others, but they have in common certain effective behaviors. The scientific community in Western cultures does not regard telepathy as a real phenomenon, so these common happenings between the sick and their caregivers are simply there to be learned and utilized by experienced clinicians. This closeness, however, requires very careful respect for boundaries. (There is a more complete discussion of this in Chapter 2, "The Person.")

David Schenk and Larry R. Churchill, in their excellent book *Healers: Extraordinary Clinicians at Work*, questioned 50 clinicians considered by their colleagues to be the best healers, to see how they worked with patients. They discovered that these effective practitioners mostly all did the same things. First, they introduced themselves by name in a personal manner, shook hands, smiled, sat down, and made eye contact. They took time and were patient—they did not act rushed or impatient. They were quiet—creating a quiet conversational space for the patients' utterances. They acted obviously and genuinely interested. They allowed the patients to be as authentically themselves as possible. After an initial and inviting word or two (I usually say "How can I help you?") they made themselves open and they listened without interrupting. What does it mean to be open?

Schenk and Churchill do not discuss this kind of openness in their book, but this is how it has worked for me. What does it mean to "be open?" What I am about to describe can be taught in lectures and in person; let me try in print. To learn to do it, sit opposite someone else (start with a spouse or a close friend) who will be doing the same thing. Both palms facing inward, fingers curled, and the backs of the fingers of both hands touching, place the tips of your curled fingers on your mid-sternum. And then, as though you are opening a pair of doors to your heart, pull your curled door-opening fingers in a small arc about 8 inches away from your chest and say—to yourself—"open." Then with the "door open," make yourself as fully receptive to the other person as possible.[10] You will probably feel a sort of light pleasant feeling in front of your chest. The other person, doing the same thing, will also feel that light pleasant sensation. You are now "open" and receptive to the other person. If this were a personal maneuver between you and someone emotionally close, it might be felt as a mildly loving feeling. It is *not like*

---

10. You are not actually opening a door—there is no door to open. I find that when I teach this it is easier to visualize yourself actually opening a door and closing it. When you are comfortable doing the maneuver you can simply consciously think yourself open or closed without your hands doing anything. It may take some time to learn.

that with a stranger or a patient. To some doing this it will feel threatening—as though vulnerable or unguarded. In this state of "openness" you are more fully aware of the other person and the other person's feelings. If it is at all threatening, swing your curled finger tips back to the sternum and say—to yourself—"close." The feeling will disappear. Then repeat the maneuver of "open," and then "close." It cannot really threaten you if it is that simple to "close the door." Practice this until you have the confidence that you can really do it, and that that feeling of openness is within your conscious capacity. When you are sitting opposite a patient, particularly in the opening interview, make yourself open (unobtrusively). The patient will experience you as "really listening," trustworthy, and caring. Patients used to say to me after only a few minutes of that "openness" before I could possibly have actually manifested it in any other way, "You're the first person who has really listened to me." Ultimately, that is the way you should always be when you are with patients. If you find a particular patient threatening, simply close the "door." (And think about what it is that is threatening.)

We all know that when you are with patients the telephone can be an obtrusive presence. Sometimes it is not possible to stop calls. Here is how I solved this common problem. I had read that Henry Kaiser, whose company built Liberty ships during World War II, taught himself when interrupted to come back to *exactly the same point* in the conversation as before the interruption. I thought that I could also learn to do that. When the telephone rang, I would memorize the few words I (or the patient) said just before the call, and return to *exactly those words* and continue the conversation. It took awhile to learn. Now, many, many years later I still habitually do the same thing. Sometimes, I repeat to the patient his or her exact words prior to interruption, and wait for them to continue.

There are almost always barriers to attentive listening and things that intimidate the patients and keep them from feeling like themselves or speaking freely. Learn what they are and get rid of them. That is not so easy to do, especially when you are less experienced or working in a group work space. When starting out we rarely have the confidence that goes with our authority. We are often—in the beginning—happy to have the desk between us and the patient so we do not feel so exposed (or ignorant). As soon as you can, get rid of whatever is getting in the way of your experiencing the patients. Sometimes it is something the patient says that seems to require comment. Must you say anything? Most often you can let it pass. Sometimes it is the feelings—anger, sadness, suffering—that may be swirling around the patient and the dangers they may seem to pose to you. What are the dangers? Anger can seem very threatening, but the patient cannot really be angry at you, there has not been time. Sometimes, in the face of obvious anger, you may ask quietly, "Why (do you seem) so angry…" You will almost certainly learn something about the patient that is important. Then there is the depth of the sickness itself and its awfulness in which you will soon be caught up. Be courageous even in the face of impending death, agonizing pain, terrible malignancies, dangerous infection, awful dyspnea, and overwhelming jaundice and ascites.

You learn courage by facing these things and discovering how well you did. Courage is catching—so, in the other direction, is fear. Family dynamics can be very challenging. Patients or others commonly want to draw you into difficulties that may have been going on since childhood. Fights, unknown unhappinesses, unmet needs that seem to be hanging off the patient, and others—the last thing you want to do is to take a part. Still, you should become aware of these things, especially in serious illness. Looming over everything else may be the awful thoughts of your own ignorance. When you start out you may be trying to be the super chief resident, as though that is the goal of patient care. Chief residents know a lot of medical science and about diseases and their management; this is necessary knowledge—given a disease problem. Of the things in this chapter, they are as ignorant as everyone else. Worse, because they may think they know more than they do. We all, to a person, hate to appear dumb. Ignorance is not good, but ignorance of ignorance is reprehensible.

Patients today often come to us thinking they really know a lot about medicine and doctors in general, the failures and faults of medicine, their own symptoms, and treatments in particular. They may react to their physician, especially a doctor new to them and young, as though they know just as much (and maybe more). Physicians find this very irritating—who would not? Physicians want to tell their patients that if it was so easy to know so much, why were they in training so long. Under these circumstances it is even more difficult than it has been since Hippocrates to sit and listen—really attentively listen—as you let the patient explain the illness and tell you all about everything. The doctor should be asking only occasional short clarifying questions that get at the meat of things and yet not let the interview go on and on. My favorite questions are as follows: "Oh…" "And then…" "So…" "And…" (All with an upward ending inflection—this is a request for an answer.) "Why do you think that was?" "That must have been upsetting…(Or painful…or distressing…or awful…)" "Wow…" Very specific questions, although, of course, sometimes necessary and productive, cause the patient to answer within the framework and words of the question, which may miss the important facts. Questions asking for a yes or no should be used sparingly—only when checking something—"Did you say it was swollen?" Especially with a crucial issue, you do not want to be in a situation in which the patient says no and you think the answer is yes. What are you going to do, call the patient a liar? My favorite follow-up questions—maybe just my favorite question is "What does that mean?" Remember, the patients know what the matter is and what you need to learn; they just do not know that they know. Your questions develop their knowledge. Clinicians who can patiently listen, listen to the fears and the outrages, listen to hopes and expectations, are unusual and patients know this, especially if the clinician is open. Patients also know that clinicians who are not defensive, who can allow patients to "look good," who do not have to display how much *they* know, probably are, paradoxically, really knowledgeable.

If you are working in a group space, there may be a lot of people going back and forth, sometimes actively interrupting and sometimes just noisy. There may be no actual office but only a desk, chairs, and an examining table. Focusing intently on the patient in the personal manner described and making yourself open to the patient create a circle of privacy enclosing the two of you that is surprising impermeable. This is also true for interactions that take place in Emergency Departments, hospital rooms with more than one bed, and other public places. Move in closer in these circumstances so that you hear what is said and so the patient knows beyond question who your primary interest is. When necessary, include the family or others also present. Some clinicians widen their circle of intimacy to include these variably important others. I do not. The patient and I are going to be working together over some time period—I want us to be and see ourselves as welded together for the coming struggle with sickness.

It has become common for clinicians to present themselves as part of the team and to introduce everyone to the patient and indicate that it is "the team" that will be caring for the patient. Realizing that the days of the lone clinician fighting off disease are over has been part of a big step forward. We know now that the nurse, nurse practitioner, social worker, and others together are necessary for good patient care. I do not believe, however, that a team takes care of a patient. I believe individuals with various skills each working with the same patient and coordinating their efforts provide the best care. The relationship with the patient, however, is an individual matter. There should be *one* person with whom that patient has the primary relationship. Where possible, that person should be the physician. Having said that, sometimes it is the nurse, the social worker, the physical therapist, or sometimes another to whom the patient will look as his or her primary caregiver. Each has to learn to listen, not only to the patient, but to each other—as *attentively* as to the patient.

Physicians are sure that attentive listening takes up a lot of time and they are very aware that the clock is always ticking. They do not have the time, they think, to *really listen attentively*. The evidence is that attentive listening is the most time efficient way. I have seen it written many times that in most patient interviews the doctor interrupts after 20 seconds or so. That is very inefficient, especially if you want to find out from the patient what the problem is. It takes longer than 20 seconds for people to tell their story. Mostly physicians ask a set of directed questions requesting specific information. Those questions usually have the possible answers already specified. Give the poor souls a chance, and they will tell you what is important. If you cut them off, they will keep trying to tell you and more time will be wasted. Doctors sometimes wonder why patients do not disclose the real reason for the visit until they are on their way out the door. It is because they were not given a chance to talk earlier or to tell it their way. So as they are about to leave the visit their question is still unanswered. It may be difficult to realize that patients have been thinking about what they wanted to say—even rehearsing the words—on the way to seeing the doctor, and maybe even the day before. Time-wasting interviews come from doctors who talk too much, use too many words, and ask unnecessary questions, from clinicians who do not know what they are after and as a consequence are inefficient, and from patients who ramble and are allowed to talk too much. Respect, patience, and attentive listening do not mean surrendering control of the interaction. You and the patient have a common goal, and the two of you working together with shared authority toward that aim (which you have made clear) allows you to direct the process, albeit unobtrusively. When there is a talkative family member or friend present and you have demonstrated your attentiveness and concern for the patient, you are permitted, if necessary, to directly request silence.

It can be very difficult to observe the virtues that go with attentive listening when you dislike the patient. Some patients (some people) are really obnoxious. More often, however, the unlikable patient is someone who, as they say, "pushes your button." Then you have the interesting problem of figuring out what it is about the patient that got to you. It is interesting because it changes the subject from "I don't like..." to introspection and that always teaches you something—if only how to self-examine. Sometimes it is because the patient is just like some unpleasant relative, or has outspoken political opinions that are upsetting. Looking for who or what becomes the problem. Solving the difficulties raised by an unpleasant patient represents an interesting issue in itself. However, a patient interview is not a debate. If you do not like what the patient said about (say) doctors, medicine, your office, staff, Democrats, or whatever, *learn to be silent*. Let it pass. Stay focused on the interview (and not on the clock, the crowded waiting room, another patient, money, difficulties at home, or whatever). I often ran behind my schedule so patients would complain about waiting. I told them, "I am sorry you had to wait, but let's make sure I spend enough time with you so that we can solve your problem."

It may seem strange, but even when you are examining the patient you should be attentively listening. Here is when a quiet mind, always helpful, is most important. There may be, as it is said, no such thing as telepathy, but there is no question that information is pouring in during a physical examination. Your conscious attention may be focused on the eye-grounds, and now on the ear (through the otoscope), and now the mouth and throat, but outside of awareness you are registering other facts (say) about the face or skin—color, texture, lesions, healthiness—that never come to consciousness. And so it is about the neck, chest, ribs, general motions, abdomen, and so on, and so on. If you are talking, or your mind is filled with other thoughts, this wealth of information probably bounces right off and does not register even below awareness. Suppose you finished your history and thought that there was something wrong—the patient was sick. On examination you find nothing that would indicate what worried you. But you are still uncomfortable about the patient and you continue to think that something is not right. You may well be correct—something is wrong. Reassure the patient that the examination is negative—but say, "I want to be on the safe side so I think we should get a... (naming another test or suggesting a consultation, or whatever). If you get the strong feeling (in the same setting) that the patient is fine, that is also probably correct. These are intuitive thoughts, but do not confuse them with magic or allow yourself the happy delusion that you have magical fingers. Intuition is an excellent source of ideas, but it should *never be the sole reason for action*. If you think something is true, as noted below, there is probably a reason. Now, go get the information from another source that will nail the thing down.

In attentive listening, in addition to the patient, you yourself are always both subject and object of your attention. You are the subject because you are attentively listening to the patient's responses as they occur—not just to their meanings, but to the language. You are focusing on the pauses, pitch, and speech rate (called the paralanguage), the words and word palate (simple, fancy, educated, sick, etc.), the sentence structure, and the logic of the utterance (which reveals the patient's underlying premises). You are accomplishing this at the speed of natural speech—hard to do until you train yourself. You are also the object because you are observing yourself in the interaction. This requires paying attention to your own words, mannerisms, and presentation to the patient, which is another taxing skill. There is a reason it is called *attentive* listening. It is fun to learn to do all this at the same time as you are listening to hear the patient's problem and clues to its solution. The impediments also clarify why it is so useful to have a quiet mind. If you are listening to all the speech and its meanings flowing from you and the patient while at the same time attending to the ideas and noise of your own wayward thoughts, that seems like too much to ask. (See Chapter 2 footnote 5 to learn the skill of a quiet mind.)

While you are attentively listening you are also observing—seeing what the patient looks like—all the details that tell us so much about other people.

When you are listening, asking questions, and listening again, you may be uncertain about what was said. Check what you think you heard with the patient. "Do I have this right? The pain first started the night before you began coughing?

Tell me." Or "Tell me again why you are having trouble with your friends since you got sick." "I'm sorry to have to ask you again, but I want to be sure I understand..." Remember, you and the patient are in this together and you want to understand the patient and the patient wants to know you know. Some people speak in a way that can only be called opaque. You do not want to appear like a dope, but if you fail to question again (and again, and again) you will not know what happened. It will not be the first time such patients experienced others as not understanding them, but it may be the first time they came across a doctor who really wanted to comprehend.

This widely diverse information comes together to form a narrative—a story with a timeline about a person and his or her sickness and life. You should tell yourself this story inwardly to see if it hangs together and to see whether it seems reasonably attached to this patient (person) about whose way of life and being you have discovered so much. Instead of relating the narrative to yourself, you can tell the story to the patient so that the two of you are together in checking the authenticity of the narrative. There are many times when you are writing the history of the illness and describing the patient and the pertinent details of a life that you will want to go back and ask more questions. Although in the hospital you can probably do this, in other settings the opportunity has probably passed. That is why getting in the habit of telling yourself or the patient the story is useful. Some believe that what needs to happen is not recounting the story to yourself or to the patient; rather it is not shortcutting the information-gathering process before you *really* have all the relevant facts. Either way, the question you are asking is, "Do I *really* know the story; do I *have all the details?*" If the answer is no, or there is doubt, you are not yet finished asking questions and listening to the answers

This vast amount of information forms itself into the pattern(s) that are the basis for the remarkable pattern recognizer that all physicians contain within themselves.[11] In the next chapter there will be a more complete discussion of pattern recognition and the part it plays in the clinical thinking of clinicians.

For attentive listening to do its best you must learn to trust your mind. If you heard it, you heard it. If a pertinent idea comes to mind, if you suddenly want to ask a strange question and are not sure why, if you seem to get an idea about the patient or the case out of the blue, pay attention. If you get an intuition as noted above, do not dismiss it unless you have reasoned the matter through. Pay attention to emotion that arises as you talk with a patient. Anger? Why? Whose anger is it, yours or the patient's (which you have caught). Warm or loving feelings, perhaps sexual feelings—this is the way connecting closely to the patient announces

---

11. Pattern recognition is a universal attribute of thought. It has been copied by automated systems, computer diagnostic programs, and all sorts of algorithms. It can also be very sophisticated, so do not let others or yourself disparage it.

itself—are not about sex, they are about connection to the patient. There is a reason something comes to mind. Perhaps, the ideas or feelings are screwy and wrong; if so, why did they push into your thoughts at that time? On the other hand, as you have been asking questions and attentively listening, your mind has been processing and the processing does not always go in a direction you would have consciously chosen. Cognition does what it does for good logical reasons. Logic here means a set (however small) of premises leading to a conclusion. We, as a profession, have become so enamored of the objective, that I believe we have actively devalued the subjectivity of unspoken cognition—quiet thoughts and emotions working in the background. If this kind of mental activity, like intuition, leads to conclusions that seem dubious, find objective evidence that supports or defeats them. Pay attention to the evidence, *all the evidence*, inside and outside of you. Some people love intuition. That is fine as long its conclusions are put to the test of evidence for and against. Be careful of strongly held opinions that seem so true that it does not matter what other evidence says. One time, in a sick patient with abdominal pain, I became convinced that he had pylephlebitis—infective phlebitis of the portal vein. Nothing, *but nothing* could change my mind—including a normal white blood count. He did not have pylephlebitis. I learned my lesson. Diagnostic hypotheses are just that, hypotheses open to test.

I have written about pattern recognition as an inherent part of how physicians think. Pattern recognition provides the basic diagnosis and opinion about the patient based on facts gathered primarily by listening attentively to what the patient says in recounting the story of the illness—and in response to careful questions. It is the beginning—not the end—of the medical thought processes. The large literature in the field of clinical epidemiology that was born of Alvan Feinstein's writing in the 1960s provides many tools that markedly increase the sophistication of medical decision making (Feinstein 1967). So much of value has been written about the subject that we have become much better in our diagnostic thinking and its tests. Jerome Groopman's book has much of value on the subject (Groopman 2007). Although generally forgotten, Feinstein wrote that clinicians were involved in a science that is characterized by an $N = 1$. To most of us, a science of $N = 1$ is an oxymoron; medicine has left behind sciences like the old botany that consisted of finding and characterizing plants like a new species of violet. Medical science, moving forward, has embraced mechanism and reductionism and objective measurement of both qualitative and quantitative dimensions. We forget too often that what makes contemporary reductionist medical science important is that it came into being because of the individual sick patients that inspired it in the first place. Yet each of our patients, the subjects of clinical medical science, is an individual—particular and unique—which is a description of an $N = 1$. Understanding starts with knowing what has happened to a particular patient—the experience—to the degree possible. Alvan Feinstein (1967, p. 312) wrote, "Thus, the clinical counterpart of qualitative precision in measurement is effective *communication* of the sensation [the patient's experience of symptoms]; the clinical counterpart of quantitative precision (the "significant figures" of the measurement) is *specification* of detail." (Italics in the original.)

Yes, there is a primordial truth in medicine, knowledge of the individual sick person. The secret of knowing that truth is to listen, and listen *attentively*.

References

Feinstein, A. R. (1967). *Clinical Judgment*. Baltimore, Williams & Wilkins Co.

Groopman, J. (2007). *How Doctors Think*. New York, Houghton Mifflin Company.

Schenk, D., and Churchill, L. R. (2011). *Healers: Extraordinary Clinicians at Work*. New York, Oxford University Press.

6

The Evaluation of the Patient

Persons Are Sick Who Are Unable to Pursue Their Goals and Purposes Because of Impairments of Function That They Believe Are in the Domain of Medicine

THE DEFINITION OF sickness determines the goals of the evaluation of the patient. In the beginning of the nineteenth century, when the modern disease era started, sickness was defined by diseases—sick persons had a disease. The purpose of the evaluation was to find the disease. The examining clinician was looking for this "thing" that had got hold of the patient. This is the ontologic view of disease—disease as an entity that entered the patient. This perspective has alternated throughout the history of medicine with a physiologic view—disease is a result of an imbalance of the forces of nature in and around the sick person. From the nineteenth century until relatively recently, diagnosis—naming the disease—was everything. Even before medicine started to enter the era of effective treatment in the 1930s, however, it was becoming evident that diagnosis as the name of a disease was not sufficient. In the 1930s the importance of the socioeconomic determinants of disease was uncovered. As a consequence, discovering the social context of the patient became a part of diagnostic evaluation. After World War II, physicians began to understand that the persons who were the patients were not merely bystanders in their own sickness, but that they played an active (although usually unwitting) role in the unfolding stories that were their illnesses. That was the beginning of moving the person to a central position in clinical medicine.

This book is based on a further step, accepting the fact that a sickness is not solely the unmediated impact of the pathophysiology of a disease on the body. Sickness, as importantly (and sometimes only), expresses its effects by interfering in the web of functions by which individuals live their lives among others and pursue or accomplish their purposes and goals. The evaluation of the patient should, therefore, reveal the disease process (the pathophysiology), the impairments of function (from the molecular to the spiritual to the degree that they can be discovered), the way they interfere with the person's life, and the degree to which they impede the pursuit of the patient's goals and purposes. It seems like a tall order. In some ways, however, it is easier than contemporary diagnostic efforts. It is, for example, about the patient's sickness and what it is doing to the patient. The evaluation of a patient with chronic obstructive lung disease, for example, does not stop at understanding the severity of the pulmonary disease, but shows how it has an impact on muscle strength and thus on walking and other tasks of everyday life, and also an effect on work, social life, and the family. It is primarily about the patient and is not focused on the disease. All the findings about the disease, the impairments of functions, and the nature of the patient fit within and can be seen as belonging to *this particular* person. The findings should provide avenues for patients to return to the pursuit of their goals even when the underlying disease resists treatment. I once made the diagnosis of scleroderma and was quite pleased with myself until I realized that I could do nothing for the patient (aside from telling her what a great disease she had). Scleroderma fits the ideal of disease—interesting pathogenesis and interesting pathophysiology. Reflecting on it afterward I realized that scleroderma was a doctors' kind of disease for those fancy reasons, whereas osteoarthritis, about which I knew next to nothing, had no intellectual standing at all. Yet osteoarthritis caused much more trouble to many more patients and offered real opportunities for treatment. The evaluation and its results described here have to do with what is doing the patient harm. In addition, the patients' expressed needs, desires, and concerns lead to still further questions about what the patient wants and requires at this time and what will make this patient better by his or her own lights. In this view of sickness patients are helped to be better even if nothing can be done to change the course of their disease.

A little bit about this chapter. This is not like a chapter from a textbook on physical diagnosis. It will not spell out in detail the complete set of actions required of clinicians. It is meant, instead, to provide sufficient detail so that a clinician knows what is different about the evaluation of the patient when using the concept of sickness described in this book. Most of us, in fact almost all, have been, in the past, evaluating our patients from a different perspective so that many of the details here will be new—at least the emphasis will be different. I have found this change of perspective interesting and challenging—and not easy. I hope you also are captured by both the interest and the challenge.

In the past, it has been common to start talking about taking a history of the present illness. This acknowledged that the clinician's first contact with a patient was most often when the patient was admitted to the hospital or made an initial office visit. These more formal occasions are still important, but they may not be the start of our work with patients. The answers to questions about the persons who are our patients start before our opening questions about the illness. They begin with the first contact: on the telephone, in the office or hospital, in the hallway, or even in email or text messages. Almost automatically, everybody forms an opinion of someone on their first few moments of interaction. These judgments are reflexive for most people, but should be a part of a conscious clinical process. A telephone conversation, answering an email, introducing yourself, and the invitation, "would you like to sit here," are each opportunities to start the clinical interaction in a polite manner that invites a trusting connection. They are also an opportunity for conscious observation of the patient and the beginning of the acquisition of information. When the disease was the primary focus of clinical medicine and the patient was secondary these facts about the patient seemed less important than clues to the patient's disease. Now both pathology *as well as* the patient command our attention. The patient's presentation of self, mannerisms, clothing, voice, and word choice, as well as what the patient is actually saying, are of interest. I say conscious observation because early on, while learning clinical medicine or changing goals, it is necessary to actively register these things in the few moments during which they take place. That seems impossible because so much information is flowing by, but, of course, in time it becomes second nature. It is information and knowledge about the patient that drive our efforts now and will do so in the future.

Note how the patient walks (coming into the office, for example), sits down, and assumes a posture. Some patients (but not too many) boldly put themselves in your face whereas others sit modestly or put their head to the side (mostly women), cross their legs or do not, fidget or do not, and so on. Clothing and style are always present. There is no such thing as no presentation of the self—no attention by the person to all these details from hair to shoes—except in the very sick or in patients who have given up and no longer care about anything. In a short time you will likely see the patient in an examining room and be able to observe the patient without clothes, observe (or smell) hygiene, watch the patient getting on a table and off, and then dressing, and so on. You learn to be discrete while observing—people do not like to be stared at. (But, believe it or not, most clinicians do not really look carefully at the naked person in front of them—probably because of cultural ideas about modesty. It takes discipline to continue looking until you really see the person.) Visual observation brings many human functions directly to our eyes. The process I am describing also makes available smells and the feeling of things under our fingers. Because we are speaking of patients who most likely have chronic health problems we are talking about multiple visits during which things can be compared from one visit (or one year or more) to the next. Clinicians tend to have very good memories for these details. Bedridden patients at home or in a hospital provide opportunities to listen and observe, but also to see what is at the bedside: cards and pictures from family and friends, books, newspapers, electronics, or perhaps (unusually) nothing. House calls offer the best opportunities to listen and to see where and how the patient lives. For example, a disorderly environment speaks of a disorderly person for any of several reasons.

One of the reasons the process of observation becomes faster is that patterns of knowledge about patients are being formed in memory against which each new patient is measured. These observations are also the foundation in memory of the comparative evaluation that occurs with each subsequent contact with the patient—or the assessment against which the statements of others about the patient may be measured. This increasing knowledge forming the memory basis of the evaluation of new observations also occurs in other aspects of clinical observation. Patients would sometimes ask how I could see so rapidly what was in their throat in the few seconds that it had taken me to look. The speed comes from the fact that I have in memory a pattern formed over time and repeated examinations of mouths and throats against which theirs is compared. I am not examining the oropharynx so much as looking (outside of awareness) for deviations from what has become my knowledge of usual (normal). The formation of patterns against which new information is measured and evaluated (while central to the way doctors think) is both a good thing and a problem. It is good because it allows rapid assessment, but it is a danger because it gets in the way of conscious awareness and reappraisal of (information about) the patient on each contact. You should be *consciously* aware of the patient, if only briefly, with each interaction and that takes *conscious* effort. I put (information about) in parentheses because physicians are aware of their interest in the patient; however, it is really information about the patient, which is the raw, almost invisible, material substrate of that interest, that is forgotten. Information management is done best when it is a conscious process.

This vast amount of information forms itself into the pattern(s) that are the basis for the remarkable pattern recognizer that all physicians contain within themselves. It seems probable that pattern recognition is an integral part of clinicians' thinking (and the thinking of everybody else, I'm sure). Furthermore, most doctors probably have an extensive library of patterns—sets of facts representing diseases, clinical states, and patterns of patient behaviors that grow and grow with experience. These patterns in an experienced physician, which include the element of time, cover most of the afflictions with which the doctor is going to come in contact. In fact, patterns—stable sets of information—are everywhere: in the sound of voices in people who are anxious, sad, happy, or sick and even in just the sound of a person's voice that allows you to identify the person by voice alone even years later. The same mechanism causes clinicians to recognize the significance of important evidence during a physical examination. It is crucial that the evidence comes from the *actual discovered facts* and not from the imagination or advanced expectations.

In the face of an individual patient who is sick, clinicians question, and question, and question again, listening attentively for clues. They examine and examine and examine again. Then they seek other facts and more facts and then suddenly as things all seem to fall into place they may say, "I've got it!" Remember, the goal of this process is not a disease name (although that may be a result), it is an *understanding of the case*—a way of comprehending—of tying together—all the facts that occurred over time in this unique patient in this particular context. "Oh," says the questioner to himself or herself, "That's why it (the symptom, the loss of function, the patient's behavior, or the whole gestalt) happened—that makes sense." The process of seeking information in diverse places and of questioning and examining has served clinicians well over time so they keep at it and get better and better. Sometimes physicians and other clinicians are constrained from so much questioning because they are afraid that it will alienate the patient. As though by so much "going at" the patient, the poor soul will feel attacked and distrusted. A patient once said, "So many questions, it's like you're the district attorney." "Except," I said, "I'm the one on your side." If you heeded the advice in the previous chapter about making the patient comfortable, making it clear that your concern is that person, and if you have learned to be open, all these questions and pursuit of details are evidence of your undivided interest in *this patient, this person*Everything you do should be (at the time or with the future in mind) building trust and establishing or strengthening the relationship. In the context of a trusting relationship the patient is more likely to feel cared for by questions rather than challenged.

If this careful elicitation of facts is available to all and is so effective, why are some doctors not good diagnosticians? It is tempting to say that it is ignorance, but that is probably not most important. Most disease diagnoses are not difficult, which is why medical students are so often correct. Five reasons for error stand out. The first reason for error is the simplest. The clinician is not committed to this method for the discovery of clinical information. Doing what is described here is difficult, it takes time to get good at it, and it quickly evaporates. The dogma of medicine for more than a century has been that the most important diagnostic act is taking the history of the illness. In recent times, history taking and physical examination skills have fallen from favor and become generally poor. Instead, there is increasing reliance on sophisticated imaging techniques and the laboratory. When the diagnosis includes discovering patients' goals and purposes as well as their impairments of function *there are no technological methods* that are a substitute for asking questions, listening, and examining.

The second reason is that the diagnosis comes to mind and then is dismissed because of biases or preconceptions. Jerome Groopman, in his book *How Doctors Think,* tells of a young forest ranger who presented to an Emergency Department physician with a story typical of acute myocardial infarction (Groopman 2007). He was sent home because the diagnosis was unlikely in the face of the patient's youth, physical fitness, normal electrocardiogram, and absence of risk factors. He returned later with an unequivocal heart attack. He had what these days would be considered a low pretest probability of myocardial infarction. The old saw is that hoofbeats more often portend horses than zebras. Unless the possibility of zebras is zero (pretest probability of zero) it is wise to give more consideration to horses but also to look out the window. The *most important consideration is not the probability, but the facts of the case*—the "hardness" of the evidence.[1] The initial diagnosis for the young man was based on the hard facts of the case, which were classically those of an acute coronary syndrome; the reasons for disregarding the diagnosis were generalities based on statistical probabilities. We could say that the hard facts also lead to a statistical inference, but based on those facts alone, the inference is very strong. This leads to two other conclusions. If the facts are so important in a diagnosis then clinicians must be certain that they have *all* the facts and that they are correct. If the diagnosis seems improbable despite its strength and you are tempted to dismiss it, remember that the most important question is not what if I am right, but what if I am wrong. For example, in the case of the forest ranger with chest pain, the price of error could easily have been his death. Experienced clinicians think more often of the danger of error than the pleasure of being correct. You must not only listen attentively and assemble the facts but question yourself, following thoughts to wherever they lead.

The third major reason for error is impatience—personal, organizational, systemic, or social. Getting *all* the facts takes time and you are busy, people are pressing you, you want to get home—the list is long. Perhaps the time your organization allots for each patient—10 or 15 minutes—does not permit taking the time to ask all the necessary questions and really listen to the patient. Most visits fit into that structure, but a difficult or time-consuming interview requires more time. What do you do? First, become more efficient and do not waste time. That is easy to write and difficult to accomplish; but if you work at making every question count, avoiding unnecessary words and acts, and keeping a single-minded focus on the patient, it is doable and pays dividends. Getting more efficient creates

---

[1]. Yes and no. Yes, because in considering one case the facts of that *one* case are what count. No, because even considering one case there is always a denominator—the population of persons with the suspected disease state. The denominator—the base rate of the disease being considered—determines the pre-facts-of-this-case chance that such an event can occur. When evaluating a fit young man without risk factors (a population of similar young men has a very low base rate of myocardial infarction) it is especially important to weigh the facts of *this particular case to make sure you have them correctly*. Finally, there is the threat as a factor versus the risk. If the danger (threat) of the event—here a heart attack—is high we might consider the diagnosis even when the risk—the base rate—is low.

time but it diminishes time for schmoozing with the staff, and similar fun things. It is not a reason to be less polite, however, or inconsiderate of the patient. When patients require less time than allotted, be personable and focused on the patient, but shorten the visit. Put the time in your personal time bank for those who take longer. If there seems to be no opportunity within your schedule to spend the time, have the patient wait while you find time or find a way to keep going with the patient. I was seeing a new patient who came with a large stack of records and previous diagnoses, but to me, her history did not seem to jibe with what other physicians had concluded. Her answers to each question were so oblique that I kept asking and asking and assessing the answers without coming to a reasonable understanding of the case, much less a diagnosis. I sent her back to the waiting room. During the next several hours, every time I had a few moments I would bring her back to my consulting room to query her further. The interview took a total of almost an hour (out of a visit time of 3 hours) but in the end the simple diagnosis (of recurrent diverticulitis) seemed correct. Did she like being repeatedly put back in the waiting area? No, but she was pleased to have what seemed a firm diagnosis. She was grateful that I had pursued understanding her problem more diligently and with a better outcome; she knew that I had given her the time necessary. At the end of the process, I also had learned a great amount about her.

Sometimes the reason for impatience is that in your system—hospital, clinic, medical service, or whatever—technologies such as sophisticated imaging or special studies or other test methods are in favor and have a high priority whereas history taking is denigrated. There is no technology available that matches talking to or questioning a patient in search of illness as defined in this book. If your history taking has gotten rusty (if you do not do it all the time, your skill will decline) then get back in the habit. It is really very satisfying. There may be social pressures in your environment suggesting that this kind of patient interaction is not "cool." What is fun is crowding around a computer terminal and looking at images and numbers and talking about the patient with everybody. Social pressure is as real as water pressure. You must decide what matters most to you—good patient care or the approval and smiles of your colleagues. None of us wants to be in conflict with other staff or the group, so it may require some careful politics to show others the interesting things you have been learning from patients—*and* that you are still "one of the gang." Fortunately, it is usually not either/or. If you have read this far in this book, the patients' needs are probably winning.

Jerome Groopman provides an example that highlights another source of error. He describes a woman with diarrhea, other bowel symptoms, and an inability to gain weight that went on for many years. During that period she was considered to have functional bowel syndrome and "anorexia nervosa" by her doctors until a wise consultant finally made the diagnosis of nontropical sprue. My friends who read the case all thought she had nontropical sprue within a sentence or two of the description. So why was a diagnosis made that derogated the patient? Preconceptions, biases, amateur psychologizing, and other reasons for forming negative (or even positive) opinions of the patient that have little relevance can get in the way of interpreting the pattern correctly. It sometimes seems that the doctors who know the least about psychogenic determinants of sickness are the quickest to blame the patients' emotional states for their illnesses. However, if the details of the case—all the details—have been discovered and entered into the pattern these errors can be avoided. Biases and preconceptions about patients whisper in your ear, "Don't believe her, she is just neurotic." Or "You know these people; they are always just looking for sympathy," and so forth. If you have so completely and carefully detailed the facts that would explain the case, and just as carefully looked for facts that would have defeated that interpretation, then the thing is what it is unless the patient is actually lying or trying to mislead—both uncommon. That is what *attentive* listening is about, finding how the facts fit together to support an hypothesis: listening below the surface, seeking flaws in the patients' logic, and paying attention to unexplained gaps, words that start to go in one direction and are then retracted, or statements that contradict earlier statements. If these or others are present and following them down does not clarify the situation, there may be something about the patient that places in doubt the pattern that you thought you had detected. Then you have two problems. The first is the original question about the diagnosis. The second is just as important: What is it about the patient that gave rise to the doubts? State to yourself just as explicitly as you would state a diagnosis: Things do not just happen. They have causes and temporal relationships. If you think the patient has certain symptoms because he got angry, did the symptoms start right after the anger? If they started a week later, it probably was not the anger, or the parent's death, or losing her job, and so on.

The final reason for error is that in searching for the trouble and its origins, the net is not cast widely enough. Finding a diagnosis, even in the wider sense used here, is sometimes not sufficient. How does this patient live her life? What are the patients' behaviors in regard to their illness? Do they take their medication regularly, is money for medical care a problem, do they go to emergency rooms and, if so, how often, do they have a regular doctor and do they see that doctor (or others), and are they still smoking, drinking, or using drugs of abuse? The ultimate question really is what is the basic issue? It takes remarkably few questions to uncover difficulties, but a lot more questions to characterize problems once discovered.

Is what I have written merely saying for the umpteenth time in the history of medicine, "Take a good history?" Yes, you should take a good history. As discussed in the previous chapter, what I am pointing toward, however, is not merely a diagnosis in the classical sense, but a much more detailed knowledge of the patients: their purposes and goals, their function and functional impairments, and the afflictions at the root of their trouble. The information is necessary for considering the patient as an $N = 1$—the information necessary for clinical science. Good clinicians may utilize very complex patterns that cover all the variations in patients and clinical states that they have encountered (including patterns learned in medical school that last into old age about diseases never seen). Clinicians utilizing the cognitive tool of pattern recognition, and the other available tools of information science and analysis, are after a clinical science that can encompass the individual patient. Patterns, to repeat, are about people, emotions, personal and social behaviors, and other aspects of patient behaviors, not only diseases or diagnoses.

What I have described is a process, *not an event*. It takes place over time. What is often written about diagnostic and clinical thinking makes it seem as if a diagnosis is a thing a doctor arrives at like landing at the correct airport. It is true that for medical students or physicians in training that one-step diagnostic "gotcha" quality is too often true. But as physicians gain increasing experience, they may write down a diagnosis and some alternate possibilities, but unless the diagnostic thinking served its purpose perfectly and all questions have been answered, they continue to think and work on the diagnosis.

Recalling the description of the person in Chapter 2 in all its complexity, what I described is but a small fraction of what there is to learn about a person. Still, it is a beginning and like the sculptor's armature for a statue, it provides a base for a more complete description of a person and the sickness as other facts are added over time. Some things, such as the content of the train of thought that tells you what the patient thinks about unfolding events or what thoughts occupied the patient in anticipation of this visit (keep in mind that most patients have been actively thinking of this moment and what they were going to say for some time) to the physician, can be known only by asking, "So what did you think about as you were coming to see me?" This is a perfectly reasonable question whose answer may tell much. Or "What do think about what I just said."[2] There is something else that directs our attention to the patients themselves and what is important to them—their needs, desires, concerns, and interests. The patient is there because of impairments of function—which the patient most likely thinks about as illness,

---

2. Please, use the words "What did you think?" when you want to know the content of thoughts and reserve "What did you feel?" for when it is emotion that you are after. In these circumstances you may have to remind the patient when it is thoughts versus when it is feelings that are the object of inquiry.

the fear of illness, concerns about health, or other things that someone goes to doctors about. We know that who this person is, in concert with the pathophysiology, is a major determinant of the nature of the illness.[3] Knowing this patient is essential to understanding why the sickness is the way it is and presents the way it does—why these particular impairments of function are prominent at this time. Knowing the patient helps answer how we are going to go about making a diagnosis and deciding on treatment. In the process of learning who the patient is— what kind of a person our patient is—we are not primarily interested in the usual facts of social interaction—niceness, politeness, charm, and so forth. (Although politeness is *always* important.) As the interaction is going on, things are happening around and to the patient—the inquiry itself is a stimulus. Clinicians are interested in how the patient responds—thoughts and actions, as well as mood, emotion, attitude, and affect. How do these barometers of response change (or do not) and what they say about the patient and the content of the visit; how do they square with what the patient actually says.

As clinicians who are, perforce, information managers, we want our information "clean" and truly representative of the thing we are after. We look for information in more than just what people say. People have much more control of their words and the expression on their face than they do over the mood, emotion, attitude, and affect that they project. Just as looking at the unclothed upper back may be a more reliable indicator of tenseness and apprehension than the face because, again, patients do not know that their back speaks for them while they may control their facial expression. The gait, motion of the extremities, and the body of someone walking into a room, moving about on a bed or in a chair, sitting down, or climbing on to an examining table may reveal impairments of which the patient may be unaware or consciously trying to disguise. Where impairments are longstanding patients may conceal them out of the long habit of attempting to look unimpaired (while usually unaware of that intention). Understanding that information is flowing all the time should make us more conscious of what we are after and what information will best convey that knowledge. In these instances it is knowledge about the patient.

It is in the evaluation of the patient that the shift to a concern with impairments of function and their disruption of the patient's pursuit of purposes and goals is made clear. The evaluation is initiated by allowing the patient to say what the problem is in response to questions such as this: "How can I help you?" "How did you first know that something was wrong?" "What made you decide that you were sick?" The high priority given in this discussion to the person who is

---

3. This sentence may seem strange if you have acute diseases in mind. It is clearly correct if you keep the chronic diseases in your thoughts.

the patient (and the fact that it is really information about the patient that is processed) highlights the difference between our direction and the emphasis of the diagnostic process that primarily looks for the name of a disease. Clues to the nature of the disease often had to be separated out from the particularity of the patient. The particularities of the patient were treated as if they were contaminants that got in the way of clearly seeing (or hearing) the symptoms or signs of disease. In those circumstances the history-taking questioner's skill was manifested by how clearly the symptom could be revealed—freed of its subjective impact on the patient (and vice versa). Now we still want that clarity of the information about the symptom, but its effect on the patient is also important because what the symptom may do is impair the patient's function. And we cannot know that unless we know more about the person that is the patient. For example, in a man with important chronic back pain we want to know about the details of the pain itself (as in the past), but also how the pain is impairing the patient's function at work *as well as* his function as a parent and as a husband. Fatherhood is a complex function and so is being a husband. (For example, does the pain get in the way of sexual activity?)

We are also interested specifically in the impact of an illness on the activities and participation of the patient. Fortunately, questionnaires have been designed and evaluated for assessing the limitation on activities of the sick patient. This is important, because the International Physical Activity Questionnaire–short form (IPAQ-SF), which is widely used to determine the physical exercise status of healthy people, may not be useful in sick patients. Their physical activity status may simply be too limited. However, a questionnaire has been developed for patients with chronic fatigue syndrome that appears to offer a reliable measure— The Chronic Fatigue Syndrome Activities and Participation Questionnaire (CFS-APQ) (Nijs 2005). However, the IPAQ-SF is very brief and is useful for evaluating the activity level of healthy persons. In Chapter 2 I said that the sickness that brings a patient to a doctor is marked by difficulties in accomplishing the goals and pursuing the purposes that the patient interprets as sickness. *What the patients actually have, independent of any assigned meaning, is a disorder—"a derangement or abnormality of function"* (Dorland 2011).[4] Physicians confronted with a sick patient try and find a disease that will explain the patients' symptoms[5]

---

4. The definition of a disorder as a disturbance in function goes back centuries.

5. In contemporary parlance a symptom is the report of something that the patient experiences as abnormal and that is attributed to illness—e.g., shortness of breath or chest pain. It could also be a patient's report of something that the patient sees or notes that is considered in the realm of illness—e.g., a skin rash or a limp.

and the abnormalities that are found on physical examination, laboratory tests, imaging, and various other methods.

Neither the patient's interpretation of the disorder as it is experienced, however, nor the doctors' interpretation of the disorder as it is uncovered—both objectively and subjectively—is the whole story. They are both readings of the text that is the actual complete-in-the-patient disorder. The entire story of the disorder and its impact on the patient cannot be known, of course, because of the technical inability to know about everything and because the disorder inevitably existed in the past and extends into the future, both of which are inherently uncertain. More important, however, is what is not seen because of lack of interest or ignorance in both physicians and patients. The greatest obstacle is acting as though the disorder is confined to the body—to its physical manifestations. Healers know, however, that the full spectrum of the disorder includes not only its physical, but also its psychological, personal, social, and spiritual impact.

The evaluation of the patient must include these other domains of function because some important human activities share in each of these dimensions. A loving relationship, for example, is personal (it is an exercise of the person) but it involves the emotions, it is social, and it is spiritual—loving relationships transcend individuals. Spiritual things transcend individuals. Religion is a spiritual activity, but spirituality has a larger meaning. Human suffering—personal, individual, self-conflicted, and lonely—is marked by failures of human function. It is a state of social and spiritual deprivation and an experience of meaninglessness. How are all these things to be evaluated by a healer in the real world, under pressure of time, and focused on making his or her patient better? This chapter describes not an alternative but an extension of the classic aspects of the clinical method devoted to a disease diagnosis. The focus is wider. Knowing the disease, the healer is concerned with establishing the functional status of the patient—what the patient can and cannot do. What is interfering with the accomplishment of the patient's goals? How does the patient attempt to surmount these impairments? These questions apply not only to the initial contact with the patient. They are important in visits to hospitalized patients, to those coming for an office visit or for a consultation, and also for (the increasingly common) telephone or email contacts.

I would like to start on a tangent by discussing the relationship with the patient, which is crucial in facilitating (or not) the evaluation. It was discussed more fully in the previous chapter, but there are points to be made in the present context. As healers make initial contact with a patient, they are starting a relationship that will be the medium through which everything else is accomplished, and the first moments of a relationship are very important. The old saw about having only one chance to make a good first impression is true. This opening sentence is too often disregarded; "Hello, Mrs. Denis, I'm Dr. Bill Osler, and I'm going to be responsible for your care while you're in the hospital." Or whatever introduction appears appropriate. Even in an initial office visit when the patient knows full well who you are, it is appropriate to stand and say "Hello, Mr. Steeple, I'm Bill Osler. Won't you please sit down?" In the hospital, people commonly walk in and out of patients' rooms without saying who they are or why they are there. Consultants may fail to tell the patient who they are and the purpose of their visit. These are failures of politeness. These behaviors treat the patient as a nonentity. To be polite to someone gives that person status. Healers are dealing with wounded human beings who frequently worry that their illness has robbed them of the ability to act in their own interests. Patients may feel powerless or unimportant—defensive bravado notwithstanding. Sincere politeness suggests that the patient *does* have status and that the patient counts for something in the healer's eyes.

Every question asked or answered, everything said or unsaid, every action in regard to the patient should further the relationship (now or in the future). I believe this is true of every doctor–patient interaction but it is especially true for healers where we correctly say that it is not only what they do that matters, but who they are. The therapeutic efficacy of healers (or lack thereof) arises out of themselves. There can be no pretense of a "magic bullet." We will discuss this further in later chapters, but healers cannot entertain the belief that what they accomplish really stems from the power of their drugs or treatments—no matter how effective those things may be. Walsh McDermott, who was a famous clinician and scientist of a previous generation (and my teacher), has written that the most important characteristic of physicians is trustworthiness, at the root of which is trust itself. Trust is hard won and easily lost. Therefore, I strongly believe that clinicians should adopt the attitude that they are working with an eye on the patient and on their relationship every moment they are involved in patient care. Their attitudes, actions, and words, therefore, should be chosen carefully to advance what they are trying to accomplish. This does not ask too much of busy clinicians. If nothing else, the fact that they are busy means that they cannot waste time; everything they do counts. If this is done from the start it soon becomes a habit. Nothing prevents making light conversation about sports, or joking—as long as the healer is always in command of what she or he is saying and doing. Living this makes you choose your words and actions more carefully, which pays off in clinical effectiveness and better relationships with patients.

The evaluation of the patient, like every patient history, starts with the narrative story of the illness. "Tell me the story of your illness, please." It is rare that a diagnosis does not suggest itself in the first moments of hearing the narrative. That first idea of what is wrong is often correct, but here it is not merely a diagnosis that is the object. We are after three things: (1) a diagnosis in a classical sense; (2) a description of the functional impairments related to the sickness in any domain of the patient; and (3) a description of who the patient is—the nature of the person who is the patient. As noted previously, this means that the usual mode of obtaining a history where the symptom description is "cleansed" of the patient to provide knowledge of the disease process is merely one aspect of the process. This requires changes in the style of questioning.

"Your hip is sore (clarified as to nature and timeline)." "Does it interfere with anything you are doing?" "Gets in the way of your running (clarified)?" "What happens with your hip when to try to run?" "How long have you done that?" "Are you a regular exerciser?" "How long have been doing that?" "How did you get started?" "What does your spouse, parent (etc.) think about your exercise routine?"

"Fatigue (or dyspnea, heartburn, or abdominal pain)?" "Does that get in your way?" or "Does that interfere in your life?" "How?" "Tell me about it." This is a very different style of interrogation than usual. It does what clinicians have tried actively to avoid in the past—finding out about the symptoms themselves as symptoms, about the patient's function, and about the patient's person simultaneously—thus taking more time and pursuing three lines of inquiry simultaneously. Commonly, at least a tentative diagnosis will be possible at the end of the narrative, as well as considerable information about the functional impact of the disorder on the patient and the person and his or her relationships. In addition, the added questioning will reveal why the patient has come to be seen at this time, what urgency the patient feels, and what the patient believes would meet his or her goals for the care. All of this is the information that clinicians should elicit in their first contact with the patient in the hospital, office, or clinic. It is the background against which the next steps in the healer's evaluation occur. This same style of questioning, however, could take place with a patient who is already hospitalized and coming under the care of the healer who might be a palliative care specialist making a consultation, or perhaps a long-established patient already in treatment who is not doing well—perhaps someone who is sicker than expected, or a patient who is expected to die because no effective treatment of the disease is possible. Whenever responsibility for the patient's care is assumed, these are appropriate essential lines of inquiry.

The remainder of what was called the history of the present illness is done in the same manner as I just described. There is no illness, however, that is separate from the patient and the patient's relationship to others. What does your spouse (father, mother, siblings, friends, etc. as appropriate) think about…? What is the effect of the present illness and its impairments on what the patient thinks about self, and what the patient does, wants to do, and is striving for? (Striving is universal—as purpose is universal in all persons except in severe illness and suffering where it remains but is attenuated.)

We are trying to uncover anything in any dimension of the patient's existence that is interfering with the patient's ability to achieve his or her goals or purposes. In what sphere do we find these purposes? Those in which people strive to make life worth living. For example, love and human connections—does the patient feel left out, isolated, wanted, or loved. ("Who, doctor, would love someone as useless as I am now?") Or a belief that there are things larger and more enduring than the self—fulfilling purposes in work (e.g., medicine, art, machine shop, or finance), social existence, or family. This is expressed in the ability to communicate, be creative, or fulfill expectations of the self or others and in doing things that the patient has identified as important, or other things that are central to particular individuals. Each of these depends on many subsidiary functions and on the meanings—the significance and importance—persons attach to other objects, persons, events, and circumstances.

We are not only in search of functional impairments; we are also seeking what patients can do, not only what they have lost but what remains or has been gained. We want to know in what setting or circumstances they feel they will be able to regain the ability to live their lives as they wish—even when functions have been lost to sickness. What context or environment will best enable the return of or regeneration of function? This probably happens when patients are feeling safe rather than endangered; are not experiencing irresolvable worries and fears; have a sufficiency rather than unmet basic needs; are physically presentable and acceptable to others; feel affirmation by others and an acceptance of the validity of their infirmities and complaints; are not lonely; have meaningful human interactions with others of their choosing; have a stable community of choice and a world that is orderly and coherent; understand the reason for things; and have a sense of self-worth and are not feeling hopeless or like a failure. Patients should, like other people, experience a realistic desire to be like others and admired; have a true sense of identity (the opposite of anomie); have the ability to do things and make things happen (the opposite of helplessness); and have a sense of overriding purpose in their lives. We will revisit these same characteristics in Chapter 9 when we discuss the State of Illness and the attributes of sickness.

This evaluation would also be appropriate for a patient who troubles the clinician, such as a case that does not hang together or make sense. Everything that has happened to the patient from the beginning of the illness to the present should fit together. What happens next in the unfolding case should not be a surprise—not expected, perhaps, as a matter of probabilities, but not a surprise. The clinician should not have the feeling that there are aspects of the illness or patient behaviors, past or present, that are difficult to understand. Not that we can always know everything about the case and its details, because that is not possible. Even then, however, the unknowns should be expected or at least acceptably possible or a not surprising consequence of medical ignorance or inadequacies. Thus, if something unexpected happens, if some unexplained fact or event suddenly sticks out it should be evaluated, not brushed aside or rationalized. Justifying something rather than explaining it hides more serious possibilities. Perhaps a patient is confused or manifests other evidence of brain failure that is not expected. Suggesting that the confusion is because the patient is an alcoholic is a rationalization unless it explains why brain failure is occurring *now*. There are some, but very few real mysteries in medical care. (I do not mean to imply that we know so much, only that generallywe have an idea of how things work, what things can happen, and the huge amount that we do not know. A mystery is something out of the blue, no apparent explanation, occurring in a domain of ignorance. Fortunately, this is unusual.) There are, however, many situations in which evaluation has been insufficiently complete to reveal the correct explanation.

As the history continues, the clinician's pursuit of multiple goals continues: habits, such as tobacco, alcohol, drugs of abuse, and medications; not just the behavior, but the impact of the behavior; allergies, past illnesses, and surgery; and not just what they had, but how it affected them. Did it change their lives, abilities, aspirations, or goals?

The family history is asked in the same manner. "Tell me about your parents, are they both alive?" "What is (or was) your mother like? Can you describe her?" The same questions are asked about the father. Then we want the patients to describe themselves. "What are you like? Can you describe yourself? What is important to you and what is *most important?* Where are you going in life?" They should also talk about their purposes and goals (if the question has not been answered by this time) as well as their troubles or problems and things liked or not liked. The mode should be more like conversation than interrogation. (The patient has probably never heard a physician speak like this or ask these kinds of questions so the clinician should have a brief explanation prepared.) Throughout, the healer is watching and listening in order to learn who this patient is.

In this list of questions to elicit problems common to many sick people, clinicians will quickly recognize difficulties that they avoided discussing in the past. There are personal, psychological, social, and spiritual issues that clinicians are often ill equipped to handle or even discuss. Patients voicing complaints allied to these may be dismissed as "neurotic," "complainers," or "difficult." They may be further stigmatized because their physical symptoms, such as pain or nausea, do not respond to medication as expected. Here these are presented as underlying failures of function (as well as creating misery, unhappiness, and despair). Their contribution to impaired function places them clearly in the arena in which healers do their work. Clinicians will find themselves asking questions about, for example, emotional problems that they may have avoided in the past as they look for information that will help clarify both the relation to sickness and to the patient's diminished function. Serious, life-threatening, or fatal illness frightens patients (how could it be otherwise). Fear is an emotion. So too are the sense of danger or being at risk, the emotions of anger, sadness, melancholy, dread, despair, and many other feelings found in the very sick. Patients experiencing these feelings may have difficulty functioning. The generic kind of reassurance clinicians commonly offer (e.g., "don't worry") is probably not going to return patients to function who are feeling (say) constantly at risk or powerless to act.

The task may seem overwhelming. How is any clinician to explore all the possible reasons why function is impaired in all the possible domains underlying the difficulty—physical, psychological, social, or spiritual? Seen that way, the job is impossible. Furthermore, the way clinicians habitually seek to discover what underlies other symptoms such as pain or dyspnea is different. They do not start by asking questions about pain in the abstract ("do you have any pain anywhere?"), rather, they ask about pain in a specific area or dyspnea in a particular context—symptoms suggested by the illness or the disease that has been diagnosed. The solution here is somewhat different. We start off by asking general questions and when we have found an area in which dysfunction is manifest, we work backward to discover the sources of the impairment.

Here are some sample (and simple) questions to uncover disordered function.

- As you go about your days, how are things different than before you became ill?
- How is this [the symptoms or illness] getting in the way of doing things that you want to do? For instance...?
- [Since the onset of the symptoms or illness] What things are important to you that you can't do anymore? For instance...?
- [Since the onset of the symptoms or illness] What activities can't you do or take part in anymore because of...?
- In what way, if any, does [the symptoms or illness] get in the way of things at work?
- What difficulties do [the symptoms or illness] create for you with your family?
- In these past [weeks, days, months] when you've been sicker, how does it interfere with your activities, [doing things, being with people, working, or playing]?

- Is it your illness [symptoms, illness, pain], or is it other people [their attitude or behavior] or the environment that keeps you from doing things you want to? What holds you back? Is it your fear [worry, embarrassment, questions about your ability] about participating that holds you back or is it something else?
- In the past [weeks, months, year] how much of the time has your physical health or emotional problems interfered with your social activities? In what ways?
- In the past [weeks, months, year] how much of the time has your physical health or emotional problems interfered with your family life? In what ways?

You will recognize, in their lack of specificity, that these questions are meant to elicit information in a general way—to provide an opening for the follow-up questions. Clinicians often avoid vague questions because they seem too open ended and too liable to produce time-consuming answers. Purposely vague and open-ended questions, on the other hand, are meant to get information you might not tap into with specific questions. It is up to the clinician to maintain control of the conversation—keep it focused, but most of all make it produce information that will lead to productive next steps. Generally it is a good idea to avoid questions that have a yes or no answer because they are conversation stoppers. If the patient says no, but you think the answer should be yes, it is hard to move on without contradicting the patient.

If the general questions elicit a positive—even a vaguely positive—answer, follow-up questions are in order. The healer should make sure a negative answer is truly negative. If there is even a possibility that something is wrong—for example, there is a delay in the answer, it is insufficiently forceful, and the patient's facial expression says something different than the words—then probing deeper into the problem is important. My favorite questions are "What does that mean?" "Why do you say it like that?" "That doesn't sound right." When nothing is forthcoming but you believe there should be interference with the patient's life from what you know of their illness, it is appropriate to be more direct. "It must be difficult [a problem, hard, unhappy making, sad, lonely] for you to be in this situation. It would be for me." When evidence of difficulty or any kind of disturbance in the patient's life surfaces that is the time to find the disordered function and trace it to its roots.

Here is an example. A previously active and engaged elderly patient with balance difficulties fell and broke his hip. After surgery and a period in the hospital for rehabilitation you discover that the patient is avoiding participating in (say) family activities. "*Why is that?*" "I just don't feel like it; it's no fun anymore." "*Why is that?"* "I don't think they really want me there; I'm a party pooper." *"Why, in what way."* "I just don't have the energy I used to have—I wear out in half an hour." *"Do you wear out or is it that your leg gets tired."* "Well, both, really, plus I'm afraid of falling again." *"Do you use a cane [walker, wheelchair]?"* "I don't like those things 'cause they make me stand out like a sore thumb. Plus, everybody is always rushing to help me and I don't like that either." *"How long since your discharge from the hospital?"* "About three months."

A patient with that history should be more functional than this man. When we speak about difficulties with activities or participation, this kind of problem is illustrative. Further questioning may reveal that he spends a lot of time in his bedroom and he does not do the exercises prescribed or go to the physical therapist. Examination might reveal weakness in the operated limb as well as general unsteadiness. It is an insufficient response to his dysfunction to suggest again that he exercise. The functional problems may involve his family, the way he has dealt with obstacles in the past, transportation, finances, other organic problems such as bladder and bowel dysfunction, and perhaps clinical depression. Each possibility will reveal itself to further questioning, discussions with the family (for which the patient must give permission), and perhaps appropriate consultations. Sometimes the problem is that the person can no longer fill the role he occupied before he fell. Previously, (say) he was the last word in the family—the referee, the arbiter, the humorist, or the wise voice. Now (in his eyes) he is just a weak old man. Perhaps a child or his spouse has usurped the role. Such matters are rarely spoken of openly in the family, but discreet questions will often bring out what has happened. Then the task becomes attempting to repair the family problem, getting him to participate again, and restarting his physical therapy to strengthen the operated leg and increase his general exercise capacity. Getting him out of the house and more active is vital. If dizziness continues to be troublesome, starting suitable therapy might be necessary. All of this will take time and the efforts of others including the therapist and the family. Sometimes the healer might have to be the orchestra leader here because too often the absence of a coherent plan or anyone leading it means that it does not happen. Each individual action and the overall effort follow from the impairment in function that was discovered by questioning and examining the patient. As in this instance, action is often required to change the more general dysfunction—in this case in his family—and the increasingly particular problems down the chain of causation. Despite the list, these things can be accomplished parsimoniously and the patient can be returned to much better function. The alternative is progressive functional decline. If the patient is returned to function, however, one of the benefits is that future difficulties (further problems are inevitable) will be easier to resolve because there is now a history of success, pathways of conversation may have been opened, and there is a strengthened relationship between patient and healer. The goal of treatment is not merely function in the abstract, but *participation*—in the family, the social world, or the workplace.

Healers may say that they do not know all these things about persons or families, certainly in the manner that they know about the liver or the heart. Actually, they know much more than they think because they too live in a family and live a life among others. They may not consider it "medical" knowledge, but for healers it does not take long before they have made it part of their working knowledge because their patients' needs have been a force for learning.

It does not always require questioning to uncover impaired function. Sometimes, when a clinician walks into a patient's hospital room, dysfunction is apparent at first glance. A patient lying on the bed with face turned away from the door who does not acknowledge the clinician's presence is acting in an unusual manner. In hospital rooms, because it is the patient's "space," the patient usually speaks first. If not, the clinician, after introducing herself, should begin looking for problems. "Tell me, what's the matter?" "Tell me about your morning (your appetite) (your discomfort) (your visitors)?" Any question should be asked to elicit some kind of response that will permit follow-up inquiries. The issue should be pursued until the problem has become clear. Is it the pain, fatigue, other physical symptoms, depression, problems with a staff member, or something else? The tone of voice and the healers face and body language can be the prompts that remind the patient of the existing relationship and that it is within this connection that the patient is more likely to reveal herself in this moment. Perhaps, after all the queries and examining the patient to look for trouble, you leave without an answer. In that case, return later in the day if only for a few minutes so the patient knows that you are *really* interested. It is uncommon, after pursuing the issue, that you will not discover what is wrong. The patient wants you to know, but the patient often does not want to be a bother or disappoint you. You may suspect that the patient has started to suffer. Yes or no questions generally are problematic but asking "Are you suffering," may be helpful. If the patient says, "What do you mean, suffer?" "Is it more than the pain?" "Are you so distressed today because the pain is so bad or because of the whole thing; how it's gone on and on, or that you've just gotten so discouraged? Tell me. Don't you feel like yourself anymore? We are not in a rush; this is important. You weren't like this before even though you had a lot of pain." The exact words are dependent on the particular patient, the illness, and the situation. It is not the specific words that count, but the fact that you keep at it until you find out. You do not want to badger the patient so if you have tried and the problem did not clarify—yet you know there is something wrong— pick it up again another time later in the day or the next day. Get the opinions of the nurses or other staff—why do they think the patient is behaving in this way—withdrawn, not communicative, unhappy, or melancholy. Do not be too quick to make diagnoses; diagnostic words, especially psychological diagnoses, mostly obscure the problem. A description of the behavior will tell you about what you do not yet know and it will help others tell you more. You are after dysfunction and its reasons so it is reasonable to ask about other symptoms, family, friends, or loss of faith or hope.

Here is another example. As you come into the room the patient is sitting in his chair with the bed sheet and cotton blanket draped over the top of his head and pulled around him like a tent—as though he is cold. The room is warm. This is not a common sight; something is wrong. This patient was admitted with invasion of his lumbar vertebrae with tumor pressing on a nerve root. On admission his pain was awful. Anesthesiologists put in an intrathecal opioid pump and he had a good result with control of his pain. Not today! Examination and further conversation confirm that root pain in his left leg is even worse than before the intrathecal pump. Reassuring him that the anesthesia pain staff will increase the medication again is necessary but not sufficient. Just pain, even though severe, is unlikely to account for his behavior, which raises the suspicion that something else has entered the picture. Has he started suffering? If so, further inquiry is in order because suffering always involves not only the symptom, but ideas about the future and the meaning of the symptom. It is common for such patients to believe that increasing pain means that his disease has worsened and thus death is closer. It is important to clarify that worse pain does *not* mean the disease is worse (there are other reasons) and does *not* mean that death threatens. If, on the other hand, the disease *is* worse and death *does* threaten find out what these words mean to him and relieve his fears by addressing them directly. Even if you do not think he is suffering, it is important to discover what has entered the picture along with the increased pain. *Meaning is as much a part of pain as the nociceptive mechanism.* Although the source of the pain may not be susceptible to change, meaning can be changed.

Thought and emotion may also be impaired by sickness and are as important to the patient and to the patient's care as other functional impairments—and are often more evident than other limitations. In the course of asking questions and listening to the patient's answers it may become apparent to you (and sometimes to the patient) that there are defects in thought. Numerous studies have shown that persons with severe illness, either acute or long-term chronic symptomatic illness, have defects in executive control. Executive function is a loosely defined collection of processes responsible for planning, initiating actions appropriate to a task, decision making, error correction, and trouble shooting. In general, executive functions come into play when actions are undertaken that are not routine or habitual but are responses to novel situations. Piagetian tests responses appropriate to children age 10 or so are routinely found in persons who are sick enough to require care in bed. They can handle only a limited amount of information at one time and they cannot deal in abstractions or make decisions involving more than two simultaneous choices. They cannot "decenter"—take the perspective of another—so that they continually see things only from their own point of view. They focus on particular states and cannot grasp the logical reversibility of transitions, such that a thing that goes from one state to another could go back to its former state. These cognitive problems are discussed in detail Chapter 13.

The defect in emotion has not been studied systematically, but patients may state that they know that they should feel love for someone as in the past, for example, the spouse. They know it and may say the words but they do not feel the emotion. Patients with these cognitive deficiencies will characteristically pass a Mini-Mental Status Exam (have a score higher than 25) and be considered cognitively intact. In Chapter 12 I will discuss the ethical problems raised by these cognitive problems. The simple summary statement about all this is that significant illness impairs thinking. Clinicians often say that these cognitive changes happen because the patient is regressed. Aside from the question about what those words actually mean, these are changes found in sick patients. This is what sickness does to people.

The evaluation of the patient by this point will probably have yielded a disease diagnosis hypothesis including possible alternative diagnoses much like a conventional history. In addition, however, the patient's impairments in function that form the basis of the patient's belief that he or she is sick will be evident. Furthermore, the exploration will have revealed the impact of these impairments on the patient's activities and participation that interfere with his or her purposes and goals. In addition, and in the opposite direction, the clinician will now be aware of possible other impairments of function as far back in the hierarchy of function as the clinician has pursued them. Just as the disease diagnosis provides clues as to what will be found on the physical diagnosis, so too do these explorations of function. An idea will have emerged of how the patient functions in life—work, family, and other relationships. This will also be important in the healthy person being seen for a "routine physical." Finally, the clinician will have a lot better idea of what kind of person the patient is.

The patient will also have a better idea what kind of a doctor (and person) he or she has been sitting opposite. At the very least the patient will know that this clinician is much more personally concerned than most clinicians in her or his experience and much more attentive to the whole range of problems that have been the source of the patient's sickness and worry.

The Physical Examination[6]

Precede the examination by an explanation of what will be done and why. Stress the emphasis on function.

Observe the patient actively for a few moments before starting the examination. Pay special attention to gait. Students will have been taught the basics of gait analysis. This not only teaches them specifically about gait, but inculcates the importance of observation and brings attention to function, normal and abnormal. If there is not sufficient space in the examining room, go out into the hallway so that the patient can be observed walking. At some point while walking, the patient should be asked to walk as fast as possible so that gait speed can be observed. After walking, the patient's balance should be assessed.

If feasible be present as the patient undresses and observe the process. (Through all of this, you are not just observing the patient; the patient is observing you.) Observe the face and its expression. Observe general development, muscles, and posture. In all of this you are adding to your assessment of who the patient is.

Measure vital signs (blood pressure, pulse, respiration, and oxygen saturation). Measure vitality signs (grip strength with a dynamometer, timed sit to stand, forward reach, and balance assessment).[7] The attitude of the clinician during the physical is closest to that of a teacher enlisting the patient in this interesting process. Just as there is no symptom apart from the person your examination should not estrange the patient from his or her body. What does that mean? The examination is accompanied by a running commentary about findings in a manner that makes the body a friend—and tells of its responsiveness to change.

Continue and complete the physical examination. Include a pelvic examination for women and a careful examination of the male genitalia. The examination is not only a hunt for abnormal findings as in the past, but also for function. We used to look in the mouth and throat for lesions. But they are organs that function

---

6. The physical examination remains vitally important to the evaluation of the patient. There are eight reasons for the physical examination: 1. It is a diagnostic method. 2. It is the only diagnostic method available for most abnormalities of the skin, fascia, and the muscles. 3. It is the only practical way to follow an abnormality on a daily basis. 4. It allows the examiner to constantly remain aware of the normal and normal variation. 5. Done on a regular basis it allows examiners to continue to have the necessary skills. If it is not done regularly, when physicians must examine a patient, they will do it inadequately. 6. It is a necessary aspect of knowing a patient—there are things about patients that can only be known by examining their bodies. 7. It is the only practical method for evaluating many human functions. 8. It gives physicians the all important opportunity to lay their hands on the patient

7. Muscle strength, gait speed, and balance should fall within normal parameters. Progressive changes over time beyond norms are important indicators of disease, loss of fitness, a pattern of difficulties aging, and predictors of future disabilities (Guralnik 1995).

and we will be developing the habit of evaluating function. "Open your mouth, please. Swallow. Stick out your tongue." The vagina functions: "Bear down, please." With two fingers in the vagina, "Please squeeze my fingers." The same applies for the penis and the rectum, the limbs, etc. Listening to the lungs and heart involves not only listening for abnormalities, but listening to them functioning.

The examination is done from a very different perspective than in the past where the point was to find the disease. Remember, we have three concurrent objectives. All three will be recorded at the end of the process of patient evaluation. (1) We are looking for a disease in the classical sense so the diagnosis line will contain a disease name and an International Classification of Diseases (ICD) code. (2) We sought out impairments of function so the second diagnosis line will contain International Classification of Function (ICF) codes or text descriptions of functional impairments and/or impairments of activities and participation. (3) The third diagnosis line will contain a parsimonious description of the patient that includes the patient's purposes and goals that are interfered with.

The perspective from which the evaluation is done is the need to search for information that allows the diagnostic statements. The major changes for the clinician are seeing everything from the point of view of function and impairments of function, much as we currently see everything from the point of view of the search for pathology. We will still look for pathology but we will see it in functional rather than primarily structural terms. The other important change will be seeing the patient as a person who is like this, or like that—a person in descriptive terms.

The most fundamental change that emerges after doing this kind of evaluation is an altered attitude that carries over into all aspects of the clinician's work. I commented in an earlier chapter that descriptions of pathophysiology are often static—as though what was being described did not occur over time. The results of the classic history and physical share that characteristic. Although they are describing what is happening in a living patient and may result in a diagnosis of a disease that is unfolding over time, clinicians tend to act as though the disease is a static in the moment object. The findings of the evaluation of the patient that I have just described—focusing, as it does, on function—should necessarily be seen as occurring through time. As the story of the illness and the story of the patient's life as lived can be written as narratives, function is also narrative in nature from the molecular to the social. Part of learning this mode of evaluation is learning to think in terms of change through time. This kind of thought lends itself naturally to prognostication, which is thinking of the narrative as it extends itself into the future. It is important for clinicians to teach themselves to see the patient and what is happening to the patient as moving forward in time. Whether looking at a wound or some lesion and picturing how it will look tomorrow or next week, or at a patient's face and surmising how the appearance will change, prognostication is important. It keeps the clinician ready for what will happen next or is predicted to occur over time. If the prediction is incorrect, that also is important because it puts in doubt the original ideas about what ails the patient—or the physician's prognostic accuracy.

I cannot leave this subject without responding to the comments of readers who cringe at the thought of the time all of this might take. It seems, on the face of it, a very time-consuming evaluation. I believe that will ultimately not be the case. When I was beginning my first clerkship in the third year of medical school, I had to evaluate a new admission. Between my time with the patient and writing it up I consumed three hours! Of course, like all other physicians, as I became more experienced I got more efficient and I could do the same work in a fraction of the time. I had to get faster, I had no choice, because I was a busy practitioner and my most important commodity was time. I got faster and faster as I became more efficient and more knowledgeable. This was necessary because I wanted to continue to practice the kind of medicine that was time consuming. This type of evaluation will be the same. We are not accustomed to looking for functional impairments, and certainly not in the habit of looking for them in patients' social life or family, so at first it will take forever. The students who learn this *will* be accustomed to the search and will learn to do it rapidly.

References

Dorland. (2011). *Dorland's Illustrated Medical Dictionary*. 32nd ed. E. J. Taylor, Ed. Philadelphia, W.B. Saunders Co.

Groopman, J. (2007). *How Doctors Think*. New York, Houghton Mifflin Company.

Guralnik J et al. (1995) Lower-extremity Function in Persons over the Age of 70 Years as a Predictor of Subsequent Disability, New England Journal of Medicine 332:556–562.

Nijs, J. V. P., and De Meirleir, K. (2005). The Chronic Fatigue Syndrome Activities and Participation Questionnaire (CFS-APQ): An overview. *Occupational Therapy International 12*(2): 107–121.

International Physical Activities Questionnaire. www.ipaq.ki.se/questionnaires/IPAQ_S7S_FINAL_MAY_01.pdf.

7
Knowing the Patient

What is spoken of as a "clinical picture" is not just a photograph of a man sick in bed; it is an impressionistic painting of the patient surrounded by his home, his work, his relations, his friends, his joys, sorrows, hopes and fears.
FRANCIS WELD PEABODY 1881–1927
(quoted in Swartz 2002, p. 3)

Is It a Patient or a Person?

UNTIL RECENTLY IT would have been said that medicine begins with the disease. Even in the late twentieth century it was disease and medical science that were considered most important—they were the subject and object of medicine. Now, as the profession has further evolved, it is the patient who has taken center stage. Others say that it is not the patient but the person of the patient that counts. Often, patient-centered medicine and person-centered medicine are spoken of as if they were the same. The conflation of person and patient is partly a result of the general trend in which persons see themselves as independent individuals, and partly a consequence of contemporary bioethics in which patients share all the moral perquisites of persons and are therefore equivalent. We have two issues; first, is it the person or the patient who must be known? Are they the same? Second, person or patient, what is the necessity of knowing? Start by fixing clearly in your mind that in clinical medicine when we speak of patients or persons it is so that we can ultimately refer back to one of these specifically.

We will start with what may seem a digression. Clinicians must train themselves, it is generally agreed, to take care of patients. It is not just the long arduous journey of learning the voluminous and essential knowledge and skills, but also the habits of mind and temperament necessary for the care of individual sick— sometimes terribly sick—patients. William Osler believed that two personal traits had to be acquired by clinicians, which he described in his book *Aequanimitas*

(Osler 1910). The first was imperturbability. Imperturbability means coolness and presence of mind under all circumstances, calmness amid storm, and clearness of judgment in moments of grave peril, impassiveness. When clinicians know that terrible things have or will happen to patients, matters of great sorrow, frightening portents of awful events, failures of treatment that signal impending death, we insist that they have their nerves well in hand. The last thing that patients in the face of such dangers need is a visibly shaken or frightened physician—one whose courage has failed. Osler believed that the other habit of mind essential for clinicians was equanimity—the ability to remain calm and good natured, with an evenness of mind that allows dealing gently and kindly with patients even if they are angry, demanding, clinging, ungrateful, ungracious, or worse (Osler 2010, p. 4ff). These qualities are not much mentioned these days because they seem to point to emotional distance and hardness, whereas we now want to emphasize empathy, compassion, and shared humanity. There is no conflict between these habits of mind and compassion and empathy.

It is no surprise that the personal traits that Osler is demanding are not asked of patients. We understand patients with tears, paralyzing fear, denial of unacceptable truths, and failures of courage—things generally kept far from daily life. At the least then, doctors as professional persons are not the same as patients as persons. We know enough about sickness to realize that sickness changes people—changes their desires, concerns, and interests to matters related to or altered by the sickness. Chronic serious illnesses such as cancer, stroke, heart failure, rheumatoid arthritis, ulcerative colitis, or chronic lung disease change the lives of patients often irreparably. Patients such as these are persons who may be autonomous and yet different from healthy persons.

Osler was a working doctor who knew that these habits of mind and presence concealed deeper emotions of fear and anxiety that trouble clinicians who care for the sick. From the earliest days in medical school the fear of doing harm, of hurting someone (or worse) is drummed into us. Fear that something will go wrong, is going wrong, already has gone wrong, that error is waiting to pounce all the time. Fear is the companion of every clinician—almost always. "Even under the most serious circumstances," Osler says, "the physician[s] or surgeon[s] who... show in [their] face[s] the slightest alteration, expressive of anxiety or fear, has not their medullary centers under the highest control, [and] is liable to disaster at any moment" (Osler 1910, p. 5). Patients do not need a visibly frightened doctor. As a subintern, I watched the chief Ob-Gyn resident do a paracentesis on a woman with late stage carcinoma of the ovary. Her abdomen was hugely distended with fluid and it caused her distress and difficulty breathing. Her belly was so large that she could not see the trocar he inserted. Nor could she see the gush of bright red blood that followed the removal of the obdurator. She was looking at his face throughout the procedure as he quickly removed the trocar and pressed gauze pads to stop the still flowing blood. Not a flicker of concern passed over his face as she rapidly became increasingly anxious and he helped her lie down on the gurney. The bleeding must have continued and he spoke calmly soothing words as she died not many minutes later. We can only guess at his feelings, but he was imperturbable. The lesson never left me.

What this means is that the word *person* is not sufficiently precise for our purpose. A person who is a clinician behaves one way; the clinician's patient behaves differently. Perhaps an acutely ill person behaves differently than a chronically ill person, and both of them behave differently than someone who is well. If a person consistently behaves differently, the person *is different*. Same name, personal facts, and history, of course, but for the clinician the person is different. The being of persons—the way the persons are—is, in an important manner, dependent on the context in which these persons find themselves. And different context is another way of saying the *meanings* of a particular situation are different. So, to pick a dramatic example, when the clinician confronts the situation of the patient bleeding out under his hands, it means something vastly different than for the patient who is exsanguinating. The being of a person is always a person's being in the world—and even more—being in a particular world. Particular worlds are particular because each is constituted of different meanings. As I have said before, people do not act in response to specific things, but *to the meanings* of those things. Meanings, although they may be in part general and common to many, are always particular to individuals. Patients are persons who are in relation to a doctor because of illness or its threat. That fact defines a world of meanings different for a patient than for just any person in the general world. This chapter is about knowing a patient.

It is imperative to understand *why* knowing the patient is so important. The patients we care for will have to act in response to their illness, its impairments of function, our diagnostic and therapeutic actions, and all the things that happen on the way toward their getting better, if they do get better. They are also going to be interacting with us, other caregivers and staff, family, friends, and so on, over a period of time and in relation to their illness and its impairments. These interactions and their outcomes will often have an impact on their illness and their function. Because what happens to patients and how things turn out over the short and the long run are also our concern we have to know enough about them to be able to predict the possibilities and intervene effectively. That means knowing a lot about patients and what things mean to them.

I started this chapter about knowing patients with paragraphs about the healer's demeanor. In Chapter 5 on Listening I explained how the patients you are trying to know are the way they are partly in response to the way you present yourself. I discussed the importance of introducing yourself, being seated, being polite, and being open, and so on. Some of the patients you are trying to know, however, may be quite sick. Sick patients, especially when their afflictions are life threatening or when brain injury is present—whether from intracranial bleeding or trauma—require special attention to speech and behavior from their clinicians. Above all, patience and gentleness are necessary in the first and the umpteenth contact as well as trust that the patients are trying their hardest. Patients in this state require people to speak quietly, slowly, in short, straightforward, and unambiguous utterances, while maintaining eye contact. When choices are presented to them they should consist of two options at a time. They are easily overwhelmed and disturbed. A noisy, action-filled environment confuses and tires them. In the face of all of this, busy clinicians tend to speak louder and talk to the patients as though they were children. This makes things worse. As Jill Taylor said of herself in the same situation: "I am not stupid, I am wounded" (Taylor 2008). The medical care environment, especially special care units, is mostly noisy, filled with activity and busy bustling people, who may be impatient at anything that slows them down. In that setting it takes discipline to accommodate yourself to the patient's special needs. If you come to the sick patient's bed slowly and quietly and introduce yourself speaking softly and leisurely, your patient will be grateful before you have asked a question. If you are also open in the manner described in Chapter 5, the patient may well respond to you as an island of safety and understanding in an otherwise threatening world. Seeing how effective this is with the sickest may lead you to do the same with all patients. I hope so, because the clinician's behavior toward the patient is part of the context that determines how the patient behaves—and thus who this patient *is* in this illness.

Who Is This Patient?

Hospital clinicians may have a chart to tell them the patient's name, age, diagnosis, and maybe even family status. Sometimes there are legible chart notes that have other personal and family facts and a useful history of the illness and the hospitalization thus far. Other clinicians may have to start from scratch. That is not necessarily a disadvantage. Discovering a patient's name and basic personal facts provides the opportunity for the healer, in but a few moments, to make an impression as open, caring, kind, interested, and *also focused*. I emphasize this because of the times I have listened to interviews that started with a few minutes of polite, nice, but useless chatter. What is true for the patient is true for the clinician. He or she is not a just a person but rather a doctor, or nurse, or another clinician, and so the patient hearing the opening words is forming an opinion about a clinician. Whatever the opinion is should move the work forward. The clinician is starting to enlist the patients in their *mutual* endeavor and the healer's seriousness of purpose helps do that. Do not waste time. You are working and you are serious and the patient will appreciate that. That does not preclude being open, kind, nice, or even funny.

By the time you have asked questions about a person that tell you about, for example, origins, where the person lives, works, family (mother, father, sibs, marital status, spouse, and children), education, medical care, present health status (including functional status), and you have followed up with other questions when facts of interests appeared, you know about the patient in the usual medical sense. Your questions have also given the patients the opportunity to present the structure in which they live their lives. You have allowed them to be real, in-the-world, rooted persons. That is important to all of us, even when it is usually invisible because we take it for granted, and especially when patients have entered an alien world such as a hospital.

The patient you are about to see may be a stranger, someone new to you. If that is the case, your opening questions should offer them the same opportunity as the questions in the previous paragraph. This will provide structure, and enable them to be someone from somewhere who does something and has a family and roots. It may also be a chance to show how you and the patient share things in common— mutual knowledge, acquaintances, interests, or whatever. The patient could be someone you know well from previous visits—even yesterday. If the patient is getting sicker, someone you knew previously, or is well-known to you (especially a patient you know well), every visit should be treated as a fresh observation. There was a period when I was photographing every hospitalized patient every day. In reviewing those photos I was struck by how much change could occur from day to day and how much change the pictures revealed that I had not recognized while visiting the patient. Patients are altered in response to changes in their sickness, what has happened to them in the previous 24 hours, the impact of new news or information they have gotten from the staff—or just from their interpretation of events, which may have changed. You do not want their change to be a result of anxiety or fear they have picked up from you. You might be unsettled by what happened to another patient but this patient will interpret your words and the way you look in terms of himself, not anybody else. You want to be sufficiently aware and observant so that every time you see the patient it is as if you have not seen her before. It takes conscious effort to do that—as it does to heed Dr. Osler's advice. Continued attention to such details creates good clinical habits. You need these habits—this and others—to carry you through the inevitable periods of fatigue, annoyances and upsets, and other distractions. It is not necessary to know every patient in the detailed manner described. Some interactions with patients are brief and superficial. But it is important to get into the habit of observing.

The healer must see the person and convey to that person by interest in personal details that she is being seen—not only her patienthood or sickness but her personhood. The open-mindedness that you bring to each encounter allows you to *see* the patient freshly each time and not behave as though it is the first occasion. You are also conveying to the patient by small remarks and references to past visits that the relationship is growing and deepening. This increasing connection helps develop the patient's trust, which encourages revealing more.

Be Continually Observant

Knowledge of the patient comes first from the senses. You usually see the patient first—although you may have already heard about him from others, or read what is in the patient's chart. In the everyday sense of the verb, when we look at people they are usually in motion and we look and wonder what they are doing. After that, or when they are still, we perceive the chest area first as a sort of unfocused sighting and then almost instantly switch to the face. Rapidly we take in the features. If something is striking—for example, an unusually big or strange nose, scars, striking nail color or the like (on a woman), or other distortions—it holds our eyes and briefly sight becomes seeing, thus keeping our attention for a moment longer. Quickly we switch to the body clothing. All of this is automatic, takes moments, and is useless—or at best, inadequate. The object is not to look, *it is to see*. Seeing takes conscious effort—certainly before habits of observation have been established. You want to look at the patient, really see the face, focus, see, and comment quickly to yourself on something that seems noteworthy. Perhaps the patient really looks tired or sick, or perhaps sad, angry, or even in tears. Sometimes what you see deserves a comment by you other than introducing yourself (unnecessary with a patient who knows you), making eye contact, saying hello, and extending your hand. (Until you get good at this, it helps to make a note or two about appearance on your pad.). As your interview or conversation goes on, your eyes should be on the patient at all times. If you are recording notes, look up frequently.

To be examined, patients have to climb onto and later off the table or move from bedside chair to bed, or around on the bed. Some move effortlessly while for others it seems to be an exercise in clumsiness. Pain, difficulty in moving, or other impairments may be obvious. Other movements or movement mannerisms might be apparent. If questioned, we usually cannot remember the details of what we saw unless a striking feature is present. This is why someone who does not want to be remembered might wear a vividly bright red hat or scarf—the casual observer recalls only the hat or scarf. Clinical skill lies in both being aware of and then remembering noteworthy visual findings. Sometimes, clinicians think it is not polite to comment on something abnormal. If you have questions about something ask—ask nicely, but ask.

Vision or seeing is not the only sense involved. Voices have very distinctive qualities—so much so that in contrast to the impact of aging on appearance, the voice remains unchanged, unique, and recognizable over many decades. The language that individuals use is frequently quite characteristic—for example, word choice, sentence structure, and conversational logic. People also have characteristic odors. In the contemporary world of special soaps and perfumes an individual's odor may be altered or hidden, but the odors of the sick are usually not concealed. Poor hygiene may announce itself by smell, something also true of fear. Casual observers frequently do not detect these odors unless they are striking because they do not pay attention.

In the course of the physical examination, clinicians also naturally observe the external body—for example, skin color, skin tone, and texture, but also mucus membranes in the mouth, the vagina, and the rectum. The person's hygiene is apparent but so is the development of the body, especially the musculature, the limbs, and the distribution of fat, including a general sense of fitness. This includes the way the person moves, but also the patient's responses to the examination and to the clinician's words and instructions.

Thus, all of the senses are receiving information about the patient—often simultaneously. There is no choice in this because sense organs do not have an on–off switch. On the other hand, eyes can be seeing and ears hearing, but what is seen or heard is neither attended to nor registered. Choosing to be aware of what is seen causes a mélange of visual, auditory, olfactory, and tactile information to flow toward us. Perception is not merely the result of sense organs; it is also a cognitive function. In addition to sensory awareness we have to recognize what we sense as a *this* rather than a *that*. That woman has a pink turtleneck tee shirt, an oval face, and blond curly hair that reaches to her shoulders. She is writing on a pad and is right-handed. That man pulling along a piece of luggage seems to be having a hard time of it. It doesn't seem that heavy, I wonder why? Look at this lady in her hospital bed. What a mess. There are newspapers all over the place and the bed clothes are mostly on the floor. Somebody seems to have brought her some take-out food but half empty containers are strewn everywhere. This is more disorganized than I can remember seeing. I wonder if she is just as disorganized about her medications. I better ask her. Gradually habits of observation develop. If they have worked at becoming good observers (and it takes continued effort), by the time medical students are on the wards, they register almost everything. As they come to know more about clinical medicine, their observations acquire increasing clinical import—recognizably abnormal gaits, body habitus, skin colors, and behaviors. Hand in hand increased observational skills grow with increased knowledge about persons and increased knowledge of medicine.[1]

In addition, sensory information expanded upon by cognition and intuition contributes to our knowledge of others.[2] You are talking to someone and he does not really look at you—or sometimes he talks right to you and other times he does not. It suddenly enters your mind that he is lying about some of the things he said. You will have to take that possibility into account. You are seeing an older lady you have seen before. She seems to be walking funny, like an old lady with little short steps. She did not walk like that the last time. You say, "Did something happen that is making you feel old?" In fact, that is just what happened and you help change her interpretation of events. Intuitions are not just guesses; they are another kind of information to take into account when you try to know what the matter is and what you should do about it. These things are learned over time. It requires attentive and skilled observation to make use of the sensory and intuitive information surrounding you.

Asking Questions for More and More Precise Information

Classically, taking the history of an illness is asking questions about symptoms and the time and manner of their appearance. Much more information usually flows from the patient in addition to just the answers to those questions. People usually provide additional information in the form of little anecdotes and questions answered that were not asked. The way in which questions are answered—paralanguage, word choice, syntax, sentence structure, and the logic of their conversation—tells more about the person. It is possible to ask more questions

---

1. How do you learn to be a good observer? The best way is to make an ongoing game of it. As someone walks by say to yourself, "What is his hair color (shoes, coat, or anything obvious)" then turn and confirm. Do it several times a day every day. Gradually over the weeks and months you will become a very skilled observer. Once acquired, the habit of observing increases the skill, or least keeps it intact.

2. Intuition is a difficult word. On the one hand, it is used to signify a kind of knowing that is akin to instinct: the alleged possession of information without any demonstrable source. As such, it has been (justly) disparaged in medicine as a kind of magical knowing that is the opposite to the logical marshaling of information acquired by observation. A better description of the process of intuition is that some perceptual information is acquired and quickly attaches itself below awareness to the memory of previous similar experience. The judgment that results returns to consciousness as the intuition. Another way of saying this is that intuition is the process by which the mind directly grasps forms of things, recognizes them, and brings to awareness the similarity of some percept to a known form, relationship, and meaning. John Locke said of intuition: "Such kind of truths the mind perceives at the first sight of the ideas together, by bare intuition, without the intervention of any other idea; and this kind of knowledge is the clearest and most certain that human frailty is capable of" (*An Essay Concerning Human Understanding*, Book IV, Chapter ii, Amherst, NY, Prometheus Books, 1995, p. 433).

to find out directly what is important to patients, what they think and feel about what happened to them, what their goals for treatment are, and what are their fears and concerns. Patients are usually (but not always) truthful when they speak to physicians—it is one of the social rules not to lie to the doctor. The attitude of the doctor in seeking information has an impact on how much he or she will learn. At the end of the questions and the sensory information, if it is skillfully attended to, an amazing amount can be known about a patient. It is, however, but one perspective on the patient. In another setting, at another time, or for a different purpose, a different viewpoint might emerge and the person would appear to have changed. Both perspectives of the same patient might be correct. Patients are not trying to fool you, but the stresses of illness and medical care bring out different behaviors from time to time in the same person. That is why predicting a future behavior from what you learn about a person in a short time is notoriously tricky. It is also why written records are so important. Nonetheless, as we utilize all the sources of information we have from our senses, cognition, emotion, and intuition, our questions, what others tell us, and all we know about people in general, we are trying to find out what we have to know to do our work.

An Illustrative Example

The man in the chair opposite our desk has been having trouble walking. He says he is just weak and "runs out of breath." He is an 81-year-old widower whose wife died less than a year ago. We have asked a lot of questions and know that he is well-educated and that he used to read a lot. He does not go out very much but he does his own shopping. He is basically alone in the world. He is immaculately and carefully dressed. He answers questions slowly and carefully and he seems proud of his knowledge and his status. He avoids talking about money and whether he can afford his medications. His hair is carefully combed and he is clean shaven. But his collar seems about three sizes too large and in general his clothes, for all that they are neat and pressed, are clearly too large. He is fun to talk to because he knows a lot about sports and what the teams used to be and who was great and so forth. We think he could be in heart failure, but maybe he is just old and frail. Or maybe he is wasting away from some disease. Or maybe he is just not eating. Perhaps it is a result of years of eating as two people and now he is alone. If he has heart failure, will he be able to afford the medications and will he take them if he can buy them? There is no test that will answer all the questions, only what we come to know as we spend more time with him. The answers to these questions are crucial to his care. Maybe helping him back to better health is possible, but even if he has heart failure it is going to take more than medication. It is going to require healing. Knowing him will be necessary.

Observation as Part of the Clinical Method

The use of the senses and the flow of information from them are systematized in the skill of observation, one of the central skills of the physician in knowing patients. William Osler called it "That most difficult skill." How is it done? Seeing (knowing) a patient is an act of observation and observation has certain characteristics. Observation is not staring or ogling; it is careful and attentive. It is goal oriented—here the focus is the patient, just as was described in observing the man having trouble breathing mentioned above. Skilled observers as much as possible allow the thing they are observing to "come to them." They are "open" to seeing (and hearing, smelling, and feeling). They see little cues in the face and its changing expressions, motions and gestures of the person and the person's parts (hands, fingers, and limbs), postures, and behaviors. To be open is as much as possible to be aware of and prevent preconceptions, prejudices, biases, and inhibitions from prematurely closing the observation—"Oh, she's crazy…," "he's an old man…"—or being inhibited by unpleasant odors, sights, and feelings; or sensing great sadness, suffering, or pain; or becoming aware that the patient is angry or hostile. In these and similar situations, attentive observers become aware of their reaction and, relaxing their muscles, turn back to observing the patient. It requires real effort to suspend assumptions and interpretations and remain open to the "primitive" elements of experiencing the patient. Here, as in the remainder of clinical medicine, it is important to distinguish between the observation and the interpretation. Nonetheless, it is almost impossible for the mind not to be continually inferring things from what is observed. Consequently, the observer can heed the inference (as though listening to a background sound) but keep moving on. With increasing experience observers do not have that "noise" running through their thoughts. Observation strives for completeness. Some things are seen that have sexual meaning and people naturally shy away from really seeing such things (like the genitalia on a naked body) so as to avoid the appearance of ogling. It is important to learn not to turn away from things that might not be polite to look at in everyday life. Observation is continuous; we do not look for a few moments and then go back to business as usual—attentive observation ultimately becomes almost constant, a clinical habit of thought. Of course it occupies the time of *this* observation, but it continues on comparing this observation of the patient to the last and the next.

Observation occurs at different levels. The primary and organizing level of all observation is *the patient*. The next level is a *part*—if one part or some pathology stands out. But *the part is always in the context of the person*. Many clinical illustrations show just the pathology—dermatologists show skin lesions and rheumatologists show the joints—but only rarely is the whole patient shown. The third level of the observation is *the context; where is the patient?* A hospital room, the emergency room, in an office examining room, or a consulting room—context has an impact on the observation. The fourth level is *the patient interacting with others*—for example, friends, family, and medical staff. The fifth and final level of observation is *the observer* himself or herself; what feelings or thoughts did the observation invoke in the observer. Part of observation is description; learning to describe what you have observed is very important. This also requires continuing practice. Everything in the observations must refer back to the patient. The patient—the person—is the context for anything that observation reveals. Observation has an ethical component. The type of close observation being discussed, wholly revealing the patient behind all the masks of everyday life, is an invasion of the person's privacy and it has, therefore, an ethical dimension. Observers must remain polite and *never* seem to find what they see funny, repulsive, upsetting, or sexually attractive.

A primary mode of observation is verbal (and nonverbal) communication—talking, asking questions, and eliciting information about the patient's sickness and the patient. The central message of Chapter 5, Listening, bears repeating. Above all, listen, patiently and attentively listen, persistently. Then listen some more. Sometimes making empathic statements helps when listening quietly does not bring out the sick person. "It must be an awful thing to be here alone without your children here to help you," may evoke a response when sitting quietly waiting for the patient to say something does not work. Empathy is greatly dependent on verbal cues as subtle as any other observational datum in the usual nonconscious appraisal of another's state. Much has been written about communication and does not have to be repeated here

Barriers to Knowing Persons Can Be Overcome by Teaching

For physicians, then, knowledge of persons is right in front of their eyes yet many physicians do not practice medicine based on such knowledge. Why? Each of the reasons—and there are many of them—should raise questions about how these behaviors and failures of knowledge can be changed.

The most common reason is disinterest. Clinicians want to know the details of the patient's symptoms, the results of a physical examination, and the findings from the laboratory, imaging, and other tests. They need this information to make a diagnosis. It is impossible, however, to listen to patients' symptoms, see their presentation to the world—how they dress, sit, walk, and interact with others—without knowing something about them. Doctors characteristically take but a small part of this information and discard the rest without thinking about what they are doing.

They also frequently lack an observational focus on the patient as a person. When most of us look at something, we tend to see what we are interested in and little else. Looking intently for information on which to base a diagnosis, the doctor may not perceive the details that would help characterize the person, even while looking straight at them.

There are some social reasons that interfere with knowledge of persons. It is believed by some that knowing about persons infringes on their freedom. Describing persons inevitably registers characteristics that place someone as a this rather than a that. This person, because he or she is of a certain age, gender, personality, character, talents, profession, life history, and so forth may live one kind of life and have some future possibilities. Just those characteristics preclude other possible life choices, futures, or ambitions. It is as though the limitless freedom North Americans like to believe is their birthright has been foreclosed because the person has been described—as though just by characterizing them you have closed the door to other possibilities. Because of this common belief, of which the observer is usually unaware, observation may be inadequate. Reminding yourself of the issue a few times may break the habit of not registering obvious details about the person.

Stuffing everyone into a category keeps you from knowing them. All people, not only physicians, cherish their categories. But observation that is merely an attempt to find an applicable category is not really observation of a person. It is difficult, however, to avoid applying categorical descriptions of people as though the category really was the equivalent of a description. Categories are so pervasive that they meld into fixed beliefs about people—like biases and preconceptions. And categories can be evoked by many personal characteristics. In men, for example, the way the hair is worn may evoke in the viewer categorical distinctions. In one era, long hair on a man was a sign of countercultural status, a few years later the same hair length might be found on a construction worker, and another few years and long hair was worn by academics. Closely cropped hair in the "hippy" era of the 1960s signified the military or allegiance to the military worldview, but within a decade businessmen wore short hair. Now closely cropped hair (or a shaven head) may signify a fashionable person. Clothing styles also lend themselves to the assignment of categories as do some interpersonal behaviors. It is as though the true description and true knowing of persons are hidden by the categories—as though they were costumes or masks.

Although that may be true, it is not only the observers trying to know persons who hide behind categories; perhaps also hiding behind categories are the persons who are the objects of observation. A person has a public persona, a way she appears in public that is meant to represent her in a certain manner that may be different from her private self. (That is the "true" self, as she sees it.) So one has to wonder, seeing someone striking, has he revealed himself to us or are we seeing a public (but not a private) persona? By way of contrast, look at the smiling 7-year-old child in overalls walking toward you. I believe you do not see him hiding anything; he is as fully revealed as can be. We acquire our public self as we mature because just as everybody is inquisitive about other people, they do not like to be known themselves. The public (versus private) self is a way to hide. Clinicians have an interest in penetrating the disguise.

Knowing the Patient's Emotional Response to the Illness

Sickness is an emotion-filled state and sick persons present many emotions to the physicians in front of them. Patients who are not sick may also present overtly or covertly many of the same emotions because in the medical setting thoughts of illness, disease, and death may not be far away. Worry, fear, happiness, sadness, grief, tearfulness, love, anger, and other emotions are often present and are frequently evident in the patients or in the patients' interactions with staff, family, and friends. Some physicians actively avoid their patients' emotions or repress and avoid their own. This is not a surprise since medical students are too often told or receive an unspoken (or overt) message not to get involved with their patients and not to show emotions or grieve. They are, thus, usually unprepared for the intensity and variety of emotions they experience in their patient interactions. Too often they get little support from their teachers and colleagues for their own emotional disturbances caused by their patients' emotions and by the things that happen to their patients.

Patients think about their illness, symptoms, treatments, physicians' actions, the nurses and other staff, procedures, diagnostic tests, their hospital room, other patients, their families' responses, visitors, and on and on. Often they tell us about these things and we may listen attentively, listen, half-listen, or not listen. In this book I have been encouraging attentive listening because of how much it helps in knowing about patients. Just as events produce thoughts, they are also accompanied by emotions or feelings—and affect. The emotions are evaluative, a commentary on the events and the thoughts, in two ways. One is an emotional comment we might make about something; it (whatever it is) makes me sad, happy, angry, or any other emotion. Similarly, it is sad (happy, upsetting, delightful, or whatever) that he had.... The other evaluative function is automatic. It is the emotion that is evoked by an event or thought and it occurs almost instantaneously with its stimulus. The affect is the subject's visible response to the emotion. The emotion pervades the person and the person's body while the affect shows. People have control over what they report about their emotions, but they rarely control their affect as well. Emotional reactions can be instantaneous and subside as rapidly, hang around for a bit, or serve as the background feeling for even long periods of time. You hear about something that makes you sad for a bit, or you are sad while you think about it on and off for a few hours, or sadness becomes your lasting mood.

Patients may be aware or unaware of their emotions, but as you ask about them, the emotions or the memory of the emotions come to consciousness and people can tell you how they feel or how they felt (say) in response to something. Their emotional response may be distinctly different—even at odds—with their thoughts on the subject. Both thoughts and emotions are as real as sand dunes and tell you things about how your patients are doing in response to their illness or the things and people associated with it. As I have noted a number of times, being open will eventually allow you to be aware of patients' feelings and that is very valuable information. Patients may be loathe to overtly express anger—especially at you—but it is vital that you know its source. Euphemisms such as "irritated" or "aggravated" may be their substitute safe words. Some clinicians actively avoid knowing about their patients' anger (or any other emotion) but that is, I think, as unwise as not heeding the early signs of infection. Just as you monitor physical responses to illness, you will be wise to stay attuned to your patients' thoughts and their emotional responses.

We have determined some reasons why clinicians fail to come to know the patients they care for, but arguably, the overriding reason is that they are not trained about persons in the same systematic way as they are trained in other aspects of clinical medicine. Disinterest and lack of perceptual focus, so common, can be overcome by training as can some of the other social reasons. The problems caused by having either patients or physicians (or both) hide behind categories can be helped by showing how the many different aspects of persons present themselves and what categories are. The more sophisticated physicians and students become about the nature of persons, the easier, I believe, it will be to teach them to *see* them. More difficult are the problems created by an avoidance of knowing patients because of the moral and emotional burdens—such knowledge threatens. In this aspect of knowing persons, students particularly require personal support. Most students and young physicians have difficulty with their own emotions so it is unfair to burden them with patients' feelings without both providing emotional support and *teaching them to be supportive of each other.*[3]

---

[3]. Students entering the world of sickness are often confronted by their own shyness, diffidence, and self-doubt; they wonder why any patient would trust them when they do not trust themselves. They have not yet developed a distinction between their doctor self and the other parts of themselves—this may also be a problem for postgraduate trainees. They have not yet accustomed themselves to the role of physicians even though patients may see them that way and have expectations born of the role of physician. In the past, medical schools have not actively helped students and house officers with these difficulties. Teaching students how to know patients without aiding them in overcoming the personal barriers to that knowledge is unfair.

Issues of trust are also important for both clinicians and patients. Levels of trust vary according to the patient's need, experience, and general nature, and even from day to day. Some patients are more trusting than others while a small number are unable to trust anyone. Inability to trust is a terrible state in a sick patient because it thrusts him or her into a dangerous world. In the uncertain and the dangerous state of life-threatening sickness, on the other hand, most patients develop trust *very* quickly because they so badly need the help of others.

Assuming the difficulties in knowing patients that I have identified have been overcome, clinicians will find themselves in front of patients who are in the emotionally, socially, and often physically *naked state of the very sick*. It is easier now to understand why knowing a patient in this vulnerable, ultimately exposed human state—rather than sticking to strictly disease-related actions—might be threatening to the knower. The patient's vulnerability creates a sense of vulnerability in the physician. The patient's helplessness may make the physician feel helpless. At this point, in addition to the explanations listed above, there are three more fundamental reasons for the failure of physicians to know their patients as the persons they are (Hall 2000).

The first route of escape is the denial of the problem of the vulnerable helpless humanness of deep sickness. This physician sees all patients through the special lens of his or her special interest. Doctors such as this are absorbed in seeing patients as examples of the sick role, or the regression of illness, or how all the patient is doing is manifesting unconscious needs. Such physicians may also be interested in, or alternatively be more interested in, their special scientific interest—genetic manifestations of disease, protein abnormalities, or other special aspect of the sick body. Two examples may make the point. An attending physician in a palliative care unit was with two students outside the door of the room of a patient suffering terribly from unrelieved pain. It was difficult to look at her writhing or listen to her whimpering, so he discussed what had happened to her liver function over the previous week. Another case involved a patient caught in the vice between shock and pulmonary edema. The resident stayed by her side caught in the unsolvable dilemma while the elderly woman wondered aloud why it was so difficult to die. His attending physicians came to the bedside and instead of addressing both the woman's suffering and the resident's helplessness, they discussed her electrolytes for awhile and left. This is a not uncommon behavior; seeing all patients as examples of the phenomenon they manifest and not as sick human beings. It is also common in relationship to the suffering patient in which the suffering itself is not addressed but only some manifestation such as pain. At first this would seem a poor example of the physician as dilettante—doctors who care more for the performance of the acts of medicine rather than and divorced from the fundamental definition of doctors as persons who take care of other persons who are sick. After all, pain is a common source of suffering and its relief would appear to be a response to suffering itself. Here, however, the physician is interested in pain, not *the patient in pain*, is interested more in the pathophysiology and pharmacology of pain than pain itself. In this explanation of why these clinicians avoid the patient, the special interest is used as a buffer between the patient as a patient and the physician.

A second fundamental explanation is the substitution of *the "universal" patient* for the particular patient. This doctor sees all patients as human beings with all the dignity and ethical attributes that belong to them. Patients are bearers of rights, examples of the nobility of even the sickest person, but they are not those nakedly sick patients in those beds over there. What should be done to and for them is obvious in the ethical details of the case. Doctors should treat all patients as having the freedom of choice their autonomous status promises. It matters little to these physicians whether *this* patient, burdened by sickness, is able to make autonomous choices. Doctors should always tell the truth to patients. It is the truth that counts, not the importance or impact of the information on *this* patient. The ethical principles come before the patients they were meant to serve. *Treatment guidelines* are another example in which the universal comes before the individual. Patients are seen as fitting into one or another set of guidelines that then determine the treatment. Individual differences and patient particularities are seen as less important than the universal principles of treatment. Treatment should be based on good and applicable evidence; there can be no argument against that. But equally true is the importance of being sure that the evidence applies to *this* patient and *this* presentation of sickness. No two patients are the same; no two episodes of sickness are the same; no two responses to treatment will be exactly the same. It requires knowledge of the individual patient to decide whether these differences warrant changes in therapy.

The third fundamental reason why physicians do not know patients is the belief that the *only evidence of importance is scientific evidence*. Only science, this view holds, provides information sufficiently reliable on which to base diagnostic and therapeutic action. Scientific information is above all objective, that is, it is measurable in that peculiarly medical sense of the term objective. Any other way of knowing the patient, in this perspective, is inadequate. The fact that the subjectivity of physicians is necessary to knowing a patient condemns the general endeavor from this "scientific" perspective. Physicians who believe this general principle cannot truly know their patients. In fact, they cannot see or know anything in full unless they acknowledge other valid sources of knowledge. This stance and its clinical implications were more common in past decades, but they remain in force in many physicians. The problems in the care of patients with chronic illness are particularly resistant to resolution through only the lens of scientific knowledge. Patients themselves in all their complexity shape their chronic illness by the lives they live, their habits, their relationships with doctors and the medical establishment, their abilities, their intelligence, and their store of knowledge about their disease. Doctors sticking to what scientifically derived data tell them about, for example, diabetes, chronic obstructive lung disease, or heart failure but who know little about their patients will fall short of optimum management of these illnesses.

Exercising the definition of illness used in this book, there is a new reason for ignorance. Here, function is preeminently important, yet we are still too often amateurs in its assessment and amateurs in its enhancement. These are not reasons to turn away, but rather motivations to stick with it and learn more. We will all benefit.

Adding these last four reasons why physicians do not truly know their patients to those previously described creates quite a lengthy list. These last—a kind of dilettantism that puts the physician's special interests between them and their patients, universalizing patients by thinking of them as embodying (say) their ethical standing rather than as particular patients, denying validity to any knowledge of patients (and therefore the actual patients themselves) that does not meet scientific criteria, and ignorance or amateurism about function—should be added to those listed earlier—disinterest, lack of a perceptual focus on the individual patient, the social blocks to knowing such as the restriction of freedom or converting the patient into an object by the act of knowing, and applying categories to the patient by the knower or hiding behind categories by the patient. In the face of the fact that knowing the very sick is in itself threatening to physicians, it is clear that truly knowing a sick person is a difficult task. But it is very rewarding.

Knowing as Empathy

What I have described as coming to know the patient through multiple channels, avoiding the excuses and the barriers that keep the physicians from closeness, and ultimately reading the patient's physical, emotional, and cognitive state while making a connection to the patient is what is generally meant by empathy. There is a large literature on empathy (not always called empathy) going back to the nineteenth century. The idea of one person knowing the cognitive state of another reaches back into antiquity where it was usually called sympathy. Knowing the *emotion* of another entered the meaning with the appearance of the word empathy in the twentieth century. Terminologic confusion continues. Nonetheless it is generally believed that observers can know the thoughts of others as well as their feelings. Empathy plays an important part in knowing that a patient is suffering. Physicians (and others such as nurses and physical therapists) may also experience the physical sensations of their patients. Despite this and the wealth of recent research it is not clear how physicians (and others) come to know how the patient, as a unique individual in a specific setting, came to experience specific affective, cognitive, and sensory states (Omdahl 1995). None of the explanations is quite adequate based on the fact that such empathy, as noted below, can occur over the telephone before there has been a chance for what would seem to be adequate information on which to base appraisal.

Physicians must sometimes simply be open in the presence of the patient as described in Chapter 5. This has sometimes been labeled sympathetic listening, empathic communication, or empathic attentiveness, and it can be taught and learned (Platt and Keller 1994). This stance is not something you do as much as something you are. It may seem threatening to clinicians at first, as though their defenses were down. Remember these physicians are working. It is the doctor-person doing and being this way, not the personal-person. What can be learned? For one, what the patient is feeling—ultimately physicians become so attuned that they can feel their patients' feelings even over the telephone. It is important at times to identify those feelings specifically, to name them. Mostly, however, we avoid putting words to what is being learned in order not to foreclose the experience. Over time physicians come to trust the intuitive thinking that takes place below awareness as the mind continually processes the experience (Lauer 1978, p. 7ff).

Responses suggestive of empathy are found in young babies who cry when another baby cries (Overton, Jean Piaget Society. Symposium et al. 1983) or young women in groups whose menstrual cycles have been reported to become synchronized over time. Other components of the response to the emotional and cognitive states of others develop as children mature. In adults the response to others is complex and includes the ability not only to feel the various distresses of another but also to share the other person's perspective. Thus physicians, as persons, come into their relationships with patients already able to be empathic. From what we see in medical students and house officers, empathy may be suppressed as they acquire increasing clinical experience. On one occasion during the research that led to the book *Talking with Patients*, the patient's visit was being recorded on tape. It happened that I was incising and draining a boil while the tape recorder was running. The patient responded to the distressing experience with loud cries of pain. I hardly remember hearing them while I was doing the procedure. The next day in my language laboratory by chance the tape recording of that set of office hours was played. Without warning the patient's awful agonized cries were broadcast on the laboratory's loudspeakers. Although the episode lasted only a few minutes it was very difficult for me to listen to her expression of pain, which I had hardly noticed the evening before. My staff was even more upset by her cries.

The episode suggests how physicians may deal with the empathic response to the distress of their patients. They suppress it. Unfortunately, that solution also denies them the information from their patients that empathy would otherwise provide. But if empathy is encouraged and further developed as suggested here, how can the physician and particularly the student survive the onslaught of emotions, suffering, pain, and distress of the sick individually and as a group? Is the knowledge that is gained, which is necessary for really effective healing, worth the personal price? Knowing patients in this way in detail and in depth, with all the senses and intuition sharpened, moves the physician to a next dimension in effectiveness. Therefore, the personal price the physician might pay for this increased ability to make patients better must be reduced. Empathy is a wonderful and necessary skill, but the cost is high for an unprotected physician. Janus was the Roman god with two faces who protected the doorways of the house. One face was turned inward and the other outward. Physicians who care for the sick must develop the same facility to protect their inner self while not retreating from facing straight into sickness. Gradually there develops a physician self facing the patients and the physician's personal self separate and relatively untouched by the difficulties afflicting their patients. This is an inner detachment that preserves physicians and their families, while maintaining the connection to the patient. These qualities are acquired only by consciously working at them and they take time to develop. They distinguish clinicians from other physicians.

It may seem that physicians are being asked to detach themselves from patients and to harden themselves, like the accusation directed at William Osler's suggestion of imperturbability and equanimity as essential demeanors for physicians with which I opened this chapter. This is *not* what is required. An inner separateness permits the distance necessary for clear thinking. Freud called this a combination of objectivity and empathy. Yes, objectivity is required, but the evidence for which objectivity is required is a combination of empathic subjective responses that tell physicians about the patient and reasoned thought about their significance. Remember, in all of this process the physician is gathering evidence and authenticating judgments for which more evidence must be acquired. Clear thinking needs a cool mind focused on the goals of care. The patient needs a physician who is so empathically connected as to be able to provide safety or its illusion, continually acquire information, and at the same time lead the patient in the actions required. If we want physicians to have these skills they have to be taught and emotionally supported while learning. There is some evidence that the experience of positive emotions over time can build enduring social resources such as empathy and altruism (Snyder and Lopez 2005). Their future as effective healers requires it.

In this discussion it may be difficult to discern the patients as autonomous agents who have the right (some would even say obligation) to make decisions about their health care. I have spoken only about the difficulty faced by physicians in coming to know their patients. What about the patients' difficulties in coming to know their physicians and their own situation? The patient's right to choice in medical decisions *cannot* be denied. Yet this discussion has been primarily about sick patients, patients whose symptoms (including pain), distressed emotional state, fears, and even suffering are what mark their faces to the world. The evidence is clear that in such patients the ability to think is impaired (Cassell, Leon, et al. 2001). Although they have the right to make choices, they may not have the independent ability to think straight. This is discussed more fully in Chapter 12.

Knowing the patient requires a *relationship* of some kind with the patient. What interests us here is not a general discussion of the doctor–patient relationship, but what attitudes toward the patient might be considered ideal in the setting of the clinician's efforts to know the patient. First, and most obvious, the physician *should treat the patient as an equal*—avoiding the common tendency to treat sick patients as though they were children by patronizing and talking down to them. The physician should see the patient as *a "co-worker,"* most commonly using the "we" rather than "I" or "you," as in, "I hope that doesn't happen, but if it does *we (you and I together)* will do the best we can." The physician should be able to *participate completely in communication* with the patient, even though, cognizant of the possibility of defects of thought and emotion, the presentation of information and ideas to the patient should be as simple and clear as possible. There should be no jargon, and choices, when presented, should be in pairs ("this versus that" rather than in threes or more). Physicians' comments should be in line with what the patient is trying to say. The physician is trying to understand and *acknowledge the patient's feelings* (Rogers 1951). None of these are easy; they take knowing their importance and then practicing.

Becoming close to the very sick person is a way to gather necessary information, but perhaps most importantly, close connection is a requirement for healing. Closeness allows information to flow both ways

After all this complexity there is one statement that is simple. Learning what it means to know patients and then how to know patients in all these dimensions, avoiding the pitfalls, remaining connected to the patient yet self-protected, meeting the requirements for a therapeutic relationship, and doing it all in the flow, urgency, and confusion that is clinical medicine are difficult. But it is possible to do this with education, dedication to the task, persistence, and a lot of patience. With time and experience physicians get better and better at it. Whatever the physician accomplishes along the way, even if short of ideal, will make him or her a better healer.

References

Cassell, E. J., Leon, A. C., et al. (2001). Preliminary evidence of impaired thinking in sick patients. *Annals of Internal Medicine 134*(12): 1120–1123.

Hall, R. L. (2000). *The Human Embrace: The Love of Philosophy and the Philosophy of Love; Kierkegaard, Cavell, Nussbaum.* University Park, PA, Pennsylvania State University Press.

Lauer, Q. (1978). *The Triumph of Subjectivity: An Introduction to Transcendental Phenomenology.* New York, Fordham University Press.

Omdahl, B. L. (1995). *Cognitive Appraisal, Emotion, and Empathy.* Mahwah, NJ, Lawrence Erlbaum.

Osler, W. (1910). *Aequanimitas*, 2nd. ed. Philadelphia, P. Blakiston.

Overton, W. F., Jean Piaget Society. Symposium, et al. (1983). *The Relationship between Social and Cognitive Development.* Hillsdale, NJ, Lawrence Erlbaum Associates.

Platt, F. W., and Keller, V. F. (1994). Empathic communication: A teachable and learnable skill. *Journal of General Internal Medicine 9*(4): 222–226.

Rogers, C. R. (1951). *Client-Centered Therapy, Its Current Practice, Implications, and Theory.* Boston, Houghton Mifflin.

Snyder, C. R., and Lopez, S. J. (2005). *Handbook of Positive Psychology.* New York, Oxford University Press.

Swartz, M. H. (2002). *Textbook of Physical Diagnosis: History and Examination.* Philadelphia, WB Saunders Company.

Taylor, J. (2008). *My Stroke of Insight.* New York, Viking.

8
The Patient's Reaction to Illness

SICK PEOPLE ARE different from healthy people in many ways that are not related specifically to their diseases. The way sick persons differ and their individual reactions to their illness offer healers an opportunity to make patients better when their disease or even their symptoms cannot be helped. In addition to the effect of medical therapeutics and surgery, healing acts primarily on the full range of responses of persons to their sicknesses. The ways people react to being ill depend on the persons they are, on the interrelated conditions in which the illness occurs, on their medical care, and on the disease or the pathophysiology that underlies their illness. Numbers of studies have been done on psychological reactions to illness. Other research has characterized pain, cough, nauseas and vomiting, gait disturbances, and on and on. The meanings that people attribute to their illnesses, their sick bodies, and their treatment including medication should be of considerable interest to their clinicians because these things often determine their behavior and how well they are able to live despite being ill. Patients' relationships to their bodies, doctors, hospitals, and others involved in their care also have an effect on their well-being and thus should be important to healers.

There will never be enough research to determine what *this particular patient is experiencing* and exactly why the patient cannot pursue or achieve his or her purposes. No matter what the circumstances, medical science *cannot* predict, describe, or explain why the sickness has the precise characteristics it has in any individual patient, any more than it can say why H_2O is wet or why oil is oily. If you want to know, you have to ask. As we go about describing the nature of illness—the things that sickness does to individual patients and their responses to it—we enter the arena of the irreducible individuality of both patient and healer. It may seem paradoxic that where individuality counts is also the arena in which the relationship between the two is of paramount importance. This is because as a result of their interaction the individual who is the healer is best able to discover the precise nature of the expression of illness in the individual sick person. It is on the details of the patient's response to illness that the healer has his or her impact. Are all these words just to say that illness and healing are individual matters? Yes, because in the contemporary world of medicine, the emphasis is on systematizing, objective facts, and evidence (as in evidence-based medicine), not on the characteristics of *this* individual patient or what precisely is happening to the person.

When people are sick they have symptoms that are characteristic of the disease. Most people know about symptoms and they are accustomed to their importance in diagnosing disease. Doctors are used to asking patients about symptoms, but when they do inquire, they are going after specific things called symptoms; they are not skilled in finding out about the patient in the same detail. There may even be the belief among physicians that they are not supposed to go rooting about just to find things out. That would be nosy and doctors are not meant to be nosy. These inquiries are not intrusive; however, they acknowledge the complexity of human sickness and the fact that illness involves all parts of a person. Learning how to find out the details of the illness, therefore the patients' symptoms, their psychological reactions to sickness, the meaning of events, the changes in their relationship with their bodies, and the patients' behaviors in reactions to it, all seems a tall order. As your knowledge increases about illness and how people deal with it and how it alters their behavior, the task of discovery becomes more manageable—and your effectiveness as a healer increases. That is, after all, what it is all about—healers do things to make their patients better. The knowledge described in this chapter is about making patients better—even dying patients.

Psychological Responses to Illness

Things that are psychological, by definition, have to do with the mental life. Some might say that clinicians taking care of the sick are focused on the body, not on the mental life, and so psychological responses are not their business. This is not true. If I care for patients with newly diagnosed malignancies and they are frightened, should I ask for psychiatric consultations? Should I acknowledge the universality of such fears and reassure the patient that it happens to everybody—then move on? Or should I learn how to deal effectively and thoughtfully with fear because it is such a common reaction to serious illness, surgery, hospitals, and so on, and because unrelieved fear will get in the way of other things the patient and I must accomplish. I believe that is in the healer's province to handle psychological responses to illness if for no other reason than their widespread physiologic or pathophysiologic consequences. Healers, particularly those who deal with the seriously ill, should become adept at managing human illness and that means following its tracks and effects in the mental and emotional life, into meanings and their importance in individual instances, and helping shape patients' behaviors in response to sickness. I am well aware that we were not trained in those skills, but it can all be learned. When it is, you will find it interesting, I believe, and you will find its use gratifying.

Fear

Fear is not just one thing and it does not come in just one size. People may have brief fears about common things such as needle sticks, doctors, being inside of an MRI, certain medications, and medical procedures. Such fear may cause them to avoid the fearful thing to the point of not having an important test, procedure, or treatment. Discomfort at being afraid may lead to embarrassments or rationalizations that further get in the way of doing the fearful thing. Making fun of such fears or even their possibility wastes time or makes them worse. It is safe to assume that fears such as these are common events and deal with them in advance. "Many people get fearful in anticipation of IVs or procedures," you might say, "so if that happens don't hesitate to tell the nurse or technicians. Nobody is going to laugh at you, so just take a deep breath, and ask them to help, like, 'I get scared of needles, so can you just be patient with me.'" The important thing is that fear is not fun or funny. Handled with patience and empathy this kind of fear is usually not a problem. Sometimes what should be a small fear turns out to be terror that cannot be sympathized away. Many times patients will have had experiences of a similar kind in the past so you can ask them how it has been handled in the past; act on their advice. Profound fear almost always has a history and may occasionally require the help of a psychiatrist. Nobody likes to see a tight schedule disrupted, but a really frightened patient is not going to do something frightening (and is in danger) so forget the schedule and reschedule the patient—but always be graceful and kind—the patient is almost always embarrassed.

When fears are about the disease or bigger things such as surgery or chemotherapy in general, it is important to find out exactly what the person fears. General reassurance is usually useless. Ask what exactly it is about cancer, heart attacks, surgery, or chemotherapy, or whatever that is so fearful—and ask the patient to describe it in precise detail. Often such discovery leads to solutions to the fear. The most effective treatment is information, information, and more information. Specific information should be given in jargon-free language with time for the patient to ask questions and receive further information. The patient should also be clear that you (or someone designated) will be there as things go on—reassurance is an unfolding process.

The fear of death requires special attention. Clinicians sometimes say that they worried about talking about death and the fear of death because it is believed that patients are so afraid of the subject. Sometimes, however, it is not the patient who is afraid of death or talking about it—it is the clinician. If that is you, work it out, think it through, or get help because it is important to get over it. The word will not hurt you. Patients seeing that you are not afraid of the subject generally have less fear themselves. Patients newly diagnosed with cancer will think about dying from that moment on (often in that lonely time in the middle of the night). They think about it for themselves and for its effect on others, especially what the patient's death will do to young surviving children. Death is on their minds; how could it not be. Notwithstanding that generalization, there are patients who are so afraid of the subject that they push it from their consciousness. The source of the fear may seem obvious because of the ubiquity of death; however, as I pointed out elsewhere, the fear of death may instead be a fear of the loss of the connection to others. Sometimes when suggested, patients may suddenly realize that is what they are afraid of. If fear of social disconnection is important to the patient, then remain aware, so that there are plenty of visitors and other tokens of connection to the social world. The conversation can go further in that direction exploring what it means and how to deal with it. Again (and again, and again) patients need to know that you will not abandon them. Patients sometimes stay with physicians they really do not like because they are afraid that their life depends on that particular physician. One of the ways that sick people deal with the uncertainty of their future is to make the doctor into the all-knowing expert who can save them. Even when they want to change physicians, they are afraid that they will be leaving salvation, despite evidence to the contrary. The worse the disease the more this is true. This can be made worse by doctors who tell patients that *they alone* can save the patient. If you discover this of your new patient, do not dismiss the concern; explain why it happens and why changing physicians is appropriate. And of course, assure the patient that you will be there for them.

A lot has been written about a state called *death anxiety*, popularized by Ernest Becker in his influential book of 1973, *Denial of Death* (New York, Simon & Schuster). Becker wrote that our inevitable knowledge that death come to us all literally drives us to distraction. Because of that we all have to deny it, but its effects linger as a universal underlying anxiety. I have not been as impressed by its importance as some and I think the research on the subject is contradictory. I prefer to discover what concerns *this* particular patient and not deal with general fears unless they actively raise their head. Having said that, you can convey by your attitude toward fear or psychological concern that you are interested in hearing about the subject; conversely, if you are abrupt or dismissive of what is said, you will probably not hear another word on the subject, and the patient will lose an important source of support. All clinicians are worried about time—about how long these disclosures and the attention paid to them will take. You can hear and respond while you examine the patient or you can sit down and listen and then terminate the conversation when necessary. I usually say, "This subject is important. It will take time to really figure it out and decide what to do. So let me think about it and we'll talk later." Having said that, you must come back to the subject. I believe, as you get good at these psychological issues, you will be gratified at how much better your patient does when they are discussed and how much more efficient you become.

Some diseases raise fears in patients about social stigma. That used to be associated with cancer and tuberculosis; it is still attached to HIV/AIDS. Stigma injures in two ways. The patient who fears that he or she is discredited by having a disease is socially hurt by the stigma and afraid of the opinion of others. The stigmatized patient fears that there is something personally defective about him or her as an individual and that the flaw may hinder treatment and recovery, not by some magic, but by the fact that the patient—feeling less worthy—does not do what is necessary or see physicians or other clinicians. Do not underestimate the damage that may follow patients' beliefs that they are stained by a disease, impairment, or disability. Your acceptance does not eliminate the problem, but it is a step in the direction of patients accepting themselves. Remember how the problem of erectile dysfunction was made (more) acceptable when an ex-Senator was the spokesman for Viagra. Coming up with an innocuous name did not hurt, either. Because of the Americans with Disabilities Act, persons with disabilities were relieved of much of the stigma previously associated with their impairments and disabilities. The fact of the legislation meant that the problem of disability had become socially acceptable. If they were acceptable to society then, their impairments became more acceptable to the persons themselves.[1] There are countries now in which disabled persons are not seen on the streets. In Nepal, children who sustained bad burns from the cooking fire and were disfigured as a result—a common event—are hidden from view. If they believe themselves to be unwelcome or worthless in their social group, they will usually have the same opinion of themselves. There are no persons who do not see themselves as seen; how they conceive of what that means, however, may not conform to objective facts. Shame and guilt are very potent and arise, sometimes, when you least expect it. You may discover that your patient feels guilty, maybe intensely so, because his or her treatment is consuming the family's resources. Patients may also feel deeply guilty about failing you when they do not improve from your treatment.

---

1. Some persons with disability have come to see themselves as a special and separate group, like an ethnicity. The problems of the disabilities, they say, are not with them, but are society's problems.

How Do You Learn about Patients' Psychological Problems?

How do you know these things about your patients if they do not spontaneously tell you? It is not feasible to ask all patients whether they are fearful of death, just plain fearful, guilty, feel stigmatized, are worried about being contagious or of passing their diseases to their children, are shamed, fatalistic, emotionally numb, are having trouble thinking, are pessimistic, sad, depressed, hopeless, feel helpless and worried, have doubts about everything, are tired of it all, are anxious, panicky, angry, have a wide range of sexual troubles from impotence to dyspareunia, have family difficulties, or have problems with relationships. This is particularly so if working with these problems is not the line of work for which you were trained. Yet every one of these, severe enough or going on long enough, spells trouble—sometimes enough trouble to determine the outcome of the case. Perhaps surgeons and organ specialists usually do not have to concern themselves about these things. Healers, who usually take care of sick patients or the dying, do need to understand what is troubling their patient because that often determines what else is happening to the patient. Most clinicians think that the problems worrying the dying patient must have to do with the disease or its symptoms or the impending demise. Maybe, but maybe what is worse, for example, is a brother who is still angry about some difficulty of a generation ago that some effort of yours, a social worker, or a psychiatrist could set right. You can know about these frets only because the patient tells you. Once again, how do you know to inquire?

Knowing when to ask depends on *careful observation* of patients. You should be training yourself to observe carefully using all of your senses—there is no substitute. Look at the patient's face and body—including posture, clothing, motions and activities, and (in the hospital or at home) the bed and surroundings. Listen attentively to the patient's speech and voice for the sound as well as the words. Smell them (unobtrusively) and touch them. Within several weeks to a few months you will have begun to acquire the habit of careful observation. (This is discussed more fully in Chapter 6 on Evaluation.) Each time you see the patient you will see and hear or maybe smell and feel whether they have changed. The sweat of frightened patients' smells worse and terror has its own smell. Sometimes changes that you observe are because of disease, but if something is bothering the patient, you will almost surely see the change in looks and in presentation of self, and hear it in the voice. It is a very rare patient whose mood and emotional interior do not exhibit itself for you to observe. Years later you will probably still remember the patient's voice so that if it sounds different on the phone, something is probably the matter (or maybe better). Observing the change you can safely say, "What's the matter?" or "Is everything okay, you sound (or look) upset?" or, more carefully, "You look a little different today, why is that?" Or just, "Is something going on?" Remember you are a clinician, you are allowed to ask. (Try to do this when the patient is alone.) The patient may then tell you, but a more likely response is "No, it's nothing, I'm okay." "People," you say, "don't usually look troubled when everything is fine. Tell me." Remember, the patient will almost certainly appreciate that you care and that you take the time, and will be grateful also to have a chance to talk to somebody about whatever it is.

When the patient begins telling you what is troubling, do not just start giving advice. *Be quiet and listen.* (I want to say it three more times.) Almost surely you are going to hear more. Then ask simple, direct, and straightforward questions until you *really* understand what the patient is telling you. Avoid psychological diagnostic language. Please, do not be afraid of the time this is taking because the patient is most often acutely aware that your time is valuable and will err on the side of not saying enough. (I am aware that there are exceptions.) It has seemed to me over the years that when it was really clearly apparent what the patient was saying, the resolution of the problem was not too difficult. Or I knew that I needed help from others or that we had to get the family at the bedside. As in the rest of clinical medicine, as the years go by, you learn more and more about patients, psychological problems, worries, and, best of all, what to do about them. Of course, just when you think you have heard everything, a patient will tell of a problem that you would have thought impossible. Just like the rest of medicine—right around the corner....

Meaning

The words that most need to be said in response to what you hear are "What does that mean?" "What does that mean to you?" "What does what I just said mean to you?" Or "What did you think the doctor meant when he said..." (Please do not say "What are your feelings about that?" Those are words from another specialty.) As soon as you notice a patient acting in relationship to symptoms, illness, or the like in a manner that seems foolish, remember that foolishness and bad judgment are less likely than incorrect meaning. Similarly, denial is usually manifested by the attribution (usually below awareness) of the wrong meaning. There was a fuss made a few years back about how patients spoke from the "life world" while physicians spoke from the "medical world" and because of the difference physicians did not understand patients. That is simply another way of saying that the same things may have different meaning to patients than to doctors. Or, to be necessarily repetitious, everybody acts on the meaning of objects, events, circumstances, or relationships rather than the things themselves. It follows that we should be searching for what things mean to our patients (and ourselves) as well as what we believe they in fact are. Everybody would already know this except that meanings are "invisible"—we believe we are seeing (hearing, feeling, etc.) the thing itself but instead we "see" the meaning

Here is a typical event. A 78- year-old man had become accustomed to some numbness in the toes and lateral aspects of both feet. When he first noticed it several years previously, his physician, after looking for common causes, told him it was age related and of no consequence, "As long as there is no muscle weakness." One morning he became aware that he had mild numbness further up the lateral aspect of both legs. He thought this was something new and became alarmed. On his morning walk that day he thought his right foot was "moving funny." He was sure that it was weaker than the other foot. The more he walked the surer he became that his foot was weak and "maybe dragging." That afternoon he was seen by his doctor whose physical examination revealed some extension of the previous mild neuropathy, but no weakness. Asked what he believed was the meaning of the weakened foot, he said: "I thought for sure I'd had a stroke." Why did he go to the doctor? He went because of the stroke.

Some years ago, one of the founders of the now vast Kaiser-Permanente medical organizations said that his medical groups and many others would all run fine if they were not besieged by "the worried well." Patients who really had nothing wrong with them, he thought, were consuming medical services meant for the sick. Wrong. Some patients with weakness in a limb like the patient just described have had a stroke and some have ascribed the mistaken meaning, "I think I've had a stroke." Some patients with headache have meningitis and some think they have meningitis but just have headaches and a cold. They, I suppose, are the worried well. Some ascribed meanings are wrong, but some are correct. Making the distinction is our job, but assigning meaning to events is universal. That is why it is so important over the telephone to ferret out exact descriptions of events given by persons who believe they are sick—teasing away the facts from the meanings that have been assigned. (Especially since if the patient has a symptom or knows something about the incident that does not accord with the meaning he or she has assigned, it may not be mentioned unless you dig for the facts.) The advantage of the telephone is that you have only the spoken language, forcing you to really learn how to attentively listen.

In the earlier years of the hospice movement, many patients became alarmed and even refused treatment when they learned they were getting morphine for pain. Some thought they would become addicted and others thought that morphine meant imminent death. The assignment of meaning to the morphine changed it from simply an opioid analgesic to a drug with dire meanings. Attaching meanings to experience is in part a prediction of future events. Like the old man with worries about muscle weakness, it was not the (spurious) weakness but what the weakness foretold. Or the patients who did not want to take morphine because they would become addicted. This implies that every time you tell a patient about something and the patient attaches meaning, the meaning is predicting the future. Asking what something means to a patient is also asking what the patient believes the future holds.

Given the choice between a meaning that predicts a good future or a bad one, people generally opt for the worst interpretation. Because of the internet, choices for the interpretation of events have greatly increased. This is another way of saying that the opportunity to find reasons for pessimism has also increased. This whole discussion is meant to impress you with the importance of pursuing what meanings your patient has attached to an event, your words and actions, and suggestions for diagnostic or therapeutic actions. As mentioned previously more than once, you may not be able to change events—what happened happened—but you can change meanings.

Purpose

There is also meaning in the sense of purpose. Patients, particularly those who are severely ill, suffering, or approaching death, may seek the *meaning* of what is happening to them. We hear this when someone asks, "What is the meaning of all this?" or "Why do I have to go through this, what purpose does it serve?" or "Am I being punished, is that what all this sickness means?" or perhaps "Is all this sickness just a trial?" Perhaps "I see all this as a test that I am determined to pass." Clinicians too often avoid such questions, which is unfortunate. We are hearing something deeply important to the patient. If it is important to the patient it is consequential to the healer. You are going to know more about this patient at the end of the exchange. What if the patient asks if it is a punishment, or perhaps a test? Is seeing something (negatively) as a punishment the same as seeing it (positively) as a test? Would there be the possibility of the patient behaving differently in these two situations? Do not rush to terminate the question or to find someone else to respond. The first step (as usual) is to listen. What is the patient really asking (or saying)? Here again, "What do you mean by that?" The healer may find that a theological question is not being asked, but something that can be answered or acted on by the clinician. If not, then perhaps ask the chaplain (if the patient concurs).

A patient with breast cancer that had spread to adjacent lymph nodes was surprisingly unruffled by her diagnosis. She refused chemotherapy because she was positive and had no doubt that it was unnecessary in her case. Further spread of her disease also did not seem to disturb her. Her trajectory to death was relatively rapid—with every advance of her disease accepted with equanimity—and definitive treatment rejected as "unnecessary." Not surprisingly, her mother, whom she worshipped, had died of breast cancer. (We do not know, however, why she had to follow her mother's example.) An older Albanian immigrant was equally tranquil about dying from cancer of the lung. He knew it was his destiny since his father and two brothers had died similar deaths. (Physicians are not happy when patients do that; not smoking, from our perspective, would have changed their destiny.)

"Are You Angry at Your Body?"

The mind–body duality flourishes in the thoughts of many—especially when they are sick. It is, for them, as though the body is something (somebody may be more accurate) apart from themselves. Rarely it is adored, sometimes liked, and occasionally hated. Patients also develop beliefs about themselves, their abilities, the way their body works, and about themselves in relation to their bodies. These ideas—that the mind, for example, fully determines whatever happens in the body—are often anatomically and physiologically in error. They are most important in long-lasting or chronic disease. Clinicians are usually unaware of what thoughts patients hold about the sickened body. Yet feelings and ideas that patients have about their own body are important determinants of their behavior in relation to their function, their disease, and its treatment. Does this matter? If you had a caregiver who hated the patient, a mother who hated her child, or a spouse who hated the sick husband she cares for would you think it mattered? You might worry that the best was not being done—or if done, then it was being done with resentment. Remember, the body has to be given medication, has to have sufficient sleep, and has to be fed, clothed, and bathed. It has to be brought to the doctor on time, its dressings (ugh) have to be changed, to say nothing of the messy, smelly, noisy, embarrassing things it does. It does not take long in chronic (or even acute) illness for clinicians to begin to hear complaints about the body—as though it was someone else. That might be the time to ask, "Are you angry at your body?" Do not be surprised if the patient answers, "Yes, I'm furious at my body, it betrayed me. Wouldn't you be angry considering what it's done to me!" The body, it turns out, gets the blame for the degradations of disease. It is not the disease, the patient says, it is the diseased body that is the enemy. Worse, the body is often assumed to have intentions—animate in the sense of actively doing things to the patient. It is useless to argue with the patient and simply denying the belief is ineffective. You might say, "That is a mean thought. It doesn't seem to have occurred to you that the disease attacked your body. A perfectly fine body was injured by this disease and instead of sympathy it gets your hatred and scorn." You want your patients to know that they and their bodies are allies; that their bodies need their help and also their concern and constancy. The patient and the body are in it together. You are sending another crucial message at the same time: "You have choice."

Sick people may—often do—feel passive about the disease and all that is happening to them and passive also to the doctor and to medicine. Here you are saying they do not have to be passive they have choice. The disease is attacking both the patient's body and the patient—now the patient is not a being divided, but a unitary being. An inner conflict is resolved and the patient can come to the defense of the body. The body needs care, it needs proper nutrition and exercise, it needs its medication, and so on. The patient's perspective has changed—the whole meaning of the illness has changed. The patient can learn to love the body like an injured child. This is an active on-going process. There is another message in all this. The patient may not be able to control the disease or the body but can control how he or she responds to them.[2]

Pain can be looked at in the same way. If the patient sees the use of potent analgesics, including opioids, as the problem rather than the pain itself, then the patient's pain will probably control the patient. Avoiding pain medication just results in worse pain, and it garners no medals. It is true that potent analgesics—not solely opioids—can result in trouble from side effects to habituation. The dangers of nontherapeutic effects may be overstated out of concern for the patient's welfare. Similarly, the threat of addiction may be held over the patient's head. Both dangerous side effects and progression to addiction in medical patients taking potent analgesics are uncommon. Poorly controlled pain is more common.[3] When patients learn that pain is just pain and, for example, not punishment, and that the use of medications—including narcotics—to control pain has no moral significance—they are what they are and nothing else—they change from being controlled by their pain to being able to control their pain effectively (and generally with less medication). Here again patients learn that they have choices. The same is true for other symptoms and other treatments. The less passive to the disease and body and the more control the patient has, the more functional the patient will be.

Patients with chronic diseases often have many doctors. People can be afraid of physicians and distressed when they have to see them. Because of this they may

---

2. A wonderful book by Ellen Schecter, *Fierce Joy* (New York, Greenpoint Press, 2011) describes how the patient's relationship to the sickness can change and improve the patient's welfare.

3. In the early days of postoperative intravenous narcotics controlled by a pump, it was thought that it would be unwise to let patients control the rescue or breakthrough pain dose because patients would self-administer too much. It was found that the total of patient-activated doses was less than when controlled by the staff.

behave in a way that displeases themselves, varying from being too aggressive to too meek. Doctors' offices may elicit these behaviors because of waiting times, the intimidating nature (from the patients' point of view) of the office, the staff or the clinicians, discomforting (or worse) treatments, and other problems. Even telephone calls may be distressing. The patient speaks to the secretary who speaks to the doctor who speaks to the secretary who speaks to the patient. (Fortunately email may sometimes make direct communication possible when doctors will not speak on the phone.) You may have to teach your patient that he or she is an adult going to get help from another adult (and no longer the little child afraid of the pediatrician). Teaching people how to behave in doctors' offices in a way that both pleases them and elicits the maximum effort from the clinicians of various types really changes the patients' experience—done well, clinicians like it too. The same is true of hospitalized patients. Learning how to manage the staff and themselves makes patients' in-hospital lives better (and is usually easier on the staff at the same time).

We have seen the large range of reactions patients may have to their illness, its treatment, clinicians and other staff, and the context of care. Discovering when these things trouble the patient is largely a matter of listening to what is said (and not said) and observing patients carefully in order to know when to probe further. I cannot stress too strongly the difference actively and effectively dealing with these can make to the patients well-being and trajectory through illness. Healers are primarily concerned with the relief of impairments of function resulting from illness. The range of reactions to illness discussed here has a direct impact on patients' functioning and well-being and they deserve your attention.

9
The State of Illness

AS ILLNESS DEEPENS, patients enter a *state of illness*. In *The Healer's Art*, more than 30 years ago, I wrote that patients with serious illness have certain characteristics: Foremost is disconnection from the world, a loss of a sense of omnipotence (a sense of indestructibility), a loss of the sense of omniscience (a sense of the completeness of one's knowledge), an impairment in the ability to reason in the fashion of normal adults, a loss of a sense of control. Since then we also have learned that sick persons lose executive function—an impairment of cognitive processes responsible for planning, decision making, cognitive flexibility, rule acquisition, initiating appropriate actions, and other functions involved in handling novel situations. In addition, the sick have an impairment of emotive thought. Now I know that these characteristics are descriptive of a special state of being that I will describe in detail in this chapter. Does this imply that all persons with serious illness have or will enter a state of illness? I believe that it does. It applies to anyone sufficiently sick to require care in bed and who is unable to care for himself or herself or who requires special care and assistance and the equivalent of institutional or hospital care (this corresponds to 50% or lower on a Karnofsky Performance Status Scale and is equivalent to a Zubroid/WHO/ECOG score of 3 or less). Any person who is sufficiently sick or injured can enter a state of illness. In *The Healer's Art* I called this the distinction between disease and illness. I no longer think that is a good division because it implies a dualism between the disease and the person that is artificial. These are simply things that happen physically or psychologically and that occur in persons who get sick enough. Many years ago I had a patient who was hospitalized and on bed rest for months because of cardiomyopathy. At the time I did these tests of cognition she was without symptoms (although still on bed rest), yet she had the characteristics of the state of illness.

Here is an example of a patient in whom the disease and its impact in producing the illness state are typical and also show their separate nature. A woman who had been living an active life despite her poorly controlled ovarian malignancy was hospitalized after coming into the urgent care area of her cancer center because of dehydration from chemotherapy-related nausea and vomiting. The patient was despondent and crying as her spouse and she wondered whether this is when she would die. They had previously distanced themselves from actively dealing with her impending death. As difficult as it has been to speak about death they have things to talk about now—issues that they have been putting off that have become immediate. So around and between the symptoms and the medical care they discuss what needs to be done. She tires very easily and fades off and falls asleep from time to time, but soon returns to awareness and the conversation. The next morning is different. She appears feeble and complains of being weak and fragile. It is difficult to talk to her because she does not appear to understand, for example, why she should care about the difficulty her mother and siblings are having getting to her bedside. She wants, "my *mother to come—now*." The doctor came in to discuss her medications, her pain control, and whether she was moving her bowels, but as simple as the questions seemed, she could not focus on answering. She is more withdrawn. All this frightens her husband who cannot figure out why she is so different, particularly as nothing has happened to her since coming to the hospital except that her symptoms—the nausea and vomiting and the pain—are, if anything, better. He slept in her room and he knows that nothing out of the ordinary was done to her.

She has entered a *state of illness*, a qualitatively different state of being. Before she was severely ill from her malignancy and its treatment; today she is not more ill, but now has this new phenomenon. A state is *"A combination of circumstances or attributes belonging for the time being to a person; a particular manner or way of existing, as defined by certain circumstances or attributes"* (*Oxford English Dictionary*, 2nd ed., electronic). The essential characteristic of a state is a redirection of all of the person's thoughts and actions to focus on the state. In a state of hopelessness it is on hopelessness. In a state of grief it is on grief. In a state of love (sometimes described as a "crush") it is on the object of love. In a state of sickness it is on a state of illness. States of being are dynamic; they are not events but processes that evolve over time. They may last a brief time or for a longer period. The impact on the person of a state of being is widespread from the social to the molecular levels. What is happening to the patient includes the entire range of things spiritual, emotional, social, and physical that happen in sickness. It is the personal, the experience, as with this woman, of feeling decrepit, fragile, vulnerable, weak, without energy, and feeble even more than the nausea, vomiting, and abdominal pain that were present prior to her entering this state that makes her know she is sick. One further characteristic of states of illness marks her; she has become completely focused on herself, her pain, her distress, and also on the "fact" that (for example) the nurse did not pay attention to *her*, just to the IV.[1]

---

1. What is the advantage of calling this a "state of illness" rather than simply illness as in the distinction between illness and disease. States, as defined, are separate entities that happen to

In other words there are sometimes three distinct and separate aspects of being sick. There is the disease and its symptoms, the reactions to those discussed in the previous chapter, and the state of illness. The severity of illness is one determinant. For example, everybody has been ill and everybody knows that illnesses can be anything from mild to severe and from brief to very long. The condition of ill patients—the symptoms they have and how sick they are—seems naturally to depend on the underlying disease. People may have minor symptoms, for example, stuffed nose, sore throat, mild cough, and a draggy feeling when they have an upper respiratory infection (a cold), but they do not generally characterize themselves as sick. They know what it is and they expect it to be gone in a week or two. If it lasts for awhile, or if they become febrile, they may think they have gone on to an infection and maybe ought to see a doctor and get antibiotics; they may even go to bed with their illness, but they usually do not consider themselves to be really ill. Aside from their symptoms and annoyance about them, they act like the well. Even with more annoying things, where, for example, the person has to urinate all the time, persons think they have a bladder infection and know antibiotics will stop it. Again, they do not consider themselves sick. The majority of everyday illnesses and injuries fall into these categories, especially because of the internet and the ability to look up symptoms. Persons know (or think they know) what the matter is and they know (or think they know) that the symptoms fit the disease.

Serious illness, for example, diabetic ketoacidosis, may cause someone to be hospitalized and be quite sick in a short time. Some patients will remain their usual recognizable selves. They will be alert and cognizant enough to see and think about what is happening, ask questions, and understand the answers. These patients will not enter a state of illness. However, despite the short duration of their illness, others will slip into a state of illness and consider themselves to be sick, weak, and fragile. Another example that is frightening is a sudden collapsed lung from a large spontaneous pneumothorax with sudden pain and breathlessness. Despite the brevity of the illness, patients such as this may quickly begin to behave like the sick and enter a state of illness whereas others do not. In accidents in which multiple fractures and overwhelming pain are predominant the characteristics of a state of illness may appear in minutes. Both those who became sick and those who do not usually recover rapidly and soon behave normally. The state of illness is spontaneously and sometimes rapidly reversible.

---

persons and they are similar from person to person. They allow you to define the parameters of a state so that it is possible to do research on them as we would do research on (say) dyspnea or chronic obstructive pulmonary disease. I selected these two because although it is known that they exist and can be defined, their definitions do not rest on structural characteristics.

Although the state of illness occurs independently of the disease and has its own subjective effects, the symptoms of disease may be taken personally, making things worse. The experience of the symptoms is as if they are things done to the patient. This is true above all and especially of pain, but also nausea, vomiting, dyspnea, or perhaps any symptom if it is severe enough to dominate the patient's attention. Add to these fear and uncertainty and a full-blown state of illness will be apparent. Physicians have classically seen symptoms as the disease speaking and thus in their attempt to control them, they think of themselves as attacking the disease. Symptoms should also, however, be seen as events in themselves that come to dominate the person. If their effect is destructive enough, suffering will ensue and then the major problem will be suffering, not the symptom that incited it. Short of suffering, however, patients may cower in fear of their symptoms. What does that mean? If profuse watery diarrhea develops, it rarely occurs without abdominal discomfort and it means endless trips to the toilet (or shifting on to the bedpan)—each one a drain on the patient's small and shrinking reserve of energy. The same is true of vomiting. A state of illness will be better understood if you see each of these symptoms as the *experienced drawing away* of energy and engagement with the outside world. This means that symptoms offer two avenues of relief, the symptoms themselves, but also the impact of the symptoms felt personally. Clinicians may be impatient with what seems like whining. It is not whining, it is a cry—help *me*. The sympathetic clinician might say, "I know that it is like the vomiting isn't bad enough, it feels like a low blow!" "We'll get through it, you'll see. The medication will soon help." Especially with a patient in a state of illness—we, we, we.

The healthy person generally does not even notice the world and its quotidian intrusive manifestations of television, telephones, smartphones, newspapers, magazines, topics of casual conversation (sports, politicians, famous people, and things of the moment); these are like the air, like water to a fish. It takes energy for a fish to move the weight and push aside currents of water, and energy for us to deal with gravity and move through air. If pointed out you may acknowledge this, but otherwise these things are invisible. The quotidian demands require still more energy. The healthy person's energy is boundless compared to the very sick, but the patient's energy is constantly drawn down as the day and the weight of symptoms and the needs of their care and the caregivers always want more. Each detail feels like a personal demand against an empty account. Visitors, including friends, acquaintances even family, even the most loving family members, further sap the waning strength of the sick patient. When I point out what seems to be the function, the utility of a state of illness, it will seem a reasonable thing. In a state of illness, *the patient withdraws from the social world*—from the world of us, of others, and of demands, denying the pull of community.

American culture endorses individualism and has done so since our beginnings. In this culture individualism has moved through stages, but no matter in what manner we are proud of our individualism. Most recently ties have also loosened to class, political, social, and ethnic group identities. Individualism, taken alone, leads to a false picture, however, because everyone has strong ties to others—stronger than most know—family especially, some friends, work associates, and others, that they hold dear to a varying degree. Martin Buber described this when he said that "In the beginning is the relationship." (We have a name for deviants in this regard, we call them hermits.) When people are sick, on the other hand, they need others to help in many ways, although the circle of relationships may be becoming smaller. Lying in a hospital bed patients may feel alone, even lonely. Then the spouse walks in or a favorite relative or friend and a broad smile erupts spontaneously on the patient's face. This is not true of patients in a state of illness who may look up or not—their world has contracted to the size of the bed and barely more. Even the box of tissues just beyond the hands seems out of sight. Their field of view narrows from 160° or more to about 30°.[2] There is a profound loss of interest in the outside world. The patient remains connected to caregivers—to the physicians or other clinicians responsible for care. Within a day they know the sound of their doctor's footsteps in the hallway. Other impairments in reasoning and emotive thought were noted in earlier chapters and they occur with any patient who requires care in bed.

Are there patients in a state of illness who are as diseased as this woman but who remain active, do not go to the hospital, or who resist the call of the sick bed? I believe not. There are many questions about the state of illness, but our focus has been so much on the disease, its diagnosis, and its treatment that our knowledge of the sick patient is really lacking. On the other hand, that there are patients who are much more engaged in the world and able to function suggests another goal of treatment aside from the disease. The state of illness and related impacts of sickness on the behavior and capacities of the sick cry for research to truly characterize what happens to people—in all domains—when they are sick. Here is a patient who provides at least a partial answer.

A 56-year-old woman had stage four breast cancer and toward the end of her life her bone marrow was filled with tumor cells with all the usual hematologic sequelae. Her pain was well controlled. She had been very busy before her tumor and in seeming disregard of her disease she continued her active life at home and some part-time work as an administrator. Her oncologist was concerned,

---

2. Give a camera to the sick person and ask him to take pictures of the visitors. The patient can do it, but the horizon will not be preserved—the pictures will be tilted. Indoors or out, healthy people make pictures level—or close to it. They preserve the horizon.

however, that she did not realize the gravity of her situation. During an office visit the oncologist spent time explaining in explicit detail what was happening and how serious it was. On returning from the visit the woman took to her bed and stopped eating. Her husband and daughter were unable to hold conversations with her, receiving only monosyllabic answers. She acted in all respects like someone in a state of illness and acted drastically different than she had before the visit to the oncologist.[3]

Within a day or so of her going to bed I was asked to see her. I spoke to her husband and her daughter who were already grieving, sure that death was imminent. Her daughter had returned from across the country with the man she planned to marry. She wanted to have the wedding in the house before her mother died; now she was overwhelmed with sadness that the wedding would be too late. I went alone into the room—which was darkened—and found her lying in bed face turned away from me. I introduced myself and asked her why she was in bed. She was too sick to get up, she said in a monotone, and besides, she would die soon. I asked her to turn around and sit up so I could talk to her; it was not polite not to face me when we spoke, I said, as I reached over to help her (not waiting for an answer). (Politeness is one of the last things to go.) Besides, I said, I was told she was running around doing things just a few days earlier. After she was sitting I gently reached out to hold her arm and asked her to let me help her over to the chairs where we could talk better. In doing this I started to physically breach the disconnection and move her away from the narrow world of the state of sickness that is the bed. I spoke quietly and easily, but directly to what I wanted from her. My actions were started slowly and calmly, but before I received permission, as though my physical reaching and touching were part of the request. For healthy persons such behavior would be an impolite intrusion into their space.

We spoke awhile, sitting in the chairs, about her work, what kept her busy (before she went to bed), her lovely daughter and what she thought about the groom to be, her husband, and so on. My questions to her were simple and straightforward. I answered her questions in a direct and uncomplicated manner. After perhaps 10 minutes I asked her to take me downstairs and show me the house. She did. After a little while I asked if she wanted go back to bed. I said that I knew of no medical reason why she could not return to the activities that had absorbed her before she saw the oncologists. I told her that I would speak to

---

3. The oncologist, when asked about the conversation, explained repeatedly that she believed that patients' well-being required knowing the truth and therefore it was her obligation to make their situations clear. She believed that this patient was "in denial" and blocking out the truth. That is why she had been so explicit. She also called the patient's husband to explain the importance of telling the truth. She did not specify what goals other than truthfulness should motivate her communication with patients.

the oncologist. Her daughter and husband came in and we made plans for her dinner and for the next day when I said I would return. Within several days she was as active as she was before the visit to the oncologist. In total, I probably saw her three or four times. I spoke to her a number of times on the telephone. I last talked to her a few weeks later, a day after the wedding about which she was delighted. She died at home not long after that, returning to her bed only a few days before her death.

My behavior was tuned to her as a sick woman and my actions were directed at the state of illness. It cannot be said often enough: the sick are different from the well and the actions of clinicians should be adjusted for the characteristics of sick persons. They are, to repeat, disconnected from their world; they have the feeling that they have no control over their lives, they have lost the normal feeling of indestructibility, their cognitive function is not what it was, they are filled with uncertainties, and they do not really understand (as hard as they try) what is happening to them. Patients can leave the state of illness even though the disease is not better. An important therapeutic goal is ending a state of illness. The primary modalities for the relief of the state of illness are the connection to the clinician, symptom relief, and talking with the patient—communication. Get them out of bed if at all possible. Symptoms must be relieved to the degree possible. When they cannot be made better the patient should know that you are trying and why the symptom is resistant.

The first step is to make a connection to the patient. Make eye contact and touch the patient. Be open to the patient (as described in Chapter 5). Speak directly, clearly, and quietly. Be aware of your body language so that it does not contradict what you manifestly intend. Communication with sick patients is not ordinary conversation. The spoken language acts on the person—every part of the person. *Every word matters.* But *do not waste words*—say what you want to say and not what you do not want to say. Say everything you want to say and nothing that you do not want to say. Remember, you are not just talking, you are working—working at making a sick person better. We all speak differently and we all have different accents and speech mannerisms. These only establish each of us as an individual. It is what is said and how that matter, and the intentions of the utterances. Intentions are conveyed not only by the words but by the clinician's presentation to the patient. A gentle hand on the patient while you are speaking connects you physically and conveys your interest. If you have a question about whether the patient will accept being touched, ask permission. The conversation should be straightforward, direct, and to the point, but also kind and gentle. (Humor is perfectly acceptable.) When an answer is called for, give the patient enough time and do not step on the utterances. Do not finish the patient's sentences. It is common when the listener speaks slowly, to talk loudly and talk down. Remember, the patient is sick not dumb.[4] He or she is another person and sickness does not remove the need for respect. Have no illusions; this way of speaking and communicating is difficult to learn and it takes practice and patience over months and years to get really good at it, but it will not be long before you will have no doubt about its effectiveness. When you say something it should be true as you know the truth. The point of what you say, however, is not that it is true, telling the truth is a moral imperative, the reason for the words is to convey information that you believe will help the patient. Your speech, the information, and your conveyed intentions are reaching out to the patient who has, as it were, moved into a different space and you are bringing him or her back to where you (and the rest of us) are. In talking with patients physicians themselves are the therapeutic agent. The vehicle through which almost everything that physicians do to and with patients is the relationship between the patient and physician. That relationship is best if it is built on trust and trust is best engendered by the truth. That is not the end of the story; it is the beginning.

Talking to patients necessarily transmits information and *in communication it is the information that counts*, and the manner in which it is conveyed (which is also information); therefore clinicians should be aware that they are involved in information control. There are specific tasks in addition to informing the patient that should be accomplished by information flowing to patients. First, it should reduce uncertainty. Second, it should improve the patient's ability to act. Finally, it should improve the relationship between physician and patient. It follows that information you provide to patients should meet certain tests. Does it reduce the patient's uncertainty now or in the future? Does it improve the patient's ability to act now or in the future? Does it improve your relationship with the patient (now or in the future)? If information wisely used can do those things, then information poorly used can create uncertainty, paralyze action, and destroy the relationship. Going back to the patient with breast cancer, the oncologist telling her the entire (and dire) nature of her disease had all those negative effects, *even though it was true*.

When speaking with patients in a state of illness remain aware of their cognitive impairment. They are concrete, they can attend only to a limited amount of information, they cannot deal in abstractions, and they cannot take the point of view of another.[5] That is why the patient discussed above with ovarian cancer

---

4. Good advice on how to be with sick patients is given in Appendix B in *My Stroke of Insight*, by Jill Bolte Taylor, 2008. New York, Viking.

5. Patients who think like this are unable to take transitions into account, so that having been shown and acknowledging that two containers (such as two urine cups) have the same amount of water, when the contents of one is poured into a different shaped container (such as a test tube) they will believe that the new container has a different amount of water. They cannot

could not understand why her mother and siblings were having trouble coming to see her. She could speak only from her desire to see them *now*. In light of this it is not useful to emphasize the mother's transportation problems, but it does help to reassure the patient that you know how important seeing her mother is and that you will do everything you can to help solve the problem—and whatever else needs doing.

If you tell a patient a fact about themselves—a laboratory test result, a physical finding, or something about their disease, the statement is not finished unless it includes the fact itself, the significance of the fact, and what you will do about it. For example, "Your tongue and your mouth look quite dry. This is because you lost fluid while vomiting. The dryness, in itself, will do you no harm, but it tells us that you need more fluid. We will be giving you fluid intravenously to make up for the loss." First, however, ask yourself why you are telling the patient about the fact in the first place. We are in an era of truth-telling that is certainly preferable to when we hardly told patients anything, and what we did say was often not the truth. It does not help patients to know, however, every little fact about themselves that you know unless it serves the purposes of their care. You are trying to move a patient out of a state of illness. Stay on the point. If asked, for example, why you are looking into the mouth so intently, that would require an answer. If not, let it pass and keep going. Conclude sections of your examination or questioning by asking if the patient has any questions.[6]

You have dealt with the foremost problem of your patient in a state of illness, the disconnection to others and the world, by actively making a connection to the patient.[7] The importance of this cannot be overemphasized since you have probably become the most important being in the patient's new world of sickness. Perhaps you do not like this idea—it seems like too much responsibility and it seems to involve you too much as an individual. You have heard since your student days that you should not get too close to patients. Besides, you have

---

grasp logical reversibility (take a ball of clay and roll it into a sausage—then know how big it will be when rolled back into a ball) and they cannot see one side of an ABCD child's block and know what letter is on the other side. They can, however, pass tests of cognition such as the Mini-Mental Status Examination (MMSE). It is startling the first time you see this in what is by all accounts a cognitively intact sick person.

6. Having said that, there are patients whose way of staying in control is to know everything. Then tell them everything, but leave no mysteries in the wake of your information

7. This is also a discussion of empathy, since as you learn to make the connection to the patient that I am describing you will also develop the ability to know his or her emotions and meet the other demands of empathy. Although known and described for almost two centuries, recent studies in neuroscience have confirmed the ability to mirror the acts and experiences of others—including emotion. Some have a greater ability to be open as I have described than others. As noted previously, sick patients are usually more open to others than healthy people are.

seen other clinicians seemingly take good care of patients without getting that close, although do you really know how good their care was, aside from technically? What should you do—get close to patients, keep your distance, or get even closer?

Closeness: Healing the State of Illness

The issue of closeness to patients is important and must be looked at in more detail to understand the solution that I will offer. This question is especially pertinent with patients who will die. It is said by some that palliative care clinicians develop "burnout"—the experience of long-term exhaustion, diminished interest, and a reduced sense of personal accomplishment—because of repeated loss after attachment and repeated grief reactions, however weak or strong. The opposite experience, a sense of personal gratification, is also reported by many who care for the dying. Generally, palliative care physicians find their work more personally rewarding than other specialties in internal medicine. What accounts for these opposite responses to the repeated experience of loss by those who care for the very sick and dying?

To understand this and resolve the problem of emotional closeness to sick and dying patients I believe we should first see how physicians are affected at different stages of their development. Medical students, house officers, fellows, those in the early years of practice, and experienced practicing physicians who care for the dying all are different in important ways. Medical students, as they start their clerkship, are very excited to finally have their own patients, even though in the beginning they are generally nervous and inefficient. The learning curve is steep and in a short time they are more comfortable with patients. I was like that and I enjoyed patients immensely. Late in my medicine clerkship I admitted a woman with end-stage malignancy. She was really sick and in great distress. In those days control of pain and other symptom was inadequate. Her family was not there that much because Bellevue Hospital did not make things easy outside of visiting hours. Her bed was moved to the front of one row of beds, which was a bad prognostic sign on those big wards. I spent hours at her bedside feeling mostly helpless. The intern warned me that she was going to die soon. That seemed all the more reason to help because she required a lot of care and the house staff had moved on to more rewarding cases. When she did die I found the experience really sad and painful, more than I had expected. There was nobody to talk to about my feelings and when I finally got up enough nerve to talk to the resident he told me that it was a lesson not to get too close to patients. I was not sure how you did that since being close to patients seemed one of the best parts of being (even an almost) doctor.

Through my internship and then residency I entered a mode of superpragmatism in which my primary focus was on diseases and disease treatment. Sometimes we lost a lot of patients and that was difficult, but mostly we were all focused on technical medicine. We were not attentive to dying patients, although we did our best to make them comfortable—or what we thought was the best. We were not concerned with suffering or suffering patients—we did not know what suffering was. Who would have taught us? I had learned my lesson about getting too close to patients and getting hurt when they died. The lesson was memorable but not really helpful because I really liked my patients and their loss continued to be a source of distress. Like my friends I mostly managed to avoid seeing the end of life problems of patients with malignant disease or other chronic diseases. Not infrequently when a patient with a lot of symptoms, including pain, at the end of life required more doctoring than we were prepared (or knew how) to give, we found a way to blame the patient. I would feel badly when someone died an especially bad death, but we did not talk about it. I knew no solution so I just felt badly and tried to push it away.

As I started practicing, I thought my goal was to be the equivalent of a chief resident—to know so much medicine and to be so good at it (whatever that meant) that patients should choose me as their doctor because I knew so much. I soon discovered that patients took it for granted that doctors knew medicine. They came to me because they thought I was less busy and could spend more time with them—which was true. Spending more time with my patients caused me to know a lot more about them, so when they were sick I was much closer. I learned that I had to be emotionally close to my patients because if I was not close I could not really do all that I believed should be done. I knew their families and often the family members and friends were also my patients. When one of my patients died—which was uncommon in the early years—I would be upset and worried that I had done something wrong. The upset feeling would last actively a week or more and it was not pleasant. Fortunately, I could talk it out with my wife. Other doctors were no help. If I made a mistake I learned to immediately tell someone else about it so as not to rewrite events in my thoughts when I was not to blame. (It really was my fault.) Again, other physicians were no help. They would say, "Forget it, it happens to everybody." There was no comfort in that.

I started actively caring for dying patients in the fall of 1971. I had been asked to give a talk about the care of the dying in January 1971 at the Hastings Center (then a new organization). As a result of the presentation I began to wonder whether it was possible to take care of a patient when the diagnosis was (so to speak) "dying patient." I learned, as has everybody else by now, that not only can you do that, but you should. The major advantage I discovered is that because you cannot effectively treat the disease, you must learn to work with the sick persons to make them better (even though they all die). I discovered, as have so many others, that it was the most satisfying and rewarding medicine I had ever done. To do it well required *greater* than ordinary knowledge and expertise about the disease, prognostication, symptom control, making things happen in the patient, changing the patient's relationship to the disease, and on and on (as detailed in other parts of this book). When you do all those things, closeness to the patient is an essential element in the care. Unfortunately, I paid a price when they died—it hurt. I had a physical symptom as a token of that price. When I received a telephone call from one of my mother's neighbors that my mother was dead (at age 81) I developed a very severe knife-like pain between my shoulder blades. Whenever a patient was soon to die, I would get a recurrence of that pain. It was an accurate prognostic sign, but the price was high.

In Chapter 5, Listening, I described how to be open to patients; it is also pertinent to this discussion. I first learned about it in the course of caring for a particularly saddening patient. She was a 35-year-old woman dying of breast cancer who I started taking care of late in the course of her disease. She was married to a psychiatrist and she had a 5-year-old child. One day she came to my office because of pain in her left upper back caused by pathologic fractures of several ribs; as a result she had pain with every breath. This kind of pain is difficult to control. Looking sick, jaundiced, and with a distended abdomen, she was a sad sight as she walked by me to the consulting room. Moments later I was handed the printout of her blood test results. Looking at them I got a chill of fear and I realized I was afraid of the pain I would soon feel as she died. I thought that the feeling was a preamble to putting some distance between us—the opposite of what I wanted to do. Minutes later, seated across from her, I had an idea; I actively imagined putting a teacup inside my chest in which she could sit, as if it was a safe place. Although I had never done it before, I tried creating the "open" feeling discussed in Chapter 5. I could easily feel the connection between us and I was gratified to see her relax and hear her say how much the pain had decreased. The feeling lasted the whole visit and her subsequent increase in trust made working with her and controlling her pain easier. I had no idea what I had done and I did not know what to make of it, but whatever it was, it helped. On the other hand, I had no doubt that her death was going to be for me a source of worse than usual distress because I was so close and connected to her.

My closeness to her persisted but I *did not get my back pain,* although as she approached death I would usually have been in pain when I saw her. She died, and although I was sad (who would not be), I was not in as much distress as I expected. I thought it would get to me as I signed the death certificate (my symbolic last act). It was not so. This unhappy death with a mourning husband, family, and very sad child, all of whom I had to see, caused me less anguish, surprisingly, than I had become accustomed to. I believe the answer is that my symptoms in the past and the distress so common in other physicians, and probably also in "burnout," do not come from being too close to patients, but by *not being close enough*. With the patient I just discussed I could not be accused of not being close enough, of not giving everything of myself, or not using all my resources, the way *an ideal physician should*. Whereas in other situations, in common with other clinicians, to avoid getting hurt I had always held back—even though I was not conscious of doing so. The pain of loss, I realized, was not a pain of loss it was a *pain of recrimination* for not doing as well by a patient as demanded by the ideal of physicianship.[8]

You cannot ask physicians—clinicians—to put themselves in harm's way every time a patient is going to die. What I am suggesting will not, however, cause physicians harm because they are protected by the ideal of physicianship as selfless that is part of the ideals of the profession that go a long way back. Medicine has professional ideals that are inculcated in doctors during their training whether they know about them consciously or not. It happens as part of becoming a physician. The usefulness of roles is that when the role of physician is in force the self is asked by the task to meet demands that go with the role; at the same time the self that is the physician is protected by the role. *It is the physician self making the connection to the patient and that self is protected because it is a doctor working.* In Chapter 2 in the discussion of what persons are I said we are all more than one self. This has been a concrete example. I used to get offended when I was asked what I as a physician thought of this or that. I would say there is only me, Eric Cassell. That is not true. There is a physician self as part of Eric Cassell. In the past I was having symptoms when I lost a patient because *I failed to meet the role expectations*. Medical students have not yet developed their physician role, which is probably also true of house officers, at least in their early years, so they do not have the protection of the role-related self. Everyday Eric Cassell, ordinary person, father, husband, etc., is not in a physician role, and does not get close to patients in the same role-related way. When close associates, friends, or family die he has (I have) the pains of loss and grief like everybody else.

To return to the patient in a state of illness. How do we deal with the patient's feeling of having no control. You, the physicians, are the patient's agent of control. That is one of the functions of using the word "we" with the patient. "What

---

8. The experience of getting close to that patient and the salutary outcome had an important influence on me. It gave me permission to try giving more of myself with an assurance that not only the patients would benefit, but I would too. It used to be said that medicine is an ennobling profession. I am not so sure of that, but it is certainly true that taking care of sick patients has taught me a lot about myself and how to live my life.

needs doing that I can help you with?" No one is asking you to run errands for the patient, in fact, the feeling of not having control is just that, a feeling (and not a pleasant feeling). The feeling is relieved by the clinician acknowledging the problem and offering to help—patient and physician, the we as the "team." If things have to be done, others should be enlisted where possible—and it usually is easier for others than for you. One area of potential difficulties is problems with the patient's family. Who is and who is not coming to visit? Who is making problems and what are the problems? The social worker, the nurse, other family members, or even the patient not feeling so helpless can often solve these problems. Or maybe you can. On the other hand, at a death-bed it is difficult to resolve family problems that started in childhood. The symptom of feeling no control is the sense of things being impossibly difficult and that feeling is often not difficult to relieve.

You cannot do anything for the loss of the feeling of omnipotence, of indestructibility, with which we healthy people are blessed. Even when people recover, it takes quite some time to return. You can, and should, however, make sure the patient does not feel endangered. Sometimes what you think should make patients feel in control—giving decision making over to them—has the opposite effect and evokes the idea that when they need help, they are being abandoned. That can be frightening. To find out, ask what the patient thinks or feels about your process of making these decisions.

The cognitive impairment of illness is a challenge—figuring out what to do about problems the patient raises about medication, going for X-rays or other studies, family visitors, and so on. The patient may have difficulty coming to a conclusion for an endless or confusing variety of reasons. The staff often become annoyed at the patient's seeming indecision.

Here is an example of a conversation at 9:00 A.M. with a patient with who had a total knee replacement several days previously. "How is your pain?" "Better, but maybe the Tramadol worked even better." "What did you take last?" "Dilaudid 8 mg an hour ago." "Did that help?" "I think so, but I'm not sure I should take that and Ambien when I go to sleep. I think the Ambien makes me very groggy." "Yes, but was your pain controlled over the night?" "Yes, but I can't be sure because I was so sleepy from the Ambien. And when I went to the john in the middle of the night it [the pain] was an 8 or 9. Maybe I should take less Dilaudid and use Tramadol instead." "Why change when your pain is controlled. And Tramadol does not mix well with Dilaudid." "I never had trouble with Tramadol before—Tramadol helps me." "What would you like to use for your pain now?" "I'm not sure, especially because of the Ambien."

You are hearing the cognitive impairment of the state of illness. You are asking what you believe are concrete questions and the patient does not stay on the subject. Because there is no evidence of true lack of capacity, we tend to forget what illness does to thinking. It is not fair to ask someone to reason well who cannot. Duck the issue altogether and put in a patient-controlled analgesia pump (PCA) so the patient has only one dimension of choice. Please do not give a cafeteria of choices because you believe patients should exercise their autonomy. (Chapter 12 will discuss the issue of autonomy at length.) To repeat, it is not fair to simply lay out information and then ask the patient to make the decisions. In addition, it takes away from clinicians one of most their most important functions, working actively *with* patients about therapeutic and diagnostic decisions. When decisions have to be made you bring to the case technical knowledge, knowledge about other patients in similar situations, your knowledge about this patient, and clear thinking. The patient brings something vital that only the patient can know—his or her values, past experiences, and what is important and means the most. When patients' thinking is impaired you can still discover what is important to them based on what is happening at the time, previous decisions, previous statements of values, and clearly and simply stated questions or choices (never more than two at a time). If the patient wants other people to take part in the decision making, cause that to happen if you agree. If you disagree, discuss it with the patient until the two of you come to agreement. Decisions about important choices are among the key elements in the care of any patient. They take time, but, done well, they help strengthen your relationship (and increase the patient's confidence). If you work with a team, during this process of decision making they should stay quietly in the background.

Patients in a state of illness are filled with uncertainties. The uncertainties flow not only from the inherent uncertainties in severe illness, but from their inability, as hard as they try, to understand what is happening to them. Generally, as you explain things to them they will appear to be following, but when you ask, "Tell me what I just told you," what they say may not correspond to what you said. Try not to get impatient, or look as though you are about to leave, or look at your watch. They do not intend to be opaque, they are having cognitive difficulties but they are unaware of their impairment. Simplify the explanation by breaking it into separate statements that are complete in themselves. Speak directly to the issue, slowly and clearly, but remember that you are not talking to a child (unless the patient is a child). Confirm each step of the way that the patient is following. I believe you will discover that the patient is gratified with your effort.

Patients in a state of illness will have difficulty making plans—a failure of executive control. Again step-by-step choices offered in simple straightforward language and no more than two at a time will make it possible. Sometimes it is necessary to tell patients that they may be having trouble with emotions. They know they should feel love when their children or a spouse visits, but they actually feel nothing. Tell the patients that a damping of emotional feeling is simply a part of sickness. When they are better it will be better; the feelings of emotion will return.

This chapter has been an exploration of the problems experienced by sick persons and by those taking care of them (as well as family and others) because the person is sick; the problems may not specifically be related to the disease. Because of this the phenomenon of sickness and the state of illness offer opportunities for intervention that can be very effective in returning the sick to better function. So much about being sick is unknown because it has not been investigated; the focus previously has been the disease.

Characteristics of Healthy People That Sick Persons Have Lost

Patients who are hospitalized, even those not in a state of illness, experience disorder in their environment and disturbances in their way of being to which healthy people are not subjected. Think about what people who are healthy generally need and have and you will have a better understanding of what it means to be sick. And realize also that there are things that can be done to bring the world of the sick more in line with the world of healthy persons. This is especially true because, as you will see, it is often medical care itself that creates the problems that impair the sick. As you read this, you may wonder whether any of these aspects of sickness are important. Hospitals, after all, are much better than they used to be. On the other hand, think of the care with which we consider every detail of the patients' diseases, medications, tests results, and so on. This is because, it has taken time to learn, the details matter; they have an influence on the outcome. With the person of the patient, details also matter. The state of mind of the patient is not a matter of "mind" alone, because there is no such thing as mind all by itself. Remember, "We are of a piece; whatever happens to one part happens to the all." The problem is that we know so much less about the significance and the consequences of insults to the person than to the body. In terms of the advancement of medicine, this is just the beginning of knowledge about persons.

Generally, healthy persons feel safe; they have security and they are not racked by irresolvable worries and fears. Sick people in a hospital are more like someone in a strange country walking in the dark. They do not speak the language and they do not know the significance of the simplest things going on around them. Most of the time, maybe overwhelmingly, this does not matter because patients know they are in a benign environment in which people wish them well and whatever the medical problem, it is soon over. A patient in a state of illness is not a "most of the time" being. This is why such patients may cling to their healer or a nurse, or nurse's aide, with whom they have established a relationship. They are trying to feel safe. This is particularly so because they may also feel attacked by their disease. It is not that bad, you may think, we are there to take care of them. Yes, and they mostly understand that. In medicine, however, we pride ourselves on paying attention to the rare and unusual disease, not dismissing such things because they are out of the ordinary. The unusual patient who is badly frightened by the environment deserves the same special attention because fear is dangerous. When one of my children was hospitalized in an institution not my own, I walked up to the nurse's station to ask for some favor. I was suddenly aware of how high the desk was, how forbidding the staff's space looked, and how much of an outsider I was in the face of my child's need. The nurses were all busy and the busy ward clerk finally took time to look up. I suddenly had more empathy for my patients and their families in my hospital—also strangers in a strange land.

Healthy persons are not usually lonely and kept in residence among others not of their choosing. Healthy person value their privacy. Is a bed really a private space? Bring to mind how quickly patients personalize the area around the bed and the bedside table in an attempt to recreate their private world. Persons have meaningful human interactions of their choice. In fact, they have a community of choice and they can depend on others in their community. Hospitals, even the best of them, are different. There are visitors and visitors are very important, but etiquette makes it difficult for patients to say who is and who is not welcome, or to tell visitors who do not know how to leave that the time to go has come. It is the rare visitor who knows to stay 10 or 15 minutes and leave. Even beloved spouses may consume the patient's diminished energy. Experienced and empathetic nurses can help, but they are busy.

We often hear patients complain about how noisy their roommate is or how many of the roommate's visitors keep crowding into their space. The patient gets our sympathy, but usually that is all we can do or think is necessary to do—we do not live in their restricted space while sick and alone. In fact, there is nothing that can be done unless the other patient's visitors are egregiously intrusive. In such a case clinicians may complain to the floor staff. Complaining is best kept to a minimum because the clinicians need the floor staff to be happy with them so that their patients are well served. There are two different social needs to be served— the patient's needs but also the needs of the staff. Conflict is best avoided because (it is said) the floor staff and the clinicians have to get along for a long time, while patients come and go.

Healthy people are not purposeless, hopeless, and lost—they have purposes, goals and intentions, realistic hopes and desires, and realistic expectations. The definition of sickness used throughout this book has emphasized that in sickness persons cannot pursue their goals and purposes because of impairments of function. Impairments, on the other hand, can be caused externally; the environment may make the pursuit of purposes difficult to the point of impossible. A patient of mine with late stage cirrhosis of the liver was hospitalized. He had come from an impoverished slum family and had risen in the world. He told me with pride that "I know important people that count in the world of finance and business. Important people whose names you would know. And they depend on me to make really big deals and to make things happen. And I can't do it in here." He did not care whether it would make him sicker or even dead, he must leave the hospital because in the hospital he was helpless—useless. I had no choice; I discharged him and when he returned he was sicker, but satisfied that he had done what mattered.

Healthy people live in an orderly and coherent world in which they know what things mean. When they do not they can turn away toward what they do know. They have a realistic desire to be like others they admire and to be admired themselves. Healthy persons have a sense of self-worth and do not feel persistently worthless. Healthy persons have an identity and they know it; anomie is not their fate. They have a sufficiency and they do not generally feel deprived. Reflecting on these you can see that physically healthy persons can find themselves like the sick on some of these measures. Some people are even marked by defects in many of these characteristics. I previously pointed out that because historically we know sickness to be primarily physical, even if the person's basic issue was, say, persistent anomie and alienation, the wholeness of persons would make us aware of the physical dimensions of the problem and that, we would say, is the illness. Consider, also, the personal consequences of serious mental illness in terms of these properties and you will better understand mental illness.

Healers can have an impact on many of personal aspects of sickness and by so doing diminish how sick the person is. Some may say that I have been writing about psychological problems or social problems that occur in sick persons as a consequence of their disease, but I want to point out that it is a consequence of the history of human understanding of sickness to see things that way. Had the Paris doctors at the Hotel Dieu in the early nineteenth century known as much about these dimensions of persons as they did about anatomy when they were describing diseases, our perspective would have been quite different.

When sick persons emerge from a state of illness they will again be more like their everyday selves. In every respect from their mode of thought to their knowledge of what is happening they will again be "normal." Except for a fact that is not true of all the healthy people around them—they have just emerged from a disturbing experience, they have been *sick*. Recovery involves more than the body again becoming healthy. People are grateful to be better again, but the impact of the illness lives on. The memory of the illness and its depredations only gradually subside like a bad sunburn. This is the reason why people commonly cannot stop telling everyone about their illness. If people become truly well once more it goes away—the immediate effects, the memories, the resentments, and the gratitude for the actions of some—hopefully their healers. Many years later traces remain, however, because a state of illness is a traumatic experience.

This chapter has been about the pervasive nature of sickness apart from the diseases that cause it. In caring for patients in a state of illness—in healing—you should always be aware that the sick are different from the well. Adapting to the differences changes the way the healer thinks, forms the goals of healing, and also how illness is understood. Entering the land of the sick conditions the spoken language, the vital connection to the patient, and much else about the healer's actions. Mastery in these diverse elements serves the patient, but also enhances the healer. Because of the personal and individual nature of all these many elements in sickness, the healer has to be present with the sick person—has to make some connection to the patient. Healers must reach within themselves for the resources that they extend to the sick. It is the healer plus the patient that constitute the healing entity.

These efforts, which make intimate and interior demands on clinicians, are kept from injuring healers because in medicine, healing is professional.

Reference

Cassell, E. J. (1976). *The Healer's Art*. Philadelphia, JB Lippincott and Company.

10

Healing the Sick Patient

"Medicine is an art, and attends to the nature and constitution of the patient, and has principles of action and reason in each case."—Plato[1]

THE EPIGRAPH IS one of the two that William Osler chose for the first edition of *The Principles and Practice of Medicine*, published in 1892. The text starts with the chapter on typhoid fever and offers no further introduction. True to the understanding of "the nature and constitution of the patient" at the time the book was written, the chapter contains a definitive (and still very readable and instructive) description of typhoid fever, its cause, its symptoms, the natural progression of the disease in the patient, and its pathology. (He was frank about the absence of effective treatment.) Medicine, as no one needs reminding, has progressed beyond description since that date. Contemporary textbooks of medicine, however, in describing typhoid fever, understand the nature and the constitution of the patient in terms not so different from William Osler. It might be assumed from this that it is only the body that labors under typhoid fever, although we know it is a person who is infected. In our culture and in the Western world in general the disease is rare, not because of antibiotics, but because of advances in sanitation and because of profound changes in individual behavior and meanings attached to personal cleanliness and sanitation in general.[2] Why do current descriptions of typhoid fever not reflect contemporary understandings of patienthood? Probably because, as has been noted throughout

---

1. Every time the phrase "medicine is an art" arises it is useful to remember that the word art is used here in the sense of a skilled craft—what a shoemaker does, perhaps, or a sailmaker. It is distinctly not used in the sense of what Vincent van Gogh did.

2. If you believe I am stretching the point, remember how difficult it has been to get contemporary doctors to wash their hands between patients when the evidence is overwhelming that their recalcitrant behavior contributes to the unacceptable spread of infection in hospitals. Changing ideas, meanings, and behaviors (parts of the nature and constitution of persons) are as difficult now as ever.

this book, disease is still thought of in primarily physical terms—an affliction of the body.

In this chapter we will look at specific sick patients with particular diseases, none of which is curable in the infectious disease sense, to see what healers must do to make them better—even those who die. Not surprisingly, it is the person that will be acted on even when it involves the simple matter of getting the person to take his or her medication. I think that William Osler did the same thing when he had a difficult case. He was an extraordinary physician who knew how to take care of sick patients. The more you read what he wrote and about him, the more you know how acute he was about individual patients and their behaviors. His knowledge of patients was not systematized, however, nor did it depend on advances in the understanding of patients (persons) that started late in the nineteenth and grew especially rapidly during the first half of the twentieth century. Samuel Levine, a famous Boston cardiologist, said shortly before his death in 1966 that finishing residents in medicine at that time were as good cardiologists as the great names of the past because they had the advantages of all the knowledge gained in recent times. That does not seem to be true when it comes to knowing about the nature and constitution of patients. Knowing about persons as persons has not yet become a recognized part of necessary medical knowledge.

That is not quite fair as there has been medical recognition of emotional determinants of illness going back to the early twentieth century.[3] In the 1920s Georg Groddeck published books in which he reported organic disease (e.g., congestive heart failure) that he attributed to emotional conflicts. In 1927 Francis Peabody published "The Care of the Patient." Flanders Dunbar, in 1938, published *Emotions and Bodily Change*. By the 1950s and following, the idea was not novel but rather had become widespread. As I have pointed out elsewhere in the book, this and associated ideas have dropped from currency at the same time as, and apparently related to, the rise in popularity of "evidence-based medicine." What is discussed in this book is not the emotional basis of illness or bodily change. This book is about illness as an affliction of the person, not just the body. Ideas of psychosomatic medicine in any form, recent or old, treat the psyche as acting on the body as though there was a mind–body dichotomy. We are past that.

The cases on which this chapter is based mostly involve outpatients. This is because the care of patients in hospitals has become foreshortened and fragmented—delivered by different physicians from different specialties or rotating physicians who may not have continuous contact with the patient. In-patient physicians

---

3. Groddeck, G. (1923). *The Book of the It. Meaning of Illness*. New York, Funk and Wagnalls; Peabody, F. (1927). The care of the patient. *JAMA 88*: 877–882; Dunbar, F. (1938). *Emotions and Bodily Change*. New York, Columbia University Press.

may not have the freedom to determine how a patient is to be cared for. They have different nonclinical staff looking over their shoulders and may have goals not strictly related to patient well-being such as keeping the duration of hospitalization brief or their own advancement in rank. Patients in doctors' offices, clinics, hospices, and other less brightly lit venues can be given more focused care.

Let us start with cases. The functional impairments these patients experienced were intrusive problems and for each of them ill health interfered with their daily lives. Sometimes persons like this do not even consider themselves as diseased. This is common in persons with chronic obstructive pulmonary disease (COPD) such as afflicted the first. Characteristic productive cough and exertional dyspnea may worsen very slowly and set limits on everyday life. Even when activities and exercise capacities of some people with the disease are severely limited, because it has worsened so very slowly, they seem to accept it as part of their lives. An afflicted person may be irritated because he ran out of breath before he finished a task. He sits for awhile, maybe even lights up a cigarette until his breath comes back, and off he goes again. He may say to himself that it is the "damn cigarettes," or he is just like his father, or the dust, or something—everyone needs an explanation.

Inflammatory bowel disease (Crohn's disease) was the next person's problem. She had had intermittent periods of diarrhea and cramping abdominal pain "all her life"—although actually, on closer questioning, only for the past several years. She even, rarely, had some blood in her bowel movements. She wrote that off as her "hemorrhoids." The symptoms did not push her into a doctor's office because she said it was "just my colon acting up like it's done for years." Then she would be symptom-free for a few weeks. She had acquired some over-the-counter anti-diarrheal medications that seemed to work when she needed them so she would not be embarrassed by diarrhea. She did not lose weight and was able to keep working and doing the other things she wanted to. On closer questioning she had modified her activities and the things that she thought important in order to stay within the limits of her symptoms. "I know where all the clean johns are in New York—I know not to get too far away from them." Increasing abdominal pain without loose bowel movements finally drove her to see a physician.

It is amazing the burden of symptoms that people will sometimes endure without considering themselves ill. A physician, the third case, had a history of asthma that had not troubled him for two years after he stopped smoking cigarettes. On a foreign trip he started smoking again and not long after that he developed a cough that dragged on for many weeks. He was a four-mile runner and his cough was worst as soon as he ended his run—sometimes almost to the point of vomiting. He had medication from his previous time with asthma and he used that to good effect, especially for the postexertional cough. The coughing continued to a variable degree for several weeks more before reaching a peak on a weekend when he was short of breath walking across his living room. Finally, on that Sunday, even worse, he thought maybe there was something really wrong so he called his doctor. He was directed to the emergency room. As he was lying propped up on the gurney waiting to be seen, it occurred to him as a surprise that maybe his asthma had returned. The physician in the emergency room asked him how he could have been so dumb as not to realize that his trouble was asthma again. He would have been more offended if he had not agreed with the doctor.

Carrying on despite sometimes severe impairments of function is not true only of those with chronic diseases. Patients with serious, even fatal diseases and a considerable burden of symptoms will occasionally go about their lives and not consider themselves sick—by their own definition. As an extreme example, consider the fourth case, George Mallory, a man with carcinoma of the lung that progressed slowly but inexorably. He lost weight and was quite weak and breathless but was convinced, he said, that the safe deposit section of the bank and bank vault where he worked could not function if he did not continue working at the same job he had held for more than two decades. The weight of his symptoms might have put most people in bed, but the bank needed him, he was sure. He also had advanced cirrhosis of the liver that added to his troubles but it did not keep him home, much less in bed. Finally, his supervisor at the bank told him he could not come to work any longer because of his sickness and he died a few days later. He told me not long before he died (he came to see me regularly through all this) that one reason the bank needed him was that he had never missed a day's work (not true) because he had never been sick. Medical professionals love to attach names to this phenomenon, which is not all that rare. Denial is frequently invoked. Denial? On the office visit when his diagnosis of malignancy was made, as was my custom, I put the chest X-rays up on the view box before I had looked at them. There was a large irregular orange-sized shadow of a mass alongside the left hilum. "Uh-oh, you don't have to tell me what that is," he said. "I guess I should have stopped smoking sooner." What was its meaning? I looked at the films and saw what I knew to be a carcinoma of the lung. From its size and position it was very probably inoperable. The shadow on the X-ray meant he was soon to become dead—the doctor's definition of dying.

He looked at the same shadow and was sure it was cancer. He probably also knew that it meant that he was going to die of lung cancer. But dying has a different meaning for patients than it does for physicians. It is a state of being and it can go on for a short or long, long time, even preceding an event or pathology that a doctor might not be sure was an adequate reason for becoming dead. For some it tells of a forthcoming event so dreaded that the details do not matter. At another extreme it is welcomed as a long hoped for end to hidden miseries. This man may have seen it entirely differently. His drinking had for years made a mess of so many things, including his job at the bank. He had been far from an exemplary father and husband or a stellar employee. He was a drunk (his word) and he was undependable in all departments of life, not someone he was proud to be. Given this chance, see how really well he carried off his last weeks at home as well as at the bank. His children and his wife were truly proud of how he did not drink, how strong he became when it really counted, and what a wonderful example he set for them and his grandchildren. It was not play acting, he was wonderful. And he was not sick—unable to pursue his goals and purposes—except for the last few days. He required some symptom control medication and the admirable way he was managing himself was reinforced on each of his frequent doctors visits.

Evelyn Willis, a 34-year-old woman, developed non-small cell carcinoma of the lung and by the time the disease was diagnosed it was inoperable and had metastasized widely. Although far superior intellectually to most and possessed of many talents, she had achieved little in life and was a profound disappointment to herself and to her family. Alcohol and addicting drugs had both been problems, so that control of the pain primarily from bony metastases was difficult. She required large doses of opioid analgesics to achieve even modest pain control. Her family was positive that she was addicted to opioids and she was using the pain to continue her access to narcotics. Her clinician disagreed but could not miss how difficult she was as a patient—argumentative and sharp-voiced more often than charming and delightful. Before starting a significant course of radiation, an intrathecal catheter was placed and she was given opioids intrathecally. The relief of pain was dramatic as was the change in her behavior. The bright, sunny, and witty woman that emerged was, the clinician was told, like she was before her sickness. Her father acknowledged that maybe her pain had been as awful as she said and pain relief brought her back.

She remained at home—refusing to be hospitalized. Radiation was begun to control a superior vena cava syndrome and continued for the full course. She started to spend more time sleeping each day. In the beginning she slept perhaps 9 or 10 hours a day, but gradually over the next 3 weeks it increased until she was sleeping more than 20 hours a day. She insisted it had been the radiation that made her tired, citing "the well-known fact." There were no other reasons discovered to explain the sleep. Timing her medication became increasingly difficult and she requested that she be given control of her dose of subcutaneous morphine by pump. She promised that she would not exceed the dose advised and loading the pump was not under her control. The visiting nurse who was in charge of the pump was surprised because the young woman seemed to be using so little morphine. After the 3-week period she woke up—*opioid free*. She had removed the pump herself late in her sleeping period and she had had sufficient effect from the radiation and the intrathecal analgesics so that the little residual discomfort could be relieved with minimal medication, primarily nonsteroidal antiinflammatory drugs. Her parents were nonplussed and not sure what they should believe because she had been "difficult" for so many years. They decided, with good reason, to be proud. After being addicted to narcotics for so long she had weaned herself off *on her own terms*. She lived only several months longer (dying easily) and there was no question that during that period she was a different woman—interesting, thoughtful, insightful, but still bright, funny, and charming to the end. This patient raises the issue of whether the treatment of the disease is the end in itself, or in the service of other goals. In the current definition of sickness where the disease is central, treatment of the disease is usually the primary goal. Where sickness is defined in terms of the patient's function, purposes, and goals the clinician's actions should be in the service of the patient's purposes and goals. It is on the patient's terms that function should be restored. When this woman announced the importance to her of independence, then what and how things are planned and carried out should be in support of her determination.

In each of these cases someone with an important burden of functional impairments does not acknowledge the presence of a significant disease and has (in the first three) no diagnosis. None of them, including the young woman and the man who died, thought of themselves as sick. The first three might each have functioned much better if the symptoms or the disease had been better controlled. Despite their symptoms, however, they lived their lives. No clinician would have difficulty thinking of patients with the same diseases and the same functional impairments who *did* consider themselves to be sick and whose daily lives were significantly worse. Leaving apart, for the moment, control of the disease, think how well they managed and how unsick they thought of themselves. If you had been responsible for these patients, I believe you would have considered that your efforts had been successful. Why? Because despite their impairments they were able to live their lives—accomplishing their goals and pursuing their purposes. That is, after all, the primary aim of healing. With appropriate treatment of their diseases, the patients with COPD, Crohn's disease, and asthma would have had less of a symptom burden but they would not necessarily have functioned better.

Looking more closely at these instances in which afflicted patients themselves managed to be functional and live their lives will help us understand how healers might achieve similar success. (I hope with better disease and symptom control.)

Think about the physician (case four) who realized that once again he had asthma only when he was on a gurney in an emergency department. I am not recommending that the way to heal patients is to leave them untreated and undiagnosed. Actually, however, that was not him. His self-treatment of his bronchospasm when it was severe was effective, using medication left over from his previous asthma. He had sufficient knowledge of his state—that he left unnamed—to use the correct drugs. Nonetheless, he functioned better than his lungs. What did he do that allowed him to continue for so long as though he was not impaired? First, he apparently accomplished this not only by controlling his own symptoms (apparently to his satisfaction), but, second, by not calling it asthma—he did not give it a name. Third, he was initially successful so whatever process he was following was self-reinforcing. The success of one day, week, or whatever encouraged the next, and so on.

In each of these cases three things were accomplished that are almost always important. First, symptoms were controlled in a fashion that was not only effective but kept under sufficient control so that one successful day informed the next, which informed the next, and on and on. This means that the patient was not only comfortable but not afraid of the next day. Second, the meaning of events was kept sufficiently within the patients' understanding so that the patient did not feel overwhelmed by what was happening or by the name of the disease and events. Third, each of these patients continued to live life and accomplish important goals and purposes even under sometimes difficult circumstances. Symptom control can be discussed separately, but each of these is related to the others and all of them are part of and contribute to the third—that a goal for sick patients, as for others, is to continue to live life and pursue chosen goals.

Symptom Control[4]

"Control the symptoms?" That seems straightforward enough. Big, bossy, life-altering symptoms like prolonged vomiting, profound diarrhea, disabling dyspnea, and their ilk cry out for relief because otherwise the patient's well-being, indeed, the patient is destroyed by them. Clinicians know how to control symptoms such as these and a whole catalog of others that can knock patients to their knees. The available medications and tools for symptom relief make up a large catalog. There are times, on the other hand, when no matter what you do, symptoms are resistant, or the cost in side effects is prohibitive, or there is disagreement among the clinicians about priorities. Maybe the patient is so sick and usually so close to death that it is difficult to recognize what should be done, what must come first, and whose help you need, and maybe there are other circumstances that destroy your confidence and get in the way. Cases such as this can make you feel badly about how you handled the patient, especially these days when controlling symptoms, not only pain, is itself a commonly accepted goal of medical

---

4. The control of pain is a special problem and will be discussed separately.

practice. In the contexts in which these quandaries arise, the problem presented is usually not really about the particular patient, but rather the symptoms themselves and the difficulties they present, about the healer's knowledge and facilities, and about other mostly technical questions. In these cases, it usually does not matter who the patient is. None of our five test cases, however, is like this.

Our cases are a good introduction to another issue that is a fundamental aspect of symptom control. My mentor, Cyril Solomon, often said that it is difficult to make a well patient better. This dictum applies here. The man with COPD, the woman with Crohn's disease, and the recalcitrant asthmatic were not sick, at least in their own eyes. To really control their symptoms in a manner that would satisfy clinicians would require that a diagnosis be made and confirmed. If that was done, the first patient would officially have COPD, expect to die like his father, and be harangued about smoking; the next would have a threatening disease of the intestines, and the third would have to confront his asthma and the foolishness of starting to smoke cigarettes again. In these unexceptional instances the symptoms were not the issue; the problem was persons (they were not yet patients) with symptoms. The problem is not symptom control, but *right from the start* working out how to **motivate** patients to control their own symptoms.

Symptoms are generally not controlled by clinicians but by patients with the help of their clinicians. Patients are motivated best when the healer's goals and theirs are consonant and are arrived at in concert. Patients have to take the medication, do the exercises, follow the regimen, and so on. Patients usually follow instructions, although not always and not always to the full extent. Mostly, patients take prescribed medications, although doses are frequently missed and although an important percentage of prescriptions are never filled. If patients do not do these things symptoms are usually not alleviated. What I called "the big bossy symptoms" require direct intervention by clinicians, which patients permit because they are overwhelmed—by the symptoms, sickness, or fear of these. The majority of the impairments of function that we call symptoms require direct action by the sick person (usually) on the advice of the healer. We called those actions "compliance" in the past when we thought it was primarily the actions of the clinicians with obedient (passive) patients. It is the same with diabetes, chronic heart failure, cardiac rehabilitation, inflammatory arthritides, and on and on through the catalog of chronic diseases—the diseases that occupy medicine now. In the current scene, however, patients are not "compliant" or "noncompliant." Instead, they cooperate with a program of action with which they agree. And they do not cooperate when they disagree.

The basic point is that now, as always, doctors do not treat diseases, they treat patients—patients who agree to be treated if the treatment makes sense to them. The days of "Whatever you say, doctor" are long gone. On the other hand, now as then, medicine is a profession of words and successful clinicians are masters of rhetoric—the use of language to convince. Patients generally trust physicians and generally trust that their actions are in the patient's best interests. For that reason, clinicians must be careful that their words and their influence are employed with prudence and with this particular patient's good in mind. Some healers who are pleased with how convincing they are talk patients into doing (or not doing) things that are not all that important. The clinician's authority is like capital in the bank—do not waste it or use it unless necessary. That way you can say when it is crucial, "*Do not do that! Have you ever heard me speak like that before? Never! This time I must really mean it. And I do.*"[5] From the sick person's point of view (even those who do not overtly think of themselves as sick) the symptoms *are* the sickness. Therefore, if you want your patient to do the other things that are important, symptoms *must* be controlled. Controlling symptoms also shows that you are concerned about the patient's immediate well-being. Sometimes (although not very often) symptom control is delayed until other objectives are achieved. If that is necessary, explain it to the patient in a way that makes it clear that you are sorry for putting a burden on the patient. With some diseases we create surrogate symptoms. Teaching the patient with asthma or COPD to measure their forced expiratory volume in 1 second (FEV_1) is an example. Another is the frequent measurement of blood sugar or hemoglobin A_{1c} (HbA_{1c}) in diabetes. These tools provide a way to teach patients about their diseases in a manner way that lets the disease do the convincing rather than you. You want them to be interested in the results, however, not teetering on the edge of fear or of displeasing their clinicians. Patients who are properly informed can become masterful at controlling their disease and (with reason) proud of it. You, of course, must stay interested.

Control the Meaning

This more extreme example is a bridge between "control the symptoms" and "control the meaning." Marjorie Raskin, a nulliparous woman of 42 years, began to have menstrual periods with profuse bleeding. Soon she was also bleeding between her menstrual periods. As the months went by the menometrorrhagia continued unaffected by her gynecologist's many attempts at control. A year went

---

5. Some clinicians may be taken aback by that kind of straight no-nonsense talk. It does not sound like the "advice and consent" method of doctor–patient interaction that has become popular. In the previous chapter I said that the healer and patient together and united constitute the healing unit. That is an unusual specification; their conversation may be unusual also. We are talking about the care of the sick in which the stakes are high. If you can just walk away unconcerned when a patient does something that you surely know will cause him or her real harm, citing the patient's autonomy, you have better nerves than I have.

by and the problem only got worse. She had consultations, diagnostic and therapeutic curettages (D&Cs), and hormonal therapy, all to no lasting effect. She was advised, despite her age, to have a hysterectomy. She refused, even though she ultimately required multiple *simultaneous* tampons and sanitary napkins to keep the blood from public display. Her physicians urged her to have the hysterectomy and her husband and other family members pleaded with her, all to no effect. She is extremely smart but was frightened of the idea of going to the hospital and even more frightened of the surgery (although she admired her gynecologist), haunted by the memory of her mother after her hysterectomy (even though that turned out alright), and worried about its after effects. In the second year, bleeding was so heavy that she had to bring an extra pairs of pants to work when she had a menstrual period. At that point she realized that the whole situation was "too much"—the bleeding and its effect on her personal life, on her marriage, and physically. She consented to surgery (which was uneventful).

The surgical end of her symptom—the abnormal bleeding—was repeatedly delayed by her fears. Her fears, which controlled the patient and her doctors, came from the meanings she attached to hospitals, surgery, and hysterectomy. If the case had turned out badly who or what should be blamed? Of course, the patient would be blamed for not agreeing to surgery in a timely manner. (It is usually not useful to blame the patient.) Or perhaps her fears would be blamed—she was so frightened her fears killed her. (I doubt that you could even say the words.) Ultimately her doctors would bear the blame because in their own eyes they know they should have more effectively reassured her. That might seem acceptable except that sometimes reassurance can be difficult to the point of impossible. Why? Because the fear is not the primary issue; *fears are always based on the meaning of the feared thing.* If you do not change the meaning, you will probably not lift the fear. Finding out the meanings of bleeding, hospitals, surgery, hysterectomy, mother's hysterectomy, or whatever else lies behind the fears may not be so easy. This is, however, a smart and articulate woman and such patients are more than open to such discussions. (A useful hint is that the underlying problem is usually not multiple meanings, but one more basic than the others. Sometimes it is very simple.) It may take time and it may even require more expert help. Think how much time and energy of many people were consumed in *not* solving the problem because fears were considered primary, not secondary to meanings. The question to be asked is not what are you afraid of, but "Tell me what you know about having a hysterectomy." Then questions should follow about the meaning of the details that are elicited in what should be a comfortably sitting down unrushed conversation. The meanings should be pursued until it is clear what underlies the patient's behavior. Then the meanings themselves become the focus of discussion until they are clarified and action becomes possible.

Here is another example. The patient is a 23-year-old woman who is dying from renal carcinoma with many metastases to the lungs. She is a recent immigrant to the United States who speaks some English but is fluent in Mandarin (although it is not her native dialect). She was told through an interpreter that no further chemotherapy was possible and that she was to be transferred to a hospice. She became very tearful and frightened and it was assumed that she was afraid of dying. The sincere sympathy of the nurses and doctors over her plight did not relieve her anxiety. It is unusual for patients who are as sick as this young woman to be frightened of death itself—their fears are more concrete and detailed.

It is such a sad scene you may not even want to go into the room. The room itself feels heavy. Her mother, who speaks neither Mandarin nor English, sits in the corner with her head turned away. The patient is wearing an oxygen mask, but despite the oxygen her breathing is obviously labored and rapid. With every motion in bed or spell of coughing her breathing becomes faster and she winces as though in pain. When that happens, she struggles to sit up higher and her eyes grow wide with fear. In English and in Mandarin the resident gradually discovers that it is not death that frightens her; she knows she has only days left to live, which she thinks is very sad because she is so young. She is terrified that she is going to choke to death and that, strangling, no one will hear her and come to save her. The resident patiently explained why she would never choke or strangle because that is not the way the disease works. Furthermore, if she gets more short of breath she can press the button on her morphine pump and she will get relief. The resident explained she would also give the patient some new medication that would help. The whole explanation took about 15 minutes and as the resident was talking, with her hand on the patient's arm, the shortness of breath subsided, her respiratory rate decreased, and the patient became calm. Shortness of breath is uncomfortable and strangling is awful, so the patient's terror is understandable. By changing the meaning of events, however, through the explanation and the resident's concerned presence, without any other intervention, the symptom abated. Of course, the resident must keep her promise and make sure the symptoms are controlled.

In the past we would have said that the patient got better as a result of the calming effects of the resident's behavior and because her explanation to the patient had been reassuring. The actions of the resident had their effect because they *changed the meaning* of *the events* that had been frightening the patient. As you reexamine many situations in which it seems that the psychological effect of something is the explanation I believe you will see that what has really happened is a change in meaning.

We come now to the last two of the opening cases, the man with cirrhosis and carcinoma of the lung, and the young woman with carcinoma of the lung.

Sometimes the most important thing the healer does in the care of a sick patient is to stay out of the way—a variant of and sometimes dependent on being quiet and listening. (In Chapter 5, on Listening, I discuss how this is done.) George Mallory is first. The diagnosis was not a mystery to me or to the patient—that is if by diagnosis you mean the name of the disease(s). The man had advanced alcoholic cirrhosis of the liver and non-small cell adenocarcinoma of the lung that was fixed to the great vessels of the left hilum. It was inoperable and no treatment of his disease was available that would do more than perhaps add a few months to his life. He came to know all of that as rapidly as the information was apparent. He decided that this was his opportunity to make up for a lot of things and die looking good. Even though his drinking made a mess of his life, his family stayed with him because he was funny, endearing, and smart (all when he was not drunk). He had also managed, despite the odds against it, to remain employed at the bank and bring home his salary. Accomplishing his overriding purpose and the subsidiary goals required his doctor's help because he did not want to be radiated and he adamantly refused chemotherapy. This was the patient's definition of the problem rather than the usual disease definition. If you cannot accept the patient's perspective you should discuss it with yourself first. Clinicians are accustomed to defining the problem in disease terms. Try redefining the issues in terms of the patient's goals, purposes, and subsidiary functions. Seen that way, what the patient says may make more sense. If not, do not try and force the patient to accept your viewpoint, it isn't fair because you have too much power—the patient needs you so badly. Negotiate. If that still does not produce agreement, get the patient another doctor.

Mallory said he wanted to die looking good. What does that mean? He wanted to be able to go to work "until the end." He did not want to spend a long time as an invalid, bedridden, or "lingering." No one can promise these things in the face of his two diseases. When patients ask for that sort of thing it may annoy doctors. On the other hand, refusing treatment of the cancer is reasonable in the face of its prognosis. As for the rest of his goals, why not? "I'll do the best I can. If you do not drink alcohol, you continue to be honest with me, keep me very closely informed about what is happening—symptoms and such—we'll try. (There is that "we" again.) It is possible. No promises and we are going to need some luck. What are you going to tell your family because I do not want to lie for you?" And that is the way it turned out. Lucky? If you ally yourself closely with the patient you will probably be lucky more often than you might think.

Evelyn Willis' situation was more complicated for a number of reasons. Her disease was more complex, she had too many doctors, her father was a doctor, I did not know her before her terminal illness, she was referred to me by her mother, she was negative about any suggestions and suspicious of my motives, and her pain was difficult to manage because of her addiction and because her father and others did not believe her. And she was extremely intelligent. The first necessity was to make a connection to her. Despite all the negatives and her suspicions, patients such as this need help and they know it. Given all that has been said about a patient such as this before even the first visit, too often the clinician has already developed an overly cautious attitude apparent to the patient. It requires special discipline to be open on the first visit. On the other hand, patients such as Evelyn are so used to being met by clinicians with a protective wall that when the healer is open the patient will respond—if not too much is asked of her, and if she gets a reward. Why the reward? It is for good behavior, of course. Tiny step after tiny step needs to be taken toward the goal of trust. Hopefully there will be enough time. Trust is especially important because her disease promises a difficult course and probably a bad end unless she permits therapeutic moves that may be uncomfortable. Her reward is the clinician believing without question what she says about her pain. In this instance that meant dispensing narcotics adequate to the considerable bone pain of which she complained. Her response to the intrathecal analgesic showed that to be correct. Much of what must be done for her involves negotiating her problems with the family (parents and two siblings) and getting the other physicians to be more openly on her side rather than on her father's side. It was a sad day when examination revealed the distended veins on her anterior chest wall announcing the superior vena cava obstruction. She turned the ensuing radiation into a good thing in her own way. Her goals, although opaque, needed support. It was not evident why she was sleeping so much but after looking into it, I seemed reasonably sure that it was not disease related. We had done what was useful for her tumor. That she would die was evident from the beginning. That she would come out a success on her terms was not obvious.

Pain Control

Learning how to control the pain may start with knowing how to use the growing number and increasingly effective analgesic drugs and modalities available. Controlling the pain of *this particular patient* starts with understanding the pain in *this patient*. One of the difficulties in understanding symptoms is the persistence of the idea that the pain (or other symptoms such as dyspnea) *as experienced* is the unmediated result of the pathophysiology (the physiologic chain of events leading to the abnormal state). For pain this means the persistence of the model of acute pain and the idea that pain is always secondary to tissue damage. It is exemplified by what everyone experiences as a result of an acute injury such as a burn or twisted ankle. There is no doubt that in acute pain there is usually a direct relationship between pain and tissue damage and that where there is tissue damage, pain often follows. But acute localized inflammation and rapidly expanding lesions (such as abscesses or fast growing tumors) are present in only a small fraction of instances of seriously ill patients in severe pain.

One part of the problem of understanding pain is that in medicine we love mechanism and it pulls us along, as though based on what has been written about acute pain physiology we really knew more than we actually do about patients with pain in serious or terminal illness. The amount of research about the mechanism of pain in the past decade or two is so amazing that it is difficult to avoid returning again and again to the research findings to explain this or that manifestation of pain or to serve as a basis for the choice of treatment in an individual patient or to explain the patient's response (or lack thereof). Another thing that impedes understanding is how easy it generally is now to control pain (particularly in a hospital or hospice) in addition to the efficacy and safety—at least in the short term—of many of the increasing numbers of pain-relieving modalities. Although pain is often controllable (at least in good part) in most patients, physicians tend to move the pain that is not easily relieved into other categories by emphasizing, for example, the psychological aspects of the patient's problem. Too many physicians act as though there are only two possible mechanisms involved in pain—physiologic or emotional: if you cannot explain some feature of a patient's pain physiologically, it must be psychological in origin.

It is commonly believed that when a physical basis for pain cannot be demonstrated—no lesion sufficient to explain the pain can be found, or the pain does not conform to expectations—then the pain is emotional (psychogenic) in origin. Unfortunately, illness caused solely by psychological difficulties has wrongly come to be seen too often as not real illness; real illness (from this perspective) is something that can be found in the body and that is associated with tissue pathology. Psychogenic pain—in this view—is imaginary pain; the patient feels pain that does not exist. There are rare patients who report pain when nothing else in their behavior or activities supports their claim. Their activities are unchanged; their use of pain-relieving medications is not increased, they do not utilize medical services, and their interactions with family and others are unchanged. In other words, all the behavioral changes that usually accompany pain are absent. These are not patients with serious disease or patients in palliative care programs, whether or not lesions to cause the pain they report can be demonstrated. Similarly, problems of malingering or using pain as part of drug-seeking behavior are uncommon in chronic illness and should not distract from the central problems that get in the way of understanding pain and suffering. I sincerely hope that by the end of this book (wishfully long before that) no reader will see *anything* in a sick patient as either psychological or physical as though there were really two separate domains.

Fear, panic, depression, or even anger, on the other hand, may aggravate pain, as may suffering, and make it difficult to control. Increasing the opioid or analgesic dose for pain that is unrelieved because of concurrent emotional distress, anguish, or suffering leads to the persistence of the pain or opioid toxicity, escalating drug costs, diminished patient quality of life, increased family distress, and greater demands on caregivers. This is not rare—and in patients such as those on palliative care services it is a common problem and often accounts for inadequate pain relief despite doses of opioid analgesics that are sometimes astonishingly high.

Think, however, how the research has revealed an ever increasing complexity of the phenomena we lump together under the one word: pain. A simple conclusion can be drawn from the intricacy of the physiology—there is not a one-to-one correspondence between the stimulus that elicits pain and the pain itself. In fact, it is evident that there exist many pathways by which the person's experience of pain can be enhanced, diminished, and/or changed in character or distribution. If there are so many different physiologic ways to alter the nature of the pain as felt, what determines the person's actual experience? It cannot simply be the pain stimulus itself—whether there is evident tissue damage or not—because that does not match the complexity of pain physiology. It cannot be what is happening in the person's body alone—although physical phenomena such as fever or other discomforts may change the person's experience of the original pain; it must be something about the nature of the person in pain.

I believe it is the phenomenon of meaning (first discussed in the Prologue) that brings together what is known about pain—the physiologic mechanisms and the role of emotion—with the experience of the person in pain. There can be no understanding of persistent pain, however, without considering the place of meaning in these states. Indeed, despite the fact that nonpsychiatric symptoms are body sensations, it is difficult to separate a body sensation from the meaning that has been assigned to it. Or put another way, symptoms, which are bodily sensations, must have meanings associated with them. This would also be the case because meaning is attached to all events, and symptoms are events. Because of this, symptoms, perhaps especially pain, are not simple brute facts of nature; they are actively influenced by preexisting meanings of the persons in whom they occur. To see this clearly it is necessary to understand that meanings are not fixed or static; they are dynamic—in two senses of the word. First, the content of the concepts that make up meaning includes ideas of where things come from and what they become. To say of chest pain that it means coronary heart disease is to invoke ideas the person has of why coronary heart disease arises and what it leads to (e.g., heart attacks). Thus meanings contain predictions and predictions lead to the foretaste of experience. Think, for example, of how your foot feels when the next step going down is not in its expected place. It is like walking down a stationary escalator. The failed expectation of sensation produces its own sensation. The second way in which meanings are dynamic is that learning modifies them. Whenever something is experienced it confirms or modifies meanings. Therefore, meanings and their resultant predictions are not only results of sensation but modify the ongoing sensation (over moments to months) so that it is reinforced, amplified, other sensations are recruited, or it is diminished.

Pain is not only a sensation, it is also an experience imbedded in beliefs about causes and diseases and their consequences (e.g., cancer, rheumatoid arthritis, fibromyalgia). Today's pain has a past that contributes to ideas about what is happening and will continue to happen. It may bring to mind an event of yesterday and its emotions (maybe anger, or perhaps guilt). It occurs in a setting (e.g., home, hospital, or hospice) and in a context that includes relationships with others (e.g., family, strangers, or doctors) that make it perhaps lonely and estranged for one patient, or supported, cared about, or loved for another. Each of these features combines and coalesces over time to personalize the pain and to make the ongoing pain the unique experience of this particular person. The pain is personalized as it enters into the creation of meanings that, like all meanings, include not only the physical sensation (pain in this instance) but also the emotions evoked, cognitive attempts to understand the significance of the pain, and even transcendent thoughts such as pain as punishment. An element of value or importance is an aspect of the experience and its meanings. As meanings are created, they begin to modify the experience on every level from the molecular to the communal.

The meanings have physiologic concomitants; mechanisms can enhance, diminish, alter the character, or change the distribution of the pain. For example, anxiety modifies the nociceptive process leading in very acute situations to analgesia as in some traumatic wounds. In longer lasting pain, however, anxiety increases the distress. In general, anxiety, depression, and fear increase the experience of pain. It is important to understand that anxiety and its physiologic correlates do not cause the increase in pain; the increased or altered pain is part of the meaning of which the anxiety is also a part. Meanings with their associated beliefs, interpretations, and predictions lead to activities in response to the pain. Patients change their behaviors to decrease the pain, avoid things (e.g., activities or postures) that worsen the pain, or adopt ways of standing, walking, or sitting that decrease the discomfort. They initiate other countervailing activities such as taking medications, visiting doctors, changing occupations, seeking information about their disease and the pain, or starting or stopping exercise programs. All of these have varying success and their outcomes also become part of the meanings. Below awareness, psychological mechanisms such as dissociation may almost hide the pain while catastrophic thinking may aggravate it. On the other hand, fear may lead to actions that aggravate the pain such as body part changes—guarding, muscular tightness, postural change, and so forth. These modes of personalization—through meaning, interpretation, prediction, avoidance, and countervailing or aggravating behavior—are also part of the process of pain. Why is all of this not part of our everyday knowledge? Because when we consider pain we think of it in the short term and within the preexisting medical categories we learned in training.

Personalization thus means that the symptom as experienced is almost always an interpretation of its meaning. The pain as experienced is itself the interpretation. This is not easy to get our head around, especially if, like myself, you have spent most of your medical life understanding pain as an impersonal thing, such as bleeding, that results from tissue damage. This interpretation of pain, however, much better fits the clinical settings in which pain is severe and often difficult to manage or pain occurs in patients with life-threatening or fatal disease and is often resistant to opioids. This means that when your patient with pain does not respond in the fashion that would be expected from the analgesic and dosage that are being employed, rather than continually raising the dose or changing drugs, it is time to stop and find out what the patient believes the increasing or resistant pain means. If the patient believes that increasing pain means that the disease is worsening and that worsening disease implies an increasing threat of death, it is little wonder that the pain is resistant. Death is not relieved by narcotics. Again a few questions about what the patient thinks is the meaning of the resistance of the pain to treatment will usually answer your question. The meaning must be changed. "Your pain does not have that meaning at all. The pain is worse because there is more swelling (or inflammation, or tissue change, or whatever you can think of) not because you are closer to death. Pain is not about death it is about pain, pure and simple. Do you understand?" The dose of analgesic necessary to control the pain will be reduced by tomorrow. If not, you still do not understand the patient's pain. If you want to tell the patient he is dying, do it directly, do not use the dose of medication to carry the message. Remember that when you cannot change the thing, change its meaning.

Pain is also responsive to the behavior of the staff. If, making rounds, the first words from the clinician are about how bad the pain is, the patient soon learns what the clinicians think is important. Next, before the question is even asked the pain may say, "It's an eight this morning and it was seven all day yesterday." Or if they think you are angry because their pain is not responding, they may tell you it is a four when it is really more severe. Their clinicians have trained them. Ultimately, if things are getting worse, you will learn about it, but you will already be behind the problem. Start off always by demonstrating your interest in the patient, not the disease or the symptoms—symptoms can come next.

There is so much written and easily available about pain control and the use of opioids and other analgesics and ancillary agents that there is no need to repeat the information here. One thing bears repeating. Wherever there is pain there is almost invariably muscle spasm making it worse. So it is important to learn to use, when appropriate, local treatments such as Xylocaine patches, heat and cold, massage, and trigger-point injections. It is also worth finding out what behavioral things may be aggravating the pain, such as sleep habits, beds, pillows, chairs, and all the rest.

When Seeing a Sick Patient

When I was a third year medical student I went on teaching rounds with one of our admired teachers. The resident, who was to present the new patients, said that we did not have any interesting cases that day. The teacher asked to see the new patients. The first patient was an elderly man with a stroke with dense right-sided paralysis and aphasia. By the end of the discussion the teacher had made this seemingly mundane case fascinating in its complexity and the questions it raised. The remaining "uninteresting cases" for the day served to make the same point. Looked at really closely all illness is interesting. I have, in this book, extended "the case" to include the person who is the patient and I believe you will see that enlarging the idea of "case" and "sickness" has made the care of sick persons even more interesting, challenging, and often difficult. Here are three patients with serious disease, but each of them, as the persons they are, puts a stamp on the case that is individual and personal. Care of them requires attention to their being as a person.

The First Case. A 47-year-old man has been newly admitted to the hospice from his home. He has end-stage renal disease secondary to childhood nephritis and has been on home peritoneal dialysis for 7 years. He apparently managed his dialysis well. He is in the hospice because he refused further dialysis. His last dialysis was 6 days ago. When he discontinued dialysis he stopped all his other medications. From the admitting sheet it is apparent that many individuals from his family, clergy, social workers, nurses, two psychiatrists, and his nephrologist have tried to convince him to change his mind. He says he is "tired of it." He complained that he is no longer able to work (3 years) because he does not have the strength or stamina to be an electrician as he was before. Things have been apparently difficult at home because of his sickness and because of inadequate resources. He has been married for 22 years and has two female children age 18 and 21 years who no longer live at home. He was alone when he was examined. He says his wife could not be there because she is working. (This is unusual. Usually the wife would be present.) What kind of work does she do? Or, more directly, "I expected that your wife would be here—is there some problem between you?"

Examination reveals a hypertensive male who appears pale, apathetic, and severely chronically ill. He has diminished muscle mass in all groups and 3+ pitting edema of the lower legs. Muscle testing shows his strength is diminished and in addition it was difficult to get him to try. His eye grounds show hypertensive changes and his heart is enlarged.

He said that he did not want the healer to try to convince him to restart dialysis. Anyway, it was simple. He was not really anybody anymore, he could not work, and he could not even help around the house. He and his wife had stopped having sex 6 months ago and even Viagra had stopped working. He could not stay home and die because it would be too much of a burden on his wife. He wanted to know what would happen to him and when. Asked what he had been told, his response suggested that the information he had received was reasonable. Except that his nephrologist explained that it would be a very unpleasant death, but the patient was not sure why. The healer corrected that misinformation and explained what would probably happen; it would be an easy death because his uremia would make him progressively sleepier. He was asked whether his wife could be present on the next visit since there appeared to be problems. The healer and he discussed that it seemed not to be a good way to end things for him and certainly not for his wife. The healer was quite insistent that all three talk and that, if necessary, the healer would call her. The patient agreed that she would be there tomorrow (Saturday) and the healer and he made a firm date. The healer told the patient that he would be seen regularly.

What did the healer do? The patient was evaluated. The chart was reviewed. The history was reviewed and a physical examination was performed. The patient's goals and purpose were ascertained and functional impairments were assessed. In this instance the illness follows from long-term impairment in renal function ending in its functional cessation, impaired blood pressure functions and cardiac functions, and impairment in sexual function. The patient did not want to maintain dialysis because of his stated inability to meet personal goals of participation in work, household, family, and spousal relationship. His concern involved the goal of dying well. Notice how many goals and purposes are involved and the many different impairments of functions that are involved. Also, note how far afield from the usual concerns of physicians many of these impairments of functions are that are crucial in this patient. Notice also that the healer chose to intervene in the patient's concern about dying well and also in the spousal relationship. The relationship should be addressed because it cannot be repaired after death and failure to improve the spousal relationship before death may result in irreparable impairment in the spouse.

The Second Case. A 37-year-old orthodox Jewish woman was brought reluctantly to the office by her husband. She carried her records from another physician because her husband had insisted. She was upset because she had been going to the other doctor for years and she liked and trusted him. She was afraid he would be so offended that she was seeing another physician that she would not be able to go back to him. I insisted that her husband leave the room while I took her history, which he did unwillingly. I made myself open to her and started with some small talk about friends and other family members who were also patients of mine. Her history disclosed two episodes of congestive heart failure that had resolved quickly and without difficulty. The second, recent, episode, had taken longer to get better than the first. Her doctor told her that the episodes had occurred because of a viral disease of her heart that was now better and would continue to get better. She took no regular medication. She was otherwise well, although she seemed to intentionally avoid physical activity. She was a social worker who was not working because her children (four daughters ages 8 to 15 years) were still at home. I took a long and careful history about her illness, her past, her parents, and so on, not so much because it required so much time, but because I could already see where the visit was going and I was trying to build her trust in me that would be a basis for her acceptance of the recommendation. She was a sedentary woman who was attentive to her diet and that of her family. My physical examination was also careful and deliberate. The only important findings were an enlarged heart with mushy heart sounds and an innocuous systolic murmur. There was no evidence of congestive heart failure. The chest X-ray showed moderate enlargement of her heart—certainly more than might have been expected. The EKG revealed only nonspecific changes. The reading of an echocardiogram done after her recent congestive heart failure resolved reported an enlarged dilated heart with a low ejection fraction. Her laboratory work, including chemistries done at this visit, was normal.

    I asked whether she wanted me to tell her what I thought when we were alone or with her husband present, even if it was unpleasant. She was insistent that I speak to her first and then with her husband. "He may not know it," she said emphatically, "but I am my own woman. And my girls will be that way too!" I reviewed her history and showed her the chest X-ray. I read her the report of the echocardiogram and explained what it meant. I told her that her doctor was correct about his diagnosis, except that her heart was not going to get better. I believed that she would ultimately need a heart transplant. She was taken aback and frightened. Together we spent the next 30 minutes going over what that meant in detail. I answered every question and probed to find out what everything I had said meant to her and then responded to those meanings. When we were finished she realized that she could take control of the situation, see the necessary specialists and transplant center, and then decide for herself what she wanted to do. I asked if her husband could come in and whether I could tell him. She agreed and with the husband present we went through the whole thing together. I told her that I would happily remain her doctor if she wished even though she was going to need the transplant center. We made a deal toward that end.

I would like to say the whole thing came out well, but it did not. She was scheduled for transplant about a year later, but died suddenly a few months after scheduling—perhaps 18 months after our initial visit. During the whole period we were in regular contact by phone and visit as she gained increasing confidence in her own capacity to make decisions and to stand up to what was to come. She had expressed the intention of becoming independent in her decisions and actions. Although this is unusual in her cultural group, I was careful to support her ambition. This may not seem important, but it is not how large a functional ambition is that is most important, but that it is the patient's own goal.

The Third Case. Rosalind Dreyfus, a married 50-year-old woman, has had serious medical problems since early childhood. She had ulcerative colitis as a teenager and required a total colectomy and permanent ileostomy at age 17 years. The rectal wound of her colectomy never healed properly leaving her with a chronic draining sinus. She was careful in her ostomy care but she continued to use an old-fashioned rubber ostomy bag so that odor was never entirely absent. She developed rheumatoid arthritis in her late twenties but the disease quieted down in her thirties leaving her with reduced joint motion of her hips.

She graduated from college, the first to do so in her extended family. She worked as a photographic darkroom technician and was prized by her employer of many years because she was bright, very hard working, and was liked by her co-workers. She was an only child. Her father was an alcoholic and was abusive and her mother was a menial worker of limited capacity. In her early thirties she married an accountant and he remained devoted to her. They had no children until regular physical therapy increased the motion of her hips permitting her to have intercourse. A son was born, now 13 years old and difficult, who was healthy and developed normally. He towered over his father and mother, who were both shorter than five feet.

At age 42 years she developed hidradenitis suppurativa, which produced chronic draining sinuses in her right axilla and right side of her groin. The lesions resolved after more than two years. In her late forties her liver enzymes, especially the alkaline phosphatase, began to rise and a liver biopsy confirmed the diagnosis of sclerosing cholangitis with significant cirrhosis. The degree of cirrhosis made it clear that she would ultimately require a liver transplantation. She was told this and accepted it with her usual mixture of irony and stoicism. The transplant center confirmed her need for transplant, but would not put her on the transplant list until her draining rectal wound was resolved because it was a site of infection. Clearing and closing the rectal wound sinus represented a major challenge, which she was willing to accept.

This patient has multiple medical problems each of which requires consideration and care. Closing the draining rectal sinus seems to be a logical immediate focus for the clinician's (and the patient's) interest. In this, she is similar to many patients with serious or terminal illness; there is much to do and many things that seem to call for the healer's full attention. On the other hand, focusing on these problems, making disease diagnoses, listing the goals and purposes, and making a list of current impairments, all the usual things we are asked to do when a complicated patient is seen, somehow push the patient out of sight. With this patient, indeed, with many of this group of patients—complicated illness, many impaired functions, multiple diagnoses, and probability of dire outcome—the last thing we want to do is lose sight of the patient herself, as herself because *she herself* is the main resource that will be needed in order to accomplish the therapeutic goals. The idea of a transplant in itself is not easy to face for this woman who has had so much trouble and illness in her lifetime. The fact that she requires the transplant indicates that her life is threatened. She has a child, and as with all mothers the idea of leaving him by dying is awful, a problem that is worsened by his challenging behavior. She is going to need to irrigate the draining sinus repeatedly herself if there is even a chance of closing it. Doing that will require her healer's support. Her husband, because of all these problems, becomes more significant than just someone sitting in the waiting room for her. Our training is all in the opposite— reductionist—direction. In this instance we have to see *her, this particular female person, Rosalind Dreyfus, the woman in full*, not just a female patient with serious medical problems.

It is common, when people are describing others, to use labels rather than true descriptive language. In medicine our labels are often diagnostic or semidiagnostic. Words such as anxious, depressed, or hyper as personality descriptors are actually diagnostic labels that do not indicate to others seeing or hearing the words how the person will look, sound, or act except in the most general terms. Rosalind is short and thick in build. She is plain-faced with many old acne scars, but, despite that, she is not unattractive. She walks with a waddle because of limited mobility of her hips. Her general hygiene is excellent despite her old smelly rubber iliostomy bag. She is attentive to and interested in what is happening around her. She is acute and clearly intelligent but given to somewhat humorous slightly sarcastic irony in her comments about other people and especially doctors and nurses with whom she has had a lot of interaction in her life. She is patient and grateful when things are done for her and accepting of discomforts and unpleasant experiences if they are in her service. She learns quickly when shown how to do something new. For example, she quickly learned how to irrigate her draining rectal sinus using a catheter attached to a Waterpik with an irrigating solution of peroxide and saline. She expressed her apprehension about the transplant, but did not hesitate to see the surgeons at the transplant center. She accepted with resignation their decision to postpone surgery because of an infectious locus, but did not hide her real disappointment from me. She wanted a frank discussion of the dangers of postponing surgery and was apprehensive without appearing openly frightened about the esophageal varices that the transplant service's work-up had revealed. As is usual with her, she is not optimistic that things will work out well. She and her husband seemed close but not demonstrative. We come away from seeing her and reviewing her life story and recent illnesses with admiration for her obvious strength of character. This is her greatest asset in her life circumstances including her illnesses. But she needs to be dealt with honestly, supportively, and with admiration openly expressed.

This patient had an emotional investment in her son even greater (if possible) than usual for parents of an only child. He was, unlike her, "normal" and she expressed her profound hopes that he would have the normal life that fate had denied her. Against this background she discussed her disappointment at her son's openly dismissive behavior toward her, hoping it was "just a phase." She died at home a few months after I last saw her. She had an episode of hematemesis and quickly bled out from her varices. Her husband came to see me shortly after she died. I expressed my admiration for her as the strong, intelligent, interesting woman she was. He was very grateful, he said, because "Everybody just looked at her and didn't realize what a wonderful special woman she was." She was. I told him I was worried about his son but he said he and the boy were now very close and he believed it would work out.

In this chapter on healing the sick person, the examples have progressed from patients who did not call themselves sick, despite being symptomatic from significant diseases, to patients with considerable functional impairment requiring major changes in their life goals. Healing required symptom control sufficient so that the patients could face the coming days with confidence that their distress would continue to be manageable. The discussion of pain control demonstrated how patients with lasting impairments personalize their symptoms—make it *this particular* person's symptom rather than merely the symptom itself. That fact allows the intervention to be directed at the particular patient: not pain in general, but *this* person's pain. The meaning of the patients' illnesses and the events that occurred were also targets of intervention. Sometimes, as with the first three, the patients themselves controlled the meaning by avoiding awareness of threatening disease diagnoses. In the young woman with difficulty breathing from metastatic renal carcinoma, changing the meaning of her symptoms relieved a terrifying fear of choking. Clinicians frequently try to reassure frightened patients, but that patient and Marjorie Raskin, the woman with menometrorrhagia, demonstrate that finding and changing the meanings that underlie the fear are more helpful than reassurance. Sometimes meanings were managed by taking advantage of a fatal illness to change the way the patient appeared to others. The maintenance of self-image is an important human function.

In all of these cases, finding out about the person who is the patient is an important aspect of the healer's work. This helps you avoid making your judgments superficially, like those who, as her husband said, "Just looked at her and didn't realize what a wonderful woman she was." It is important to learn how to describe the patient (even if only to yourself—although it is better written). In important ways, this clinical task is different than the largely reductionist pattern of thinking and integrated logic that leads to correct diagnoses. Here, it is important to fashion a narrative of the patient that tells you who the patient is—what the patient is like—free of diagnostic terms and personality clichés. This picture of the patient aids in fashioning your actions and therapeutic aims in harmony with the patient's functional abilities as well as goals and purposes. The therapeutic "we" should be a we in fact, clinician—healer—and patient, with a common understanding and common goal.

11
Healing the Suffering Patient

THE MOST IMPORTANT part in caring for suffering patients is understanding suffering. To that end I will review what makes suffering the unique form of distress that it is. This is especially important because of the persistence of the traits of mind in which all Western clinicians are trained—particularly the habit of focusing on the physical problems in very sick patients almost to the exclusion of the person. You might think that unnecessary to say, but because these patients are by definition very sick, their illness seems to pull the healer's attention almost exclusively to the body. As a result of that, with the best intentions in the world, the suffering is not lifted from the patient. On the other hand, we hear discussions about different kinds of suffering, for example, existential suffering, in which the person's suffering is said to be caused by the inability to bear existence itself, or psychological suffering in states of extreme grief, loneliness, or unhappiness. Making these distinctions between supposedly different forms of suffering seems called for because, for example, the American Medical Association's guidelines for terminal sedation sanction its use when physical suffering is present, but not in the case of these other kinds of suffering. What we actually learn from these discussions is how poorly understood suffering is. Suffering is suffering. There may be different causes of suffering, but not different kinds. Suffering is suffering.

Suffering has most commonly been associated with pain or other physical afflictions. It is now generally accepted, however, that pain and suffering are distinct and different. Despite this again and again you will hear people speak as though the stimulus *is the suffering*. For example, "He is suffering from terrible pain," instead of "His terrible pain started his suffering." In general, very severe pain results in suffering as much because of the distress itself as fears that severe pain often generates. The magnitude of pain, however, is only one factor in the distress it causes. People will tolerate even very severe pain if they know its significance—what it is—and they know it will end or that it can be controlled. Pain of a lesser degree may be poorly tolerated and lead to suffering if it appears to be endless or it is considered by the person to have a dire meaning. For example, it is not rare to have a patient who has constant right or left lower quadrant abdominal pain—frequently described as more like an ache (sometimes severe) than a pain—that has continued for weeks or even months and nobody has found its source. Usually many doctors of different specialties have been consulted and there have been endless diagnostic studies but no diagnosis—only more pain. If it is a woman, gynecologic sources have been endlessly considered, and, sad to say, even organs removed with no relief. Pretty soon the patient whose pain is not validated vacillates between thinking that it is "just mental," or that an undiagnosed malignancy is present from which death will ensue. In these circumstances if there is sufficient pain, patients may begin to suffer.[1]

Suffering may follow from pain even when it is no longer present. Patients who have pain secondary to metastatic disease to the bone may have dreadfully severe pain in which suffering follows from both the severity and its meaning. When the pain has been effaced by radiation, for example, the idea that it might recur sometimes precipitates suffering. The example in Chapter 1 of the woman with initially undiagnosed pain from metastatic disease from the breast is an instance. I have used pain as the inciting cause of suffering, but suffering may follow from any symptom—dyspnea, profound diarrhea or vomiting, neurologic symptoms, even weakness or fatigue in certain circumstances—if it disrupts the person sufficiently. People who have no symptoms may suffer, for example, from the suffering or even pain of a loved one (particularly a child), especially if they feel helpless in the situation. Suffering may be caused by helplessness itself, or hopelessness.

There are two constant features of suffering, the place of the future and the meaning of the source. People say, "If this pain continues I won't be able to take it," even though, at that moment, they are "taking it." Or "What if the pain recurs, I can't even stand the thought of that." Or "What if the diarrhea starts up again, or maybe even gets worse?" "If this pain is that cancer again, I'm finished." "I can't bear the thought of being tired like this the rest of my life; I'll have no life." We all can sympathize with those thoughts because everybody has trouble keeping the future out of mind, even (or especially) when they cannot know what the future will bring.

Meaning is also a necessary component of suffering. People have distinct ideas of what cancer, multiple sclerosis, Alzheimer's disease, paralytic stroke, and many other bad things mean. Remember also that meaning always includes ideas about the future as well as the thing itself. Given the possibility of thinking bad or good

---

1. This particular pain in that location has a name, ilioinguinal causalgia, and arises from a muscle knot or triggerpoint in the paraspinal muscle entrapping the ilioinguinal branch of L1. A similar pain syndrome may arise from nerve entrapment after inguinal herniorrhaphy. Nerve entrapment pain syndromes occur in many other places and defy diagnosis—a particularly troublesome location is in the right upper quadrant of the abdomen arising from entrapment of fibers of a thoracic nerve. It is troublesome especially because of all the other afflictions that are falsely indicted as the cause in that region.

outcomes, human nature settles on the worst. Thus, the distress that is the inciting cause of suffering is not only the thing in itself but what it is believed to mean for the person's future. These two facts, that suffering always includes ideas about the future and suffering always rests on the meaning of events, give us the most important fact about suffering; bodies have no sense of the future and bodies do not assign meaning. Only persons have a sense of the future and assign meaning. *Bodies do not suffer, only persons suffer.*

Suffering is the specific distress that happens when persons feel that their intactness or integrity as persons is threatened or is disintegrating and it continues until the threat is gone or intactness or integrity is restored.[2]

The key term is *person* and the concept of person is central to the discussion of sickness and healing in this book. It is important to keep in mind that in order to suffer a person must be aware of the past and the future and be able to assign meaning. This is why animals may suffer[3] but very young infants not suffer. They can have pain, even terrible pain, but not suffer. The existence of pain is enough to make us relieve it, but it is not suffering. The profoundly demented may, if they no longer have awareness of the past, future, and ideas of meaning, have pain, but do not suffer. The pain should cause us to relieve it, but it is not suffering. There is a central concept related to personhood that is important in understanding suffering and that bears repeating: Persons are of a piece; whatever happens to one part of a person happens to the whole—every part. All this time—more than 450 years—since Rene Descartes and many still act as though there is a separation between mind and body. Now, however, it is between the physical–biological of medical science and the "psychological" or the "personal." With that historical background it is easy to see why it might not be simple to comprehend that "All persons are of a piece, what happens to one part happens to the all." With that concept in mind, it is obvious that there cannot simply be "psychological" or "existential" suffering. If there is suffering in a part, for example the mental life, then there must also be manifestations of suffering in every other part, the social and the physical, for example, and the characteristics of suffering manifested by suffering persons described below will also be present.

---

2. There are threats to our integrity or intactness as persons that occur frequently but are small, just as the integrity of the skin may be broken by a small cut, bruise, or burn yet the importance of the skin as a barrier integument is not compromised. If the wound or burn is large enough, however, then the skin fails its function as a barrier. So it is with the integrity or intactness of persons.

3. Some animals have a sense of both the future and the past. How long into the future or the past probably varies with species. Some form of meaning is probably as ancient as animality since the cardinal feature of animals is motion. Without the assignment of even primitive meaning how would animals know to desire or to fear?

Suffering can occur in relationship to any part of a person, but it is always because the stimulus to suffering threatens the integrity—the wholeness—of the person. For example, if I believed that my family is brave in the face of adversity, sickness, and death, and it is on that difficult-to-overestimate model that I have lived my life and faced up to my awful illness, but when I discover instead that the image is a myth to cover up cowardice, the person I have believed myself to be falls apart and I suffer. Or the patient finds that he cannot tolerate further pain, knowing it will destroy him, but the future holds only more pain, then he suffers. Perhaps the stimulus to suffering is the experience a patient has when she finds herself alone facing a terrible, frightening illness when she had previously believed her family would stand by her. I will give specific examples below.

Understand a basic fact. Suffering is suffering is suffering. It is suffering and not another thing. When pain is the source of suffering, the suffering is suffering, not pain. When existential issues are the cause of suffering, it is suffering, not the unbearable existence. When psychological issues are the stimulus for suffering, it is suffering, not the terrible fear, sorrow, loss, or grief. When patients suffer it is suffering, not pain, not fear, and not loneliness. When suffering starts, pain might be relieved, but the suffering continues because the problem has become suffering and is no longer primarily pain. Why is it necessary to make the same point over and over again? The converse is true. It is because healers commonly see a suffering patient and concentrate on the obvious stimulus to suffering rather than treat the suffering itself. Because persons are of a piece, no matter what the stimulus to suffering, the clinician will find physical, psychological, existential, and personal alterations that may draw attention away from the suffering itself. On the other hand, it is possible to lift off the suffering even when, for example, the pain cannot be relieved.

I have put together four scenarios that illustrate these concepts. I believe you will recognize the truth of these episodes and the patients even though the character descriptions are short. I have put them in the first person to make them easier to identify with.

> What if you have been tolerating pain for hours and hours and days and it never stops. Now you're in the emergency department. You are so exhausted because you haven't been able to sleep. You've tried so hard not to cry and call out to every passing doctor and nurse. And they don't stop anyway because they are too busy for you. When they do stop, it's just because they want something, a signature or something. It goes on and on and on. Finally you have no stamina, no strength left anymore—and no control. And you just start to whimper and you don't even hear yourself anymore because there is no "yourself" anymore, just pain.

What if you have always been proud of your appearance and the way you look, really proud, and a careful dresser maybe for a hundred years? Then lately you start having diarrhea—all the time, constantly. For days on end. And they won't give you anything to stop it because—you're not sure why. And when you finally come into the hospital and the nurse undresses you standing up there is shit just running down your legs and on your clothes and everywhere. And everybody just goes in and out of the room.

What if you've always been a good patient and tried to do everything they asked you to do. Because you've always been good and did the right thing even as a kid. And everybody always said you were special—even strangers. And you came into the emergency room because this time you're really sick. And you've been lying on a gurney for eleven hours waiting for a bed. And you're not sure what's happening. You're so thirsty and cold, for hours, but nobody helps. When people do stop they tell you how busy everybody is and to just be patient. When you try to find out what's happening nobody listens. And some are just mean and short. And you're so cold...

What if you have always been really social and have a million friends because you just love that stuff. What if you just found out last week that you had cancer in your colon and they couldn't operate because there's a lot in your liver too. And you're sure you're going to die soon. And you're afraid to tell anyone because they'll stop talking to you. Like they did when your mother was dying when everybody ran away from her—and you. And left you to take care of her alone. And that was so awful, awful. You don't even tell your girls because—you know—they have their own lives. And you're scared, really terrified about dying.

These are abbreviated, but these are like real people and the possible sources of the disruption to the integrity or intactness of these persons should also be recognizable. The fact that each of them suffers is not solely because of the stimulus to the suffering but because they are the particular persons they are. This is what it means to say that suffering is always *personal*. I say that meaning plays a part in suffering because in each of these narratives, certainly the last three, it is not just the stimulus to suffering that matters, but what it means—the personal meaning—that elicits suffering in that person. Liquid feces running down your legs is never nice, but to the vain and fastidious person it is beyond horrible. It is never acceptable to be abandoned on a gurney (although it happens all the time), but if you have always been considered so good and special it feels terribly unfair and abusive. Being separated from or feeling abandoned by others is always bad, but if you are an actively social person the threat of isolation may be perceived as terrible. As I have noted elsewhere, for many patients, the fear of death is the fear of being separated from the group.

Suffering can be present in varying intensity and duration with the differences again dependent on the particular person as well as the cause. It is the increasing awareness of the impact on the person (perhaps out of consciousness) not the physical impairments per se that causes the suffering. Does this mean that suffering is psychological, in the sense of affecting or pertaining only to the mental and emotional state as opposed to the physical state of the person? No, because just as reading, driving a car, or working as a physician may involve any aspect of a person—physical, social, emotional, spiritual, or personal—so too does suffering. It is probably true that when someone has suffered, no matter for how short a time, the memory of the suffering never goes away. In some persons it seems that once suffering starts it continues on at some level for a very long time unless it is treated. This may account for the instances in which a person wants to tell you over and over again about the awful things that happened during sickness or tragedy. Mostly clinicians brush aside or try to avoid that kind of repetitive telling. Generally, (although not always) when a patient wants to tell you something over and over again it is because you (or others) have not heard or responded to what is really being said. "Tell me that again, slowly, so that I really understand," is a response that will shorten the interaction, not make it longer. In addition, acting on what the patient says will probably bring the patient relief, and gratitude for your caring.

Characteristics of Suffering

All Suffering Is Unique and Individual. The identity the suffering person feels will be disrupted or disintegrated in the future, or it is now; that identity existed in the past and is expected to be present in the future. That identity is the self that I call me—it is individual to me. Any of the parts of the person may be the locus for suffering, for example, family including family's lived past, body and relationship with the body, personality, character, lived past, roles, political power (in relation to others), relationships with others, society and culture, work, daily activities, identity, and believed in future. Remember, all the parts are connected. Why each person suffers (not why each has pain or other disruptive symptoms) will be individual—related to the person as an individual person. So that if, for example, two men have ruptured aortic aneurysm and both have excruciating pain as the cause of their suffering, the suffering itself will be individual and unique to each. A woman in her sixties presented with a pathologic fracture of her humerus and it took days to find the primary cancer, a small carcinoma of the lung. Meanwhile she began to have one pathologic fracture after another with awful pain. I asked whether she was suffering and she said she was. What was making her suffer, I asked. To my surprise she said, "It's because of food." "We've been married for more than 30 years. Every single morning when we get up, since before we were married, the first thing we talk about is what we're going to have for dinner. Now the last thing I want to hear about is food; even the words make me sick. What is there to say?" It is not persons in general that have to be known, it is *this particular person*.

Suffering always involves self-conflict. This may at first seem strange because the source of suffering is identified as separate from the sufferer—the cause of the pain or the pain itself—the life circumstances or fate that is considered the stimulus to suffering. The clue, however, is that the threat to the person's intactness or integrity lies in the meaning of the source and persons may not be of one mind about this. The person who suffers from social ostracism or the stares of others that goes with the sickness or appearance wants, at the same time, to continue to be part of and accepted by the group. Is self-conflict present in the dying and in acute illness? Yes, because there would not be suffering if we did not resist the pain, did not try still to be ourselves, truly did not care about dying. But people want to be themselves and want to live, so there is self-conflict. There is self-conflict also in wanting to be alive but not wanting to live the only life that seems possible, or wanting to be alive but not wanting to be a burden. At a certain point it is not living that matters, but only the things in each particular life that really mattered and are now impossible.

Suffering is thus always personal, individual, and marked by self-conflict, and also by the loss of central purpose. The word purpose has for many come to mean our life purpose or what gives meaning to our life, as derived from Viktor Frankel's work first published in his influential book, *Man's Search for Meaning* (1946, Beacon Press). Purpose is also an old world with simple senses: the action or fact of intending to do something, the object for attainment that one has in the short or long view (as generally used in this book). In that simple sense each life is pervaded by purpose in every moment, and these immediate purposes, often tiny in themselves, join together to form larger purposes, which join with yet other purposes, on and on culminating in *central purpose,* being (the active verb) oneself. (Which may, in itself, involve other purposes around, for example, art or business or medicine.) Central purpose is fundamentally not only individual but social—it draws from within the person but also requires the outer world for fulfillment. What one does, wants, acts on, makes, and becomes is ultimately both social and individual, lives in time and in rhythm with the world. So that when central purpose is lost we in the surrounding world feel the sense of the absence of the suffering person. For the sufferer, purpose has become redirected on the sickness and the sick part—all purpose becomes focused on the relief of pain, sickness, and suffering. The more compelling the injury, the more complete the redirection of purpose. The loss of central purpose, related to the loss of hope, is profound.

Finally, all suffering is lonely. The sufferer is lonely for three reasons—the individual nature of suffering, the withdrawal of purpose from social engagement, and the fact that the person's suffering is not understood. Just as pain is both not understood and the person in pain is avoided, so too with suffering. Suffering, then, is always personal, individual, marked by self-conflict and the loss of central purpose, and lonely. For all these reasons suffering is also a state of social deprivation and isolation even in the midst of others; and therefore it is also a loss of spiritual connection to the world. Suffering is a spiritual injury. As I noted above, suffering varies in intensity but also in the degree each of these factors plays in a particular person's suffering.

Make the Diagnosis

For healers these characteristics of suffering offer the opportunity for its relief. As elsewhere in the healing of the sick, however, the first step is to make the diagnosis; to know that the person is suffering, and, hopefully, to know why. Start with a high index of suspicion. If the patient is in severe or long-lasting pain or the equivalent in other symptoms, if the illness has dragged on—especially without a diagnosis—if explanations do not ever seem to satisfy, if bad things have happened in a cascade without apparent end or explanation, if fear cannot be relieved, ask the patient about suffering. If the patient seems unrelievedly sad, depressed, and/or chronically anxious but antidepressants or anxiolytics are ineffective ask the patient, "Are you suffering?" If the patient seems disconnected from others, uninterested in anything but the sickness, whimpers without awareness of whimpering, ask, "Are you suffering?" If the idea that the patient might be suffering comes to your mind, inquire directly about suffering. If the patients wants to know what you mean by suffering, ask "Is your distress more than just the pain or the..." "What is there in all this that you find particularly distressing?" "What is the worst thing—I mean just anything that is especially hard for you—about being sick and being here?" "If I could do anything at all to make things better—aside, of course, from making you better or taking the pain away—what would it be?" Follow up on hesitations, distracting answers, and pauses. Ask your questions, then be quiet and wait for the answers—and *be patient*. You have more patients who are suffering than you expect. If you suspect that patients are suffering, but are not sure, treat them as though suffering is present.

In all suffering these things are present. There is a cause, stimulus, source, or something happening to the patient that might be a reason for the patient to suffer. There is a person who is susceptible to suffering because of who he or she is, or what is especially true of the person in relationship to what is happening. The pain, for example, is much worse than the patient was led to expect. The disease, sickness, or illness events are having more impact on this particular patient than you expected. The woman in the example with feces flowing down her leg seems even more overwhelmed by the event than you expected. There is apparent self-conflict—the person seems more conflicted by events than most. For example, the patient continues to express the desire to be someone or do something despite the obvious fact that it has become impossible. The patient has lost purpose—there is no interest in doing anything beyond immediate relief of distress. For example, the patient's entire attention over some time (from which distraction does not work) is focused on finding a comfortable position in bed, fixing the pillows, or trying not to move even a little. The patient sits oddly in the chair; a sheet or blanket is pulled over the head like a tent as if the patient is trying to hide (from the distress); the patient faces the wall and hardly answers questions and will not turn around. Or you cannot get the patient interested in anything. The patient is or acts lonely and isolated. Politeness is absent (which is different than active impoliteness). He or she does not seem aware of the visitors except for monosyllabic answers, does not want to speak on the telephone, and does not engage with the doctors, nurses, or attendants except the bare minimum. There is evidence of spiritual isolation—not too easy to describe. You make yourself open to the patient and feel nothing in return. Notice how similar all these behaviors (or absence of behaviors) are to the depressed patient. This is the reason that suffering is so often treated as though it is depression. Suffering, however, does not respond to treatments for depression whereas generally depression secondary to physical illness is quite responsive to antidepressants.

Treating Suffering

Symptoms must be relieved. If that is not possible, build confidence in the patient. The patient should know that you are trying as hard as possible, getting others to help, or going to special lengths (whatever those may be). However, it bears repeating that suffering can be relieved even when its source cannot be removed. The central truth about the relief of suffering is that efforts are primarily directed at the suffering *patient* because suffering is an affliction of persons, not bodies. It is understandable that clinicians are forever working in suffering patients on the treatment of the diseases, because that is what we have been trained to do and where our methods work best. Furthermore, it seems to make sense that if you relieve the disease the suffering will also be made better. It cannot be bad to lift the source of sickness, but suffering is suffering and it is best treated, no matter what else you do, by focusing on the suffering *patient*. The problems in suffering that can be most directly acted on are the loneliness and the social and spiritual deprivation. This is accomplished by healers making a direct connection to the patient. The healer is uniquely qualified to reach across and make contact with a suffering patient even when the patient has withdrawn and seems unreachable or inaccessible.

Clinicians are accepted by patients as the source of their care and the relief of their symptoms and their suffering. The social role of the clinician is the basis of that authority and power. Make no mistake: you have both power and authority by virtue of your training and the responsibility that goes with your profession and your station. The power and authority allow you to reach across the chasm that separates the suffering person from the rest of the world—even when others cannot. We are not used to speaking about power and authority and the force of a social role; it seems to lead to political incorrectness. This is because professionals, especially when they are starting out, may confuse the power and authority of their professional role as though it was their own personal power—belonging to them as persons instead of being role related. Make no mistake, you would not even be with that patient or at the bedside if it were not for your training and professional authority. When you truly understand that and accept it and know that the responsibility that goes with the role is an honor and an opportunity you greatly increase the chance that you will do everything that is within your capacity.

Sometimes the personal nature of suffering is manifest by the patient taking the suffering personally, as though it is (or was) actively being done especially to him or her (now or in the past). Sometimes that is because suffering started when the patients felt that what happened to them in the emergency department was personal (endless waiting, feeling invisible, being thirsty or cold and no one helping, etc.). You can find that out by asking what happened that started the suffering. Then sympathetically address the patients' complaints directly. (Please, do not make the common mistake of apologizing for the staff—e.g., "They have been very busy, you know." Your concern is the patient.) It is also useful to find out, if possible, the individual nature of the suffering. "Why did you find that especially awful? I know it was simply terrible, but why did it strike you so particularly hard?" Finding out the source of the self-conflict may also offer an avenue of relief. Sometimes clinicians say something like, "If he wants to keep being a distance runner and now that is out of the question, what can I do about that?" You can be sincerely sympathetic. The sympathy of someone who has power and authority is different than when the family commiserates. Just like, "You tell him doctor, he'll listen to you." Try and get the patient involved in purposeful activity—useful activity. It can be as simple as "Let's see if you can transfer to the chair."

I'll bet you can. Here, give me your arm. See! Isn't that great." "You walked in the hallway all the way to the nurse's station, wow. I knew you'd do it." Perhaps you think, he'll be dead in a few days, what does it matter? Maybe you cannot stay the hand of death, but you can relieve suffering and give the person back to himself or herself. That is not a small gift. Or, for another patient, "Would you like us to call your brother so you can talk to him? It may not be too late to say what you want to say." Why not ask the nurse to do all these things, maybe she has more time? Because it will have more effect, be more therapeutically powerful, if you do it. The nurse's caring function and the healer's healing function are *both* very important, but they are different. Nothing is like the nurse's *caring touch* on some sick person announcing caring. Nothing is like the healer's words bringing the suffering patient back among the rest of us. They are different functions—too often forgotten by both professions.[4]

Let us return briefly to the examples I presented. The patient in pain was reduced to a pitiable whimpering object by her suffering. That memory will never leave her and her suffering will continue even if her pain is relieved unless the healer specifically and sympathetically addresses the fact that what happened to her is not because of her, or specific to her, it can happen to anyone whose pain is sufficiently severe or long lasting. Then elicit in detail the things she has to say about what happened that were so bad, so frightening, and so destructive so that you can address them individually and change their meanings. She will want to talk about it more than once, in all likelihood. It must be addressed each time.

The good and special person lying unattended on the gurney feels herself humiliated and abused. The humiliation and the memory will never go away unless you change its meaning. How will you know she is suffering? Hearing her problem by itself you may be tempted to dismiss it because many people wait, seemingly forever, on gurneys in emergency departments. But she will not look like an indignant self-concerned woman. Most probably she will seem withdrawn and disconnected even from your best attempts to connect. She will, however, want to tell you what happened. When she does it will not sound like an ordinary complaint. It will certainly be worth a simple, "Tell me why that felt so awful to you." I would be surprised if you do not hear her tell, like a theme, how hard she always tries to be good. Listen carefully and ask yourself whether you have ever heard that from a stranger, probably accompanied by tears. How much "right" someone has to suffer is not the question; the issue is to relieve her suffering. If you do not, it will go on, because one of the foundations of her way of living in this world has been severely threatened.

---

4. In this book a nurse practitioner is considered a clinician and a healer if that is the role he or she is inhabiting.

The fastidious person is undressed and had feces running down her leg *with an audience present.* That trauma, and everybody can recognize its awfulness, has to be relieved. She will tell you what you have to do and say as she undoubtedly tries to reclaim herself as fastidious and special in looks and action. She deserves your profound sympathy (so does every suffering person) openly expressed. If, instead, she is just withdrawn and apathetic, be careful and watch her closely. The apathy tells you that the trauma was worse than it might have seemed (which was bad enough). Adverse events happen to patients like this. Also, please, tell her you will control her diarrhea and do it. Some things are worse than the threat of megacolon.

You can do good things for the patient who believes she will be abandoned by the world because she has cancer. Reach out to her and make a connection. I think she will be responsive and very grateful. Whatever else you do, reunite her with her daughters. Once she discovers that she is truly not a pariah you will, I suspect, see a different, social, open, and friendly patient emerge. Of these four patients she will be the one from whom suffering is most easily lifted.

The fundamental warrant of medicine in every culture is the relief of suffering. As you can see, it is not often difficult. Perhaps the treatment of the inciting cause or the underlying disease is problematic, but the suffering can still be made better by focusing on the patient and finding out specifically why *this* patient is suffering. What future is anticipated and what meanings are involved? As with fear, simple reassurance is inadequate. You are the treatment—your understanding, your actions, and your words. You will find it among the most gratifying things you do.

12

Respect for Persons and Autonomy

*"Into whatsoever houses I enter, I will enter to help the sick, and
I will abstain from all intentional wrong-doing and harm."*
From the HIPPOCRATIC OATH. GREECE,
5th century BCE

FROM THE BEGINNINGS of Western medicine the overriding ethical precept has been benevolence, the desire to do good for the patient, tempered by the necessity to avoid harm. The reason for this is that sick patients are made vulnerable by their sickness and are in need of protection and help to be well. From Hippocratic times it has been known that for sick patients to get better—even in the face of death— it requires more than just medicines or surgery, it requires the aid of a skilled, careful, and caring doctor. In no other profession, not the law or even religion, does the benevolent relationship count for so much. This is as true in this time of cure and effective technology as in antiquity. This storied relation is less frequent and more difficult to see at present than in the past because of the intrusion of advanced technologies between doctor and patient and, of greater importance, the emphasis on the autonomy of the patient that started in the United States in the 1960s and has increased since that time. Until then, as I have said previously, patients were considered to have lost agency—the ability to act in their own best interest—because of sickness. Generally, doctors made what medical decisions they believed necessary for their patients, with or without their patient's assistance. Now that is called paternalism and is rightly condemned.

It is forgotten, however, that in American culture prior to World War II, the personal individualism that we prize today was not the norm. The United States, from the late nineteenth century, welcomed the acculturation of and assimilation of many immigrant and native groups (but not all). The doctor in a neighborhood was often considered not only a representative of medicine (and science) but a cultural standard bearer. Decision making on his (mostly) or her part was not only about medicine but about society. Wealthier and more educated patients were even then active (but not sole) participants in medical decisions.

The growth of individualism throughout American society and the civil rights movement after World War II provided impetus for the transition of patients to personhood and the rise of autonomy. The bioethics movement starting in the late 1960s focused heavily on the importance of autonomy. With the celebration of autonomy and the end of paternalism, the close relationship between patient and physician began to be less celebrated and to diminish in practice. It is commonplace at this time for physicians to present the alternatives to the patient and leave the task of choosing which course he or she desires to the patient. This is called the exercise of patient autonomy and in this view autonomy is seen by most as the equivalent of freedom of choice.

Other changes in medical practice, methods of payment, and systems of delivery of care have further obscured the nature of sickness, the nontechnical needs of patients, and the importance of the patient's relationship with his or her physician. Some aspects of American medicine have become commodified and the idea of medicine as a business has spread. The influence of these alterations on fragmentation of and worsening patient care while maintaining high utilization of new technologies is exaggerated by an increasing lack of primary care physicians. Medical students graduating with a high level of debt not surprisingly gravitate toward higher paying specialties. Primary care, whether general internal medicine, pediatrics, or family practice, provides the lowest income.

Other factors should also be considered. We are a society with a large burden of chronic illness that, despite this fact, seems to perceive itself as healthy. This, too, may diminish the perceived value of the patient–doctor relationship. It is surprising that with illness as common as it is, *illness itself* is not widely represented in the media. Advertisements for managed care organizations are notable for their emphasis on healthy people not the care of the sick. A billboard advertising an Immediate Care facility pictures a smiling healthy appearing dad, a daughter hugging him and mom smiling close by; what do they need acute care for? Pharmaceutical advertising and even advertisements for breakfast cereals and other foods emphasize health claims, and elements of a healthy life style, such as weight loss and exercise, and are prominent on public media. Television shows about medicine are popular but are focused on emergencies and the unusual not every day care such as the shows of the past that featured, for example, kindly Doctor Welby (and similars) taking care of the sick. High level medical and scientific technology are prominently in the public eye.[1] I believe the vision of

---

1. There has also been, I believe, a growing belief that modern technological medicine is more widely and completely effective than it is—that everything can be cured and if not that there are effective treatments for everything. Similarly, things are seen as white or black. There are no grays. Uncertainty is intolerable and believed to be unnecessary; there must always be another test to settle things. These myths are not surprising given the publicity and widespread

medicine and sickness that is portrayed is unreal—it is as though (unless unconscious or such) we continue to have independent choice, as though a sick person is just like a well person despite being sick. This is understandable because freedom, liberty, independence, and absence of hindrance or restraint are all words for an American value so fundamental and cardinal that any limitation on it is seen in negative terms. Thus it was on the nation's founding and even more so now. The current form of individualism is more marked by belief in the freedom of persons than even in our past.

All illness, depending on its nature and severity, may limit freedom, sometimes profoundly. Sick persons (and their families and friends), physicians, other caregivers, and those who work throughout medicine know this well. From self-limited illnesses such as the infectious diseases, through common problems such as the impairments of arthritis, diabetes, heart failure, and stroke, to the dreaded neurologic diseases such as multiple sclerosis, amyotrophic lateral sclerosis, and Alzheimer's disease, sick persons are hindered in their daily lives. Their freedom to live as they wish is sometimes extremely restricted. Actually, of course, everybody knows this, so when it seems to be kept out of common view it must be because as a society we do not wish to be reminded of it. Perhaps you think it was always so. This is not the case; illness was more commonly spoken and written about in the past—maybe even three decades or less in the past. The reason I am emphasizing this point is that I believe that seeing autonomy in patients as only freedom of choice—the right of patients to choose by themselves—may *restrict* rather than further autonomy. This is such an important point that it requires in-depth clarification.

Before we get into the meat of a discussion about autonomy, it should be clear that autonomy and liberty are not the same. I may be at liberty to do something even though in that situation I cannot be autonomous. As a simple example, I may be free to walk out either door but I have been given false information about what lies behind those doors. Because the information is false I cannot make an autonomous decision, a decision that is the same as I might have made if the information was true.

Here is a quotation from the British philosopher Isaiah Berlin that gives an idea of the goal of understanding autonomy and shows that it is larger than freedom of choice.

> I wish my life and decisions to depend on myself, not on external forces of whatever kind. I wish to be the instrument of my own, not of other men's,

---

dissemination of medical advances and wonders. Combined with the ubiquity of medical knowledge on the internet and other easily available sources this has created a public that has optimistic and exaggerated views of its knowledge.

acts of will. I wish to be a subject, not an object; to be moved by reasons, by conscious purposes, which are my own, not by causes which affect me, as it were, from outside. I wish to be somebody, not nobody; a doer—deciding, not being decided for, self-directed and not acted upon by external nature or by other men as if I were a thing, or an animal, or a slave incapable of playing a human role, that is, of conceiving goals and policies of my own and realizing them. This is at least part of what I mean when I say that I am rational, and that it is my reason that distinguishes me as a human being from the rest of the world. I wish, above all, to be conscious of myself as a thinking, willing, active being, bearing responsibility for my choices and able to explain them by reference to my own ideas and purposes. I feel free to the degree that I believe this to be true, and enslaved to the degree that I am made to realize that it is not.[2]

Reading this it is immediately apparent that aside from his wanting to be his own person, Isaiah Berlin does not want his self-governance to be impeded, "acted upon by external nature," "not by causes that affect [him]...from outside." He wants to depend on himself, "not on external forces." In those few phrases he is describing the fate of the sick person and certainly the hospitalized patient. On the other hand, the body of the quotation describes what many mean by saying that "I want to be my own person," and roughly speaking what it means to be autonomous.[3]

In April 1979, The National Commission for the Protection of Human Subjects of Biomedical and Behavioral Research, created by an act of Congress in 1974, issued The Belmont Report, which contained principles and guidelines for the protection of human subjects of research. The Belmont Report was immediately popular and widely influential not only in research ethics but as providing general principles that should guide the practice of medicine. The three principles were Respect for Persons, Beneficence, and Justice.[4] The principle of respect for persons in Belmont reads in part as follows:

Respect for Persons.—Respect for persons incorporates at least two ethical convictions: first, that individuals should be treated as autonomous agents,

---

2. Berlin, I. (1958). Two Concepts of Liberty. In Berlin, I. (1969). *Four Essays on Liberty*. Oxford, Oxford University Press.

3. An excellent, accessible small monograph on autonomy was written by Gerald Dworkin. It should be read by anyone who wants to go further on the subject. Dworkin, G. (1988). *The Theory and Practice of Autonomy*. Cambridge, Cambridge University Press.

4. Tom Beauchamp was the philosopher who actually wrote the Belmont Report. The principles in the report, beneficence, nonmalificence, autonomy, and justice, were quickly adopted by

and second, that persons with diminished autonomy are entitled to protection. The principle of respect for persons thus divides into two separate moral requirements: the requirement to acknowledge autonomy and the requirement to protect those with diminished autonomy.

An autonomous person is an individual capable of deliberation about personal goals and of acting under the direction of such deliberation. To respect autonomy is to give weight to autonomous persons' considered opinions and choices while refraining from obstructing their actions unless they are clearly detrimental to others. To show lack of respect for an autonomous agent is to repudiate that person's considered judgments, to deny an individual the freedom to act on those considered judgments, or to withhold information necessary to make a considered judgment, when there are no compelling reasons to do so.

However, not every human being is capable of self-determination. The capacity for self-determination matures during an individual's life, and some individuals lose this capacity wholly or in part because of illness, mental disability, or circumstances that severely restrict liberty. Respect for the immature and the incapacitated may require protecting them as they mature or while they are incapacitated.

The idea of a person is cast more narrowly in the Belmont Report than by Isaiah Berlin (20 years earlier). In this book the idea of person is as central as the understanding that persons may become sick and be unable to live their lives as they wish, and unable to pursue their goals and functions because of sickness-induced limitations of function. I do not believe that Tom Beauchamp and James Childress would disagree with Isaiah Berlin; they might say that deriving a principle from what Berlin said would be very difficult. They are interested in stating a Principle to guide action and principles require a certain simplicity not to get bogged down in all the details and counterdetails that the principle is meant to cover—parsimony in writing principles is a virtue. Let us restate the principle of autonomy as it is in Belmont: *To respect autonomy is to give weight to autonomous persons' considered opinions and choices while refraining from obstructing their actions unless they are clearly detrimental to others. To show lack of respect for an autonomous agent is to repudiate that person's considered judgments, to deny an individual the freedom to act on those considered judgments, or to withhold information necessary to make a considered judgment, when there are no compelling reasons to do so.* When Tom Beauchamp and James Childress state their principle of autonomy, it is followed by two obligations: Negative obligation: *Autonomous*

Tom Beauchamp and James Childress in their justly well-known book, *Principles of Biomedical Ethics,* whose first edition was published by Oxford University Press the same year as the Belmont Report, 1979.

actions should not be subjected to controlling constraints by others. Positive obligation: *Requires respectful treatment in disclosing information, probing for and ensuring understanding and voluntariness, and fostering autonomous decision making.*[5]

You can, perhaps, derive autonomy as merely freedom of choice from that statement but if you do you are not saying what they said. For these authors, respecting the autonomy of someone includes *probing for and ensuring understanding and voluntariness, and fostering autonomous decision making.* I believe that means that where sick patients are concerned, respecting their autonomy will require other people to help the sick patient by, at least, providing information, ensuring that it is understood, and making sure that the sick person's choices are voluntary The current model of freedom of choice and what is obvious in most clinical settings does not promote the participation of others beside the patient where necessary.

Respect for Persons

Persons are richly diverse, many-layered, complex, and interesting. When, however, they are lying in their sick bed, sitting in the chair opposite and so obviously ill, or calling on the phone about symptoms quickly recognizable as important, they just seem like a "person-thing" housing sickness or impairment—just who they are in the moment, not like someone out of whose mouth might come words like those of Isaiah Berlin's quote. It is natural that we should see persons that way in the moment—healers have a job to do and they see and hear what informs them of the task. It is not just healers. It is human nature to see just one facet at a time, or even to keep regarding someone in that oversimplified manner that may be necessary to get some task done. Making sure that a patient's expression is autonomous—of opinion, choice, and presentation of self—is, therefore, not a simple task. It is a vital task if the patient is to be autonomous.

Think back to the descriptions of person in Chapter 2. It starts by saying that sickness changes persons if for no other reason that a person in relationship with a physician (or with medical care) occupies a role that has a corollary in the healer's role. Because patients are in a role (that is invisible) they may not behave exactly as they would in their daily circumstance. They may not present their usual daily self to the world in which they find themselves when sick, or the self they wish to be. They may not find themselves to be a subject but instead an object of the care process; they may not be moved by reason or by their own conscious purposes and goals. They may not, in fact, in the alien setting of their care, and in the stressful

---

5. Beauchamp, T. L., and Childress, J. F. (2001). *Principles of Biomedical Ethics,* 5th ed. Oxford, Oxford University Press.

moment remember what their purposes and goals were. Sick enough, or in the sickness–care environment long enough, they may not think or feel themselves to be self-directed and responsible for their own choices, a deciding, thinking, willing, active being—a somebody not a nobody. More probably, they will not have even given thought to most of those descriptors, even though they are true. These patients will simply be. There is a reason that patients were not considered persons before our current era. Make no mistake, there is for good reason (the world has changed) no going back—*patients are persons*. Contrary to the behavior of many in the sickness–care setting, this has not diminished the responsibility of clinicians for their patients, *it has increased their responsibility*.

The central concept of patient-centered (person-centered) care is respect for persons. The increase in responsibility comes from the necessity to maintain not just the integrity of the sick body but the *intactness of the person*. It makes a caricature of that necessity to believe that it is fulfilled by telling sick persons their options and turning choice over them. Remember that Isaiah Berlin and most (if not all) others do not want their self-governance to be impeded by causes that affect them from the outside or by acts of an external nature, or things that make it difficult for them to depend on themselves. These phrases describe the fate of the sick or hospitalized patient. Now consider what meliorates outside forces: the truth—truthful information—above all. Sick persons, in order to make choices, must understand the truth of what is happening to them now, what happened in the past, and what is forecast for the future. This is easy to write but not so easy to fulfill. The essential descriptive word (aside from truth) is understand. When a patient asks a question, the answer should be true; that is an obvious moral imperative. More important is that the patient must understand what is being said as well as *what it means* to the patient. The patient must understand not simply what the words of the utterance mean but what the significance is—the implication of the utterance, simply spoken and jargon free. Things are happening, external forces are acting, and there is usually more to come.

There is another circumstance. Patients have a right to *not* be told the truth if that is their desire. For example, a patient had rheumatic heart disease and subsequent congestive heart failure and also metastatic carcinoma from the bowel. At one point she said that she never wanted to be told that she had cancer no matter what happened. That is quite explicit. Following that, all conversations about arrangements for her care if, for example, she became sicker were done in terms of her heart failure. Respect for persons does not stop just because they knowingly want or do something of which you disapprove. Nor are you required to tell them a painful truth that they seem to be actively avoiding. Too often physicians feel obligated to "set the patient straight." With not too many exceptions, the patient's clearly stated desires rule.

The problem is that self-governance—being in control of yourself and your fate—may be impeded by external forces. Self-governance is crucial. Outside forces impede people from the beginning to the end of their lives; that is what it means to live in the world. The problem is self-governance—choice. Protecting oneself, defending oneself, rising above, taking advantage of opportunities, altering course, getting ready, enlisting aid, and on and on. Choice. Sometimes, it is true, things happen to sick people and there is literally little choice except bad or less bad choices. Even when there is no apparent choice there is choice of attitude—brave or cowardly, equanimity or cowering, calm or scared. All of these choices that can define the person in his or her own eyes as well in the eyes of others are influenced by the way truthful information is conveyed: the mode, form, tone, content, completeness, timing, and the affect of the delivery of information. Did the patient get the message about the malignant biopsy result by voicemail or email. This happens, but it is not good; or even worse, it is unkind. Did they get the message standing or sitting down, on the run, or in the fullness of time; brusquely, abruptly, or calmly; coldly, matter-of-fact, disinterestedly, or kindly. Look at all the varieties of conveying truthful information and each one of these modes happens, seemingly without thought by the clinician about their impact on the patient. If your main interest is in the information perhaps it makes no real difference how it is delivered (apart from a general need for kindness). Because the focus is not merely the information but the maintenance or enhancement of the person (and voluntariness), then the impact on the patient is crucial. The content should be true, complete, clear, understandable, and delivered in the most humane manner. There are many reasons to be kind, but a pertinent justification is that persons are most likely to actually hear what is said and be themselves when treated kindly.

The information rule of three: It is not complete until it has covered at least these three points: (1) What the information is. (2) What the information means (implies or portends). (3) What **we** are going to do about it.[6]

Now we understand that information is itself a therapeutic tool and is meant to benefit persons. Respect for persons, self-governance, requires not only

---

6. Must what clinicians say always be truthful? I trained and started practicing medicine when untruths were common. A woman might have anesthesia for a breast biopsy and when she awoke she realized she had had a mastectomy. She would ask, usually panicky, whether that meant that she had cancer. "No," the surgeon might say, "but there were some suspicious cells so we had to take the breast off to prevent cancer." A lie. Another patient had surgery for a tumor of the stomach and at operation he was found to have widespread cancer from the stomach. After surgery he asked the surgeon what was found. The surgeon said, "We did some cuttin' and schnitten, and now you'll be fine. It will take a little time, but you'll be fine." I took care of that patient until his death some weeks later. A few days before his death after steadily losing weight he said to me, "Sometimes I don't think I am getting better." Neither of those patient stories is

truthfulness, but the patient's trust in the truthfulness of the healer—trust, always, that the healer has this patient's best interests as a paramount guiding force. The importance of the patient's trust cannot be overemphasized. Truth does not mean blind trust. Trust also does not mean "The truth, the whole truth, and nothing but the truth." What is said should be in the patient's interest, should respond to requests for information, should form a solid basis for decision and action, and should be tuned to the patient's ability (at that time) to process the information. It is necessary to be sure the patient understands: "Tell me what I just told you. Tell me what it means," and so forth. If bad news must be shared, some times are better than others—when the patient is going to be able to hear, understand, and as far as possible process the information. Sometimes there is nothing you can do but say it, no matter how bad it is. I always tried not so much to tell patients things, but to answer their questions. That way I knew they were ready. The trick was to get them to ask the questions. When the question seemed to ask for information that might be badly received, I might say, "Clarify that. Ask me that question another way." If ultimately the patient wanted the information I said it as clearly as possible, following the rule of three above. Sometimes I hear doctors tell a patient bad news with an undertaker's tone of voice. The information is hard enough, why make it sound even worse by your tone of voice. For the same reason be careful of your voice with good news, especially in a patient for whom things are generally not going well. A bright and cheerful tone with some good news makes the bad news voice portend even worse. A nice even tone of voice conveying that you will be there for the patient good news or bad is best.

The whole process of information transfer—which is much larger than merely words—has to be attended to. What are the nurses saying, how is medication delivered, and what does the care setting say? Is the patient in bed because it is necessary or because that is the way we do things? Is the patient unnecessarily awakened at night and is the patient getting enough sleep, food, and other necessities? Are all the medications *really* necessary? In other words, is the information,

---

conceivable now. You may think that is because patients know more now and because doctors tell the truth. Yes, but back then (the early 1960s) there were no effective treatments for cancer, pain was inadequately medicated, there were no hospices, and there was no palliative care. People, including doctors, believed that the diagnosis of cancer was a hopeless painful death sentence. Patients who were told that they had cancer, we believed, would become depressed and might even commit suicide. Those things did happen sometimes, but not commonly. Terminal care took place in the hospital and it was inadequate or worse. The whole ethos of medicine was different. Patients, at that time, kept their emotions and their emotional reactions to themselves. People did not talk about *everything* the way they do now. The guiding spirit of medicine now—about listening to patients, positiveness, hope, cure, and effective treatment—started after World War II, but it did not pervade medicine until around a decade later. In other words, the lies of the past took place in a very different medical setting. I did not like lying even in those days, but it was considered a necessary part of medical practice.

the staff, the procedures, and the way things are done to and around the patient all conducive to the being of oneself for the patient. Sometimes things are done to and for patients that are dreadful, painful, frightening, difficult to comprehend, and even infantilizing, but necessary. Sickness and injury may require unpleasant (or worse) medical acts, but nothing in medicine necessitates lack of kindness, impatience, put-downs, unnecessary silence on the part of clinicians, chattering among staff as though the patient was not present, or other manifestations of unthinking or uncaring attitudes. Generally, the meanings of patient-centered medicine that are most common—meeting the patients needs, desires, wishes, and concerns—although certainly less than what this book means by patient-centered, have produced better actions and attitudes on the part of the medical staff. "We put patients first" has had positive results.

Much more difficult for the clinician is the following question: "Who, or in what state, is this patient I am speaking to." Is this patient authentically himself or herself? The persons they wish to be; the beings that if they could look down from above or could regard themselves and their state of being from the outside, are really them. Or are influences acting on them such that what they say or do does not truly represent the persons they usually are? For example, a patient who is (say) in an ICU with a tyrannical head nurse may become much more compliant with requests and demands than he or she might usually be. The patient knows that it is better than arguing or disagreeing because the nurse will make unwanted trouble. The behavior may be chosen (and thus autonomous), but it is still a false picture. Suffering patients or patients who are in great distress, frightened, or altered by medication may not be able to authentically represent themselves, even though they have cognitive capacity. Realistically, how can we know all these things about patients. It is difficult and may be impossible at times. What is always required is awareness of its importance.

Respect for persons requires respect for the other aspects of person discussed in Chapter 2. First, is the patient thinking well? On a number of occasions throughout the book the impairment of thinking that occurs in bedbound sick persons has been mentioned. A Mini-Mental Status test is an inadequate measure by which to judge how the patient is hearing what is said and how the information must be modified so that the patient understands. The finding that the cognition of bedbound sick patients is impaired (as described) does not mean that they lack capacity to make judgments that are in their own best interests, it means that their healers and other clinicians must be very careful in finding out what the patient believes is in his or her best interest. It takes time to determine what these patients want because of the constraints on decision making. It does not take much time, however, to discover what is important to the patients—their values—because nobody except the patients know this. It is not technical choices that are wanted from patients, it is value choices to which clinicians should adapt their technical decisions. The problem of the number of different selves also requires that the clinician carefully explore why the patient wishes this rather than that. All of the time this takes is not to enable the clinician to make a better decision but to ensure that the decision is authentic to the patient.

I have devoted time to this subject because it is central to patient care. I sometimes see clinicians explaining things to patients as though they cannot get away from that bedside fast enough. If a patient is bleeding, the same clinician will take all the time it requires to staunch the flow and care for the lesion. Information transfer is as vital as anything else a healer does. For example, it happens that more than one team is making rounds on the same patient. This team comes to the bedside and tells the patient what is happening—but leaves before the patient's questions are answered. Here comes the next team and tells the patient something different, and leaves before the confusion is clarified. Here comes the attending physician and the patient leans on every word trying to find out what is happening. The attending physician is busy and also leaves before the questions are all answered. This is not rare, it is common. Uncertainty is bad for people. Everybody works hard these days to minimize medication errors—for good reason. Information errors are also dangerous.

Benevolence and Respect for Persons

Benevolence is a disposition to do good, a desire to promote the well-being of patients, it is kindness and generosity of spirit toward patients. This is simple and straightforward enough. In medicine, in the care of the sick, it is asked of people who have acquired a large, difficult-to-master, and technically sophisticated body of knowledge, who have been trained and further trained, just how to apply that knowledge. Sometimes it happens that the knowledge and the skills become central to healers and the reason for it all becomes peripheral. That is unfortunate. It is true that we would not have the opportunity and privilege of attending to patients were it not for the training and the role it prepares healers for. But the overriding reason for the healing professions and the devotion to the healing of the sick is benevolence and respect for persons. Medicine has progressed in our era not only by continued technical advancement but by increased respect for and knowledge of persons.

13
Purposes, Goals, and Well-Being

THREE WORDS APPEAR in this book—well-being, goals, and purposes—that are not usually the focus of a clinician's work. They are so important that they need to be defined again. Purpose is the reason the person wants or aims to do something—the action or fact of intending to do or be that thing. Purpose is, however, often more or of larger or more intimate dimension in the lives of people—an ongoing or underlying pursuit of a theme in someone's life—like medicine in my life and for many of my friends or music for Bob Dorough. Many people have such a purpose, but it may seem too ordinary or quotidian like the family or religion for the person to take manifest note of it as an ongoing purpose without your help. The point is that purposes such as these or in this sense are hardly separable from the person. Take away that purpose and the person is diminished, not whole. That is the reason it is so important to focus on the person's purposes. Goals are things that people pursue to further purposes. Well-being is the state or being of or doing well in life. It is always relative to the person's situation. In the Preface I pointed out that well-being is a difficult treatment goal from a clinician's point of view. There is not anything there, I said, that clinicians could sink their teeth into. Purposes and goals are not so easy either. Impairments of function—what gets in the way of purposes and goals—are just fine. The reason function is congenial is that clinicians are used to measuring function. Muscle strength, joint range of motion, peak expiratory flow rate, and cardiac output are the kinds of function with which we are familiar. This is because these are body functions.[1] Clinicians, medicine in general, have had almost three generations of focusing on

---

1. Physicians are used to measuring function these days, but it was not always the case. Cardiologists prior to perhaps the later 1950s listened carefully to the patient's heart to determine what murmur was present in order to make the structural part of a cardiac diagnosis according to the widely accepted New York Heart Association (NYHA) criteria. Those same criteria provided for an overall estimate of a patient's function status on the basis of the patient's statements. NYHA Class I. "No symptoms and no limitation in ordinary physical activity, e.g. shortness of breath when walking, climbing stairs etc." Class II. "Mild symptoms (mild shortness of breath and/or angina) and slight limitation during ordinary activity." Class III. "Marked limitation in activity due to symptoms, even during less-than-ordinary activity, e.g. walking short distances (20–100 m). Comfortable only at rest." Class IV. "Severe limitations.

physical function, delving, in its pursuit, as far down into the cellular and then molecular basis of function as our technology will go—which is pretty far. On the other hand, we are not accustomed to considering in the same terms public speaking, carrying out daily routines, using the internet, driving a motor vehicle, respect and warmth in relationships, intimate relationships, being a father, community, and social and civic life. These are activities and participations listed in the *International Classification of Functioning, Disability, and Health* (ICF). They describe activities and participations that are part of the world in which our patients (and we) live. These must become matters of concern for healers once they become interested in a person's purposes and goals. What clearly distinguishes the first set, in which muscle strength was listed, from the second set, in which respect and warmth in relationships is found, is not that the former involves body functions. What activities and participations do not require bodily functions? Everything human requires the body. The contrast is that the first set, which included cardiac output, is a *reductionist account* of human functions that, in the aggregate, may eventuate in "community, social, and civic life." Perhaps your patient has been (say) a regular church-goer and that remains vitally important to her. You know that in the ordinary course of things, going to church requires an almost normal cardiac output. Once you are aware of the importance to her of going to church, you can figure out a way, despite her currently reduced cardiac output, to get her there regularly. However, you will not know the high priority she gives to regular church attendance unless you are really concerned about her goals and purposes. Living her religious faith is an important purpose in her life, one of her life's most vital aspects. Once you act on that concern you will see her and know her differently.

I would be tempted to say that reductionism is the enemy, except that it would be foolish. No reductionism would mean no science and science brought medicine out of the dark ages. However, even very good things sometimes have unforeseen consequences. The reductionism that is part and parcel of medical science has had negative consequences for aspects of patient care. Healers like general internists, palliative care clinicians, nurse practitioners, and other primary care clinicians should be patient centered. The whole patient gets lost in the tendency to shift away from the patient toward the patient's parts, or primarily body functioning. This is not good. That it happens frequently, however, is generally appreciated.

Experiences symptoms even while at rest. Mostly bedbound patients." The Master's two-step test for angina was as close to functional testing as things went. Along came cardiac catheterization and cardiac surgery and everything changed. Knowing a patient's functional status *with accuracy* became vital. By the late 1960s physical exercise became popular, and exercise testing became commonplace. Function became an important word.

When Dr. Balfour Mount (who invented the name palliative care) founded the hospice in the Royal Victoria Hospital in Montreal, which today, because of Dr. Mount's influence, we call a palliative care unit, it was based on understanding the patient in terms of "body-mind-spirit." When the large influx of physicians into the field of palliative care started—attractive because it is devoted to patients and is so rewarding—despite their good intentions it began to be a specialty focused on pain and opioid analgesics—mind and spirit got lost as subjects of concern. Old habits die hard. Good palliative care physicians, however, see their patients in wider terms and push against the restraints of reductionism in clinical medicine. It remains a struggle. The high degree of specialization and subspecialization in internal medicine and other fields is also a reflection of the same reductionist mind-set.

There is no inherent contradiction between reductionism and holism. Reductionism has been—is—successful when you want to understand how parts of a problem work. It is also a good strategy when dealing therapeutically with one aspect of an illness, especially over the short term. Patients—persons—on the other hand *are more than the sum of their parts*. To understand them and to take the best care of them, especially over a period of time, it is best to know them as the persons they are. It is unfortunately true that our ability to understand wholes—whole persons, whole families, even whole illnesses—is not nearly as well worked out or as effective as reductionism. That is not a reason for not keeping in mind the need to know and learning how to understand sick patients using both approaches. It is true, however, that the more you know about the person, the better you will be at adapting therapeutic goals and actions so that they have the best chance of success in individual patients.

Focus on the patient's goals and purposes and keep them in mind as you find, treat, work around, or resolve underlying impairments in function and you will necessarily be patient centered. To do that it is helpful to make a change in the way you start with a new patient whether healthy, sick, or dying. Early on ask questions about goals and purposes rather than, as usual, immediately starting to unravel the presenting symptom. Notice that I said unravel, not asking about. A good opening question with an ambulatory patient is "How can I help you?" A good opening question with a hospitalized patient is "What is your trouble?"

After a few questions to establish the problem and your interest in helping, ask the patient "How do the [symptoms or illness] get in the way of reaching your goals or doing what is important to you." Purposes are things that are important for the patient to accomplish or be and goals are subsidiary to purposes. Then move on to "How is [the symptom or sickness] getting in the way of pursuing your purposes and goals [restate the patient's purposes and goals in the patient's words]?" Usually, a few utterances will follow this and you will know more about the patient. Economy in the use of time and words counts here as everywhere, so remain in control of the conversation, but get the questions about purposes and goals answered.

Let me enlarge on the issue. "Are there things that are especially important to you that you cannot do? Or something you wish you could accomplish these days?" "Do you have some goals in mind? Some special purposes or things that are really important?" In the past, clinicians' questions would pursue the symptoms and other manifestations of illness until they had taken the problem apart into easily manageable small parts. It is practical to do that—if you are interested primarily in the parts and not the whole person. When you reduce persons to their parts, you lose the person. If medicine is person-centered for all the important reasons, both medical and because of respect for persons, then we do not want to lose sight of people's goals and purposes. The goals the patients tell you about the patient and provide avenues for follow-up questions (or actions) directed at the purposes and goals themselves. They give you an entrance into details and immediately ally you with the patient. You are interested in what the patient is interested in. Do not be concerned that you will hear some lofty goal or high-flying purpose; sick persons do not do that.

Here is an example. The patient is a 53-year-old woman who is single and worked as an independent contractor, building residential houses, for many years. She has had carcinoma of the ovary for nine years. She has required courses of chemotherapy on several occasions when she had recurrences, but was always treated back into remission. Last year she had an episode of intestinal obstruction and required surgery. She now has a colostomy. She is in the hospital because she is presently maintained on intravenous Dilaudid at the insistence of an oncologist who recently took over her care because the previous oncologist moved. Apparently the Dilaudid was chosen because the oncologist did not approve of the morphine she had been taking for pain. Her total daily dose, however, including IV push rescue doses, is equivalent to more than a gram of morphine. The palliative care physician admitted her in order to reduce and rationalize her opioid dose and route of administration.

In the usual course of events, after initial introductions and pleasantries, the questions would have centered on her pain and narcotic dose. Narcotics are like a red flag for clinicians, who are often immediately suspicious that patients are taking too much and not specifically for pain. Clinicians almost automatically want to lower the dose. There often are reasons from their past experience for these attitudes. Patients soon learn this, so they become defensive just as quickly. It is not a good strategy to start with the narcotics, whatever your intentions. A defensive patient is difficult to win over. Instead, the clinician's next questions were about goals. "Are there things you really want to do that you cannot or that cause you difficulties?" She replied, "I really want to be able to walk outside—it's really, really important to me. I want to watch the sunset but I'm stuck inside and I feel like a prisoner. And I really want to be able to sleep through the night." "Why can't you do those things?" "Because my bag has to be emptied so frequently because it fills up so fast." On request, she uncovered her abdomen and it was obvious that her ostomy bag was too small. The clinician assured her that the problem would be solved; the ostomy nurse would help and make sure she had a larger bag so she could go outside and also sleep with fewer interruptions. There were a couple of other illness-related problems that interfered with her goals. They were solvable and the clinician explained what would be done. On several interspersed occasions she said how upset she was with the surgeon because he had, she believed, "taken out too much intestines." Suddenly, she erupted in a fury at the surgeon—saying again and again, while crying, how angry she was. The clinician remained quiet, neither defending nor criticizing the surgeon nor discouraging her show of rage. The clinician let it explode and then simmer down over 2 or 3 minutes. In fact, the anger was not addressed directly, except to acknowledge it ("I hear you."). The clinician focused on the goals. She wanted to sign out of the hospital (which she had done many times in the past), but meekly agreed to stay in the hospital, which she did. She was eager to have a colostomy appliance that fit into her life. The whole interview with three other clinicians in the room lasted less than 20 minutes. Her attitude had changed from antagonistic to embracing. I believe that if the interview had started in the usual manner about the narcotic, its dose, and its route of administration and her pain, this patient would not have been willing to work with the clinician (who would also have known a lot less about her). She has a lot to teach us. Her history tells us that she is an unusual woman, intelligent, and used to doing things her way. She is, however, sick. Sick patients desperately need to trust, but if they have been sick long enough they are almost always untrusting—generally with good reason. Sick persons desperately need to be cared for, but find it very difficult to establish a good relationship with their clinicians. (Also, for good reasons, arising from their past care.) Establishing the conditions for a relationship comes first. Starting with *her concerns* rather than ours is a good first step in that direction. (How about her wanting to "watch the sunset." I suspect you are hearing a person saying, like Isaiah Berlin in Chapter 12, "I wish to be somebody, not nobody; a doer—deciding, not being decided for, self-directed and not acted upon by external nature or by other men as if I were a thing…" The way to know would have been to ask.)

In finding out about these patients, all the usual questions about the family, the past history of health and illness, and the other aspects of evaluation discussed in Chapter 6 are as pertinent here as always. They should be helping you enlarge what you have discovered about this patient. With the knowledge of the patient's goals and matters of overriding purpose in your mind you will have the opportunity to better understand the patient. Facts and details that patients have told you in the past but that were not pertinent may now have a home in your thoughts. The larger the picture you have of the patient the better previously disregarded information fits in. Why? Look at all I learned about the disease, pathophysiology, medication use, etc., because I shifted the focus to the person. Those other facts are important now because they too are part of the person, but persons are more than those facts about (usually) the body.

Other changes in the initial evaluation follow from the need to have a better overall view of the patient. Healers should be interested in and record the way patients present themselves—an initial impression of the person. Learning how to write a succinct description of a patient is an important skill not quickly acquired. To become proficient you have to practice to get past the first almost inevitably clumsy attempts. In the beginning choose one patient per office hours or hospital rounds, or even less frequently, until the skill is mastered. Include a *brief* personality description. Follow with a description in succinct terms of the patient's background, education and employment, current family (married or single, children), or other significant relationship. Following that there should be a *brief* description of the patient's physical appearance. Start with the patient's appearance prior to undressing. If there are distinguishing features of speech or presentation of self they should be mentioned. Then focus on the unclothed appearance—body habitus, general development, musculature, and prominent distinguishing features such as major birthmarks, scars, or deformities. The whole description is usually not more than a paragraph.

Here is an example. The patient is a 42-year-old woman who is attractive despite the signs of illness. Her face is pale and drawn and appears older than her age. She is wearing some make-up carefully applied. Her face and speech are animated especially when angry. She is articulate and obviously educated and smart. Despite its long duration she does not really accept that she is sick. She seems always ready to argue. She is sort of beaten down pugnacious with humor at the edges. Her intelligence is quick to engage and when the defensiveness eases she becomes an important helpful partner in deciding about her care. She wears an attractive bedjacket. She uncovered herself for examination without hesitation. She is thin and without much body fat. Her breasts are small and sag. The abdomen has numerous surgical scars. There is a colostomy bag that is clearly too small. Muscular development is better than might be expected in someone with a long illness suggesting that she exercises. She stood at the bedside without support and without difficulty. She accepted help returning to bed.

Clinicians may find this difficult because good clinical habits, as we all know, are slowly gained and painfully changed. Too many have forgotten how to write complete sentences without abbreviations, much less a coherent description. But it is possible. I have noticed how easily I fall into old habits of focusing on parts of the patient and neglecting a larger perspective, but with concentration on the goal, I have changed. Many of these habits of viewing the patients as their parts are still necessary and helpful; it is the context into which they fit—a larger view of the patient—that requires adopting.

Here is another example. The patient is an attractive 86-year-old woman with thinned dyed red hair wearing glasses and considerable make-up. She dresses neatly and is obviously attentive to her looks. The bulkiness of her pants at the seat suggests that she is wearing diapers. Her speech pattern, repetitiveness, and topics suggest cognitive impairment. She is witty and interested in talking about politics and current events. Asked about goals she replied that "I have to get someone to take my car to the garage. I want Scott to feed the cats on Thursday when I go to the doctor. Some things are hard for me to do now, I am 86."

The simple question about goals reveals the cognitive defect even if nothing further is added. "What is really important to you?" "I want to stay alive for a long time." Adding the questions and the information suggested earlier changes the understanding of the impact of dementia on this woman. Clinicians tend to think about dementia as a cognitive difficulty of memory and reasoning, which it unquestionably is. But in even the brief description of this woman's office visit, it is obvious that the effects of the defect in thinking are more global. She may be interested in politics, but the absence of details (of which she is unaware) immediately makes her interest superficial. Her wittiness is also a shadow of what it must have been in the past. The narrowness and concreteness of her goals indicate that the problem is not merely cognitive ability but that it is her world, which has contracted to a small space around her. The sadness of dementia is that you need a working brain to live in the world.

Here is another patient who is 60 years old and generally healthy. "I want to be happy. I know I have to be healthy to be happy and do all the things I love with my family, especially with my grandchildren." A few more questions are necessary to flesh out her purposes, her place in the family, and what is of most importance to her. More details emerge about her more immediate goals—what she tries to achieve in the family and what she likes to do. The whole set of questions and follow-up conversation took only several minutes. Incidentally, one question, answered affirmatively, was, "Would you consider yourself as having a state of well-being?" The tenor of the entire visit was changed by the opening questions moving away from merely the usual search for signs of disease to a focus on worries and concerns. However, as the previous patient made clear, you are hearing how a person is functioning. Here, also, is an opportunity to talk about health and how it is pursued. It is true that physicians have not been taught about health; instead their training is about disease. It will not take long after the focus changes to the whole patient rather than a diseased (or not) part before clinicians will know a lot more about health. It is also easier to learn about normal function of many body systems from this vantage point. In addition, the questions make more sense to patients.

Generally, patients' perspectives are strongly influenced by their clinicians' outlook. Why are so many patients with cancer narrowly focused on survival instead of the more pertinent (and more inclusive) question of how to live their lives most fully in their present state? If their clinicians reduce them to their tumor they will soon be doing the same thing. Goals and purposes are universal. If clinicians ask about them and show real interest in helping patients reduce the impediments that are keeping them from achieving their goals and pursuing overriding purposes that will change the patients also. Particularly as over time the clinician becomes familiar with the patient's purposes. Freedom from cancer, as important as it is, is an intermediate goal; returning to living life and achieving well-being is a truly human purpose. A primary focus on cancer is a focus on fear. On the other hand, the malignancy is real and it must be dealt with. The question that can be raised at this point is what is the frame of reference surrounding the vital concern with the malignant disease. As long as the definition of sickness is the presence of disease and medicine's role is the treatment of disease the focus will be on disease. Change the definition of sickness to the presence of impairments of function that interfere with the pursuit of purposes and goals, and it will be the healer's task to help patients achieve their purposes and goals.

The Patient as an Arena for Therapeutic Action

In these pages, from beginning to end, the sick or well person has been the focus. There have been descriptions, questions, issues, problems, and suggestions all focused on the person, both sick and well. The person has been described in some detail, and the changes in persons that occur in serious illness—all illness to some extent—have been highlighted in the book, particularly in Chapters 8, 9, 10, and 11. All of this leads to the importance of sick persons, as the persons they are in their illness, as a place to act directly—a field for therapeutic action. In the Preface I said that this concept pervades the whole book and gains substance chapter by chapter. This chapter is not as much about details of clinical action as about a reflective consideration of both goals and learning about the sick person. The overarching goal is maintaining sick persons to the extent possible as the persons they know themselves to be—or returning them to that state. I believe that sick persons whose overriding purposes still occupy them (to the extent possible) are the best ally the clinician has in overcoming the pathophysiology or disease. I have had the feeling in the past that it is difficult for many physicians to focus on the person as a person as effectively as they do about disease. I think it is in part lack of training, but it is also because it is not clear what is entailed. In the remainder of the chapter there are ideas about what a clinician should do to learn to see patients as the persons they are. Doing this does not at all diminish the importance of acting on or attending to the disease, body parts, or functional impairments; it enlarges the field of view, the clinician's perspective about where action would be most effective. There is a person connected to that body and whatever is done to the body impacts the person and whatever happens in the person is also happening to the body—meanings, feelings, and thoughts—everything. Therapeutic action can be primarily directed to the person—to meanings, feelings, thinking, and ideas—but it is fundamentally different from many other medical acts. This is not action at a distance. Without question the agent of treatment is the *person* of the clinician. Years of watching young clinicians at work suggests that learning this may not be easy. Clinicians distancing themselves appears to be the normal mode. Exposing themselves openly to the sick person—person to person—seems endangering. The fear of being truly open to the patient is probably a carryover from medical student and postgraduate days because, as I have said before, the clinician's role, once formed, is protective. There really is no danger in being open. This is discussed at length in Chapters 5 and 7. One of the difficult aspects of this perspective on clinical action is keeping the whole clinical arena in mind—the patient and the patient's body. Obviously we cannot be consciously aware of the whole all the time, but in looking and listening the clinician has to consciously, from time to time, pay attention to—register consciously—the whole gestalt.

Most often sick persons have symptoms that are prominent and from a common patient's perspective they are the whole illness. The patient's report of these symptoms and the clinician's response tracking them down in addition to the whole diagnostic and therapeutic effort narrow the clinician's field of view onto the physical and away from the total experience of sickness. Pain, but also nausea and vomiting, or maybe any symptom if it is severe enough to dominate the patient's experience, can do the same to the clinician and push every other consideration aside. These and other manifestations of illness—including fear and uncertainty—take a central place in patients' lives and also in their clinicians' thoughts. Sooner than one wants the illness is in the center and the person of the patient has been (figuratively) pushed to the periphery of everyone's attention. This is a straightforward example of the impact of illness on the person. It is a matter of concern for us because it is not helpful (or healthy) for someone to feel diminished in this fashion. Will such persons feel themselves as strong and as able to act on their own behalf? Would you, as one test of the impact, be enhanced by being relatively diminished in power in relation to others in the scene of sickness?

Do you believe that diminished power might have some influence on the course or outcome of the sickness? Ask yourself instead whether such a patient would feel as empowered to question an unfamiliar medication, or as quick to report a change in symptoms that the patient worries will be taken as questioning your skills? Probably not. An incorrect medication or an unreported symptom might well affect the course of an illness. Rather we recognize the personally diminishing effect of pushing the patient out of the immediate field of view. Instead we want the patient to experience as much power as possible knowing that the direct effect of the manifestations of the sickness already make the patient feel less empowered. On the basis of this reflection we know that the patient must be actively returned to the center. "Listen," the clinician might say, "It is important to get your symptoms under control, and we are doing that. But let's not forget this is all about you—you are what this is about. You, not just nausea or vomiting, but you." In a serious illness there will be occasion to say that again and again.

Clinicians must get in the habit of not discounting the personal effects of illness simply because they are not physical. Clinicians may brush a patient's emotional reactions aside as not as important or as "real" as something physical such as (say) pain. In our own lives and in the lives of most if not all persons, what has hurt the most have not been physical pains but the pain of loss, reactions to fear, or perhaps profound embarrassment. Knowing these truths from personal experience as well as so many other things in our life and applying them to patients is part of what it means to use ourself as the therapeutic agent. How do I know, you might object, that my own experience applies to this particular patient? If in doubt, ask the patient.

From this stance, you will be more tuned to what you see and feel as you walk into the patient's room. The patient says, for example, "I heard you—your footsteps—coming down the hall." Think how many people are walking in that hallway. What made the patient attend so acutely to the sound of *your* footsteps? You already know that happens with hospitalized patients. Wait. Is it telling you that the patient is beginning to withdraw from ordinary life into sickness—disconnecting from the well? Look again. Has the patient looked at the newspaper? Is the television playing and, if so, is the patient paying any attention? Are there other signs of the disconnection? Does the patient seem to be more frightened—seeing this, that, and nearly everything as a peril and as dangerous and threatening. There will not be a sign above the bed. In perhaps 3 days there will be no doubt where the patient is, but by then you will be 3 days behind. You will have a patient feeling profoundly threatened. Now, having picked up the signs, and asked about fears, you will have a chance to address the fright. Is it important? I doubt that you want the patient to be subject to (say) 3 days of inadequate sleep, generalized muscle tension, and the catecholamine cascade that accompanies the fear that accompanies the loss of omnipotence. You can stop it now with some questions and directed answers. And so it is with the other characteristics of a state of illness. You may want to assure yourself that the patient is in a state of illness or use the opportunity to learn more about it—and about your own reactions to a state of illness. How? By using the opportunity to reflect on the characteristics of serious illness in *this patient*. You have probably had considerable experience with the very sick, so much of this information is already accessible to you once you know that it is part of your *clinical* knowledge. Reflect also on how you are responding to it. Have you switched to the continual use of "we" and begun actively being the patient's surrogate in connecting to others and being the patient's agent of action where appropriate? Remember that one of the most distressing elements of sickness is the loss of control. As you do these things you become the patient's agent of control. When you have become actively aware of your speech and actions at the patient's bedside listen for the quality of your explanations and other utterances. Here is where one of those small voice recorders will allow you to listen to yourself in the interaction. Nothing teaches faster.

Teaching yourself to try to see everything and hear everything is not easy. For one thing you are probably busy and have more patients to see. For another, it takes discipline to keep looking and keep listening. If you did it with every patient every day it would take forever (or seem that way). Select one patient and focus on that sick person today, tomorrow, and everyday you have the opportunity. The last time you were actively teaching yourself these skills may have been in medical school. This kind of learning takes patience and willingness—and time—days, weeks, months, and years to get really skilled. See the Preface.

This sick person, bedbound and requiring care in bed, almost certainly has the cognitive impairment of sickness. Demonstrate it for yourself. Get two containers—urine specimen cups are convenient—and fill each of them about half full making sure that the two contain the same amount of water. Get a urinometer or large test tube and go to the patient's bedside. Show the two specimen cups to the patient saying, "Do you see these two cups? They have the same amount of water, is that true?" Wait until the patient acknowledges their similarity. Now say, "Watch while I pour one of the cups into this test tube. Which has more water, the test tube or the cup?" Seeing the patient select one of the two containers—usually the test tube—as having more water is startling the first time you experience it. You can do the same thing with two same-sized balls of plasticene or playdough. Show them to the patient and get an acknowledgment of the similarity. Then roll one out into a long thin rope and ask which has more clay. Another simple test is to take a box of tissues or something similar that looks distinctly different on its opposite sides. Show the different sides to the patient—you can comment on the features of the opposite sides. Then, with the patient looking at one side, ask what is on the other side. The sick patient will not be able to tell you. This is because the patient *cannot* take the perspective of another. The published paper has other Piaget tests of cognitive function that you may wish to try. You will be impressed, I believe, by how serious illness profoundly changes a patient's thinking. Overwhelmingly these patients can pass a Mini-Mental Status examination (Cassell et al. 2001). I have described these tests and mentioned the study again and again and again. Why? Because nothing will teach you faster or more to the center of your clinician self that the sick are different. Once you *really* know that you will understand why you are focusing on the sick person and not primarily on the disease. This is not done as kindness—although kindness is always necessary—but as a clinician who wishes to be *maximally* effective in helping patients get or be better.

In speaking with sick patients, be polite but do not waste words on useless pleasantries, and honor the impact of sickness on thinking, as I have pointed out before, by speaking directly, avoiding abstractions, offering choices two at a time rather than three or four, and making sure what you said has been understood. Listen to the patients' speech—words as well as speech rate, pauses, and other nonword phenomena. Be attentive to the patients' exercise of executive control for planning, carrying out complex tasks, multitasking, problem solving, or dealing with novel situations. If you assist the patient, it should be unobtrusive, or done with the patient's acquiescence. It is permissible, if necessary, to point out that when people are really sick, thinking through things can be difficult and that is why you are there to help. If emotionality appears to be a problem it is also okay to point out that when people are sick they may not feel the emotion they expect. The patients should be reassured that their normal emotional responses and normal thinking will return when they get better.

In widening your perspective on the sick person, do not disregard what is happening to the body as a byproduct of sickness. Is the patient losing weight because of inadequate caloric intake? Should a nutritionist see the patient? Sometimes time at bedrest keeps extending and the bed itself becomes a source of trouble. Unused muscles waste and strength wanes and these defects are difficult and time consuming to repair. They are much easier to prevent with physical therapy and by keeping the patient out of bed when possible. A patient connected to a respirator will lose strength in the muscles of respiration making weaning more difficult. That also is easier to prevent than repair. Keep the patient out of bed and in a chair as much as possible.

I have discussed the problem of meaning throughout the book. Find out what the patient believes is happening and what events foretell. An ongoing explanation of things is very helpful. Using simple, straightforward, and true statements keeps the patient abreast of what is happening and what is planned. Make sure everyone is using the same explanations where possible. Otherwise ask the patients what they have been told and what they think things mean. When they ask for explanations of symptoms, provide them. Remember, given the choice, the patient will think the worst (like everyone else). Do not wait until you have been hospitalized and found yourself in a sea of ignorance or competing explanations to know how important it is to keep patients informed.

Always, and until the moment of death, *all* patients are due respect, kindness, and compassion. There is no better ally.

This book about healing has been a long journey over places for clinical action that are not often discussed. This has been necessitated by a change in the definition of sickness suggested by much that has occurred in medicine and the surrounding society in the past decades. As a result of social change, patients have become persons much as other groups have achieved full personhood. The growth of bioethics over more than 40 years has altered and enlarged the basic ethical precepts of medicine from benevolence and the related avoidance of harm to now include respect for persons—from which came an acceptance of the concept that patients should be treated as autonomous. Respect for persons has helped move the idea of persons and knowledge about them to a more central position in medicine. From this it follows that healers and other clinicians should know as much about the persons they treat as they do about pathophysiology.

Pathophysiology, itself a child of the twentieth century, introduced the idea of function into medicine in full force. The World Health Organization published its first version of the International Classification of Function (ICF) as the International Classification of Impairments, Disabilities, and Handicaps in 1980. Originally about diseases, it mutated to a classification about health. Its concern with functioning has come slowly to pervade medicine and the associated health sciences. Some fields, such as rehabilitation medicine, have embraced it fully since returning wounded World War II veterans to functioning members of society was the force for the growth of the specialty. Concepts of function have had an influence on thought everywhere in medicine and its allied sciences. Starting in the 1950s with the idea to "Treat the patient as a person," the person of the patient has gradually become the subject and object of the medicine until now patient-centered medicine is embraced by the whole profession. It is embraced, but too often is not practiced. This book endorses the idea that person-centered medicine has been held back by a definition of sickness that is dependent on the idea of disease.

The concept of disease is itself an abstraction—there are no such things as freestanding diseases to be discovered anywhere but in the pages of books and perhaps bottles in a museum. There are only persons with diseases and in such persons their impact is found in every part of the individual. Unless the definition follows the sickness caused by the pathophysiology into whatever aspect of the human condition it is found, the definition and actions based on it will not be true to the nature of sickness. The definition of sickness in this book and the emphasis on purposes and goals does that. It provides the basis, therefore, for understanding the nature of healing. It is called healing because in every language that is how helping the sick recover their health is described. In the modern era we have become aware that it is also possible for those who will die of their sickness to be helped to be better—to be healed.

These ideas can never change the fact that the relief of suffering remains the fundamental goal of medicine. Science and human understanding have so advanced that the relief of suffering is part of the task and the possibility of lifting the burden of sickness and returning patients to a state of well-being.

Reference

Cassell, E. J., Leon, A. C., and Kaufman, S. G. (2001). Preliminary evidence of impaired thinking in sick patients. *Annals of Internal Medicine 134*: 1120–1123.

Index

Note: Page numbers followed by n refer to notes.

Abrahm, Janet, 63
abstractions, 255–56
　avoidance of, 92
　executive function impairments and, 136
acceptance, 30, 171–72
activities, 52–53
acts of thought, 29
ADA. *See* Americans with Disabilities Act
adaptiveness, 33–34
addiction, 173, 199
adenocarcinoma, 8–9
advertising, 232
"advice and consent" method, 203n5
Aequanimitas (Osler), 141–42
aesthetics, 39–40, 39n4
agency, 27, 51
aging, 52
　afflictions of, xvi
　impairments and, 65–66
　postpolio syndrome and, 22
agreeableness, 75
aid, 90–91
alcoholism, 198–99, 206
altruism, 159
Americans with Disabilities Act (ADA), 27, 53, 167

anesthesia, 103n6
anger, 107–8
　at bodies, 172–74
　listening to, 247
　pain aggravation and, 209
anticipation, 99n3
　anxiety and, 47
　fear and, 165
anxiety, 41, 47–49
　death, 166
　meaning of symptoms and, 76
art, xi
　definition of, 195n1
　of medicine, 17
Asclepius, ix
asthma, 197–98
atomism, 105
attachment, 36–37
authority
　of doctors, 11, 203
　figures, 33
　treating suffering and, 228
　weight of, xxviii
autonomy, xviii
　bioethics and, 255
　growth of, 232
　liberty compared to, 233

autonomy (*cont.*)
  loss of, 189
  principle of, 235–36
awareness, 41
  body, 33
  of patients, 145

balance, xiv, 137n7
Balint, Michael, xii
Beauchamp, Tom, 234n4–235n4
Becker, Ernest, 166
beds, 90n5, 179–80
behavior
  drug-seeking, 208
  effect of childhood on, 45–46
  emotion-based, 17
  social factors influencing, 76
Belmont Report, 234–35
benevolence, xviii, 241
Berlin, Isaiah, 233, 235
Berwick, Donald, xii
biases, 119–20, 122, 150
bioethics, 232, 255
bodies, 49–50
  anger at, 172–74
  awareness, 33
  boundaries of, 54
  care for, 173
  depersonalized, 86–87
  external, 147
  function, 52
  intentions of, 172
  persons compared with, 82n1
body-mind-spirit, 245
boundaries
  of bodies, 54
  lowered, 105
  respect for, 106
Buber, Martin, 179
burnout, 184, 187

cancer
  emotional response to, xxvii
  functioning and, 62–63
  language of survival in, 67–68
  survival, 250
carcinoma, 198–99, 205–6
cardiomyopathy, 175
caregivers
  attachment to, 36–37
  connectedness of, 106
"The Care of the Patient" (Peabody), 196
categorization, of patients, 152–53
causation, 4–5
central purpose, 225–26
CFS-APQ. *See* Chronic Fatigue Syndrome Activities and Participation Questionnaire
Charcot, Jean Martin, 44
childhood, 45–46
children, 136
Childress, James, 234n4–235n4
choice
  freedom of, 233–34
  intentions and, 61
chronic disease, xvi, 55
  disablement process and, 66
  executive function impairments and, 135–36
  patient knowledge of, 100
Chronic Fatigue Syndrome Activities and Participation Questionnaire (CFS-APQ), 125
chronic obstructive pulmonary disease (COPD), xiv, 197
Churchill, Larry R., 106
cirrhosis, 198–99, 206, 215–16
civil rights movement, 232
client-centered therapy, xii
clinical knowledge, 36
clinical medicine
  observations in, 150–51
  patient knowledge in, 95
  science in, xxv, xxviii–xxix

closeness, 160
  of healer-patient relationship, 91
  pain and, 186
  state of illness and, 184–90
cognitive function, 75
  changes in, 136
  dementia and, 249
  impairments on, 17
  measures of, 240–41, 253–54
  perspective and, 254
  Piagetian tests of, 91–92
  state of illness and, 182–83, 188–89
colectomy, 215
colonoscopy, 96
colostomy, 246–47
communication
  attachment and, 37
  communities and, 11
  empathic, 158
  in observations, 151
  relief from state of illness and, 181–84
  of symptoms, 114
communities
  communication and, 11
  healthy persons and, 191
complaining, 191
compliance, 202
confidence, 75
  functioning and, 64
confusion, 130
congestive heart failure, 21
connectedness, 105–6
consciousness
  dailiness and, 44
  emotional responsivity and, 17
  objectivity and, 10n8
  problem solving and, 41
context, 2n2
  of observations, 150–51
  social, 115
  of well-being, xiv
control
  information and, 183n6
  of meaning, 203–7
  pain, 207–12
  of symptoms, 201–3
conversation, 127
cooperation, 202
COPD. *See* chronic obstructive pulmonary disease
coughing, 197–98
courage
  failures, 142
  learning, 108
Croce, Benedetto, 40
Crohn's disease, 197
cultural traditions, 96–97
curing
  healing distinguished from, 83n2
  science as, 82–83
  well-being distinguished from, xiv

dailiness, 7n6, 37n3, 44
D&Cs. *See* diagnostic and therapeutic curettages
death. *See also* dying
  acceptance of, 171–72
  anxiety, 166
  fear of, 165–66
  threat of, 48–49
decentering, 136
decision making
  in doctor-patient relationship, 102
  paternalism and, 231
  process, xiii
deliberation, 235
dementia, 249
denial, 169, 198
Denial of Death (Becker), 166
depersonalization, 84–85
  of bodies, 86–87
  of selves, 25
depression, 18–19
  disability benefits and, 63

depression (*cont.*)
   pain aggravation and, 209
   suffering and, 227
Descartes, Rene, 221
desire
   fear and, 43
   hope and, 38
   of outcomes, 58
   sexual, 37
detachment, 159
details, 112
diabetic ketoacidosis, 177
diagnoses, 6. *See also* patient evaluations
   cardiac, 242n1–243n1
   hastiness of, 135
   hypothesis, 113, 136
   impairments in, 67
   lines of, 138
   patient history and, 70–71
   prominence of symptoms in, 251
   of suffering, 226–27
   technology and, 119
diagnostic and therapeutic curettages (D&Cs), 204
diagnostic hypotheses, 113, 136
dialysis, 213
diffidence, 154n3
dignity, 156
Dilaudid, 246–47
disability
   benefits, 62–63
   definition of, 53
   prediction of, 21, 65–66
   stigma and, 167
disablement process, 65–66
diseases. *See also* chronic disease; *specific disease types*
   as abstraction, 255–56
   burdensome, 87
   cellular basis of, 3n4
   degenerative, 64
   describing, 55–58
   functional impact of, 60
   illness distinguished from, 175
   impairments and, 65
   impairments without, 20–21
   infectious, xv
   influences on, 16
   interrelationship of disorder, sickness and, 17–19
   knowledge of, xiii, 12–13
   malignant, 19
   molecular determinants of, 4
   passivity towards, 173
   patients affected by, 5–6
   personhood and, 26
   sickness and, xv
   sickness *versus*, 87–88
   smell of, 168
   theories, 1
   therapeutic focus on, 72–73
   treating of, 83
   well-being compared to, xiii–xiv, 83
disinterest, 151, 154
disorders, 5
   definition of, 125n4
   interrelationship of disease, sickness and, 17–19
dissociation, 45
doctor-patient relationship, xii. *See also* healer-patient relationship
   decision making in, 102
   deepening of, 146
   establishment of, 126–27
   familiarity in, 100n5
   maintaining of, 100n4
   myth of, 99
doctors
   authority of, 11, 203
   empathy and, 64
   equanimity of, 142
   fear and, 104n8
   fear in, 142–43
   ignorance of patients of, 153–57

inner detachment of, 159
knowledge of, 64–65
multiple, 173–74
role of, 99–100
special interests of, 155–56
speech of, 253
dominant moods, 43
Double Helix Curriculum, xiii
doubt, 44
drug addiction, 173, 199
drug-seeking behavior, 208
Dunbar, Flanders, 196
duodenal ulcers, 4
Dworkin, Gerald, 234n3
dying. *See also* death
   control of meaning and, 206–7
   denial and, 198
   pain control and, 211
   patients, 73–74, 185–86
   restoration of function when, 199–200

egalitarianism, xii, 26n2
emotional distress, 88
emotional problems, 131
emotional responsivity, xxvii, 17, 153–57
emotional trauma, 13–14
emotions
   behavior based on, 17
   defects in, 136
   detachment of, 159
   evaluative, 153
   experiences and, xxvi–xxvii
   meaning and, 76
   pain control and, 209
   positive, 159
   primitiveness of, 43
   sensing of, 112–13
   of sick patients, 153–57
Emotions and Bodily Change (Dunbar), 196
empathy, 151, 183n7
   doctors and, 64

knowing as, 157–60
objectivity and, 159
pain and, 158
suffering and, 157–58
Engel, George, xii
environment, 191–92
equanimity, 142
errors
   information, 241
   in patient evaluations, 119–22
ethics, xviii. *See also* bioethics
euphemisms, 154
evidence
   based medicine, 163–64
   hardness of, 120
   scientific, 156–57
examinations
   cultural tradition of, 96–97
   physical, 137–39
excess care, xii–xiii
executive function, 31, 78
   attention to, 254
   diminished, 43
   impairments, 17, 135–36
   state of illness and, 189–90
exercise, 90, 133
existentialism, 32, 222
expectations
   of functioning, 129
   hope and, 38
   of patients, 99
experiences
   definition of, 6–7
   emotions and, xxvi–xxvii
   fear from, 77
   labeling of, xxvi
   meaning of, xxvii

family history, 130
fear, 7
   anticipation and, 165
   causes of, 9

fear (cont.)
  control of meaning and, 204–5
  of death, 165–66
  desire and, 43
  in doctors, 142–43
  doctors and, 104n8
  from experiences, 77
  information and, 47
  inner naysayer and, 34–35
  meaning of symptoms and, 76
  pain aggravation and, 209
  patience and, 165
  physiological response to, 15–16
  in response to illness, 165–67
  of symptoms, 178
  universality of, 46–47
feelings, xxvii, 160. *See also* emotions
Feinstein, Alvan, 113–14
Fierce Joy (Schecter), 173n2
Fishbein, Morris, ix, 82
foolishness, 169
frailty, 21
Frankel, Viktor, 225
freedom, 233–34
functioning, 52–53. *See also* cognitive function; executive function; impairments
  body, 52
  cancer and, 62–63
  clinical focus on, 61–63
  complexity of, 53–54
  conceptualizing, 57–58
  confidence and, 64
  depersonalized bodies and, 86–87
  directed, 12
  disturbances of, 8
  domains of, 126
  executive function and, 78
  expectations of, 129
  interference in, 12–14
  loss of, over time, 65–66
  maximizing, 13
  measuring of, 242–43
  mental, 75–79
  pain and, 74–75
  palliative care and, 63
  pathophysiology and, 255
  patient-centered care and, 64
  patient evaluations and, 115–16, 124–25
  persons and, 68–70
  as process, 61
  reductionism and, 244–45
  rehabilitation and, 60–61
  research on, 66–67
  restoration of, 199–200
  return of, 51–52
  suffering and, 126
future, 38, 221

gait speed, 137, 137n7
genital examination, 137
gentleness, 144
germ theory, 3
goals, xiv–xvi
  definition of, 242
  deliberation about, 235
  discovering of, 88
  for dying patients, 73–74
  inability to pursue, 66
  interfering with, 126
  of medicine, 83
  mental functions and, 75
  participation as, 134
Google, 101
gratification, 184
Groddeck, Georg, 196
Groopman, Jerome, 113, 119–22
group spaces, 109
guilt, 167

habits, 130, 145
harmony, 39n4
haste, 135

Hastings Center, 185
healer-patient relationship. *See also*
    doctor-patient relationship
  closeness of, 91
  history of, 17
healers
  as authority figures, 33
  openness of, 106–7
  religious, 82
  responsibility of, 8
  role of, 65
  in society, 81–82
Healers: Extraordinary Clinicians at
    Work (Schenk & Churchill), 106
The Healer's Art (Cassell), 173, 175
healing
  continuous, 90
  curing distinguished from, 83n2
  definition of, xii, 85–86
  entity, 93
  knowledge of, xix
  openness to, 99
  power of, 81–82
  as quackery, ix
  relief of suffering and, 256
  well-being and, xiv, 84
health condition, 52
healthiness, 92–93, 191
healthy characteristics, 190–93
Helicobacter pylori, 4
helplessness, 155
hidradenitis suppurativa, 215
Hippocrates, xix
Hippocratic Oath, ix
holism, xiv, 245
Holmes, Oliver Wendell, Sr., 103
hope, 38
hopelessness, 176
hormonal therapy, 204
hospice movement, 170–71
hospitalization
  depersonalization in, 84–85

disturbance of, 190
  impairments from, 72–73
  state of illness and, 177
Hotel Dieu, 192
house calls, 117–18
How Doctors Think (Groopman), 119–20
humiliation, 229
hygiene, 147
hypnosis, 44
hysterectomy, 204

ICD. *See* International Classification of
    Disease
ICF. *See* International Classification of
    Function
identity, 192
ignorance, 101
  degrees of, 105
  of doctors, 153–57
  ignorance of, 108
  of patients, 108–9
  reasons for, 157
ileostomy, 215–16
ilioinguinal causalgia, 220n1
illness. *See also* sickness; state of illness
  descriptions of, 163–64
  disease distinguished from, 175
  emotional determinants of, 196
  fear in response to, 165–67
  memory of, 192–93
  mental, 79
  nonphysical impact of, 252
  psychological responses to, 164–65
  psychosomatic, 3
  severity of, 177
impairments, 1–2. *See also* functioning
  aging and, 65–66
  body awareness and, 33
  in cognitive function, 17
  concealment of, 124
  degree of, 54
  in diagnoses, 67

impairments (*cont.*)
    without disease, 20–21
    diseases and, 65
    emotional component of, 76–77
    executive function, 17, 135–36
    from hospitalization, 72–73
    initial evaluation of, 61
    narrative of, 71–72
    observation of, 134
    process of, 66
    questioning about, 71–72, 131–32
    understanding of, 69–70
impatience, 120–21
imperturbability, 142
inclusiveness, 26–27
individualism, 11, 85, 179
    growth of, 231–32
    of patients, 143
inflammatory bowel disease, 197
information
    control and, 183n6
    errors, 241
    fear and, 47
    gathering, 95
    management, 124
    precision of, 148–49
    processing, 119
    relaying, 165
    rule of three, 238–39
    sensory, 148
    transfer, 239–40
    transmission of, 182–83
informed consent, 92
injuries, 207–8
inner naysayer, 34–35
inner voices, 44–45
insulin, ix, 103
insurance plans, 100
integrative medicine, 4–5
integrity, 221n2
intentions, 51
    of bodies, 172

choice and, 61
interconnectivity, 11
International Classification of Disease
    (ICD), 138
International Classification of Function
    (ICF), 52–53, 66–67, 138, 244
    pain and, 74
    pathophysiology and, 255
International Physical Activity
    Questionnaire-short
    (IPAQ-SF), 125
internet, 101–2
interruptions, 107
interventions, xvi
    conveying, 181
    injurious, 13–14
    in mental function, 77–78
    unpleasant, 240
intimacy, 38
intimidation, 107–8
intuition, 42
    clinical thinking as, xxviii
    definition of, 148n2
    knowledge of others, 148
    limitations of, 111
    pattern recognition and,
        113, 123
    sensory information and, 148
    as source of ideas, 112
IPAQ-SF. *See* International Physical
    Activity Questionnaire-short

James, Williams, 44
Janet, Pierre, 44
Jette, A. M., 65
joint physiology, 56–57
*Journal of the American Medical
    Association*, ix, 82

Kaiser, Henry, 107
knowing, as empathy, 157–60
Kraemer, Helen Chmura, 6

Index

labels, xxvi, 216
Laennec, René Theophile, 3
language, xi
  cautionary, 34
  clinical, 68
  connotation of words in, xxvi
  descriptive, 216
  of events, 20
  functional descriptions in, 56–57
  observations of, 147
  of pathogenesis, 55–56
  of pathophysiology, 56
  of physiology, 58–59
  of questioning, 123n2
  of science, 59
  of survival, 67–68
learning
  courage, 108
  patience and, 253
Levine, Samuel, 196
liberty, 233
listening, 85
  active, 97
  to anger, 247
  anger and, 107–8
  attentive, 95–96, 105
  barriers to, 107
  efficient, 109–10
  in group settings, 109
  to psychological problems, 169
  questioning while, 111–12
  sympathetic, 158
  tools, 98
liver transplantation, 215–17
logic, 113
logical reversibility, 182n5–183n5
loneliness, 92, 191, 223, 226
love
  capacity to, 36–37
  state of, 176
  threat of death and, 48–49
Ludmerer, Kenneth, xviii

malignancy, 19, 67–68
Man's Search for Meaning
  (Frankel), 225
materia medica, 103
McDermott, Walsh, ix, 127
meaning, xxv–xxvi, 169–71
  clarifying, 89–90
  control of, 203–7
  dimensions of, 14
  dynamic nature of, 209–10
  emotions and, 76
  of experiences, xxvii
  incorrect, 169
  physical reactions and, xxvii
  responses to, 29
  revised, 16
  seeking of, 15
  sensation and, 41–42
  sickness and, 2, 14–16
  subjectivity of, xxviii–xxix
  suffering and, 135, 220–21
  of symptoms, 76
Medical Outcomes Study, 66–67
medical records, 20
medical school, xiii
medications
  for pain management, 75
  uncertainty and, 102
medicine. *See also specific medical*
  disciplines
  art of, 17
  biopsychosocial nature of, xii
  definition of, xvi
  effectiveness of, 103
  evidence-based, 163–64
  focus of, 27–28
  goals of, 83
  history of, xv
  modernization of, 232
  personalization of, 4n5
  rehabilitation, 255
  scientific, 82–83

medicine (*cont.*)
	systematizing of, 163–64
	Western, 4
memory, 6
	anxiety and, 48
	dementia and, 249
	emotive thought and, 42
	of illness, 192–93
	as mental function, 75
	neurobiology of, 38
	patient evaluations and, 117–18
	repressed, 46
menometrorrhagia, 203–4
mental activity, 40–41
mental functions, 75–79
mental illness, 79
Merck Manual, 18th edition, 56
mind-body duality, 172
Mini-Mental Status Examination, 78, 92, 136, 183n5
Morgagni, Giovanni Battiste, 3n3
motivation, 202
Mount, Balfour, 245
muscles
	functional descriptions of, 56–57
	spasms, 212
	strength, 137n7
	testing, 213
	weakness of, 54
My Stroke of Insight (Taylor), 182n4

names, 144
narcotics, 173, 246–47
narratives, 58n2, 112
	construction of, 105
	of impairments, 71–72
	nondiagnostic, 218
	in pathophysiology, 58–59
	of patient evaluations, 127–28
	scope of, 59–60

National Commission for the Protection of Human Subjects of Biomedical and Behavioral Research, 234
negativity, 34–35
nerve entrapment, 220n1
New York Heart Association (NYHA), 242n1–243n1
noise, 109, 150
nurse practitioners, 229n4
NYHA. *See* New York Heart Association

objectivity, 10n8
	empathy and, 159
	stigma and, 167
obligations, 235–36
observations, 111–12
	attentive listening and, 105
	of changes in patients, 168–69
	in clinical method, 150–51
	communication in, 151
	context of, 150–51
	continuity of, 146–48
	development of, 148n1
	habits, 145
	of impairments, 134
	of language, 147
	in patient evaluations, 117–18
openness, 99, 106–7, 158
opioids, 75, 170–71, 199–200
	dosages, 246–47
	pain control and, 209
	patient-activated, 173n3
optimism, xv, 75–76
Osler, William, 141–42, 150, 195–96
osteoarthritis, 116
osteosarcoma, 87–88
ostracism, 9–11
outcomes
	desires, 58
	influence of patients on, 12
outpatients, 196–97

pain
  acute, 207–8
  aggravated, 209
  closeness and, 186
  control, 207–12
  empathy and, 158
  functioning and, 74–75
  hospice movement and, 170–71
  interpretation of, 74
  local treatment of, 212
  management, 75
  patient management of, 173
  personalization of, 210–11
  psychogenic, 208
  questioning about, 131
  of recrimination, 187
  special interest in, 155–56
  without suffering, 221
  suffering and, 219–20
palliative care, 73–74, 184
  body-mind-spirit and, 245
  functioning and, 63
  pain control and, 209
participation, 52–53, 134
partitioned care, 20
passivity, 173
paternalism, 231
pathogenesis
  language of, 55–56
  scleroderma and, 116
pathophysiology, 4
  event-based, 20
  functioning and, 255
  language of, 56
  narratives in, 58–59
  scleroderma and, 116
  static descriptions of, 138
patience, 106, 144
  fear and, 165
  learning and, 253
patients. See also outpatients
  activity of, 254

  agency of, 27
  appearance of, 117
  authentic, 98–99
  awareness of, 145
  bedbound, 179–80
  care for, 83
  categorization of, 152–53
  changes in, 168–69
  characteristics of, 8
  confusion of, 130
  descriptions of, 138, 248
  diminished power of, 252
  doctor's ignorance of, 153–57
  dying, 73–74, 185–86
  emotional response to sickness of, 153–57
  entities affecting, 5–6
  as equals, 160
  expectations of, 99
  familiarity with, 104–5
  feelings of, 160
  goals of, xiv
  habits, 130
  helplessness of, 155
  human problems of, xiii
  ignorant, 108–9
  individualism of, 143
  influence on outcomes of, 12
  initial opinion of, 116–17
  interactions of, 151
  intimidated, 107–8
  knowledge of, 95, 100, 144–46
  lowered boundaries of, 105
  motivation of, 202
  movements of, 146
  with multiple doctors, 173–74
  personhood of, 27
  as persons, 141–44
  persons as opposed to, 25–26
  perspective of, 250
  politeness to, 127
  psychological problems of, 168–69

patients (cont.)
  public personae of, 152–53
  purposes of, 65
  relationships with, 160
  respect for, 181–82
  responsibility for, 128
  rights of, 27, 156
  role of, 99–100
  seeing, 212–18
  social withdrawal of, 178
  speech of, 168, 254
  standardized, 31–32
  without symptoms, 65
  therapeutic action and, 250–56
  universal, 156
  unpleasant, 110
  voices of, 147
patient-centered care, xii
  functioning and, 64
  in medical school, xiii
  responsibility in, 237
  symptom control and, 202–3
  treating suffering and, 228
patient charts, 144
patient-controlled analgesia pump (PCA), 189
patient evaluations, 115–16. *See also* diagnoses
  conversation in, 127
  efficiency in, 120–21
  errors in, 119–22
  functioning and, 115–16, 124–25
  memory and, 117–18
  narrative of, 127–28
  observations in, 117–18
  pattern recognition in, 118
  as process, 123
  purposes and, 115–16
  time and, 139
patient history, 70–71, 116–17
  detail of, 122–23
  questioning style in, 128

pattern recognition, 112–13, 112n11, 118
PCA. *See* patient-controlled analgesia pump
Peabody, Francis, 196
peer pressure, 31
pelvic examination, 137
perception, 147
  emotive thought and, 42
  lack of, 154
  sensation and, 41
personality, 69
personalization
  of medicine, 4n5
  of pain, 210–11
  of sickness, 16–23
personhood, xi–xii, 26–27, 26n2, 146
  maintenance of, 91–92
  of patients, 27
persons
  actions of, 28–29
  adaptiveness of, 33–34
  aesthetic dimension of, 39–40
  bodies compared with, 82n1
  definition of, 25–26
  describing, 152
  differences among, 30–31
  as existential creatures, 32
  focus on, 251
  functioning and, 68–70
  general description of, 28–29
  healthy, 190–93
  integrity of, 221n2
  patients as, 141–44
  patients as opposed to, 25–26
  relationships and, 29–30
  respect for, xviii, 234–41, 255
  sexuality and, 37–38
  social aspects of, 28
  suffering and, 221
  temporal dimension of, 38–39
perspective

cognitive function and, 254
    of patients, 250
pessimism, 171
physical activity status, 125
physical examination, 137–39
physical reactions, xxvii
physical therapy, 254
physicians. *See* doctors
physiology
    of joints, 56–57
    language of, 58–59
Piagetian tests, 91–92, 136
placebo effect, 99n3
polio, 21–22
politeness, 127
Positivism, ix–x
postpolio syndrome, 21–22
power
    diminished, 252
    of healing, 81–82
    suffering and, 228
precision, 114
preconceptions, 119–20, 122, 150
pregnancy, 52
prejudice, 71
The Principles and Practice of Medicine
    (Osler), 195
Principles of Biomedical Ethics
    (Beauchamp & Childress),
    234n4–235n4
privacy, loss of, 92
probability, 120
problem solving, 41
prognoses, 8
prognostication, 138–39
psychological determinants, 27–28
psychological problems, 168–69
psychological responses to illness,
    164–65
psychosomatic illness, 3
psychotherapy, 79
public personae, 152–53

purposes, xiv, xvi, 171–72
    central, 225–26
    changes in, 101
    definition of, 242
    discovering of, 88, 129
    patient evaluations and, 115–16
    of patients, 65

quackery, ix, 82–83
quality of life, xiv, 250
questioning, 22
    caring, 119
    detail of, 122–23
    in diagnosis of suffering, 226
    efficient, 109–10
    follow-up, 132–33
    of ignorant patients, 108–9
    about impairments, 71–72, 131–32
    importance of, 89
    language of, 123n2
    listening and, 111–12
    mental functions and, 76
    open-ended, 132
    about pain, 131
    for precise information, 148–49
    during state of illness, 183
    style, 128
    yes or no, 134

reason
    dementia and, 249
    kinds of, 42
recrimination, pain of, 187
reductionism, 62, 68–69, 113–14,
    244–45
regression, 91–92
rehabilitation, 51
    functioning and, 60–61
    medicine, 255
relationships, 26n1
    connectedness within, 105–6
    factors in, 16–17

relationships (*cont.*)
  with patients, 160
  persons and, 29–30
  rules and, 35–36
  spousal, 212–13
  suffering and, 222
religion, 82
respect
  for boundaries, 106
  for patients, 181–82
  for persons, xviii, 234–41, 255
responsibility
  of healers, 8
  in patient-centered care, 237
  for patients, 128
  personhood and, 26n2
  respect for persons and, 237
  of society, 11
review-of-systems approach, 88
rheumatoid arthritis, 55–60
Rogers, Carl, xii
role behavior, 35
role-playing, 98
rules
  of daily life, 44
  relationships and, 35–36

Schecter, Ellen, 173n2
Schenk, David, 106
science
  in clinical medicine, xxv, xxviii–xxix
  as curing, 82–83
  evidence and, 156–57
  language of, 59
scleroderma, 116
security, 190
segmentation, of cases, 19–20
self-conflict, 225, 227
self-determination, 235
self-doubt, 154n3
self-governance, 234, 238
self-image, 218

self-worth, 192
selves, 25
  empirical, 31–32
  knowledge of, 32
  presentation of, 248
  public, 152–53
  recognizable, 177
  secret, 30–31
sensation, 41–42
senses, 33
sexuality, 37–38
shame, 167
shoulder joint, 56–57
shyness, 154n3
sickness, xv–xvi. *See also* illness
  causes of, 2–7
  determinants of, 27–28
  differing responses to, 6–7
  disease *versus*, 87–88
  distinguishing healthiness from, 92–93
  emotional response to, 153–57
  impact of, 7–12, 88
  induced by chronic disease, 55
  interference in functioning and, 12–14
  interrelationship of disease, disorder and, 17–19
  meaning and, 2, 14–16
  patients affected by, 5
  personalization of, 16–23
  from sickness, 93
  theories, 1
silence, 110
smell, 168
social changes, xi
social determinants, 27–28
social disconnection, 166
social factors, 3, 76
socialization, enhancement of, 60
social pressure, 121
social self, 11

social withdrawal, 178
society
　healers in, 81–82
　inclusiveness of, 26–27
　responsibility of, 11
Solomon, Cyril, 202
specialists, 8
speech, 52
　of doctors, 253
　focus on, 111
　of patients, 168, 254
　patterns, 249
　utterances and, 97n2
　variations in, 181
spiritual isolation, 227
state of illness, 175–76
　beds and, 179–80
　closeness and, 184–90
　cognitive function and, 182–83, 188–89
　definition of, 176n1–177n1
　environment and, 191–92
　executive function and, 189–90
　hospitalization and, 177
　impact of, 178
　questioning during, 183
　relief from, 181–84
Stewart, Moira, xii
stigma, 167
stubbornness, 71
subjectivity, xviii–xxix, 156
suffering
　characteristics of, 224–26
　concept of, 61–62
　depression and, 227
　diagnosis of, 226–27
　dimensions of, 223–24
　empathy and, 157–58
　existentialism and, 222
　functioning and, 126
　humiliation and, 229
　meaning and, 135, 220–21

　without pain, 221
　pain and, 219–20
　personal nature of, 228
　persons and, 221
　power and, 228
　relationships and, 222
　relief of, 256
　treatment of, 227–30
sulfa drugs, 103
surcease, 49
surgery
　anesthesia and, 103n6
　impact of, 163
　infectious diseases and, xv
survival
　cancer, 250
　language of, 67–68
sympathy, 158, 230
symptoms, 3–4
　acute, 15
　communication of, 114
　control of, 201–3
　definition of, 125n5
　details of, 164
　enduring of, 197–98
　fear of, 178
　meaning of, 76
　patients without, 65
　prominence of, 251
　surrogate, 203

Talking with Patients (Cassell), 158
Taylor, Jill, 144, 182n4
teaching, 151–54, 154
teams, 109
technology, xii
　diagnoses and, 119
　faith in, 232n1–233n1
　limitations of, 96
telephones, 107
temperament, 69
terror, xxvii, 9–10

The Theory and Practice of Autonomy
    (Dworkin), 234n3
therapeutic action, 250–56
thoughts, 40–41
    emotive, 42–43
    reasoning, 42
time, 38–39
    functioning loss over, 65–66
    patient evaluations and, 139
treatment guidelines, 156
trust, 47
    control of meaning and, 207
    establishing, 127
    levels of, 155
    respect for persons and, 239
trustworthiness, 75
truth, 42, 237
    telling, 183
    withholding of, 238n6–239n6
tuberculosis, 4
tumors, 9
typhoid fever, 195

ulcers, 4
uncertainty, 38, 101–2, 189
unconscious, 44–46
unitary beings, 43–44

University of Western Ontario, xii
utterances, 97n2

Verbrugge, L. M., 65
Virchow, Rudolf, 3n4
vitality signs, 137
vital signs, 137
voice recorders, 253
voices, 147
voluntariness, 238

well-being, xiii–xv, 83–84
    definition of, 242
    promotion of, 241
    restoring, 85
Welty, Eudora, 35
Western medicine, 4
whining, 178
WHO. *See* World Health Organization
wholeness, 86–87
wittiness, 249
words, connotation of, xxvi
World Health Organization
    (WHO), 66
worried well, 170
worry, 41
writing skills, 248–49